# Torah and Western Thought
## Intellectual Portraits of Orthodoxy and Modernity

MAGGID

Yeshiva University
**THE ZAHAVA AND MOSHAEL STRAUS
CENTER FOR TORAH AND WESTERN THOUGHT**

# TORAH AND WESTERN THOUGHT

## INTELLECTUAL PORTRAITS OF ORTHODOXY AND MODERNITY

EDITORS

Rabbi Dr. Meir Y. Soloveichik
Dr. Stuart W. Halpern
Rabbi Shlomo Zuckier

Straus Center for Torah and Western Thought
Maggid Books

*Torah and Western Thought*
*Intellectual Portraits of Orthodoxy and Modernity*

First Edition, 2015

*Maggid Books*
*An imprint of Koren Publishers Jerusalem Ltd.*

POB 8531, New Milford, CT 06776-8531, USA
& POB 4044, Jerusalem 9104001, Israel
www.korenpub.com

© Straus Center for Torah and Western Thought 2015

Cover photos:
Rabbi Joseph B. Soloveitchik: courtesy of the family of Rabbi Irwin Albert z"l
Rabbi Yehuda Amital: courtesy of Dr. Na'aman Kam
Rabbi Ahron Soloveichik, Rabbi Lamm,
Rabbi Lichtenstein: Yeshiva University
Prof. Leibowitz: courtesy of Rabbi David S. Levin

All rights reserved. No part of this publication may be reproduced, stored in a retrieval system or transmitted in any form or by any means, electronic, mechanical, photocopying or otherwise, without the prior permission of the publisher, except in the case of brief quotations embedded in critical articles or reviews.

ISBN 978-1-59264-436-0, *hardcover*

A CIP catalogue record for this title is available from the British Library

Printed and bound in the United States

*In reverent memory of our rebbe, Rabbi Aharon Lichtenstein, zt"l, who was a "remarkable fusion of mastery and simplicity, of vigor and humility, and, above all, a pillar of radical integrity."*

*We are particularly thrilled to share this dedication with Heshe's mother, Helen Seif, who celebrated her 100th birthday two years ago.*

*Heshe, Harriet, Orit, and Yehuda Seif*

# Contents

*Timeline* ix

*Introduction*
Rabbi Dr. Meir Y. Soloveichik xi

*Unity, Plurality, and Human Limits:
Secularism in the Thought of Rav Kook*
Dr. Daniel Rynhold 1

*Rabbi Yitzhak Herzog's Approach to Modernity*
Rabbi Dr. Itamar Warhaftig 37

*"Founding Brothers":
The Rav, Rav Ahron, and the American Idea*
Rabbi Dr. Meir Y. Soloveichik 83

*Prof. Nehama Leibowitz and
the Revolution in Bible Interpretation*
Yael Unterman 109

*Rabbi Immanuel Jakobovits and
the Birth of Jewish Medical Ethics*
Dr. Alan Jotkowitz 145

*Torah and Humanity in a Time of Rebirth:*
*Rav Yehuda Amital as Educator and Thinker*
Rabbi Reuven Ziegler and Dr. Yehudah Mirsky   179

*Rabbi Dr. Norman Lamm on the Role of Talmud*
*Torah in a Torah Umadda Framework*
Rabbi Dr. David Shatz   219

*Halakha and History, Intellectualism and Spirituality:*
*Professor Isadore (Yitzhak) Twersky's Academic-Religious Profile*
Rabbi Dr. Carmi Horowitz   249

*Music of the Left Hand: Personal Notes on the Place of Liberal*
*Arts Education in the Teachings of Rabbi Aharon Lichtenstein*
Rabbi Shalom Carmy with Rabbi Shlomo Zuckier   281

Index   315
Contributors   325

# *Timeline*

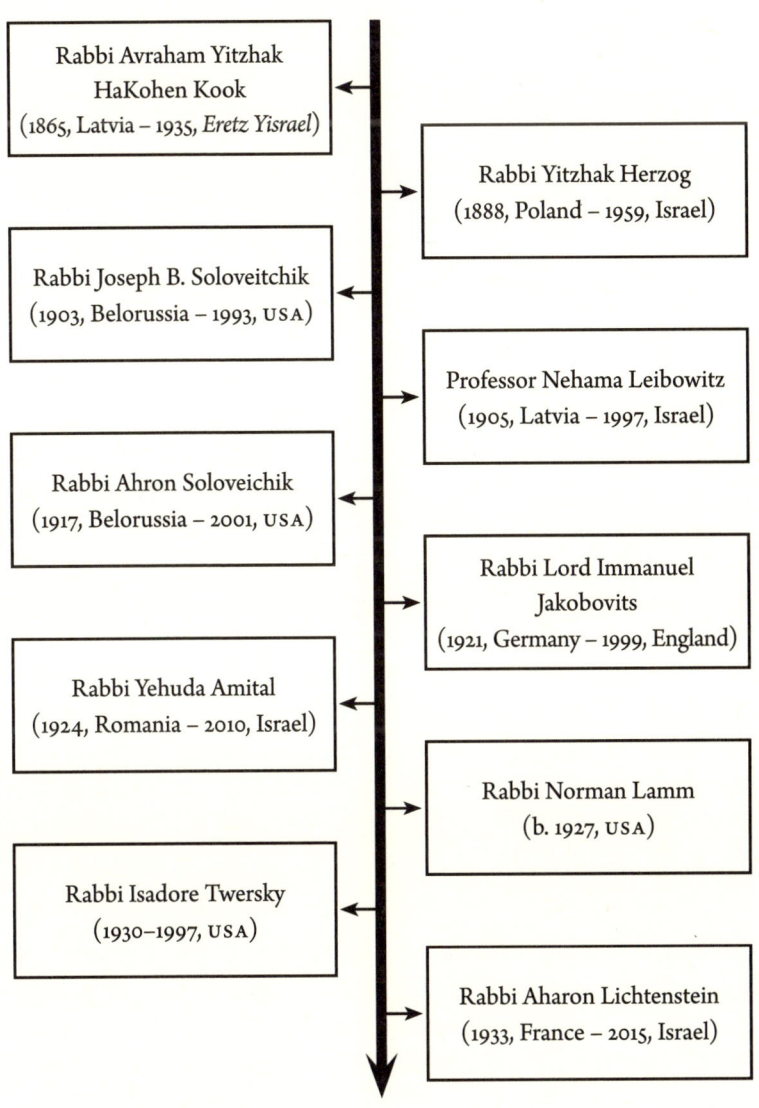

# Introduction

## Rabbi Dr. Meir Soloveichik

> *According to the way of reason, the Menora with its seven lamps alludes to the Torah, which is called "light," as it is said, "For the mitzva is a lamp and the Torah is light" (Prov. 6:23). It includes seven [types of] wisdom, which is why it has seven lamps.*
> – Rabbeinu Baḥya[1]

> *An account of R. Akiva's spiritual odyssey could no doubt eclipse Augustine's. But* his confessions have been discreetly muted. *The rigors of John Stuart Mill's education – and possibly, their repercussions – are not without parallel in our history. But what corresponds to his fascinating* Autobiography? *Or to the passionate* Apologia Pro Vita Sua *of his contemporary, John Henry Cardinal Newman? Our Johnsons have no Boswells.*
> – Rabbi Aharon Lichtenstein[2]

---

1. *Midrash Rabbeinu Baḥya*, trans. and annotated Eliyahu Munk (Jerusalem, 2003), 4:1256–57.
2. "Torah and General Culture: Confluence and Conflict," in *Judaism's Encounter with Other Cultures*, ed. Jacob J. Schachter (Northvale, NJ, 1997), 253.

## Rabbi Dr. Meir Soloveichik

**H**inc, lucem et pocula sacra – From here, light and sacred draughts. *In lumine tuo videbimus lumen* – In Your light, we shall see light. *Lux et veritas* – Light and truth.

These are the school mottos of three of the West's leading universities: Cambridge, Columbia, and Yale. These very phrases proudly proclaim what the academy used to believe: that the knowledge it safeguarded and transmitted was vital to the moral and spiritual survival of civilization; that faith and reason must go hand in hand; and that not only does religion enhance the pursuit of wisdom, but that the fear of God is the very beginning of wisdom itself.

The Straus Center for Torah and Western Thought at Yeshiva University was founded with the aim of more fully realizing Yeshiva University's mission to bridge Judaism and the West, and to illustrate how the Jewish faith in particular has so deeply shaped so many of the achievements associated with modernity. It was also born in the realization that the academy has, to a great extent, lost the will to defend the traditions and the canon of Western civilization itself.

When the Straus Center was founded, it struck me that even as the twentieth century will be remembered for the West's loss of faith, Jewish Orthodoxy itself experienced in that very time a golden age of leaders and teachers who sought to bridge the world of Torah and that of the West. Some of these Torah figures were deeply impacted by an academic field, such as philosophy or literature. Others developed a Torah-based perspective on developments within the West, such as the rise of Zionism, democracy, or biotechnology. Still others reflected on the very nature of religious knowledge itself. I therefore suggested that we invite twenty-first-century thinkers to paint intellectual portraits of these luminaries, serving – each in his or her own way – as Boswells to their own spiritual Johnsons, illustrating how each figure bridged the worlds of Torah and the West in a unique way. The essays would not comprise a complete intellectual biography of their subjects, as every one of these figures would merit a book in his or her own right. Rather, they would serve to inspire Orthodox Jews and all intellectually engaged individuals of faith to learn from their lives and to have the courage to bridge these worlds as well.

*Introduction*

The project was tirelessly shepherded and overseen by Dr. Stuart Halpern, the assistant director of the Straus Center. Dr. Halpern and I were privileged to be joined from the very outset by the very gifted Rabbi Shlomo Zuckier, who partnered with us in shaping the book and in serving as our coeditor. I am thankful to Dr. Halpern and Rabbi Zuckier for helping to make this book a reality. Special thanks as well to Rabbi Daniel Tabak for his research assistance, Meira Mintz and Elina Mosheyeva for their excellent copyediting work, Shalom Dinerstein and Ita Olesker for their careful proofreading, and Matthew Miller, Rabbi Reuven Ziegler, Tomi Mager, and the entire Maggid team for ensuring the quality of this volume.

Profound gratitude must be expressed to Moshael Straus, who, with his wife Zahava, has from the very inception shown great faith in the Straus Center's vision and in its leadership. We are grateful as well to Yeshiva University President Richard Joel for his constant encouragement and advice, and for his pride in the Straus Center's founding as part of the legacy of his leadership. We are also so delighted that Heshe and Harriet Seif, dear friends of Moshael and Zahava, generously sponsored and dedicated this volume in memory of Rabbi Aharon Lichtenstein, *zt"l*. Heshe and Harriet revered Rabbi Lichtenstein as a paragon of moral clarity, and he was, for us at the Straus Center, the ultimate embodiment of the worldview that we seek to perpetuate.

It was in the Temple that the glorious, golden Menora was kindled by the priests every day, most famously after the Hasmonean victory over Hellenism. The Ḥanukka story is often seen as a Jewish rejection of Greek achievement. In fact, the light of the Menora embodied a celebration of knowledge in all its forms; the rabbis realized that a world that had only Jerusalem, and not Athens, would be one less intellectually rich. At the same time, Judaism has insisted that shorn of the Jewish genius, we may have the Greek empire's scientific and artistic achievements, but also its tyranny and immorality. The Talmud therefore ordained that every Ḥanukka Jews kindle lights not in the window, but facing the mezuza, the small piece of parchment that proudly proclaims the foundations of monotheism that Judaism bequeathed to the world: "Hear O Israel, the Lord is our God, the Lord is One" (Deut. 6:4). The rabbis thereby expressed the demand that the light of knowledge be joined with the wisdom of religious tradition and that the search for wisdom begin with faith.

We offer this book as a menora of our own, in the hope that the luminaries portrayed herein will serve as intellectual beacons not only to the Orthodox Jewish community, but to Western civilization itself. We pray that in their merit the West will experience a rebirth of both faith and wisdom, thereby fulfilling the daily prayer of millions of Jews:

*Or ḥadash al Tziyon ta'ir venizkeh khullanu mehera leoro.*

May You make a new light shine over Zion, and may we all soon be worthy of its light.[3]

Meir Soloveichik<br/>
Ḥanukka 5775

---

3. From the morning *Shema* liturgy, with translation from *The Koren Siddur, with Introduction, Translation, and Commentary by Rabbi Lord Jonathan Sacks* (Jerusalem, 2009), 94.

# Unity, Plurality, and Human Limits: Secularism in the Thought of Rav Kook

## Dr. Daniel Rynhold

In the twenty-first century, Modern Orthodox Jews generally live in a pluralistic world. This is simply a *de facto* statement; Jews throughout Europe and North America plainly *do* live in societies that permit groups with very different – and sometimes entirely opposing – belief systems and practices to coexist in a manner that allows for the flourishing of each. Many of us have friends of other religions, of differing denominations within our own, or of no religious faith whatsoever whom we deem to be thoroughly good people. But the question for *all* religions is whether or not this *de facto* judgment can be rendered *de jure* – to what extent can we justify this pluralism from a theological, rather than purely pragmatic, perspective? While we are mostly very grateful for the friendships and freedoms that we enjoy, they depend on a system that grants those same freedoms to others with whom we disagree, sometimes on quite fundamental matters.

## Dr. Daniel Rynhold

Rabbi Avraham Yitzhak HaKohen Kook (1865–1935), known to all simply as Rav Kook, was one of the few Orthodox figures of his day to address these questions head-on, mainly in the context of another particularly modern, if not Modern Orthodox, phenomenon: the advent of political Zionism. His attitude toward Zionism and to the secular Jews at its forefront resonates strongly with many Modern Orthodox Jews who read his work. As many have noted, it is true that one would be hard pressed to call Rav Kook himself a Modern Orthodox figure, whether from the perspective of his biography, his attire, or his deep-seated mysticism, which does not sit comfortably with the majority of more rationalistically inclined Modern Orthodox Jews.[1] Yet he nonetheless grappled with the thoroughly modern issues of Jewish secularism and political Zionism in a manner that certainly set him apart from his ultra-Orthodox contemporaries and makes him of interest to all Jews attempting to come to terms with how to live their lives in the full glare of modernity. This remains the case even if, as David Shatz has noted, the extent to which we can detach those views of his to which we are attracted from their less-than-modern roots remains an issue.[2]

This chapter, following a brief biographical and bibliographical discussion, will focus on what precisely Rav Kook's attitude was toward secular Jews and will consider the manner in which it grew out of his more general theological commitments.

### BIOGRAPHICAL SKETCH

Rav Kook was born on September 7, 1865 (10 Elul 5625), in Griva, Latvia, to Shlomo Zalman and Perel Zlota. His father had studied at the famous Volozhin Yeshiva, and although his mother was of Chabad hasidic stock, Rav Kook was nonetheless primarily schooled in the

---

1. This is also true at times from a halakhic perspective. See Michael Z. Nehorai, "Halakhah, Metahalakhah, and the Redemption of Israel: Reflections on the Rabbinic Rulings of Rav Kook," in *Rabbi Abraham Isaac Kook and Jewish Spirituality*, ed. Lawrence J. Kaplan and David Shatz (New York, 1995), 120–56.
2. See David Shatz, "Rav Kook and Modern Orthodoxy: The Ambiguities of 'Openness,'" in *Engaging Modernity: Rabbinic Leaders and the Challenge of the Twentieth Century*, ed. Moshe Sokol (Northvale, NJ, 1997), 91–115, reprinted in Shatz, *Jewish Thought in Dialogue* (Boston, 2009), 118–37.

tradition of Lithuanian mitnaggdic talmudism that Volozhin represented. Rav Kook himself studied at Volozhin for one year under the Netziv (Rabbi Naftali Zvi Yehuda Berlin), who appears to have been a formative figure for the young Rav Kook.[3] One of Rav Kook's fellow students was Micah Yosef Berdichevsky, who would go on to be one of the early giants of Hebrew literature.

Amid the ferment sweeping Eastern Europe at that time, the world in which Rav Kook grew up was the Jewish equivalent of "interdisciplinary," so to speak. Thus, even in his teenage years Rav Kook was exposed not only to the Lithuanian mitnaggdism of the Volozhin Yeshiva, but also to hasidic and *musar* literature, as well as maskilic (pertaining to the Enlightenment) works of philosophy and *Wissenschaft* (the scientific study of Judaism) – all forms of literature that would continue to exert an influence throughout Rav Kook's life.[4] Without engaging in any sort of reductive psychologizing, one might say that the dialectical and "undisciplined" literary style that he would eventually adopt stemmed from the "undisciplined" (from a "disciplinary" perspective) nature of the world in which he was educated.

In 1886, Rav Kook married Batsheva Rabinowitz-Teomim, the daughter of Rabbi Eliyahu David Rabinowitz-Teomim – known by the acronym Aderet – famed rabbi of Ponevezh (and later of Mir) with whom Rav Kook studied and forged a close relationship following his return from Volozhin. It was in Ponevezh that Rav Kook first engaged seriously with Kabbala and medieval Jewish philosophical works. These, as Yehudah Mirsky shows,[5] played a formative role in his more systematic (and rationalistic) early writings, which differ markedly in tone from the writings and views with which he would subsequently become most closely identified.

---

3. Indeed, Rav Kook's first published article, in 1886, was a defense of his teacher's Torah commentary, *Haamek Davar*, from some of its more conservative Orthodox critics. See Yehudah Mirsky, *An Intellectual and Spiritual Biography of Rabbi Avraham Yitzhaq Ha-Cohen Kook from 1865 to 1904* (PhD diss., Harvard University, 2007), 107ff. Much of this opening section is indebted to Mirsky's landmark study.
4. For a detailed account of these early influences, see Mirsky, *Intellectual and Spiritual Biography*, ch. 1.
5. This is a general theme in the first half of Mirsky's thesis.

A combination of economic necessity and the exhortations of Rabbi Yisrael Meir Kagan (better known as the *Hafetz Hayim*) led to Rav Kook's becoming a communal rabbi in the small Lithuanian town of Zeimel, in 1888. There, just a year later, his wife Batsheva died tragically, but within the year, with the encouragement of the Aderet, Rav Kook married her cousin Raiza Rivka Rabinowitz. His study of Kabbala increased significantly during this period and would intensify further with his move in 1896 to become rabbi of the larger Boisk community.

In 1902, the Land of Israel beckoned. The position of rabbi of Jaffa had become available, and Rav Kook was encouraged to take up the post by the Aderet, who by then was himself assistant to the chief rabbi of Jerusalem. Despite Rav Kook's subsequent fame for his Religious Zionism, he was not a part of the Eastern European Zionist movement at this time. He opposed the formation of the Mizrachi movement in 1902, not wishing to advocate the existence of a separatist religious form of Zionism,[6] and he was not a formal member of *Hibbat Tziyon*, which strikes one as somewhat surprising given that his mentors, the Aderet and the Netziv, both had some degree of involvement with the movement.[7] Moreover, in Rav Kook's early writings there is no mention of his views on the special theological status of the Land of Israel. Nonetheless, Rav Kook accepted the role as rabbi of Jaffa, arriving in Israel on May 13, 1904.

Once in Jaffa – one of many incubators of the larger battles going on in *Eretz Yisrael* between traditionalists and modernists – Rav Kook had to contend with the burdens of communal leadership. In 1910, he upheld the *heter mekhira* (while insisting on significant stringencies), whereby Jews could continue to work their fields in the sabbatical year through sale of the land.[8] He was also involved in a dispute over the opening of the *Tahkemoni* school in Jaffa, which he initially supported, although somewhat guardedly given that it ignored the Jerusalem rabbis' opposition to secular studies.[9] In 1907, he himself began to plan

---

6. See Mirsky, *Intellectual and Spiritual Biography*, 319ff.
7. See Aviezer Ravitzky, *Messianism, Zionism, and Jewish Religious Radicalism* (Chicago, 1996), 92.
8. See Nehorai, "Halakhah, Metahalakhah."
9. Benjamin Ish Shalom reports that the school failed to live up to Rav Kook's expectations. His support for the school, although never entirely withdrawn, certainly

to open a yeshiva that would have a broader Jewish curriculum than traditional yeshivot and would even include the study of literature and certain languages.[10]

The realization of this dream would have to wait, however. In 1914, Rav Kook reluctantly sailed to Germany for the worldwide conference of Agudath Yisrael, in the hope of persuading the conference to support the Zionist initiative. The outbreak of the First World War at this time left him stranded in Europe for a period of five years, first in St. Gallen, Switzerland, and then from 1916 onward in London, where he served as rabbi of the *Maḥazikei HaDat* Synagogue in the East End. Whether due to providence or serendipity (most certainly the former in Rav Kook's opinion), it was while he was in London that British Foreign Secretary Arthur Balfour issued the Balfour Declaration in support of "the establishment in Palestine of a national home for the Jewish people."[11] Rav Kook was among those who lobbied in support of the declaration – activity that brought him into conflict with prominent members of the English Jewish establishment, including the Board of Deputies, and Edwin Montagu, a Jewish member of the British cabinet, who seemed concerned that such outright particularism might upset the status quo for Jews in Great Britain (*plus ça change…* ).

Rav Kook's European hiatus ended in 1919, when he returned to Israel, this time as chief rabbi of Jerusalem. He was immediately involved in negotiations regarding the creation of a Chief Rabbinate for the entire Jewish community of Palestine, which the British authorities would indeed create in 1921, with Rav Kook as the first Ashkenazi incumbent. This would also be the year that he created the *Merkaz*, which began as a beit midrash adjacent to where he resided as chief rabbi and would

---

waned. See Benjamin Ish Shalom, *Rav Avraham Itzhak HaCohen Kook: Between Rationalism and Mysticism*, trans. Ora Wiskind Elper (Albany, NY, 1993), 19.

10. The very style of the yeshiva was also intended to be different. Indeed, Rav Kook's description of the intended aesthetics of the place notes how the "alien Eastern garb" of traditionalists might be perceived by modern Europeans, echoing some of the secular Zionists' less flattering descriptions of the traditional Judaism against which they were reacting. See Ish Shalom, *Between Rationalism and Mysticism*, 21.
11. "The Balfour Declaration," reprinted in *The Jew in the Modern World: A Documentary History* 2nd ed., ed. Paul Mendes-Flohr and Jehuda Reinharz (Oxford, 1995), 582.

evolve into *Yeshivat Merkaz HaRav*. This was to be the fruition of his 1907 dream, although it would never take on the varied curriculum that Rav Kook had originally envisaged.

Rav Kook continued to play a prominent public role throughout the remainder of his life. On a practical level, his views were not always popular. He famously ruled in 1919 against women's suffrage, much to the consternation of some of his Zionist rabbinic colleagues, and he took an extremely unpopular stance defending Avraham Stavsky in the case of the murder of Zionist leader Chaim Arlosorov in 1933. Theologically speaking, however, he would become the major ideologue of a brand of Religious Zionism that engaged Zionism's secular roots within a broader theology.[12]

It was while yet in London that Rav Kook planned and founded *Degel Yerushalayim* (Flag of Jerusalem), a worldwide umbrella movement for all the Zionist movements of the day that would bring the spiritual element lacking in political Zionism back to the table. His time away from the Land of Israel during the war had only exacerbated his yearnings for the Land and his understanding of its unique ontological standing. The latter was presented in 1920 in its grand theological context in *Orot*, the first major publication of selections from his spiritual diaries. Edited by his son, Rabbi Zvi Yehuda Kook, *Orot* includes the announcement of this movement to "revive the mundane through the renaissance of the sacred."[13] The movement, however, would quickly be consigned to a footnote in the history of Zionism (and a short one at that), although the beliefs that inspired it would continue to form the core of Rav Kook's thought. *Orot* prompted certain overzealous followers of Rabbis Yosef Chaim Sonnenfeld and Yitzḥak Yeruḥam Diskin (the leading rabbis of the Old Yishuv in Jerusalem) to ignite a bitter controversy concerning some of its more original claims, presaging the continuous disputes

---

12. Rav Kook has subsequently been used, rightly or more likely wrongly, by followers in the *Gush Emunim* (Bloc of the Faithful) movement to bolster their political aspirations, much to the chagrin of some other Rav Kook scholars.
13. Avraham Yitzhak Kook, "*LeDegel Yerushalayim*," in *Orot*, 185. This volume contains the original 1920 version of *Orot* together with a number of other articles by Rav Kook. *Orot* itself (introduced with "*LeDegel Yerushalayim*") has been translated by Bezalel Naor (Spring Valley, NY, 2004). Translations from *Orot* are based on this volume.

regarding Rav Kook's literary and political legacy that have raged since his death on September 1, 1935 (3 Elul 5695).

## WRITINGS AND METHODOLOGY

In writing a single chapter on the thought of Rav Kook, one cannot avoid a brief word concerning the methodological difficulties that remain a constant bugbear in Rav Kook scholarship. Rav Kook's best-known works are compiled from "spiritual diaries" in which he recorded his thoughts in diary form with a measure of spontaneity, rather than setting them out in systematic treatises. His writing, therefore, is far from systematic; it is as much literary poetry as it is philosophy or theology. Reconstructing an overarching conceptual framework based on these texts is no straightforward matter, especially if one believes that the form of the writing is significant, exhibiting a man struggling to work these issues through rather than to expound a fully developed systematic theology. Aside from the difficulties emerging from Rav Kook's style, scholars must contend with the far greater obstacle of finding themselves in the paradoxical position of at once having so much and yet so little available material with which to work.

In his early years, Rav Kook composed a whole raft of books and articles covering a wide variety of topics. During the Zeimel years in particular, he composed all manner of works, many unfinished and many unpublished, all of which are significant for gaining a full picture of the development of Rav Kook's thought. While they have received increasing attention in recent years, they are still relatively little known or studied. A non-exhaustive list includes the journal *Ittur Soferim* (1888), which he edited and to which he was the main contributor;[14] *Mitzvat Re'iya*, a commentary on the *Shulḥan Arukh*; *Midbar Shur*, containing his sermons from Zeimel in 1894–96 (eventually published in 1999); *Ein Aya*, an aggadic commentary to Tractates Berakhot and Shabbat of the Babylonian Talmud (only published between 1995 and 2000); and *Ḥevesh Pe'er* (1891), an exhortatory piece on the virtues of the mitzva of *tefillin*, which he published and then publicized through sermons

---

14. Due to the death of Rav Kook's first wife, the journal ran for only two issues.

included in the 1925 reprint.[15] Also written during this period was *Musar Avikha* (published in 1946 by Rabbi Zvi Yehuda Kook), which was the first work of the elder Rav Kook to take the form of a spiritual diary, the literary form upon which he would subsequently settle.[16]

Only slightly better known than these works are his earliest attempts to come to grips with nationalism. These were published in the journal *HaPeles* between 1901 and 1904, although his fully crystallized views on Zionism only developed subsequent to his *aliya* in 1904. For our purposes, therefore, the most significant body of work is the theological and philosophical material contained within the more popularly known writings drawn from his diaries. Few volumes were published in his lifetime, the most significant being *Arpelei Tohar* in 1914, *Orot* in 1920, and *Orot HaKodesh* and *Orot HaTeshuva* in 1925. But it is here that the problems begin, for with one exception, these writings were not produced for publication by Rav Kook himself, but rather selected and edited from his diaries by his disciples.

*Arpelei Tohar*, one notebook from a set of seven, was the single work that Rav Kook prepared for publication. Publication was interrupted after only eighty pages had been printed, at which point Rav Kook's forced European exile put an end to the process. On his return from Europe, a combination of factors, including the responsibilities of his new post, his dissatisfaction with editing errors in the printed material, and pressure from Rabbi Zvi Yehuda not to publish the work in this form, led to its suppression. A small number of unbound copies of the 1914 version made their way to certain individuals – including Gershom Scholem – but the book subsequently appeared in an "edited" version only in 1983.[17]

*Orot* and *Orot HaTeshuva*, which are many students' entry point to Rav Kook's teachings, were both edited by Rabbi Zvi Yehuda Kook,

---

15. Rav Kook was known for wearing *tefillin* all day.
16. Once again, the main study of these earlier works is Mirsky, *Intellectual and Spiritual Biography*.
17. This edited version dismayed Professor Rivka Schatz, who was prevented from publishing it in relatively unvarnished form despite an agreement she had made with Rabbi Zvi Yehuda Kook prior to his death. The full story as told by Prof. Schatz can be found in an interview with Haggai Segal in *Nekuda* 113 (September 28, 1987): 20–21.

who was a leading light in the *Gush Emunim* movement and thus a figure of immense significance in the Israeli religious-political scene, with very particular interests that, one might assume, helped shape the editing process. However, *Orot* was published in 1920 with Rav Kook's full knowledge, and given that he was forced to defend it in the controversies in which it became engulfed, it is inconceivable that he disapproved of its contents.[18] Finally, *Orot HaKodesh*, viewed by many as Rav Kook's magnum opus, was edited by one of Rav Kook's leading disciples, Rabbi David HaKohen, known as "the Nazir," regarding whose heaviness of editorial hand (or otherwise) there are conflicting reports.[19]

The question for Rav Kook scholars therefore is the extent of editorial input into these works. With the publication in 1999 of *Shemona Kevatzim*, itself twice withdrawn from publication before finally becoming openly available, we now have the unedited diaries of 1904–21 from which these books, among others, were culled. This has enabled the beginnings of an informed discussion regarding the extent of the editorializing within Rav Kook's originally published works and the intentions behind it, although this remains an emerging science.[20] As more material surfaces, the picture of Rav Kook's thought might well need to be adjusted somewhat. Even now, the recently published *LeNevukhei HaDor*, drawn from Rav Kook's work before he made *aliya*, has also only emerged in a censored version, while the diaries from 1921 to 1935 appear to be closely guarded from public view and unavailable to most.

I mention these caveats since this essay will focus primarily on Rav Kook's "mature thought" regarding secular Jews. Consequently, we

---

18. That being said, Rav Kook and his son were not always of like mind regarding the book's contents. See, for example, Shalom Carmy, "Dialectics, Doubters, and a Self-Erasing Letter: Rav Kook and the Ethics of Belief," in Kaplan and Shatz, *Rabbi Abraham Isaac Kook and Jewish Spirituality*, 227n2.
19. Avinoam Rosenak, "Hidden Diaries and New Discoveries: The Life and Thought of Rabbi A. I. Kook," *Shofar* 25, no. 3 (2007): 111–47, esp. 146–47.
20. For an account of this nascent field of research, see Rosenak, ibid. It is important to note that the light thrown on Rav Kook's thought by this material is not all focused in one direction. The manuscripts include material that emphasizes *both* poles of the dialectic between universalism and particularism with which he struggled. See Jonathan Garb, "'Alien' Culture in the Circle of Rabbi Kook," in *Study and Knowledge in Jewish Thought*, ed. Howard Kreisel (Beersheba, 2006), 253–64.

## Dr. Daniel Rynhold

will be referring to the available published works, with all the attendant problems discussed above. The nature of this piece, however, means that we are dealing with broad conceptual themes that pervade Rav Kook's thought. This will allow us to construct a generally reliable picture, in the hope that (if I do my job properly) while minor modifications might become necessary as new material emerges, the general conceptual thrust of this piece will remain reliable.[21]

### GOD AND REALITY: RAV KOOK'S MONISM

The theological starting point for any assessment of Rav Kook's thought is his monism. The idea of the ultimate unity of being is an ancient one, with roots in the pre-Socratics. Parmenides, who lived at the beginning of the sixth century BCE, was traditionally understood to have presented a form of monism according to which there exists just one undifferentiated, unchanging thing (although this reading is now questioned).[22] However, Rav Kook's religious and philosophical assumption of an ultimate unity underlying the multiplicity that we encounter in our world owes its form to biblical and kabbalistic sources.[23]

For Rav Kook – indeed, for Judaism – monotheism is a fundamental tenet of faith. "Hear, O Israel, the Lord is our God, the Lord is One" (Deut. 6:4) is recited twice daily in the *Shema*. But this paradigmatic statement of the oneness of God has been understood in Jewish philosophy as more than a mere numerical statement. It has come to be viewed as a quasi-description of His nature. There is one God, and He is a unity, meaning that He is indivisible and that there is no multiplicity in His nature. God cannot be divided into parts, either physically or conceptually, since He has none. He is a simple unity beyond all division. If we combine that idea with a key element of the zoharic concept of

---

21. In the interest of accessibility for readers, I have tried, to the extent possible, to choose representative quotations from works available in English translation, although I have adjusted some of the translations. Notes will provide the Hebrew reference followed by a reference to the English translation (when there is one available).
22. See, for example, John Palmer, *Parmenides and Presocractic Philosophy* (Oxford, 2009).
23. Although it could also be parsed in more Hegelian fashion. It should be noted that the extent of Rav Kook's Jewish and philosophical influences is a matter of fierce debate among scholars.

God as the *Ein Sof* – the key element being His *infinite* nature – we end up with some significant theological implications. Before the advent of modern theories of infinity (although frankly, in the realm of actual infinite existents, many would continue to assert this), it was but a short jump from the idea of an indivisible infinite unity to the idea that this infinite being must encompass all of reality. Surely, it was thought, a being that was infinite would have no limits. But if it has no limits, it would have to be the only substance, since any other substance would necessarily limit the "space" that the infinite object could occupy, thereby making it less than infinite. This would mean that if God is reality, He must be all the reality that there is, "that all of being is divine, that there is nothing other than God."[24] He is a unified reality that encompasses *all* and grounds the fundamental unity of all existence.

> All that was, is, and will be – all is in His spirit, knowledge and desire.... It is a fundamental principle that divine knowledge encompasses what is in reality, for there is nothing that is not within reality in relation to God.... Moreover, it is in no way relevant to speak of God's knowledge encompassing what is not in reality, for since His knowledge encompasses all, He is inherent in the most excellent aspects of reality, and all existents are nothing other than tiny sparks in the light of that supernal reality.[25]

Note that in this quotation there is an important blurring of epistemology (theory of knowledge) and ontology (theory of what exists) that Rav Kook's monism demands. God's knowledge is an undifferentiated whole that reflects all of reality. But if there is no reality outside of God *and* God's knowledge encompasses all of reality, then God's knowledge and God's reality must be equivalent.

This idea of an infinite unified God, however, raises the question of where our world of multiplicity fits into the picture. Rav Kook's own view owes much to his appropriation of the Lurianic interpretation of Kabbala. Rabbi Yitzhak Luria (1534–72), known by the acronym Ari,

---

24. *Orot HaKodesh* 2:396.
25. Ibid., 1:214.

presented these themes of kabbalistic mysticism through his notion of *tzimtzum*, whereby God, as the infinite and all-encompassing being, must contract Himself in order to "make room," so to speak, for created things other than Him. Within this created "space," God's divine light is received by vessels that are ultimately unable to contain the power of the divine light, and thus shatter, in a process known as *shevirat hakelim*, scattering divine sparks throughout the universe within the *kelippot* (shells) of the shattered vessels. Thus, the created world is replete with divine sparks of good contained within shells of evil. It is through human redemptive activity – which for Luria affects the divine realm – that we will eventually bring about the great *tikkun*, the ultimate redemption, whereby the divine sparks will be redeemed from their profane shells, restoring God to His primordial unity.

The upshot of all of this is that the world *as we experience it* is, in a significant sense, illusory.[26] In the language of the Zohar, we must distinguish between our world of separation (or disunity) – the *alma deperuda* – and the world of unity – the *alma deyiḥuda*. Similarly, for Rav Kook, if God is the only reality, outside of which there is nothing, and God is a perfect unity, then despite appearances to the contrary, the world in its multiplicity must in some sense be an expression of this divine unity, a unity the perception of which has been disturbed and must be regained:

> True reality is the divine, and all existence that descends from God's ultimate transcendence is no more than the descent of will in its imperfect choice, which causes yet more deficiency until, at last, all impurity will perish, and the will in its freedom shall rise to the absolute good, and the Lord will be one and His name one. The return of all to the divine is the highest perfection of existence, and one cannot conceive its worth.[27]

---

26. In other words, the world is not simply an illusion; since it is rooted in God, it is real. The illusion lies in our way of conceiving it as independent of God. See S. H. Bergman, "On Death and Immortality," reprinted in *Essays on the Thought and Philosophy of Rabbi Kook*, ed. Ezra Gellman (Madison, NJ, 1991), 61–68, esp. 62–63.
27. *Orot HaKodesh* 2:395–96.

## Unity, Plurality, and Human Limits

There are two important points to emphasize at this stage. First, Rav Kook's view is not Spinoza's *Deus sive Natura* (God or Nature), the straightforward identification of God with nature. Rather, it is a form of panentheism, whereby everything is in some sense "within" God, but God comprises more than just our world, or indeed our universe. Second, given the fundamental truth of the "unity in divinity" that encompasses all reality, according to Rav Kook, the multiplicity of this world can only be a function of our limited perception. To make use of some quasi-Lurianic imagery, we view this world as if it is a reflection in a shattered mirror, giving us a horribly refracted version of the true reality that is to be found in God. It is, however, a refraction of something divine, and we need to recover this unified perception of divinity. Our belief in God's unity bespeaks this desire to recover the correct perception of unity:

> The affirmation of the unity of God aspires to reveal the unity in the world, in man, among nations, and in the entire content of existence, without any dichotomy between action and theory, between reason and imagination. Even the dichotomies experienced will be unified through the highest enlightenment, which recognizes their aspect of unity and compatibility.[28]

So it is our perception that creates the illusion of multiplicity; the underlying reality always remains unified. Thus, whereas our function, according to zoharic mysticism, is the theurgic one of actually reconstituting the *alma deyiḥuda* by reuniting the Holy One, the *Kudsha Berikh Hu*, with His *Shekhina*, for Rav Kook, God remains a unity throughout. We are not actually reunifying God through our actions. Rather, we are trying to align our knowledge with the fact of divine unity that does not itself change. In a characteristic Kookian psychologization of kabbalistic categories, what we are really trying to do, therefore, is reunify ourselves.[29]

---

28. Ibid., 411. Translation taken from Ben Zion Bokser, ed., *Abraham Isaac Kook: The Lights of Penitence, Lights of Holiness, the Moral Principles, Essays, Letters and Poems* (Mahwah, NJ, 1978), 225.
29. See Lawrence Fine, "Rav Abraham Isaac Kook and the Jewish Mystical Tradition," in Kaplan and Shatz, *Rabbi Abraham Isaac Kook and Jewish Spirituality*, 23–40, esp. 28–29.

For Rav Kook, *we* are the Lurianic shattered vessels that require reunification, and it is through cognition that we can achieve this. Genuine knowledge (i.e., divine knowledge) would allow us to perceive the unity in multiplicity that reflects the essence of divine reality. And it is that perception that we are able to work on in order to see reality anew.[30]

## WHAT WE CAN KNOW AND HOW WE CAN KNOW IT

If all of reality is, in fact, a unified divine realm, our purported knowledge of that reality as composed of unrelated, separate realms has to be somehow mistaken. But in what sense? To begin with, one could read Rav Kook's contention as a prosaic account of the modern tendency to confine ourselves to narrow specializations that preclude our knowledge of other realms:

> All the deficiencies in the world, both the physical and the spiritual, derive from the fact that every individual comprehends only one aspect of existence which appeals to him, and all other aspects which are outside his comprehension, as far as he is concerned, might as well disappear from the world.[31]

Thus, at the simplest level, Rav Kook could be taken to be bemoaning the high degree of specialization that passes for expertise in university departments. An Aristotle, who wrote on everything from metaphysics to botany, is no longer a possibility in our overspecialized world. Contemporary experts might know an ever-increasing amount, but on the whole they know it about ever-diminishing fields.

Nonetheless, such particularized endeavors are indeed necessary according to Rav Kook, who acknowledges that a person "must first enrich himself with the acquisition of the particulars, so that his

---

30. That being said, I believe that this standard distinction between perceiving God's unity and actually affecting God's unity is rather more complicated than this. If all of reality is God, then there is a sense in which our changing perception is indeed affecting "God." It seems to me that the distinction must be recast with greater precision, although that would take us beyond the concerns of our immediate topic.
31. *Orot HaKodesh* 1:120 (Ben Zion Bokser, ed., *The Essential Writings of Abraham Isaac Kook* [Teaneck, NJ, 2006], 152).

spirit may be liberated to contemplate general principles."[32] However, that such knowledge is necessary to gain truths is not the issue. The problem is that it is not sufficient for discovering the ultimate divine "Truth." That, it seems, is not simply because of a lack of time and energy. If this were the case, then a person with enough time on his hands and a good enough – well, probably perfect – memory might be able to acquire expertise in all manner of different fields. Rav Kook's concern, however, is more deep-seated than that of a lack of time and brainpower. The problem is to be found in the very division between disciplines itself.

If the Truth is unified, as it must be if rooted in God, then we must not only attain knowledge of all the particulars, but must also understand their underlying unity. And it is in the very nature of the division into disciplines to obscure this unity. Even if I know all the particulars in many different fields, I am not going to understand how they are in fact all a single unified phenomenon. So, for example:

> Philosophy embraces only a given part of the spiritual world. *By nature it is detached from whatever is outside its bounds. By this itself it is fragmented in its being.* The grace of perceiving how all feelings and tendencies, from the small to the large, are interdependent, how they act on each other, how separate worlds are organically related – this *it cannot portray*.[33]

From a human perspective, it appears, all items of knowledge are distinct and every picture that we form is necessarily partial.

This echoes an important contemporary view that goes by the name of perspectivism,[34] according to which all of our knowledge claims are indexed to particular interests, which are precisely the kind of factor that could "sever [our] favorite material from the larger web

---

32. Ibid., 53 (Bokser, *Abraham Isaac Kook*, 205).
33. Ibid., 9 (Bokser, *Abraham Isaac Kook*, 194). Emphasis added.
34. For example, this is a cornerstone of the philosophy of Friedrich Nietzsche, a thinker who is often referenced in relation to Rav Kook. See Naor's introduction to his translation of *Orot*, 44–47, and more significantly Jason Rappoport, "Rav Kook and Nietzsche: A Preliminary Comparison of Their Ideas on Religions, Christianity, Buddhism, and Atheism," *Torah u-Madda Journal* 12 (2004): 99–129.

of existence."[35] To take a simple analogy put forward by philosopher Brian Leiter, a driver and geologist would be interested in very different maps of a particular area in order to glean the information that they need.[36] Of course, both maps provide us with knowledge, but they do so in accordance with their different – and partial – interests.

While "interests" need not be the only prejudicial feature to yield partial perspectives, I believe that Rav Kook would agree that from a rational or more generally naturalistic perspective that only appeals to features of our human makeup, it is indeed correct to say that our claims to knowledge can only reflect a partial view of reality. All human knowledge *must* do so. To pick up on the map analogy again, a map that corresponds to *no perspective at all* would be impossible, since it would map out nothing. Moreover, Rav Kook would have to say the very same about any field of human knowledge, even science – which many moderns seem to believe has some privileged epistemological standing, but which in fact no more reflects a uniquely privileged description of unvarnished reality than anything else. Scientific endeavors reflect scientific interests, but have little to say to us regarding how we ought to live as human beings in community with others.[37]

In the above examples, the perspectivist claim might not be deemed all that controversial. The aforementioned perspectives – be they scientific and religious, or navigational and geological – can all be happily reconciled with each other. They might each be true in their own sphere. Religion can have its own aims, and science can have its own aims. To say that one better fits reality than the other may be meaningless; one better fits religious reality, and one scientific reality. Both can and should coexist, and thus these perspectives might, in a certain sense, be thought to form part of our unified picture.[38]

---

35. *Orot HaKodesh* 1:49 (Bokser, *Abraham Isaac Kook*, 204).
36. See Brian Leiter, *Nietzsche on Morality* (London, 2002), 273–74.
37. In a forthcoming piece for *Revue Internationale de Philosophie* entitled "Perspectivism and the Absolute: Soloveitchik's Epistemological Pluralism," I argue that Rabbi Joseph B. Soloveitchik's epistemological pluralism yields a similar form of perspectivism.
38. That being said, it is not clear that Rav Kook always viewed the matter in this way. See Shatz, "Rav Kook and Modern Orthodoxy," 104–8.

But Rav Kook's claims go much further than this in a number of ways. For he even asserts that competing views that *cannot* be held in parallel nonetheless both contain value, for it is inevitable given his monism that "in every subject of study, there is a spark of the general light which is manifest in all existence."[39] If everything is a manifestation of a unified God in some sense, there must be an element of truth in all such manifestations. Rav Kook notes:

> All controversies among people and all the inner conflicts of opinion that every individual suffers are caused by conceptual confusions regarding the idea of God.[40]

More than that, however, the very conflict between views propels our knowledge to a higher plane. In classic Hegelian fashion, Rav Kook sees our knowledge progressing dialectically through the clash of opposing views that ultimately yield a higher synthesis. It is only through the clash of opposites that we can progress, for it is only when separate and competing ideas exist that there is the possibility for such growth:

> Ideologies tend to be in conflict. One group at times reacts to another with total negation. And this opposition becomes more pronounced the more important a place the ideas have in the human spirit. To one who assesses all this opposition on the basis of its inner significance, it appears as illustrating the need of the spatial separation of plants, which serves as an aid to their growth, enabling them to suck up [from the earth] their needed sustenance. Thus will each one develop to its fullness, and the distinctive characteristics of each will take shape in all its details, something that would have been blurred and impaired if they

---

39. *Orot HaTorah*, ch. 3, p. 18 (Bokser, *Essential Writings*, 201).
40. "*Yissurim Memarkim*" in *Orot*, 124 (translated as "The Pangs of Cleansing" in Bokser, *Abraham Isaac Kook*, 261). This piece originally appeared in 1914 in a set of essays called *Zeronim* that were published in the periodical *HaTarbut HaYisraelit*.

were too close. *The proper unity can only result from such distance. One begins with separation and ends with unity.*[41]

Note that for Rav Kook, the conflict is not to be regretted. On the contrary, it is necessary to "awaken us from our dogmatic slumbers," as Kant once wrote, and propel us to greater heights. Indeed, no doubt counterintuitively to some, it appears that in the religious field, this underlying unity between two disputants is even more pronounced:

> In a dispute over opinions and beliefs, grounded on spiritual and abstract matters, it is more common than in other sorts of disputes for the two disputants, who appear on the surface to be very far apart from each other, to in fact be saying the same thing. And the nub of the dispute, which sometimes appears to rage to the heavens, is nothing more than verbal, with neither participant understanding the other.[42]

If we apply this to the example of two competing religions, it appears that for each of them the opposing view must have something right. This is based not *only* on the idea that everything is a manifestation of God. It also stems from the notion of His unity and the corresponding unity of knowledge for which we strive. For given this idea, it appears that the mere *existence* of disagreement between competing conceptions means that they must inevitably be partial and in need of supplementation. As long as our world is not perceived as unified, and thus as long as any form of disagreement exists, our knowledge is incomplete and we clearly have more work to do. The point here is that if we indeed reach the most exalted stage of "epistemological unity," presumably all disagreements would dissolve. Their very existence shows that we are not mirroring in our knowledge the true unity of God. That means that those views opposed to our own must have *something* right, for at the very least their claim that we are mistaken, even if itself only partial and human, is correct, or is correct at least in its assertion that we do not

---

41. *Orot HaKodesh* 1:15 (Bokser, *Abraham Isaac Kook*, 204). Emphasis added.
42. *Shemona Kevatzim* (Jerusalem, 1998–99) 1:5, no. 10 (Rosenak, "Hidden Diaries," 131).

have the whole truth. As long as there is any disunity in reality – which their very opposition indicates – we have clearly not reached the highest level of knowledge. Were our knowledge to be a *genuine* reflection of the unified divine knowledge, there would be no remaining conflict in the world. Knowledge of the divine truth would be beyond such divergences.

In this, Rav Kook might be thought to differ from the modern perspectivists mentioned earlier, for they not only argue that the notion of absolute truth in which all such multiplicity disappears is inconceivable from a human standpoint; they also argue that the very idea of an absolute truth unifying all perspectives and reflecting some form of "thing in itself" is self-contradictory. Although we might be able to view the world from many different perspectives, it appears to be impossible for us to occupy multiple perspectives simultaneously, or indeed to reconcile all the various perspectives that we have. How could there be a single unified perspective that embraces all actual and possible knowledge in a unified and undifferentiated whole? As philosopher Alexander Nehamas has noted, this would be akin to an impossible painting that includes all styles and thus all perspectives.[43] It would have to be knowledge that is independent of *any* human perspective, a description of the world that stands outside of *all* human conceptualizations. But human cognition, by definition, is impossible to conceive of in terms that avoid human conceptualization, not because we lack the appropriate conceptual apparatus to form such a picture, but because it seems impossible to formulate a coherent notion of such knowledge. It would require us to "represent" the world without taking any sort of perspective on it, and then to compare that perspectiveless "representation" to some external reality. The very idea takes us beyond the limits of coherence, requiring a representation that could not possibly *be* a representation.

Yet while Rav Kook does, of course, believe in the existence of an undifferentiated divine absolute, it is not clear that his belief really contradicts the perspectivist point just made. Rav Kook agrees that from a purely *rational philosophical* standpoint, the idea of this absolute divine conception does make little sense. We *are* beyond the rational

---

43. Alexander Nehamas, *Nietzsche: Life as Literature* (Cambridge, MA, 1985), 51.

when we speak of this knowledge. This is precisely why he retreats (or in his mind advances) into mystical language in order to discuss these ideas. No human vision can ever actually be equivalent to the divine vision, and we need to recognize that "our love for clearly established knowledge must be within limits so as not to impede us from aspiring after that which transcends it."[44] Thus, according to Rav Kook:

> Far greater is the mystical quest, which by its nature penetrates to the depths of all thought, all feelings, all tendencies, all aspirations, and all worlds, from beginning to end. It recognizes the inner unity of all existence, the physical and the spiritual, the great and the small, and for this reason there is, from its perspective, no bigness or smallness.... Because of this advantage, mystical vision, in being able to embrace within itself all thoughts and all sparks of the spiritual, is alone fit to chart for us the way to go.[45]

In this vein, the perspectivists, operating on the human level, would be correct even according to Rav Kook, since his mystical insights are indeed "inconceivable" from a purely rational perspective. It is no mere accident that Rav Kook settled on the literary form of spiritual diaries – not to mention poetry – rather than on a more typical prosaic philosophical style. The very amorphousness of his format is better suited to the non-rational nature of the ultimate truths to which he points us.

## THE LIMITS OF HUMAN KNOWLEDGE

The ideas discussed thus far have further radical implications that some of Rav Kook's formulations occasionally betray. One might ask whether finite humans could ever entirely overcome multiplicity in knowledge. Presumably, even for Rav Kook, as long as we remain with *any* human perspective, even one that is compatible with others, we would not have achieved the unified knowledge of reality at which he aims. The mere existence of different disciplines seems to be something that would not appear in the ultimate unity of God's knowledge and reality. This, Rav

---

44. *Orot HaKodesh* 1:218 (Bokser, *Essential Writings*, 158).
45. Ibid., 9–10 (Bokser, *Abraham Isaac Kook*, 194).

Kook writes, "is based on the profound truth that the very fragmentation into particulars is a mistaken notion, because creatures, even the highest among them, can see but dimly."[46]

If this is indeed the case, then *any* views that we form can be only stepping stones, for they will be opposed by their antitheses, which will, through the principle of the unity of opposites, yield yet higher syntheses, in a never-ending quest:

> There is no wisdom or perception concerning which one may say that it is enough, and that it cannot be linked to a higher illumination, in comparison with which it seems in a state of dimness. Even the supernal crown, which is a dazzling light, a pure light, is darkness in comparison with the Cause of causes, before whom all lights are turned into darkness.[47]

The "supernal crown" – the *keter elyon* – is the highest of the kabbalistic *sefirot* (emanations) accessible by humans, of which man can have mystical glimpses and which presumably allows man to reach some form of messianic cognitive "Promised Land." Indeed, Rav Kook speaks of mankind's attaining such knowledge with reference to messianic texts:

> Man's nobler future is destined to come, when he will develop to a sound spiritual state so that instead of each discipline negating the other, all knowledge, all feeling will be envisioned from any branch of it. This is the true nature of reality.... Only the limitations of our mental capacities impede us from glimpsing those aspects of the spiritual domain that are immanent in every part of it. When man rises in his spiritual development his eyes will open to see properly. "Then the eyes of the blind shall be opened" (Is. 35:5). "And the earth shall be full of the knowledge of God as the waters cover the sea" (11:9).[48]

---

46. Ibid., 550 (Bokser, *Essential Writings*, 175).
47. Ibid., 9 (Bokser, *Abraham Isaac Kook*, 194).
48. Ibid., 22 (Bokser, *Abraham Isaac Kook*, 195–96).

But if it is genuinely the case that we can never say "enough," that we can never say that there is no "higher illumination," then the ultimate divine level that hovers above our fragmented perspectives is not a possible object of human cognition at all and must remain an eschatological vision that will always remain beyond human capacity.

It is worth noting that in his recent book on Franz Rosenzweig, Benjamin Pollock has argued for such a view as the culmination of Rosenzweig's general project, from which Pollock has drawn some important implications.[49] Pollock's Rosenzweig argues that the individual philosopher realizes that his knowledge of the absolute that would unify everything depends for its formulation on the individual himself; we individuals are always going to be the ones *pursuing* this knowledge, so we must always remain as the subjects that *know* this object. But Rosenzweig understands that we cannot rise above human finitude to view the absolute from some standpoint outside of it. Our quest for knowledge, as we understand the term, must always be from a human perspective that cannot be swallowed up within some absolute divine unity if it is to be known by humans at all. Notably, however, Pollock, unlike the perspectivists, argues that Rosenzweig's problem is not with the notion of the absolute per se, but with thinking we know the absolute before it is actualized. Similarly, Rav Kook believes in the God that embodies this absolute unity. He merely cautions us against positing our partial versions of that truth as the absolute Truth, whereby one, "instead of seeing it as one phenomenon of reality, perceives it as all of reality."[50]

The idea, then, would be that the final divine vision is one that is entirely beyond human comprehension, for actual knowledge of divine unity would eliminate all individuality. Come the time of the

---

49. See Benjamin Pollock, *Franz Rosenzweig and the Systematic Task of Philosophy* (New York, 2009), ch. 5. The parallel to Rosenzweig may be more than just coincidental. In a recently published letter, Rabbi Zvi Yehuda Kook writes that his father believed that one could not understand Rosenzweig without knowing Kabbalah. See Uriel Barak, "Rabbi A. I. Kook on the Nature of Franz Rosenzweig's Connection to Kabbalah: Analysis of an Unknown Letter by Rabbi Zvi Yehudah Kook," *Da'at* 67 (2010): 97–116.
50. *Orot HaKodesh* 2:484. This particular comment is made with regard to Schopenhauer's conception of the world as will, but applies more generally to all of our partial visions.

final return to the divine source, all particularity will be eliminated. We could not possibly be there as self-conscious individual subjects *knowing* this final eschatological vision. For Rosenzweig, we humans can only grasp the final redemptive "vision" as something future or "not yet," rather than as "now," in its final realized state. To know it now would be impossible, for it would make us God.[51] Humans can only *know* the absolute unity that constitutes redemption as future – or, for Rav Kook, as an eschatological hope. While the point regarding the elimination of particularity is not as explicit in Rav Kook's work, it appears to be implied by his monism – if that monism is indeed as thoroughgoing as it appears – and by many of his statements regarding the limits of *all* human knowledge claims:

> There is no harmonization in the content of ideas except in He, who is the source of wisdom, perfect in knowledge, praised be He.[52]
>
> In relation to the highest divine truth, there is no difference between formulated religion and heresy. Neither of them yields the truth, for every *positive human assertion is lacking before the divine Truth*.[53]
>
> There is no doubt to the cultivated person that the highest ideal, which is concealed and secret, is more exalted than its fractional manifestations.[54]

---

51. It is worth noting that in the Gate that closes *The Star*, Rosenzweig does point to the possibility of an apparently immediate mystical vision of the "All," and Pollock is open about the difficulty of assimilating this notoriously problematic passage into the story he tells.
52. *Orot HaKodesh* 1:12 (Bokser, *Essential Writings*, 149).
53. Yitzḥak Shilat, ed., *Arpelei Tohar* (Jerusalem, 1983), 45 (Bokser, *Essential Writings*, 207). Emphasis added. Tamar Ross notes that this quote appears in the original version of *Arpelei Tohar*, while Rabbi Shilat's 1983 edition contains a more "muted" version. See Tamar Ross, "The Cognitive Value of Religious Statements: Rabbi A. I. Kook and Postmodernism," in *Ḥazon Naḥum: Studies Presented to Dr. Norman Lamm in Honor of His Seventieth Birthday*, ed. Yaakov Elman and Jeffrey S. Gurock (Hoboken, NJ, 1997), 479–528, 491n15.
54. *Orot HaKodesh* 2:569 (Bokser, *Essential Writings*, 176).

Moreover, Rav Kook's statements regarding the perfect unity to which we aspire speak of it as just that – as an *ideal* to which we *aspire*, that "everything aspires (*shoef*) to ascend."⁵⁵

In sum, Rav Kook's monism challenges us to expand our limited conceptual horizons in order to attain the unified knowledge of God, which is the ultimate eschatological aim. But the idea that we could arrive at this final destination from our location as individuals within the *alma deperuda* becomes, in this view, deeply problematic. That does not mean that we cannot strive toward this ultimate unity:

> The more the world becomes perfected, the more its constituent elements are seen as embraced in a comprehensive unity.⁵⁶

Nor does it mean that we cannot gain mystical glimpses of the final unity or reach a messianic point of international harmony. But it does seem to imply that the ultimate achievement of the divine end is necessarily *divine* and one that we will not experience as independent individuals, at least as we currently understand that type of experience.

It is certainly true that Rav Kook does not draw out this implication as explicitly as I have done here; he does not even speak in a unified fashion on this issue. Moreover, since Rav Kook's messianic age might well lead to a changed reality that would even eliminate death,⁵⁷ in a sense all bets are off concerning what is possible within this final unified vision. But to conceive of it in a manner that answers both to our current understanding of the unity of knowledge and our current notions of being self-conscious individuals or societies appears impossible and leads us into meaningless speculation. At this point, as at so many, Rav Kook's reflections pull him in opposite directions in a dialectical manner that might only be reconcilable for one attuned to the types of mystical ideas that confound human logic.

---

55. Ibid., 374 (Bokser, *Essential Writings*, 166).
56. *Arpelei Tohar*, 13 (Bokser, *Essential Writings*, 206).
57. For discussion of this issue and the different views taken, see Tamar Ross, "Immortality, Natural Law, and the Role of Human Perception in the Writings of Rav Kook," in Kaplan and Shatz, *Rabbi Abraham Isaac Kook and Jewish Spirituality*, 237–53.

## RAV KOOK ON ZIONISM AND SECULAR JUDAISM

With the abstract philosophical background in place, we can turn at last to our main topic – Rav Kook's attitude toward secular Jews. The ideas that we have been discussing up to this point can be straightforwardly applied to the historical realities that faced Rav Kook. Unsurprisingly, however, their application yielded conclusions that were out of kilter with both the mainstream ultra-Orthodox and Zionist movements of the decades leading up to the establishment of the State of Israel.

Rav Kook's Zionism was unique at the time for combining a religious, as opposed to secular, agenda with a messianic, as opposed to pragmatic, perspective. But while in his earliest Zionist writings prior to his *aliya* he took a relatively unforgiving stance toward the secular Jews engaging in the Zionist revolution, as Aviezer Ravitzky has noted,[58] given the broad philosophical themes of his mature thought as outlined, Rav Kook took a far more conciliatory tone after his *aliya*. Rav Kook's monism could no longer remain theoretical in the face of his actual experience of the ethical and nationalistic commitments of the people about whom he was speaking. His fundamental monistic starting point could no longer rest at giving the Zionist revolution mere accidental or pragmatic legitimacy. In its confrontation with reality, the monism that embraced opposites led Rav Kook courageously to grant genuine value to the contributions of the secular Zionists and the holiness of the "destruction" that they bring:

> There is a holiness that builds and a holiness that destroys. The benefits of the holiness that builds are visible, while the benefits of the holiness that destroys are hidden, because it destroys in order to build what is nobler than what has been built already. One who understands the secret of the holiness that destroys can mend many souls, and his capacity for mending is in accordance with his understanding. From the holiness that destroys there emerge the great warriors who bring blessing to the world.... One whose spirit cannot reach out to the wide horizons, one

---

58. See Ravitzky, *Messianism, Zionism*, 85–101, for more on Rav Kook's earlier views on secular Zionism.

who does not search for the truth with his whole heart, cannot tolerate spiritual destruction, but neither does he have any edifices he has built himself.[59]

The very designation of holiness for the "destructive" endeavors of secular Zionism itself is an important concession. Just as important, though, is Rav Kook's evaluation of those who cannot reach out to the "holy destroyers." A necessary corollary to this, rooted in the same monistic soil, is the recognition of the partial nature of his own Orthodox Judaism. The flipside of his reevaluation of the efforts of his secular counterparts is a corresponding degree of modesty regarding the status of those propositions that he holds most dear. For until such time as all multiplicity disappears, we can neither assert that opposing views are absolutely mistaken and without merit, nor assert with absolute certainty that our own views are without defect. With respect to secular Zionism, the key point is that the secular fill a breach that exists in the world of their Orthodox brethren. The secularists' "love for the nation…is adorned at its source with the purest ideals."[60] This is put most famously by Rav Kook in terms of the elements of the soul spoken of in kabbalistic writings:

> The *nefesh* [lower part of the soul in kabbalistic tradition] of the sinners of Israel in the "footsteps of the Messiah" – those who join lovingly the causes of the Jewish people, to *Eretz Yisrael* and the national revival – is more corrected than the *nefesh* of the perfect believers of Israel who lack the advantage of the essential feeling for the good of the people and the building of the nation and land.[61]

The practical ramifications of such a view show themselves in the different approaches taken by Rav Kook and his rabbinic colleagues,

---

59. *Orot HaKodesh* 2:314 (Bokser, *Abraham Isaac Kook*, 217).
60. "*Nishmat HaLeumiyut VeGufah*," in *Orot*, 122 (translated as "The Soul of Nationhood and Its Body" in Bokser, *Abraham Isaac Kook*, 277). This originally appeared as one of the *Zeronim* essays (see n. 40 above).
61. *Orot*, 84 (Naor translation, 194).

including Rabbi Sonnenfeld, during a tour of predominantly secular settlements on the coastal plain and in the Galilee conducted in the fall of 1913 (Ḥeshvan 5674). While most of the other rabbis on this tour saw it exclusively as an opportunity for *kiruv* – as a way of attempting to convince the secular *ḥalutzim* (pioneers) to repent of their sinful ways – Rav Kook records his view that the secular settlers were themselves engaged in *tikkun olam* (correcting, mending, and perfecting the world) and thus had something important to teach their Orthodox visitors, who were in need of a form of *tikkun* themselves. Indeed, the "heresy" of the Zionists is seen as a form of repentance, *teshuva*, which is essential to the ultimate universal redemption that will indicate the messianic understanding of divine unity:

> The revival of the nation is the foundation of the great *teshuva*, the higher *teshuva* of the Jewish people, and the *teshuva* of the entire world that will follow it.[62]

Of course, whether secular Zionists would understand themselves in this manner, as engaged in such acts of "repentance," is highly questionable. It is important to note that independent of our main focus on the theological motivations for his view of secular Zionism, Rav Kook generally appears to engage in a tacit form of psychoanalysis of secular Zionists, imputing religious motives to their avowedly secular endeavors – a view to which some within that camp have taken offense.[63] But for Rav Kook, any pursuit of truth and justice is ultimately religious, whether acknowledged to be such or not.

The implications of the previous quote from *Orot*, however, are that the Orthodox also require a form of *tikkun* to mend their own imperfections, although it is important not to overplay this. Even in the selection excerpted above, there is a clear hierarchy of concerns, as the continuation makes clear:

---

62. *Orot HaTeshuva*, 122 (Bokser, *Abraham Isaac Kook*, 126).
63. See Ravitzky, *Messianism, Zionism*, 115.

> But the *ruaḥ* [higher part of the soul in kabbalistic tradition] is much more corrected in the God-fearing and Torah-observant, even though the essential feeling and arousal to Jewish activism are not yet firm in them, as they are in those whose heart is polluted by a perverse spirit to the point of contacting foreign philosophies and deeds that sully the body and prevent the light of the *ruaḥ* from being corrected, and concomitantly the *nefesh* too suffers from their flaws. The *tikkun* (correction) that will come about through the light of Messiah...is that Israel should bond together, and the *nefesh* of the observant will be corrected by the perfection of the *nefesh* of the better transgressors, in regard to communal affairs and material and spiritual ideals attained through human understanding and perfection; whereas the *ruaḥ* of these transgressors will be corrected by the influence of the God-fearing, observant of Torah and great of faith, and thereby both groups will receive great light.[64]

Thus, while the observant are indeed in need of *tikkun*, they are nonetheless classified as God-fearing, whereas their secular counterparts are "sinners" who are "polluted by a perverse spirit," fulfilling rabbinic predictions that the pre-messianic era would be characterized by mass rebellion against God.[65]

Nonetheless, the central contention is that while Rav Kook would certainly assert that secular Jews are wrong, from a religious perspective, to ignore the realm of ritual mitzvot, and therefore are in need of repentance, his monistic view of the universe yields a holistic understanding of this-worldly holiness whereby the Orthodox are similarly lacking something that is present among their secular counterparts. Given the *divine* unity at which we are aiming, presumably there is a sense in which it is also missing from their *religious* makeup. Orthodox Jews are to be faulted from a *religious* perspective for ignoring the nationalistic promptings and material efforts of the secular Zionists. Indeed, a theme that we find time after time in Rav Kook is the insufficiency of mere "observance":

---

64. *Orot*, 84 (Naor translation, 194–95).
65. See, for example, Sanhedrin 97a.

Though the Torah and commandments refine one's character traits, we, nevertheless, cannot depend on this alone. It is essential to make special efforts to refine one's character traits and, particularly, to perfect one's moral state.[66]

In Rav Kook's view, there are actually four essential elements of the genuine spiritual life – the divine, the moral, the religious, and the national. This final category of Jewish nationalism, uniquely rooted in the Torah, acts as a lightning rod for all other nations, which will allow Judaism to achieve its historic purpose of unifying the world:

> The unity of reality, in its yearning to be included in the lofty, majestic, and refined life of the divine, has its bastion in the community of Israel, whose national spirit embraces all spiritual tendencies in its historic maneuvers.[67]

But while it is true that the Orthodox lack this nationalistic spirit, genuine Jewish nationalism can only be based in the recognition of its basis in Torah, which the secular are missing, and so the dialectic continues. The unfolding of divinity in the world continues apace, but as yet, Orthodox Judaism cannot rest within its *dalet amot* (four cubits) of halakha if it is to perfect itself, any more than the secularists can remain aloof from the spiritual dimensions of existence implicit in their very actions. That this would put Rav Kook at odds with the Jerusalem rabbinate of his day is perhaps unsurprising. Yet, according to Rav Kook, as long as these very divisions exist in our lower world, we clearly have not yet achieved the goals set for us, regardless of the variety of Judaism to which we happen to belong.

---

66. *Orot HaKodesh* 3:233 (Bokser, *Essential Writings*, 196). Further insight regarding Rav Kook's unease with the unthinking obsession with halakhic details has come through the publication of *Shemona Kevatzim*. See Rosenak, "Hidden Diaries," 121–22.
67. "Talelei Orot," in *Maamarei HaRe'aya*, 23 (translated as "Fragments of Light" in Bokser, *Abraham Isaac Kook*, 313). This piece originally appeared in the journal *Taḥkemoni* in 1910.

Dr. Daniel Rynhold

## TOLERANCE, PLURALISM, AND THE HUMAN CONDITION

From our discussion, we can begin to see the manner in which Rav Kook's attitude toward secular Jews can be traced back to his deep theoretical commitment to mystical doctrines of unity.[68] This, at the very least, yields a version of tolerance that we find Rav Kook representing to a greater degree than most in the Orthodox world. Indeed, Rav Kook's personal embodiment of such a stance is evidenced by oft-quoted reactions of many who encountered him from the opposite side of the Jewish spectrum.[69]

At this point, however, we need to return to our opening question. For the question that is inevitably raised in all such affirmations of tolerance is whether it amounts to a mere practical constraint of history or if it is founded upon a principled affirmation of pluralism. The difference is thought to be important in religious circles. If I am tolerant, then for a variety of reasons I might assert your right to be wrong.[70] If I am a pluralist, then I concede that indeed you are not wrong; you are in some sense right, as am I, but there is more than one way to be right – *Ellu va'ellu divrei Elokim ḥayim* (These and those [i.e., both views] are the words of the living God).[71] Can secular Jews be included within this? On the one hand, given the underlying divine unity in all human phenomena, it appears as if they must. But what is to come of religious claims to absolute truth if indeed we are confined within the theologically motivated epistemological limits we have outlined?

---

68. Rav Kook, however, sometimes also brings halakhic considerations to bear; see Tamar Ross, "Between Metaphysical and Liberal Pluralism: A Reappraisal of Rabbi A. I. Kook's Espousal of Toleration," *AJS Review* 21, no. 1 (1996): 61–110, esp. 77–80. Our focus in this piece is on the theological background, which appears to be more fundamental in any case.
69. For example, see S. Y. Agnon, *MeAtzmi el Atzmi* (From Myself to Myself) [Hebrew] (Jerusalem, 1978), 181–92.
70. The reasons for such tolerance may vary from my being powerless to do otherwise (which is not real tolerance at all) to a robust belief in the right of autonomy. For an excellent presentation of the different varieties of tolerance and pluralism and how they relate to each other, see Ross, "Between Metaphysical and Liberal Pluralism." As Ross shows, one can make more fine-grained distinctions in this realm than the simple ones I will be making here. However, such detailed analysis will take us beyond the confines of an article such as this.
71. Eiruvin 13b.

*Unity, Plurality, and Human Limits*

It is in answer to this question that I believe we find Rav Kook's most important contribution to contemporary Jewish thought. It is clearly the case that he must find some positive religious value in contrary religious affirmations given his view that everything in our reality is a refracted image of the ultimate divine unity. And yet, he does not simply equate all the various different religious and moral systems that exist. Rav Kook would maintain unequivocally that the proposition that "Jesus was the son of God" is false, for example. He is certainly no relativist who assesses every position to have equal status (though it seems difficult to decide whether the positions would be rendered equally valid or equally invalid according to the relativist). But neither is he willing to assert that he, or indeed any human or human group, has the complete and absolute truth such that all others are irredeemably false. The question of how one stakes out the middle ground has left many thinkers perplexed, unable to avoid the inexorable slide down the slippery slope from pluralism to relativism.

To begin with, we have already seen that Rav Kook is very clear in his hierarchical arrangement of the competing interpretations of Judaism. There is no question that he asserts the superiority of a form of Judaism that is committed to the mitzvot over a form of Judaism that is not. The Torah is the highest source of wisdom and a conduit to the divine, allowing its true adherents to lift others from their inferior modes of life:

> The higher thoughts of holiness that flow from the source of the holy, from the light of Torah and wisdom, refine souls and endow them with the light of true life. The few wise men that rise to this supreme delight do so because their souls are linked with the delight of the highest divine wisdom.... They know full well that the more they rise to the higher conceptions of holiness, the more they contribute significantly to elevate many souls from the depths in which they are sunk, to raise precious jewels from the lowly state to which they were brought by a host of physical and spiritual afflictions.[72]

---

72. *Orot HaKodesh* 2:295 (Bokser, *Essential Writings*, 162–63).

For Rav Kook, a life of Torah is immeasurably superior to a life without it. The problem, however, is how we can know this, given that every knowledge-claim that we make is inevitably partial. However, while it might be true that in the realm of abstract theoretical truth all views are partial, we cannot and do not live in a manner that reflects this. If we did, we would be the intellectual equivalents to Buridan's ass, which starves to death, unable to choose between two equidistant piles of hay. As human beings, we do not find ourselves in such a state of suspended animation. Rather, we find ourselves convinced by a particular view of matters that we do not deem to be simply one among many that we could equally choose to act upon.

The important point that emerges from Rav Kook's monism is that it is only from a divine perspective that we cannot state that one perspective is to be privileged over another. Despite the seemingly radical implications of such a view, Rav Kook indeed asserts just that, even in the most extreme of examples. Recall again:

> In relation to the highest divine truth, there is no difference between formulated religion and heresy. Neither of them yields the truth, for every *positive human assertion is lacking before the divine Truth*. From our point of view, faith seems closer to the truth and heresy to falsehood.... But from the perspective of the light of the *Ein Sof*, they are all equal.[73]

For Rav Kook, it is necessarily the case that heresy has a certain positive divine valence that must be drawn if we are to achieve the ultimate *tikkun*.

But we, of course, are not divine. We are human. And from a human perspective, we do indeed believe certain things at the expense of others. To quote Nietzsche, "Life itself forces us to posit values; life itself values through us when we posit values."[74] As Nietzsche recognizes, it is life that posits these values rather than our intellects. They are rooted in will and emotion as much as in intellect, which is

---

73. *Arpelei Tohar*, 45 (Bokser, *Essential Writings*, 207–8). Emphasis added.
74. "Twilight of the Idols," in *The Portable Nietzsche*, trans. W. Kaufman (New York, 1976), V, no. 5.

why Rav Kook is so keen to emphasize the greater significance of the imaginative and emotional side of human cognition. As Tamar Ross has noted, Rav Kook's claims to religious truth are "based on criteria for truth which are not primarily cognitive,"[75] though this is not the forum to try to pin down precisely what they are. There is something experiential to our particular stances that we cannot, indeed must not, eliminate from consideration.

This returns us to the modern perspectivists mentioned earlier, for similarly in their view, our cognitive claims simply cannot be separated from the evaluative frameworks in which they are situated. We might be unable to give a neutral rational proof of our beliefs and commitments, but that is because the very idea of a neutral rational proof outside of all human interest makes no sense – at least not from a human perspective. The flipside of this is that it makes no sense to view our knowledge as illusory or inadequate in comparison to some neutral independent standard, since there could not *be* any such standard against which our claims ought to be compared. In denying that there is a "thing-in-itself," such perspectivists deny that there could be any absolute perspectiveless reality that our descriptions *could* mirror. There is only human truth and human knowledge and no such thing as knowledge from *no* perspective. For Rav Kook, while it makes perfect sense to speak of an absolute divine reality, it is a mere place-holder rather than something of which we can actually conceive, or at best something that can only be understood mystically. He therefore would agree that it cannot be conceived as long as we remain bound to philosophical methods and categories, as are the perspectivists. He would, however, criticize their unbounded faith in such methods.

What remains important and distinctive with regard to Rav Kook, therefore, is that there is an absolute truth "embodied," so to speak, in the infinite unity that is God. But as humans, we cannot fully gain that ultimate divine perspective, at least not so long as we remain human. Our understanding will always remain partial. As such, even when we

---

75. See Ross, "The Cognitive Value of Religious Statements," 494. Ross takes a more detailed look at what these criteria might be, placing moral and more generally pragmatic criteria at the forefront.

are convinced by the truth of our particular perspective, we still need to respect other views – not merely for the pragmatic reason that we are currently powerless to do otherwise, but because there is an extent to which they are similarly expressions of an underlying divine reality.[76] There is truth contained within the opposing views, and it is imperative that we engage with them in order to uncover that truth and improve our grasp of our own truths.[77]

There is a sense, therefore, of Rav Kook's "using" alternative viewpoints for his own gain. However, the alternative viewpoints similarly "use" their opponents in precisely the same way. In a mirror image of Rav Kook's approach, the best-case scenario is that secular Jews similarly view the Orthodox as bringing something to the table. Thus, we all end up affirming each other's existence and difference – *de jure*, not merely *de facto* – as a necessary prod to universal redemption, in which neither of our views will remain exactly as they were prior to the confrontation between them. The ultimate truth is a higher amalgam that can only emerge out of the dialectical engagement of each view with the other.

The struggle to at once affirm this while maintaining our own rock-bottom commitments has the potential to lead to instances in which we simply cannot tolerate the practical implications of the views of our opponents if we are to live together.[78] Thus, Rav Kook's commitment to his Judaism led to certain practical decisions that might not smack

---

76. In taking this view, I align myself with Benjamin Ish Shalom's view of tolerance in Rav Kook. Ish Shalom and I have independently reached very similar conclusions via similar routes. See Benjamin Ish Shalom, "Tolerance and Its Theoretical Basis in the Thought of Rav Kook," in Kaplan and Shatz, *Rabbi Abraham Isaac Kook and Jewish Spirituality*, 178–204; for a more expansive discussion along the same lines, see his *Between Rationalism and Mysticism*. An alternative view can be found in Zvi Yaron, *The Philosophy of Rav Kook*, trans. Avner Tomaschoff (Jerusalem, 1991), ch. 12.
77. Interestingly, David Shatz has suggested that Rav Kook's notion of the superiority of Judaism might be rooted in the belief that Judaism gets this perspectivism right. See David Shatz, "A Jewish Perspective," in *The Oxford Handbook of Religious Diversity*, ed. Chad Meister (Oxford, 2011), 365–80, esp. 372–73.
78. For more on the practical limitations on tolerance and pluralism, see Ross, "Between Metaphysical and Liberal Pluralism."

of tolerance, such as his opposition to women's suffrage. But such are the conditions of life and such is the dialectical nature of the human condition and of human knowledge, as Rav Kook never tires of pointing out. Eliminating such instances is the ultimate human aim.

## CONCLUSION

As mentioned at the beginning of this chapter, David Shatz has noted that while many within the Modern Orthodox community are in sympathy with Rav Kook's bottom lines, they may not find the mystical basis of those conclusions quite as compelling. As I have indicated in the course of this discussion, however, modern philosophical perspectivists come to very similar conclusions rooted in large part in very similar philosophical assumptions, such as the inevitably partial nature of human knowledge-claims and their debt to non-rational factors. This may yield an opening for Modern Orthodox thinkers to find their way to Rav Kook's conclusions without invoking his underlying mystical monism. Mystical experience might be the experiential factor that Rav Kook invokes, but it need not be the only possible candidate for playing the role of preventing the slide into relativism.

Importantly, this view need not – and for Rav Kook, *must* not – undermine one's fundamental and non-negotiable commitment to mitzvot and the beliefs that underlie them. When you get to the most fundamental assertions regarding beliefs about one's way of life, you will always get to rock-bottom principles about which people will have substantive disagreements that cannot be tested in a laboratory for corroboration. The idea of faith in fundamental religious (or, indeed, fundamental non-religious) views will always be found beneath the surface of our practices. Such "faith" is an inevitable part of the human condition. While one might be willing to make enormous sacrifices for one's faith, one cannot *prove* its truth on neutral grounds. Moreover, in line with Rav Kook's beliefs we might know that other faiths also reflect some level of truth. It is living with this dialectical affirmation and negation of our own faith as well as that of those that surround us that is definitive for him. The spiritual diaries of Rav Kook are, in a sense, the perfect literary form for expressing the struggling back and forth between these poles.

The clear lesson of Rav Kook's writings is that as long as divisions exist, it is clear that we *all* still have work to do. There is no smug self-satisfaction with his own particular version of Judaism, however much he may have firmly believed he had access to mystical insights that would unite the world in perfect harmony. In Orthodox circles, this level of pluralism was viewed as controversial at the time, and in certain Orthodox circles, it appears to be controversial still.[79] But the idea that our human limits will always bequeath us such debates is, and always has been, the legacy of Rav Kook. Our task is to render them debates for the sake of heaven.[80]

---

79. The most notable recent example of this concerns former chief rabbi of the United Hebrew Congregations of the Commonwealth Lord Jonathan Sacks, whose book *The Dignity of Difference: How to Avoid the Clash of Civilizations* (London, 2002), was embroiled in controversy for making similar claims, leading eventually to his having to bring out a second "revised" edition. Many of the sources for his views were drawn from none other than Rav Kook.
80. I am grateful to Yehudah Mirsky for his helpful comments on this chapter. I would also like to thank David Shatz for offering me his perspective on an earlier version, a perspective that I have attempted to dialectically incorporate into my own. While it is customary to claim that any remaining errors are my own, in the spirit of the piece, I suppose I can only claim that my remaining errors are far less egregious as a result of his. In all seriousness, though, I am, as ever, indebted to his wonderful insights.

# Rabbi Yitzhak Herzog's Approach to Modernity

### Rabbi Dr. Itamar Warhaftig

**INTRODUCTION**

Considering the manner in which any particular *posek* addresses halakha immediately raises more general questions regarding the overall relationship between halakha and mundane reality.[1] The very attempt to apply halakha in the "external world" is hindered by theoretical and practical concerns. First of all, on a theoretical level, an inevitable crisis emerges whenever a conceptual ideal is transformed into reality. There are, to be sure, positive elements to this transition – for indeed our overall objective is that our dreams be translated into reality. However, the transformation from the simple "ideal" to the convoluted and complicated "real world" necessarily constitutes a compromise of the original ideal. Second, from a practical standpoint, when an ideal is actualized, it becomes safeguarded in human hands and becomes subject to the interferences that are very much functions of the heterogeneity and diversity of human beings.[2]

---

1. This article is an expansion of the author's earlier article, "Rabbi Herzog's Approach to Modernity," in *Engaging Modernity: Rabbinic Leaders and the Challenge of the Twentieth Century*, ed. Moshe Sokol (Northvale, NJ, 1997), 275–319.
2. See Rashi's commentary on the phrase "*Elokim* created" (Gen. 1:1): "The verse does not state '*Hashem* created' [referring to the attribute of mercy], since God

In our particular case, the ideal is halakha and we are actually commanded to apply this ideal to common life. In this instance, in fact, an additional problem arises. While halakha was given in the past at Mount Sinai, history itself is dynamic and ever-changing, and people generally demand change in halakha to correspond to the new reality.

One can detect two general trends among halakhic authorities who confront this challenge. The first position resolutely rejects any surrender to changing times. *Torat ḥayim*, the Torah of life, remains eternal and can be applied in its pure form in any context. Indeed, *ḥadash asur min haTorah* – all novelty is forbidden by the Torah. This position can perhaps be detected within the words of Maimonides, who includes in his Fundamental Principles of Faith that "this Torah will never be exchanged."[3]

On the other hand, the second position admits, and even embraces, change and stands ready to reform the halakha so that it can be adapted to these changes. This adaptation can be performed either through legislation – interpretation or issuing *takkanot* – or by utilizing tools that are internal to the discipline of *pesak* – such as relying on minority opinions. The principal objective is to avoid severe confrontation between halakha and the need for change.

In our contemporary condition, this broad issue can be viewed as the relationship between halakha and modernity. Advocates of the first position view modernity as a negative phenomenon from which the halakha must be protected. Proponents of the second stance tend to be further divided into two categories. Many adopt this "flexible" attitude out of purely practical concerns; they wish to rescue as much

---

had originally intended to create the world based upon the attribute of justice but realized that the world could not be sustained as such. He therefore conjoined the attribute of justice with that of mercy and built the world around the two." See also Gen. 6:5–6 and the commentaries, ad loc. Two authors who have studied the relationship between halakha and reality are Prof. Haym Soloveitchik, who discusses halakha and reality in the Middle Ages, and Prof. Jacob Katz, who deals with a much later era in *The "Shabbes Goy,"* trans. Yoel Lerner (Philadelphia, 1989) and *A House Divided*, trans. Ziporah Brody (Hanover, NH, 1998). See also *Sefer Hagut VeHalakha: Sefer Kinus LeMaḥashevet HaYahadut*, ed. Dr. Y. Eisner (Israeli Ministry of Education and Culture, 1968), which is partially dedicated to this theme.

3. The ninth principle in his *Introduction to Perek Ḥelek* (Mishna Sanhedrin 10).

of halakha as possible, believing that outright confrontation will cause greater harm. Others, however, fully identify with the various components of the modern reality. They embrace the entire notion of change and evolution, and personally sympathize with the need to consider the existing reality.

At this stage, we reach a critical question: What precisely is the "modernity" that some embrace and others spurn? This question clearly exceeds both the scope of this article as well as its author's abilities. A brief summary of this era's general characteristics will suffice for our present purposes.

The history of human civilization is generally divided into three periods: antiquity, the Middle Ages, and modernity. The modern age began with the French Revolution, an event that heralded two new movements. The first was a scientific and industrial revolution, marked by spectacular advances in science, medicine, and technology. Life expectancy increased, electricity brought greater convenience, and advances in communication and transportation reduced the distances between people. The second movement entailed an ideological or cultural revolution in which the spotlight was transferred from the communal to the individual. Man became more aware of himself and his independent powers, and fresh notions of freedom and equality began to surface. Man began to view himself as autonomous and independent, aspiring to maximize his potential. In short, one can say that modernity is the hallmark of the New Era.

Religion and modernity traditionally did not support one another. Religion was generally perceived by modernity as anti-rational and was therefore disapproved of, while modernity was often characterized within religious circles as a secular lifestyle in which theo-centrism is replaced by anthropocentrism.

Despite this, halakha never directly challenged modernity. Modernity took root in the gentile arena and wrestled with the Church more than it did with Judaism. In addition, halakha, by all accounts, contains a degree of built-in flexibility that allows it to make peace with many other diverse systems. Finally, modernity never presented itself as a religious competitor to Judaism, since religion is in no way its stated aim. Its initial movement – scientific and technological advancement – raises no complications to religion. Quite the contrary, these advancements were embraced by Judaism due to their potential to assist religious development. With the proliferation of printed matter, knowledge became more accessible and texts became more reliable. A greater amount of time now became available for various forms of religious pursuit.

The principal tension between modernity and Judaism emerged due to the revolution of values that accompanied the modern period. This transvaluation tends to, if not supplant Torah, at least marginalize it. A hidden battle is now being waged between a system that underscores the centrality of man and one that affirms the centrality of God.

This new system of values raises certain halakhic considerations. For example, freedom and equality are not always standard or universal in halakha. The status of gentiles, women, and sinners has prompted differing responses from halakha, on the one hand, and modernity, on the other.

It is incumbent on us, then, to identify the positive aspects of modernity in the eyes of halakha. Here we return to the aforementioned trends within halakha: one that repudiates modernity and is unwilling to accept that Torah is "incomplete" and dependent on some external source; and one that identifies with modernity and affirms the aphorism *hokhma bagoyim taamin* (if you discern wisdom among gentiles, accept it).[4] This second movement recognizes that halakha can learn from, and indeed assimilate, aspects of modernity.

The challenge of modernity can be observed in several ways, most notably in the expression of modernity within Jewish communities, their media, and their literature. However, the best way to appreciate the relationship between Judaism and modernity is to study those who represent the primary and original Judaism – its rabbinic leadership.

Judaism exhibits a diversity of opinion regarding almost any issue, but to Orthodox Jews, the dominant opinion is that of halakha as represented by Jewish rabbis spanning the millennia, from Moses to our contemporary leaders. Faith in halakha is based on the principle that "Moses received the Torah at Sinai and transmitted it to Joshua,"[5]

---

4. See Lamentations Rabba 2:13.
5. Mishna Avot 1:1. See also Maimonides, *Mishneh Torah, Laws of Repentance* 3:7: "In addition, one who denies the *Torah Shebe'al Peh* or one who rejects the presenters

a transmission that has been continuing uninterrupted until our present day. This rabbinic authority is, thank God, still intact, and history records the Jewish position regarding any issue based upon the perspectives and stances of its rabbinic leadership.

In the present work, we will explore the perspective of rabbinic personalities who represent the second group within Judaism noted above – namely, the group that identifies with modernity.[6] It may be safely asserted that the stance of the rabbis regarding this question might be better understood in a theoretical or ideological context. For this reason, it would be beneficial to inspect their ideological works. However, here we confront a phenomenon that is singular to Judaism. With rare exceptions, halakha and ideology (*Aggada*) are inseparable,[7] both in terms of the literature and in terms of the authors. There was rarely a great Jewish philosopher who was not also an eminent halakhic authority; indeed, each one's prominence was generally due to his halakhic abilities, while his ideological contributions were oftentimes espoused only parenthetically.

Furthermore, there were many rabbinic figures who did not compose any ideological works, and their beliefs can therefore be ascertained only through their halakhic output. To be sure, there were exceptions – men like Rabbi Joseph B. Soloveitchik and Rabbi Avraham Yitzhak HaKohen Kook, who rose to distinction in both fields. Most rabbinic leaders, however, were not exceptional ideologues in the traditional sense. Nevertheless, there were some who took interest in and wrote about ideological issues in the context of their halakhic responsa. Thus, the position of rabbinic leaders regarding modernity can be appreciated

---

    and transmitters of it, like Tzaddok and Baitos [are considered heretics who forfeit their share in the World to Come]." This is parallel to the eighth principle of faith in Maimonides' list of thirteen principles, cited in his *Introduction to Perek Ḥelek* (Mishna Sanhedrin 10). See my article, "Comments to the Thirteen Principles of Faith of Maimonides," *HaMaayan* 30 (Tishrei 5750): 12–18.

6. I wonder if it would not be more appropriate to examine the approach of a leader from the other camp, for sometimes the negation of a theory helps illuminate the theory itself.
7. I use the term *Aggada* here to refer to ideology, which is often latent within the aggadic texts themselves.

not only through the limited material that deals directly with ideology, but even through their halakhic works. As noted above, their *weltanschauung* influenced their learning as well as their halakhic rulings.

In this light, we will examine the approach taken by one of the great authorities of the previous generation, a man who was known as one of the *Geonim* of that generation and who also filled the powerful office of the chief rabbi of Israel – Rabbi Yitzhak Herzog.

## THE MAN AND HIS WORKS

We will not emphasize Rabbi Herzog's personal history here,[8] but instead mention his principal salient features: a talmudic genius, a prolific writer, a scientific writer (who received a doctorate in the field), a master of several languages, and an individual who possessed impressive scholarly talents. In addition to these personal talents, he had the fortune to head the Israeli Chief Rabbinate during a historic period of both disaster and renaissance. He responded to and actively participated in the events of this period.

Realizing his authority and the singular tenor of this period, Rabbi Herzog commented both orally and through his writings on contemporary events. However, practically all of this literary output is in the genre of halakhic literature.

I edited Rabbi Herzog's first three published volumes, entitled *Jewish Law of the Torah* (*Tehukka*). The remainder of the volumes (presently nine) include responsa and are entitled *Pesakim UKtavim*. *Teshuvot* entitled *Heikhal Yitzhak* – responsa on issues pertaining to *Even HaEzer*

---

8. Briefly, he was born in the Polish city of Lomz in 1888. At a very young age, he and his family moved first to Leeds, England, and then afterward to Paris, the city in which his father served as rabbi. He studied Torah with his father, and by the age of sixteen he knew the entire Talmud with *Tosafot* practically by heart. He received *semikha* from the Ridbaz, who predicted a great future for his pupil. In England, he studied several other disciplines and in 1919 received his doctorate in marine biology for his research on *tekhelet*. In 1916, he was appointed rabbi of Belfast and later chief rabbi of Ireland. By 1936, his name had already spread, and he was summoned to succeed Rabbi Kook as the Ashkenazic chief rabbi of British Mandatory Palestine and, subsequently, of the State of Israel. He was known as a *gaon* and an exalted figure who was accepted by all sectors of society. He served as a leading *posek* until his death in 1959.

## Rabbi Yitzhak Herzog's Approach to Modernity

and *Oraḥ Ḥayim* that have been previously published – are included in this compilation as well.

Rabbi Herzog's English works include two volumes entitled *The Main Institutions of Jewish Law*, as well as his comprehensive research on *tekhelet*, the latter published by the University of Haifa. Mossad HaRav Kook published a volume of his letters, and his son Chaim, the former president of the State of Israel, published a collection of his essays in English entitled *Judaism: Law and Ethics*.

Our principle objective in this essay will be to examine the manner in which Rabbi Herzog related to questions that pertained to modernity, specifically with regard to the modern State of Israel. We will thus examine his perspective on Israel as a modern democracy, the status of gentiles, the status of women, interaction with secular Jews, the ability to initiate halakhic decrees in our society, and other issues.

### THE STATE OF ISRAEL

The establishment of the State of Israel in 1948 (5708) was not an easy task in any realm; severe "labor pains" preceded and occasioned its arrival. In this context, we will examine the internal religious struggle within the different religious camps.

Two general sects developed within the Orthodox community at the time, each with a drastically different view of the Zionist movement and its aspirations for a Jewish state. In general, those who rejected Zionism belonged to the Agudath Yisrael movement, while those who endorsed Zionism were identified with the Mizrachi camp.

Those who rejected Zionism based their perspective upon two central points. First, from a purely theoretical standpoint, the Jewish nation is prohibited from establishing its own state at this stage in its history. This argument was often centered on a midrash cited in the Talmud, which describes three "oaths."[9] The nations of the world swore that they would not excessively subjugate the Jewish people; the Jewish people swore that they would not go up to the Land of Israel united and by force; and they swore that they would not rebel against the other nations. Instead, we are urged to bear the yoke of the exile experience

---

9. Ketubot 111a.

while awaiting the arrival of the Messiah, who himself will carry us to Israel and appoint himself as our king. Nationalism, which lay at the root of Zionism, was viewed as a foreign implant of modernity that should be thoroughly rejected. The second consideration of Agudath Yisrael concerned more practical matters. The Zionist movement, and subsequently the state itself, were directed by secular Jews whose culture did not admit Torah or its values and was therefore deemed destructive.

Rabbi Herzog belonged to the Mizrachi camp and wrestled with each claim asserted by his Agudath Yisrael counterparts. Regarding the first concern, Rabbi Herzog authored an extensive article entitled "On the Establishment of the State Prior to the Arrival of the Messiah."[10] In it, he questions the modern-day validity of the three oaths, confirms that settling in Israel is an obligation, and explains the position of Maimonides, who does not list living in Israel as a mitzva.

In terms of the validity of the oaths, he considers, among other issues, the modern reality. First of all, he claims, the validity of these oaths was limited from their very conception, and their terms have already expired. In addition, since the other nations have violated their part of the bargain – namely, not to assault us – we are likewise excused from our oaths. Rabbi Herzog adds that our establishment of a state does not constitute a rebellion in any event, since "the British captured the land both for our interest and for theirs…. The resident Arabs have already lost control of the land and during the First World War, the land was not captured from them, but from Turkey."[11]

In addition, Rabbi Herzog considers the conquering and settlement of Israel as an outright commanded war (*milḥemet mitzva*) in the view of Maimonides, since this would serve to provide haven for refugees fleeing for their lives: "Had the State of Israel been extant [during the Holocaust], hundreds of thousands of lives would have been saved."[12]

But for Rabbi Herzog, Israel was not merely a physical haven; it also served as a spiritual-religious asylum. He discerned in the establishment of the state a vital necessity for the Jewish soul. He writes:

---

10. Yitzhak Herzog, *Teḥukka*, vol. 1, app. A.
11. Ibid., 1:127.
12. Ibid., 130.

I was euphoric about the idea of the State of Israel. I concluded that it served a vital and urgent need. Not only from the perspective of saving lives – hundreds of thousands of refugees of the disaster in Europe – and salvaging our brothers under Islamic reign, the victims of religious intolerance (such as those in Yemen and Iraq). Not merely from the historical perspective, in terms of our national yearning for redemption from the exile. Not only to address the ever-present danger of Jews converting to other religions. Not only to prepare a retreat for times of crisis. Not only in terms of the Jewish people's search for substantial freedom – Jewish freedom – at once internal and external. The State of Israel is something that Judaism itself, from the very depths of its national collective consciousness, requires and demands. It is as clear as daylight to me that the terrible Holocaust, which destroyed most of our national framework – our geniuses, rabbis, *tzaddikim*, scholars, authors, and poets – caused great trauma to the bedrock of our belief, the principles of faith that are deeply ingrained in the hearts of most Jews the world over. I feared that if the dawn that had begun to break in the historic land of our fathers would be unduly hidden for too great a period of time, the consequences would indeed be grave – possibly endangering the very existence and survival of Diaspora Judaism.[13] Therefore, I recognized the notion that those who supported our heroic struggle in the Land of Israel are involved in a drive in which the future heart of our nation depends, not merely a battle to save Jewish lives (which itself is considered a *milḥemet mitzva*). Ours is not only a war for physical rescue; it is a war to preserve our nation's soul itself. Despite the fact that I realized that the formation of a state would present complicated internal problems, I was

---

13. In an unpublished responsum, Rabbi Herzog relates that when he visited the death camps after the Holocaust, he was informed that many hasidic Jews from the sect of Carpathians – simple Jews who had been reared in the lap of Hasidism – had despaired during the Holocaust to the point where they no longer wanted to put on *tefillin*. Rabbi Herzog spoke with them and encouraged their continued hope by informing them that they would one day come to Israel and that the Jewish people was on the verge of its redemption.

not fearful. I fulfilled the verse "*ufaḥad veraḥav levaveinu*," "and our hearts were filled with fear and courage" (Is. 60:5).[14]

Rabbi Herzog recognized the state as "the first budding flower of our future redemption,"[15] words that he composed which appear in the prayers for the welfare of the state. However, I do not recall within his writings any direct analysis of the messianic implications of the state. Indeed, as stated above, Rabbi Herzog, almost without exception, did not engage in abstract contemplation, but rather in halakha. His works are halakhic discourses addressing concrete issues of the day.

Here we reach the second cause for opposition to the state – its secular nature. Rabbi Herzog dealt extensively with this issue. On the one hand, he waged an ongoing battle against the possibility of a secular state not built on the foundations of Torah and halakha. On the other hand, he recognized the democratic character of the state, established at its very roots by the United Nations' mandate. Rabbi Herzog was of the few who maintained that it was possible to establish a religious but democratic state; the two values were harmonious within his conception. One might argue that most of his *Teḥukka* endeavors to prove this very point.

In the first volume of this work, he examines various forms of government – theocracy and democracy – and concludes:

> It is evident that the Jewish state, according to its traditional plan, was neither a complete theocracy nor a complete democracy, but instead a nomocracy; especially in monetary matters, it had much of this quality, and in criminal matters, it had … much flexibility.[16]

It is important to note that Rabbi Herzog averred that even if accepting the state theoretically entailed a violation of halakha, "even then I would assert that saving Jewish lives takes priority and the violation may be pushed aside in light of the condition of world Jewry."[17]

---

14. Herzog, *Teḥukka*, 1:210.
15. Ibid., 222.
16. Ibid., 2.
17. Ibid., 18.

Nevertheless, Rabbi Herzog made great efforts to demonstrate that the halakhic framework does allow democracy – even if difficult leniencies are inevitable, as we will see below.

## TREATMENT OF GENTILES

One of the areas of conflict between halakha and modern values is found in the concept of equality. Democracy trumpets equality, whereas halakha does not confirm that equality.[18] According to most *Rishonim*, the halakhic system greatly favors Jews in many economic areas. Although stealing from a gentile is prohibited, one is not responsible to return a gentile's lost item, nor must one return monies that he mistakenly acquired from him (*mekaḥ ta'ut*). Similarly, in theory, one does not violate Shabbat to rescue a gentile's life. In Israel, a gentile's privileges are limited; one may not sell him land, and his very residence in the land, according to Maimonides, is permitted only if he lives there as a *ger toshav*.[19] It goes without saying, then, that we do not have to tolerate the presence of alternate religions.

A more conservative outlook would not grant significance to "modern beliefs" such as democracy, and instead would pursue a path governed exclusively by halakha, with the practical result being the creation of a system that discriminates against gentiles. But the question of the treatment of gentiles would trouble any committed Jew who advocates democratic principles.

Rabbi Herzog dealt with these problems in the context of the establishment of the State of Israel. As noted above, he recognized the character of Israel as a Jewish democracy that includes a minority of gentiles, whose rights must be protected:

> The biggest problem concerning the democratic nature of the state (which, in any event, will be carefully monitored by the UN

---

18. The Talmud in Bava Kamma 38a relates that two Roman emissaries were sent to study Judaism. The only issue they had difficulty comprehending was the discrimination against gentiles in the area of damages. See the discussion and the associated commentaries regarding the manner in which these emissaries dealt with this concern.
19. See Maimonides, *Mishneh Torah, Laws of Idolatry* 10:6.

[so that discrimination is impossible for practical reasons]), are the rights of minorities, Christian and Muslim alike.[20]

Rabbi Herzog maintained that these rights could and should be safeguarded within a halakhic framework. With regard to the status of Muslims, Rabbi Herzog relied on the position of Raavad and *Kesef Mishneh*,[21] who consider Arab Muslims to be *gerei toshav* permitted to settle in the Land. In terms of their acquiring land (generally forbidden because of the prohibition of *lo teḥanem* [do not show them excess favor]), Rabbi Herzog relied on the position of Rav Kook,[22] first asserted with regard to the selling of land (*heter mekhira*) during the Sabbatical year (*Shemitta*):

> The Islamic Arabs, as it has been established that they are not outright idolaters, do not fall under this prohibition [of selling lands], even though they are not *gerei toshav* in the legal sense; I agree with the view expressed by Rav Kook.[23]

Accordingly, state law does not have to categorically prohibit these sales. Rabbi Herzog concedes that this reasoning is somewhat strained and, indeed, even Rav Kook included several other justifications for this position. However, Rabbi Herzog adds:

> Since it is recognized that our insistence upon these forms of discrimination will possibly hinder our chances at achieving a Jewish state and endanger the existence of the Jewish state, one can rely on the lenient opinion.[24]

This response typifies Rabbi Herzog's tendency to adopt difficult and strained positions to enable the formation of the State of Israel.

---

20. Herzog, *Teḥukka*, 1:12.
21. *Mishneh Torah, Laws of Idolatry* 10:6.
22. See *Mishpat Kohen* 63.
23. Herzog, *Teḥukka*, 1:15.
24. Ibid., 16.

Similarly, his attitude regarding the tolerance of Christian rituals, which, according to Maimonides, are certainly considered idolatry, reflects this tendency. Rabbi Herzog writes:

> Certainly, there will be intense concern both from the various powers that be and several Christian nations in terms of the rights of resident Christians in Israel. In light of the fact that the majority of Islamic nations oppose us and our only support is found among Christian nations, we cannot risk our existence by engaging in these harsh forms of discrimination against Christians. In order to solve these difficulties, it is imperative to prove that the Christians are, in fact, not considered idolaters.[25]

Rabbi Herzog goes on to engage in a thorough analysis of the concept of the trinity, relying heavily on the position adopted by the author of the work *Seder Mishna* that worshipping other beings alongside God (*shittuf*) is not prohibited to gentiles and that Christians therefore do not qualify as outright idolaters. It is more difficult, however, to tolerate Catholic ritual, which includes images in their churches. Rabbi Herzog writes that we may contend that they do not revere these images as actual deities:

> Although we are certainly enjoined against entering these sites, just as we are forbidden from *shittuf*... we do not violate the Torah if we tolerate these churches in our country.... Being that the entire issue may still be classified as a *safek* (doubt) [as to their status as pagans], even if we consider this a *safek* concerning a biblical prohibition [which we generally treat with utmost severity], in a dire situation such as this we may rely upon Maimonides, who asserted that any *safek* regarding a biblical injunction can be treated leniently. In addition, we may follow the principle that rabbinic prohibitions may be permitted in cases of *eiva* (maintaining harmonious relations with surrounding gentile communities).[26]

---

25. Ibid.
26. Ibid., 18. An interesting responsum regarding the status of Christianity vis-à-vis Communism appears in Rabbi Herzog's writings (*Pesakim UKtavim, Oraḥ Ḥayim* 117).

## Rabbi Dr. Itamar Warhaftig

An additional problem concerned the appointment of gentiles to public positions – for example, as members of Knesset or judges in the judicial system. This notion is obviously taken for granted in any democratic society, but here we confront a conflicting halakhic principle: "Any appointments shall be selected from among your brothers."[27] Rabbi Herzog relied upon the fact that the Jewish people obtained the State of Israel as partners with gentiles, and therefore have no right, nor capability, to prevent the latter's participation in public administration. He bases his defense of public appointment based on other reasons as well, such as the fact that these are only temporary appointments, they are not inherited, and they do not qualify as positions of "authority" since they are made by public election or approval.[28]

Halakhic discrimination against gentiles applies in other areas as well. For example, it is permitted to annul loans taken from gentiles,

---

Rabbi Herzog was asked by his son Yaacov Herzog if it was advisable to assist Christians and Moslems in their resistance against the Communists. In response, Rabbi Herzog first discusses the general Communist ideology, which includes several elements that he views as consonant with the Torah, such as socialism, an idea that is echoed in the laws of *Shemitta*. However, he views other components, such as forced abolition of private property, as antithetical to the Torah. Rabbi Herzog praises the social improvements that are an inherent part of Communist ideology, improvements such as strengthening the position of the weak and forlorn. These improvements, however, are healthy only when they are performed gradually, as they were in capitalist countries – "evolution, not revolution." Rabbi Herzog's principal opposition to Communism stems from its advocacy of atheism. In this context, Rabbi Herzog poses an interesting question: Which is preferable – idolatry or atheism? Rabbi Herzog does not provide a distinct answer. He notes, however, that there is no inherent relationship between Communism and atheism, although an association certainly exists on the pragmatic level, and many Jews rejected their faith under the influence of Communism. In theory, then, since no inherent relationship exists between Communism and atheism, it might be advisable to support the Communists in their struggle against Christians (who might be considered pagans)! Politically, however, Rabbi Herzog recognized that any involvement on the part of the Jews would be ill-advised and dangerous. Once again, we see that Rabbi Herzog brings a thorough understanding of the political and social reality to his analysis of a given halakhic concern.

27. See Kiddushin 76b and Maimonides, *Mishneh Torah, Laws of Kings* 1:4.
28. Rabbi Herzog bases his position on the *Knesset HaGedola, Ḥoshen Mishpat* 7. See also *Beit Yosef, Ḥoshen Mishpat* 1.

without repayment.[29] Under the insistence of Rabbi Herzog, Rabbi Binyamin Rabinowitz-Teomim compiled a codex of modern law, and Rabbi Rabinowitz-Teomim questioned whether he should insert the clause that annulment of loans from gentiles is legal, given that that is the halakha. On the one hand, this halakhic ruling is blatantly discriminatory and would be met with much negative reaction. On the other hand, according to Maharshal, presenting a gentile with misleading information regarding halakha constitutes a distortion of Torah, and doing so is forbidden even if one's life is at risk (*yehareg ve'al yaavor*).[30] Consequently, the codex should be written as accurately as possible.

Rabbi Herzog responded that the codex should be altered, enumerating several arguments:

> Although I disagree with this position [of Maharshal], we must still defer to the view of this great scholar.
>
> A. However, this [prohibition of publicizing inaccurate information] would hold true only if we were producing a modern *Shulḥan Arukh*. If that were the case, we would be forced to include the halakhic precept that annulling a gentile loan is permissible. However, we are merely presenting a legal codex to enable the uninitiated to comprehend our halakhic system, and it is therefore permitted to omit certain issues.
> B. Maharshal's prohibition applies when a gentile directly requests information; in this case, he neither asks for nor seeks information.
> C. We are not distorting the halakha, but rather omitting information.
> D. The famous qualification of Meiri that gentiles who lead moral religious lives are not included in these discriminatory laws will be of no help to us, for if the codex is absolutely

---

29. See Bava Kamma 113a; *Shulḥan Arukh, Ḥoshen Mishpat* 348:2; *Encyclopedia Talmudit*, s.v. "*goy*," esp. section entitled "*Gezel Goy*," 493.
30. *Yam shel Shlomo* to Bava Kamma 2:9.

accurate, it will still contain discriminatory elements regarding gentile communities that do not lead such lifestyles.

E. In a case of *ḥillul Hashem*, it is certainly forbidden to injure a gentile. This [*ḥillul Hashem*] is the most severe prohibition, punishable only by death. In contemporary times, when all financial interaction is public knowledge, we are responsible to avoid *ḥillul Hashem* by refraining from financially injuring any gentile [even an outright idolater], and certainly Christians and Muslims [whose status as pagans is highly questionable].

F. A principal legal condition of our modern state is that in economic matters, there will be no discrimination between Jew and gentile. The Knesset's authority certainly reflects the public decision. Indeed, the Knesset has no right to eradicate explicit Torah laws, but this applies only when they seek to contradict the Torah. In this case, the Torah merely states that when *ḥillul Hashem* is not a factor, financial harm to a gentile is not forbidden. The Torah does not state that one must discriminate. Thus, if the society accepts the law not to discriminate, this does not eradicate a Torah law, but rather helps prevent *ḥillul Hashem*. Ultimately, the law is then transformed so that discrimination is now forbidden (because of public consensus), and we could thus write in the codex that discrimination is forbidden. However, it is better not to raise the entire issue.

In sum, it is advisable to omit these references [of discrimination] entirely. In truth, precedent for doing so can be found in Maimonides and *Shulḥan Arukh*. Upon carefully examining their treatments of the laws of monetary injury, one notices that they only mention that "it is prohibited to injure your friend." We may infer that this only refers to a Jew ["friend" in the ideological sense], but from the words themselves, this is not entirely clear, since we often find the term "friend" in relation to a non-Jew (for example, in Shabbat 151a).[31]

---

31. Letter from 1952, published in *Teḥukka*, 3:278.

Rabbi Herzog's words speak for themselves. Although he mentions the famous principle of Meiri that talmudic discrimination was directed at ancient nations and not the modern ones,[32] he adds that in contemporary society, any form of discrimination must be avoided, since it entails a *ḥillul Hashem*. The novelty of Rabbi Herzog's position lies in the fact that he recognizes in governmental authority – as a representation of public will – halakhic validity in terms of prohibiting discrimination against gentiles. This prohibition does not constitute an abolition of the Torah law, but merely an addition that deters *ḥillul Hashem* – and it then becomes the halakha. Accordingly, it becomes our license to "update" halakha to the spirit of the age. Rabbi Herzog does not refer to such lofty issues as "the spirit of the age" or "modern existence," but rather only to the familiar halakhic principle of *ḥillul Hashem*. However, the guidelines of *ḥillul Hashem* are very much functions of the spirit of the age.[33]

The issue of violating Shabbat to save the life of a gentile also appears in Rabbi Herzog's responsa. Many authorities permit the violation of even a biblical prohibition because of *eiva*, the desire to maintain harmonious relations with the gentile community.[34] Rabbi Aryeh Leib Broda attempted to expand this principle to permit Shabbat violation even in cases that do not constitute *eiva*.[35] Rabbi Herzog disputes this opinion and refutes the proofs.[36] However, this response is merely theoretical, rather than practical, for in another instance, Rabbi Herzog writes:

> In general, it is difficult to equate all situations of *eiva*…. According to some, even biblical prohibitions may be violated for *eiva*.

---

32. Meiri to Bava Kamma 113a, and in several additional places.
33. The phrase *ḥillul Hashem* appears in Bava Kamma referring to monetarily injuring a gentile.
34. See *Teshuvot Ḥatam Sofer, Yoreh De'ah* 131; *Teshuvot Divrei Ḥayim* (of Sanz), *Oraḥ Ḥayim* 2:25, who writes that it is permitted to violate a biblical prohibition in this case because of the *takkanot haaratzot*. See also Rabbi I. Y. Unterman, "Darkhei Shalom VeHagdaratam," *Morasha* (1971): 5–10.
35. *Mitzpe Aryeh, Oraḥ Ḥayim* 2:10.
36. Herzog, *Pesakim UKtavim, Oraḥ Ḥayim* 63.

Yet all depends upon the particular circumstances, as evaluated by experts and halakhic authorities.[37]

In summary, it is clear that Rabbi Herzog refused to deviate whatsoever from halakha, but insisted that halakha itself allows a degree of flexibility in the attempt to apply its ideals to reality. Halakhic principles such as *she'at hadeḥak* (a time of pressing need), "public will," *ḥillul Hashem*, and *eiva* allow this flexibility. Rabbi Herzog exploits these in his attempt to reconcile halakha and democracy.

### ATTITUDE TOWARD WOMEN

Another conflict between halakha and democracy arises in terms of the status of women. In the modern world, one would never consider preventing women from voting, being elected, or holding public office. In the world of halakha, however, female appointments to public offices (*serara*) are considered problematic.[38]

Rabbi Herzog confronted this issue in the context of the establishment of the state. He writes, "Since, inevitably, the right to vote and be elected must be extended to gentiles, it is inconceivable to restrict Jewish women from these rights."[39] Even if one were to differentiate between gentiles and women in this regard by claiming that the issue of women's rights is an internal problem that should be governed exclusively by halakhic guidelines, there are still practical concerns – namely, that the United Nations as well as a large part of our own society demands equal rights for both genders.

Rabbi Herzog continues and distinguishes between his own personal opinion and the reality:

---

37. Herzog, *Teḥukka*, 1:10. See also pp. 122, 131. In this responsum, Rabbi Herzog cites the lenient position adopted by the *Mitzpe Aryeh*. In Herzog, *Pesakim UKtavim, Oraḥ Ḥayim* 207, he permits the transfer of a church located on Mount Zion to Christian owners based on the principle of *eiva*.
38. See *Sifrei* to Deut. 17:15, quoted by Maimonides, *Mishneh Torah, Laws of Kings* 1:5: "A woman may not be appointed king, since it is written, 'a king upon you' – and not a queen. Similarly, women are excluded from all public appointments."
39. Herzog, *Teḥukka*, 1:95.

> Personally, I view this issue [of women holding public office] quite negatively, even aside from halakhic considerations. However, the decision is not in my hands, nor is it in the hands of the Rabbinate.... Presumably, the majority of the population will vigorously demand these rights, and we cannot respond by prohibiting Orthodox Jews from voting altogether [so that they would not elect a woman]. This would lead to internal schisms and Orthodox Judaism would lose most of its influence in guiding the formation of the state.... We must consider the issue very carefully in an attempt to reveal a cause for leniency.... In my opinion, such a cause can be found.[40]

Rabbi Herzog continues by claiming that a Knesset appointment does not constitute *serara*, since each appointment is circumscribed within term limits. He further bases his decision upon the precedent of Queen Shlomtziyon, whose status did not elicit opposition among Ḥazal. Rabbi Herzog deduces:

> This example clearly illustrates that in instances in which religious continuance depends on women holding office, the strict halakhic clause is superseded, just as the law forbidding the canonization of *Torah Shebe'al Peh* was superseded so that Torah would not be forgotten by Jewish society.[41]

Additionally, Rabbi Herzog maintains that allowing women to hold public office requires no halakhic justification and can be defended on purely practical terms.[42]

---

40. Ibid., 97.
41. Ibid. Rabbi Herzog analyzes the various positions among the *Rishonim* and claims that according to Rashi, serving as judge in civil cases does not constitute *serara* and is not forbidden for women. According to *Tosafot* (as opposed to the position of Maimonides), there is no general prohibition of female appointments. This is also the impression given by the Jerusalem Talmud.
42. In another instance, Rabbi Herzog addresses the validity of women serving as witnesses and judges, which is justified on grounds of public approval and acceptance. In the course of his halakhic discussion, he incorporates the arguments noted above.

Opponents of the appointment of women to public office claimed that it would violate norms of Jewish modesty (*tzeniut*) and further suggested that it constituted forbidden imitation of the gentiles. To this, Rabbi Herzog responded:

> In terms of modesty, there can be no argument. Do women refrain from attending court for their own cases?... In the marketplace, is there no mixing between men and women? We have never heard an opinion that takes issue with these forms of interaction, for if so [that women and men would never be allowed to mix], life would be intolerable. Indeed, we have records of measures to separate men and women in the *Beit HaMikdash* and during a funeral, but when parliament is deliberating over issues that will determine the future of our state, there is no room for doubt. In addition, modesty will not be compromised since Knesset members are presumably occupied in their work.... We should request different benches for women, and if this is not feasible, we should avoid excess intermingling. One cannot, however, compare the standards adopted in the *Mikdash* and similar arenas (such as the synagogue) to those in mundane assemblies.... Certainly, there is no concern of *uvḥukkoteihem lo telekhu* (the prohibition against imitating gentile customs), since the prohibition applies only to activities which have some resemblance, even remote, to idolatry, which does not apply in our case. Quite to the contrary, Ḥazal have already informed us in Sanhedrin 39b, "The wise customs of the gentiles you did not follow," implying that there exist several judicious gentile customs that should be integrated within Judaism. Women's suffrage stems from the feminist movements struggling against discrimination, and there is no prohibition against this movement.[43]

Rabbi Herzog further notes that an erudite woman distinguishes herself from the general community and, in theory, can even issue halakhic decisions. However, on a practical level, no one would suggest appointing her as a rabbi. He asserts that Ḥazal's declaration that women

---

43. Herzog, *Teḥukka*, 1:97.

are light of mind (*nashim daatan kalot*) applies only to their inability to keep secrets, and in parliament there are no secrets.[44] Although Maimonides compared fools to women and children, his intention was only to demonstrate their naïveté. His statements referred to women of his time, as Rabbi Herzog notes:

> Since they had not learned any Torah and had no financial experience – which can also serve to educate – they tended to stray after false ideologies just as children would. By contrast, contemporary women … who possess wide and varied knowledge … are involved in commerce [and presumably have greater wisdom].[45]

Again, Rabbi Herzog presents his own opinion:

> I definitely believe that the appropriate place for women is the home and this is her suitable role for which she was created – to perform the will of her husband, within certain limits, and to raise the family. It is disadvantageous that women should fiercely compete in the rugged sea of society, as "all the honor of the princess is indoors." But what can be done in light of the fact that the present stream of society has generated massive changes, and it is impossible to oppose this tide outright? Had these issues been exclusively halakhic ones, the law would be otherwise, but this is not the case.[46]

Finally, Rabbi Herzog writes, "there are things that are not preferable (*lekhatehila*), but are permissible (*bediavad*)." It seems that Rabbi

---

44. Incidentally, Rabbi Herzog advised against including women in the Israeli cabinet (ibid., 110).
45. Ibid., 111.
46. Rabbi Herzog responded similarly to a proposal of Dr. Leo Cohen (*Tehukka*, 3:22): "Even though we can halakhically justify appointing a woman as a judge, it is an unhealthy idea. It is unwise to counteract nature, physiology, and psychology. With all the honor and respect that I have for Jewish women, their nature is not suited to sit in judgment. They might have undue mercy, or compensate by not having enough." See also his comments on *Tehukka*, 3:64.

Herzog did not fully identify with these changes in the roles of women, but recognized the reality and charted a course that would meet both women's demands as well as the public will.

### ATTITUDE TOWARD SECULAR JEWS

In Orthodox thought, there are two basic approaches toward secular Jews. The first regards them as heretics and *mumarim*, the treatment of whom is clearly charted in the sources.[47] The second approach attempts to defend these Jews by distinguishing between contemporary secular Jews and the *mumar* mentioned in the Talmud and *posekim*. There are a number of practical ramifications of this dispute.

## The Judicial System

Rabbi Herzog analyzed this issue along theoretical lines, in terms of the Israeli judicial system, as well as in a practical context – what should be done if and when a secular Jew wishes to testify? According to halakha, the testimony of a *mumar* or *rasha* (evildoer) is invalid, and he cannot sit as a judge.[48]

In this respect, Rabbi Herzog clearly adopted the second approach toward secular Jews, that of tolerance. In several instances in his works, he defends their character. From an abstract standpoint, Rabbi Herzog understood that the state could not strictly follow Torah law, as this would invalidate the majority of the country from serving as judges and witnesses. However, he recognized the difficulty this posed:

> The principal obstacle that presents itself is with regard to accepting their testimony. If we were to follow the absolute law, we would confront serious difficulties. While the behavior of these Jews in social affairs can be accepted (and there is no warrant to invalidate them on grounds of violating these mitzvot), their

---

47. A *mumar* has a distinct halakhic status and is discriminated against in several areas, including *sheḥita*, interest laws, and testimony. From the analysis of the original sources, it appears that the term applies not only to one who actually converts, but even to one who denies Torah or does not fulfill its precepts. See Ḥullin 5a.
48. See Sanhedrin 27a; *Shulḥan Arukh*, *Ḥoshen Mishpat* 32:2.

conduct in terms of ritual and principles of faith is somewhat less stellar (and would warrant invalidation).[49]

Rabbi Herzog attempts to validate secular Jews as judges based on the halakhic principle of *kabbala (ne'eman alai abba)*.[50] This principle allows for the appointment of judges who are generally ineligible, based upon the mutual agreement of the two litigating parties. Similarly, we find in the *Shulḥan Arukh* the possibility of accepting the testimony of relatives.[51] This precedent justifies the possibility of similarly accepting the testimony of those who are disqualified due to their sins. Once this acceptance of ineligible judges and witnesses is established as law by the assembly of lawmakers (the Knesset, Israel's parliament), it would apply automatically to all cases.[52] Although the *Netivot HaMishpat* asserts that if Jewish scholars are available as judges, this principle of *kabbala* is prohibited (as this will lead to the erosion of Torah law),[53] Rabbi Herzog argues that in this critical instance, we can rely upon this principle.

Some authorities suggested the possibility of establishing two independent judiciary systems – a court of rabbis, and a separate civil court that would operate under its own system of laws (based upon the precedent of *arkaot SheBeSurya*).[54] Rabbi Herzog strongly opposed this setup, which could lead to the formation of a completely independent

---

49. Herzog, *Teḥukka*, 1:39. Rabbi Herzog wrote similar comments in the same volume, p. 200: "If most of the society were religious, we would need no *takkana*. However, we know that our society will not accept the invalidation of moral and ethical people as judges and jurors based solely upon their lack of religious adherence. If we will insist upon the strict application of halakha in this case, rather than implementing the rule 'better they should be unintentional sinners' (Kiddushin 21b), they will inevitably be appointed judges within a system which stands in direct opposition to Torah law.... Torah law will become entirely neglected, and the state will select a gentile codex as the basis of its legal system." See also ibid., 206, 212, 215.
50. Sanhedrin 24a.
51. *Shulḥan Arukh, Ḥoshen Mishpat* 37:22.
52. The principle *hefker beit din hefker* (the license of the court to unilaterally transfer ownership or affect financial obligation) would help overcome the problem of any minority that opposes this decision.
53. *Netivot HaMishpat, Ḥoshen Mishpat* 32, *Ḥiddushim* 13.
54. Sanhedrin 23a. See Rabbi Herzog's dispute with Rabbi Shlomo Goren in *Teḥukka*, vol. 1, app. 3, especially pp. 164, 173, 200.

and foreign judicial entity that would subvert Torah law; he viewed this option as an assault upon Torah law.

Even the option of accepting secular judges who would operate under Torah Law was not completely acceptable to him, though such a possibility was not practical or feasible in any event. He writes that he begins to sense a growing "distaste for these compromises [such as *kabbala*] which, in practice, would eliminate such a large section of halakha pertaining to judges and witnesses."[55] Therefore, he saw as his principal purpose the fortification of rabbinical authority within the office of the Rabbinate.[56]

Rabbi Herzog was more lenient with regard to accepting secular Jews as witnesses, and even contemplated their outright acceptance.[57] The halakha follows the view of Abaye, who asserts that one who sins to anger God, as an overt act of rebellion, and therefore qualifies as a *mumar lehakhis*, is disqualified for testimony, as is one who sins for his own benefit, *mumar lete'avon*.[58] Rabbi Herzog reasons that this is only because one of such contemptible character would have no hesitation about falsifying information. Quite astonishingly, he concludes that if the individual is known by the court to be a righteous and virtuous man in terms of his character and conduct with other humans, he is not ineligible according to Torah law.[59] In another instance, he relies upon the testimony of an *am haaretz* (ignoramus):[60]

> In our generation, we are careful regarding the witnesses to any marriage or divorce... but with regard to monetary issues, we are not that careful. I suggest that this practice of the Israeli court

---

55. Herzog, *Teḥukka*, ibid., app. 9, p. 229; see also 212, 219.
56. Ibid., apps. 5–12.
57. Herzog, *Pesakim UKtavim*, *Yoreh De'ah* 63. Even though he was lenient regarding accepting their testimony, he still objected to any leniencies regarding their serving as judges.
58. Sanhedrin 27a.
59. Herzog, *Teḥukka*, 3:232. Rabbi Herzog relies upon many leniencies, among them the position adopted by Rabbi Yonatan Eybeschutz that unless there are formal witnesses to the sins committed by these candidates, they remain valid for testimony even though their sins are common knowledge.
60. See Ḥagiga 32a; *Tur, Ḥoshen Misphat* 34:17; commentary of the Vilna Gaon, ad loc., 39.

system is in accordance with halakha, as the Gemara writes that through the aegis of *hefker beit din hefker*, we may accept the testimony of the uneducated as long as we are not outright uprooting the law by accepting due to their immoral actions. Indeed, according to Rava's position, even *these* individuals are valid as witnesses, but we do not conclude like Rava.[61]

Rabbi Herzog observes the unique status of contemporary secular Jews:

> From the above, we may conclude an additional fact. In our time and place, due to universal factors as well as our own sins, lack of religious discipline has become widespread. Therefore, as the Ḥazon Ish already asserted, the principle of *moridin velo maalin* (we must not assist secular Jews, but instead facilitate their downfall) does not apply. The recession of the face of God from society is so severe that secular Jews are to be considered *shogegim* (unintentional violators of the law). In addition, since the majority of the Jews in our generation in Israel are secular, public violation of Shabbat is no longer an indication of their reliability in *beit din*.[62]

In another instance, Rabbi Herzog differentiates between a case in which an individual is immoral and a case in which the overall community is in a state of religious decline and individuals are drawn into these forms of behavior.[63]

---

61. Herzog, *Teḥukka*, 3:238. The ability to rely upon a rejected halakhic position (even when it only serves to bolster a position that can be supported for alternate reasons) is questionable. See *Teḥukka*, 2:158, where Rabbi Herzog considers this issue.
62. Ibid., 2:232. Rabbi Herzog cites many later *posekim* who also are lenient in accepting testimony from modern secular Jews since they are considered *shogegim* (Responsa Rabbi Akiva Eiger, *Binyan Tziyon*, *Zekan Aharon*, and several others). However, in *Teḥukka*, 1:39, Rabbi Herzog hesitates to validate the testimony for this reason, since "we have not yet reached the point where these sinners can be considered *shogegim*."
63. Ibid., 3:233. Since the disqualification of sinners is a law with reason, one can consider the applicability of the law in light of the general behavior of society. Additionally, one must consider the explanation of *Sifra* to the verse (Lev. 7:20): "*Venikhreta*

## Suitability for a *Minyan*

Rabbi Herzog did not absolutely disqualify a Shabbat violator from a *minyan*. He distinguishes between such a person and one who has been excommunicated (*menudeh*). In the case of the former, who attends *minyan* infrequently:

> We will in no way encourage greater Shabbat observance [by not counting him]; quite the contrary, we will provoke him to move further from religious observance. To push someone aside with two hands is not acceptable.[64]

## Overall Relationship with Secular Jews

On another occasion, Rabbi Herzog refused to ascribe sins to secular Jews simply because they were non-observant. In 1941, a disconcerting rumor emerged that in a secular kibbutz located in the north of Israel, a *sefer Torah* had been torn and defiled. Many wanted to take action even before the news was verified, based on the principle found in the Talmud: "We may impute corrupt acts to the depraved [even though we do not have proof positive]."[65] Rabbi Herzog opposed this view and asserted that Ḥazal refrained from imparting wicked actions even to known sinners such as Ahab when there was no hard evidence. Rabbi Zvi Hirsch Chajes, in his introduction to the work *Ein Yaakov*, takes the general stance that we may assume wrongdoing on the part of the wicked. Rabbi Herzog responds:

> From this Yerushalmi, one cannot prove the legitimacy of ascribing immoral behavior to corrupt individuals in the absence of evidence. The way of the Torah is honesty…. Altering or coloring

---

*hanefesh hahi*" (That soul will surely be cut off) – a soul, not a community. An entire Jewish community cannot receive *karet*. Once this type of behavior becomes widespread, the status of being a *mezid* (intentional sinner) is called into question.

64. See Herzog, *Pesakim UKtavim*, *Oraḥ Ḥayim* 13. The laws of *menudeh* are cited in *Shulḥan Arukh*, *Oraḥ Ḥayim* 12:55. I do not know why Rabbi Herzog does not quote the comments of the *Peri Megadim* (46, cited there by the *Mishna Berura*), that one who violates Shabbat in public cannot join a *minyan*.
65. Y. Sanhedrin 10:2.

the truth in this manner will not succeed in persuading them to abandon their present conduct, but will cause greater polarization and intransigence and will distance them even further from the possibility of *teshuva*.⁶⁶

Possibly the most ardent defense of secular Jews can be found in one of Rabbi Herzog's responsa addressing the possibility of *kohanim* (priests) praying at gravesites of *tzaddikim*. His words speak for themselves:

> The Vilna Gaon cites a section from the Zohar on *Parashat Pekudei* and comments, "Even a Jewish *mumar* is considered a *barza demehemnuta* [literally, a divine pipeline – one who serves to channel divine grace from heaven to earth]." Surely the Gaon, when referring to a *mumar*, intended secular Jews and not Jews who have converted. He intended these Jews because their behavior is due to poor education; they have never been given the opportunity to appreciate the beauty of Torah. In this respect, they are not comparable to those who have been properly educated and still reject the Torah. I disapprove of those who claim that secular Jews are inferior to gentiles; these detractors themselves are considered *megaleh panim BaTorah shelo kehalakha* (those who make blatantly erroneous mis-readings of Torah law). This statement of the Gaon serves to authenticate Rav Kook's overall ideology (*tana demesaye'a lei*). I am inclined to support this position.
> 
> I might add that, in our generation, even those who did receive a proper *ḥeder* education have been so unfavorably influenced by modernism – which, at its root, is a gentile influence – that they may be partially exonerated in the same manner as those who have not received any education. In earlier periods of history, when the gentile world was predominantly religious, Jewish youth would reason, "How can we not continue our *mesora* if the gentiles are so committed to their religious heritage? After all, our tradition is so magnificent and exalted, and far surpasses

---

66. Herzog, *Teḥukka*, 3:229.

the philosophies of other religions!" However, in the modern era, most cultures have spurned religion and the overall scientific "atmosphere" is decidedly anti-religious; this, of course, has an adverse effect, both directly and indirectly, upon the commitment of Jewish youth.

It is important to remember the governing principle set down by Ḥazal (Sota 47a), "Do not distance [sinners] with two hands; rather, let the left hand push aside while the right hand attempts to retrieve." When I was a young student, I heard from the Holy Ridbaz of Jerusalem, himself a student of Rabbi Ḥayim of Volozhin [the principal student of the Vilna Gaon], who said, "In ancient times, even when actual prophecy was suspended, society continued to employ a *bat kol* (Yoma 9b). The spirit of *tuma* was still periodically unveiled amongst the gentiles, and to counter this, the spirit of *kedusha* would appear intermittently among the Jews. In this setting, one who remained an *apikorus*, in light of these revelations, was indeed an unholy sinner. By contrast, in our own times, we have not witnessed in some time an overt revelation of *ruḥniut* – neither *kedusha* nor, *lehavdil*, *tuma*. The influence of spiritless *ḥomer* is extremely powerful and we cannot equate a modern *apikorus* to an ancient one." Similar words have been echoed by the great righteous one, the *Ḥazon Ish*, that in our era the law of *moridin velo maalin* does not apply. Being that our generation does not enjoy public miracles, these forms of punishment are ineffective and do not apply. Quite the opposite is true; we should endeavor to retrieve them with bonds of love, and, as much as possible, place them in the "rays of light."[67]

Rav Kook's words in this matter are well documented. He also was aware that modern secular Jews were not of the same variety as their predecessors. In earlier times, such Jews had completely turned their hearts away from their people, their land, and their culture. Modern secular Jews, however, especially nationalistic Zionists, are entirely committed to our legacy, to the point that they are willing to sacrifice their very lives for the future of

---

67. Ḥazon Ish, Yoreh De'ah, Laws of Slaughter 2:16.

our people. About such individuals, Ḥazal remarked (Eiruvin 21b) regarding the passage in Jeremiah 24 that when the verse refers to spoiled figs, these symbolize the wicked. One might maintain that their worth has entirely disappeared. Therefore, the verse affirms, "the flowers provide aroma" – all the plants [both healthy and rotten] will ultimately provide fragrance.[68]

Rabbi Herzog employed these sources to justify his decision to participate in the establishment of the State of Israel, "to invest all our energies to invigorate our religion...so that we may benefit from a divine assistance which will inspire all of Israel to embark upon a national *teshuva*."

To summarize, Rabbi Herzog considered the unique character of modern society in differentiating between the conventional *kofer* (heretic) and the contemporary secular Jew.

## THE ARMY AND NATIONAL SECURITY

Rabbi Herzog's perspective on the renascent State of Israel is clearly reflected in the answers he penned to halakhic questions relating to the army and various matters of national security.

On the eve of the establishment of the state, the Ezra organization turned to Rabbi Herzog with a number of questions relating to proper army procedures, particularly with regard to Shabbat, and from his response we can learn of his appraisal of these matters. Until this point, questions regarding the desecration of Shabbat were usually discussed within the framework of the laws of *pikuaḥ nefesh*, the saving of life. Rabbi Herzog, however, deemed the reality at hand as falling under the halakhic guidelines of a *milḥemet mitzva*, an obligatory or commanded war. For this category to be invoked, a battle must be undertaken with the direct consent of the king, and this would appear to be irrelevant in modern times. Nevertheless, Rabbi Herzog maintained, based on a responsum of his predecessor, Rav Kook, that to a certain degree, it is possible to view the consent of the nation (through their representatives) as equal to that of the king.

---

68. Herzog, *Pesakim UKtavim, Yoreh De'ah* 146.

This principled view has ramifications with regard to a number of questions.

## Offensive War on Shabbat

A defensive war is considered *pikuaḥ nefesh*, but it is difficult to relate as such to a self-initiated offensive that is undertaken for future considerations (unless the battle at hand is an urgent, preventative war that the officers of the army demand immediately due to a clear and present danger). In the framework of a *milḥemet mitzva*, it is permissible to conduct an attack against enemy forces even on Shabbat in order to bring about an overall victory of the People of Israel over its enemies.[69]

## Compulsory Conscription

Some authorities were of the opinion that we have no right in modern times to apply mandatory conscription of soldiers to the army, certainly not in order to fight a *milḥemet reshut*, a war of choice. We have no right to force others to endanger their lives. With regard to this issue as well, Rabbi Herzog claimed that the state has the halakhic status of a king. In his words:

> The power of the overwhelming majority of the Yishuv (the Jewish population in Israel) is similar to the power of the king of Israel… and there is no need for a court of seventy-one. According to the above, we have the power to enforce conscription.[70]

Rabbi Herzog adds that even if we were to discuss the matter of forced conscription within the halakhic framework of a situation of *pikuaḥ nefesh* relating to the general public, there is still reason to permit forced conscription. Even though the danger is localized and does not relate to the entirety of the Jewish nation, "since the Yishuv is

---

69. See Herzog, *Pesakim UKtavim, Oraḥ Ḥayim* 48, p. 213. Rabbi Herzog's responsa on this topic were analyzed and annotated by Rabbi Yitzḥak Roness in his article in *Masua LeYitzḥak* (Yad HaRav Herzog, Jerusalem, 5769), 451, the volume in Rabbi Herzog's memory commemorating fifty years since his passing.
70. Herzog, *Pesakim UKtavim, Oraḥ Ḥayim* 48, p. 217.

considered to be likened to the entire *Kehal Yisrael* (Congregation of Israel), we should say that one is obligated to endanger himself... even if there is no actual law of a *milḥemet mitzva*, a commanded war, as there is no king today."

The expression *Kehal Yisrael* is taken from the Talmud's statement that the inhabitants of the Holy Land are regarded as the "entire congregation of Israel."[71] In this vein, Rabbi Herzog answers the claim made by Rabbi Meshulam Roth that we do not have the power to enforce conscription:

> I assumed that Maimonides' explanation of the mishna (Bekhorot 4:2), which is based on the words of the Talmud in Horayot 3a... that the Yishuv is the "congregation of Israel," pertains to this matter as well. In order to bring about the salvation of all of Israel or the majority of the nation, as the majority is likened to the whole, every individual is required to endanger himself... [for this] is not only a question of the safety of the Yishuv, but rather an attempt to save the entire people of Israel and to save Judaism itself, and therefore could there possibly be any doubt in my eyes that we are obligated to endanger ourselves for this?[72]

## Conscription of Yeshiva Students

In a responsum that Rabbi Herzog published on the eve of the War of Independence, he elaborates on this topic, calling for the partial conscription of the yeshiva students, in coordination with the army representatives. Here, once again, he declares that the war being fought in our days is defined halakhically as a *milḥemet mitzva*, as it was declared by the authoritative bodies representing the Jewish population, including the representatives of the religious organizations.

Rabbi Herzog explains that after the Holocaust, the nation is in a terrible and perilous situation, and Judaism itself is in extreme danger: "Our only hope [is] that God will influence the position of the nations to grant us 'a name and a remnant' and a haven in the land of

---

71. Horayot 3a.
72. Herzog, *Pesakim UKtavim, Oraḥ Ḥayim* 55.

our forefathers." After the Arabs rose against the nascent Jewish state in order to destroy it, "who is it that harbors a brain in his skull who would not recognize that this is a *milḥemet mitzva*…in the fullest meaning of these words?" Rabbi Herzog notes that this is certainly true according to Nahmanides, who maintains that there is a mitzva even in our times to conquer the Land. It is all the more so true given that these wars are fought for the salvation of Judaism, the soul of Israel:

> Without this hidden miracle of the Land of Israel, the majority of people of Israel would either fall into the depths of despair… and the majority of them would be pushed to the depths of assimilation and disappearance.[73]

Since this war is viewed as a *milḥemet mitzva*, "everyone should go forth, even the groom from his wedding chamber and the bride from her canopy," and this law, Rabbi Herzog maintained, was true for the *talmidei ḥakhamim*, the Torah scholars, as well.

## INSTITUTION OF ENACTMENTS (*TAKKANOT*)

We have thus far reviewed several instances in which Rabbi Herzog attempted to reconcile traditional halakha with democracy. In a number of contexts, we have seen that since he viewed the state as a vital necessity, he felt that there was room to permit violations of halakha in order to save the state – a form of *pikuaḥ nefesh* – based upon the principle of *et laasot Lashem heferu toratekha*. Despite this theory, Rabbi Herzog always attempted to find a strictly halakhic parameter to justify his decision, such as the concept of *eiva* and reliance on the minority opinion (*shitat yaḥid*).

Another important element of Rabbi Herzog's response was his repeated assertion of the need for rabbinic enactments (*takkanot*).[74] He insisted that the Chief Rabbinate of Israel, in conjunction with the government and local communities, have the authority to issue these

---

73. See *Masua LeYitzḥak*, 237.
74. This section is adapted from my introduction to *Teḥukka*, 1:30 (Hebrew pagination). The topic of *takkanot* is discussed extensively in *Teḥukka*; see the index at the end of the third volume. The present article includes a summary of the ideas elaborated there.

decrees, maintaining this position even though he opposed the restoration of the Sanhedrin.[75] Rabbi Herzog greatly valued the existence of the Chief Rabbinate, and he aspired to forge this institution as a central rabbinic authority that would be invested with authority similar to the *semukhin* (officially ordained members of the Sanhedrin). In this respect, he was in conflict with many others who strongly opposed the notion of reestablishing the authority to issue rabbinic injunctions.[76] It is safe to say that Rabbi Herzog's unique perspective upon the meaning of contemporary historical events stood at the heart of this halakhic stance.

**Need**
Rabbi Herzog writes:

> Recent developments have led to the expansion and sophistication of the economic structure. Without question, in seeking to legally impose Torah law in our society, we must institute various *takkanot* and, in addition, add several laws that will complement the existing ones…as Ḥazal and those who succeeded them often instituted.[77]

In earlier sections, we examined the manner in which Rabbi Herzog validated women, gentiles, and secular Jews as witnesses in a court of law. Rabbi Herzog also perceived the need for *takkanot* regarding personal financial affairs, which fell under the jurisdiction of the Rabbinate. Without adjustments to the halakha, rabbinic authority would not be accepted, and the authority of the Rabbinate would begin to erode in light of the apparent inapplicability of its laws to the new reality.

Rabbi Herzog paid particular attention to the issue of wills and inheritance. He authored a complete work addressing the topic, in which

---

75. See Herzog, *Teḥukka*, vol. 3, part 4, app. 13, p. 260.
76. See Ḥazon Ish, *Kovetz Iggerot, iggeret* 96, in which the opposition of the Brisker Rav is also noted. Of course, it goes without saying that Rabbi Herzog recognized the severity of the issue and approached it with a good degree of caution. He writes, "These *takkanot* are a difficult *avoda* – one of the most difficult *avodot* in the *mikdash* of the laws of Torah" (cited in *Teḥukka*, 1:31, n. 17 [Hebrew pagination]).
77. Herzog, *Teḥukka*, 2:5.

he proposed several radical ideas, such as allowing a daughter to inherit equally with her brother, withholding the dual portion from the firstborn, addressing the question of maternal inheritance, and other significant issues. These areas were candidates for innovative changes based upon public need and will.[78]

In his introduction, Rabbi Herzog expounded upon the need for *takkanot*, affirming that he was not advocating change in Torah law to imitate gentile democratic systems, but rather to serve as an internal protective factor for the Torah itself. Without these changes, he argued, foreign laws that are completely dissonant with Torah law would inevitably be introduced:

> Since we desire the institution of Torah law within the State of Israel and the opposition to this is substantial – based primarily upon the discrimination against women in the area of inheritance – the danger readily presents itself that the state will select an alternate gentile codex to serve as the basis of its legal system. Therefore, we should institute *takkanot* which will serve as a fence (*seyag*) against such an event.[79]

Rabbi Herzog was sensitive to an additional concern as well:

> If no *takkanot* are formulated in the economic sphere even where there is apparent exigency, and society is aware that the Rabbinate has not properly exercised its authority, many will become disillusioned in general with Torah authority.... Society will falsely determine that similar rabbinic authority exists in the area of marital affairs, but the Rabbinate lacks the courage to implement change and is only protecting itself against criticism from more radical elements. This will induce the average Jew to seek

---

78. Additional material relevant to the issue of inheritance can be found in my introduction to *Teḥukka*, 2. See also Ben Zion Greenberger, "Rav Herzog's Proposals for *Takkanot* in Matters of Inheritance," in *The Halakhic Thought of R. Isaac Herzog*, ed. Bernard Jackson, *Jewish Law Association Studies* 5 (Atlanta, 1991): 57–112, and the other essays in the volume.
79. Herzog, *Teḥukka*, 2:3.

alternate authorities who will be irresponsible and provide errant halakhic decisions.... There is even a danger that the exclusive authority of the Rabbinate in marital affairs will be challenged.... I therefore suggest that it is vital to win the approval of the average Jew in the street.... These *takkanot* regarding inheritance will [positively] influence most of the female population and their supporters, which accounts for most of the population.[80]

It is noteworthy that, quite aside from the external pressures, Rabbi Herzog supported *takkanot* for internal reasons as well. He mentions that in previous generations, several devices were sought to award inheritance to daughters. S. Y. Agnon remarked to Rabbi Herzog that a hasidic rabbi had once passed away and his children conducted the division of the estate based exclusively upon Torah law, thereby excluding the daughter entirely from inheritance. Upon hearing this decision, the entire community scoffed at them. This demonstrated that even in earlier generations, it was recognized that estates should not be settled exclusively according to Torah law. In addition, modern women would not accept a discriminatory policy (unlike their ancestors, who humbly accepted the Torah's decrees). This friction would ultimately lead to hostility, controversy, and familial disharmony; it is certainly our moral duty to find methods to avoid such dispute.[81]

## Authority

Rabbi Herzog addressed the issue of the Rabbinate's authority extensively. In financial matters, authority stems from the talmudic principle of "*hefker beit din hefker*."[82] Rabbi Herzog dedicates a major segment of his tract regarding inheritances toward clarifying this principle.[83] He also relies upon earlier precedents, such as the *takkanot* of the exiled community of Castile, the *takkanot* of Toledo,[84] and the *takkanot* of the

---

80. Ibid., 6.
81. Ibid., 2:110.
82. On this principle see *Encyclopedia Talmudit*, s.v. "*hekfer bet din hefker*," 10:95–110.
83. See, especially, Herzog, *Teḥukka* 1:6, 2:2, 4, 5, 9.
84. Mentioned in *Tur, Even HaEzer* 118.

leaders of Morocco, all of which improved the status of women.[85] From these precedents, he infers the authority to issue similar decrees. He also deals extensively with the concept of *dina demalkhuta dina* (the law of the government is [binding according to Jewish] law) and utilizes this principle in the area of inheritances.[86]

Regarding the issue of authority, Rabbi Herzog differentiated between different domains, writing that regarding *takkanot* of *beit din* and *takkanot* of communities, such as in our case, *takkanot* of the government with the approval of Torah authorities, there is a fundamental difference between *mamona* (civil cases) and *issura* (ritual law). In cases of *issura* – such as *gittin* and *kiddushin* – we have no right to issue *takkanot*. However, in civil cases that relate to monetary suits, we have the authority to do so.

Despite this statement, however, Rabbi Herzog indeed considers the possibility of instituting *takkanot* in the realm of *issura* in certain extenuating circumstances. He seems to have hesitated to conclude that it is permitted due to doubt regarding the status of the Rabbinate. He maintains that ultimately, when *semikha* as an institution will be restored, the authority to issue *takkanot* will indeed exist.[87] Although he rejects the possibility of rehabilitating the Sanhedrin in modern times, he writes:

> In my heart, there arises the notion that even if *semikha* is not renewed, the overwhelming majority of opinions would support the concept … of conferring final authority upon the *Beit Din HaGadol* in Jerusalem … albeit not the authority of *semukhin* …. When we will achieve the approval of the majority of the Torah scholars … we will purify and sanctify ourselves through proper thoughts and appropriate lifestyles, to the point that we situate ourselves firmly in the tent of Torah. We can then embark upon heightened analysis and achieve greater halakhic resolution so that we may remove all the physical factors that inhibit our clear intellect and level all the walls

---

85. See Herzog, *Teḥukka* 2:2, 5, 7; apps. 2, 5.
86. Ibid., 2:3. Rabbi Herzog did not wish to rely on the authority of *mishpat hamelekh*. See also ibid., vol. 1, app. 3. This authority is only valid in the narrow domain of punishments.
87. Ibid., vol. 1, app. to section 6.

that separate us from Torah.... We might achieve divine assistance in clarifying the various issues that remain in doubt [justifying the ability to issue *takkanot* even before *semikha* is renewed].[88]

Rabbi Herzog raises the possibility of annulling *kiddushin* retroactively, a prospect that will be considered "when *semikha* is restored, or at least when the *Beit Din HaGadol* is established in Jerusalem, even though the Messiah has yet to arrive."[89] He also elaborates upon the authority of a modern *beit din* to mete out punishments, noting the startling fact that such authority does readily exist (more so than in annulment cases), and there are several precedents for such authority.[90] He also notes that most rabbinic authorities did not assert their authority in this matter.[91]

## The Form of *Takkanot*

Rabbi Herzog advocated cooperation among religious leaders, the government, and community leaders in instituting *takkanot*.[92] In general, the degree of participation depends upon the particular legal domain. Any arrangement that will ultimately be accepted as state law, such as inheritance or accepting halakhically invalid witnesses, certainly requires coordination with the government. However, regarding internal *takkanot* – such as those pertaining to marital affairs, which are under the exclusive authority of the Rabbinate – such cooperation is not vital.

Rabbi Herzog initiated several *takkanot* that were ultimately accepted by the Council of the Chief Rabbinate.[93] We will mention some notable cases in brief.[94]

---

88. Ibid., 1:91.
89. Ibid., 92. Such rabbinic cancellations of marriage would be considered in cases in which a husband has become mentally ill, has disappeared, or refuses to grant his wife a divorce.
90. Ibid., 1:6, beginning with p. 72.
91. Ibid., 5, apps. 3, 5.
92. See ibid., vol. 3, part 3 (9), p. 151.
93. When the wording of the *takkana* mentions that it has been approved by the Rabbinate as well as the leaders of various communities, it merely refers to their passive approval (the *takkana* having been instituted exclusively by Rabbi Herzog and the Rabbinate).
94. The background and evolution of these *takkanot* are discussed at length in Herzog, *Teḥukka*, vol. 3, part 3; see pp. 118, 168. See also the article written by my father, Dr. Z. Warhaftig, in B. S. Jackson, ed., *The Halakhic Thought of R. Isaac Herzog*, 21–32.

*Takkanot* instituted in the year 1944:

1. Every *ketuba* must contain a *tosefet* [generally, a voluntarily added sum of money] no less than fifty Israeli lira for a *betula* (virgin) and no less than twenty-five lira for a widow.
2. A *yavam* [eldest brother of one who dies childless] who refuses to perform *halitza* [thereby liberating the widow for remarriage] must pay her financial support.
3. The *beit din* may legally compel a father to support his children until the age of fifteen [prior to this enactment, the law had obligated the father only until the age of six].

*Takkanot* instituted in the year 1946:

1. Prior to marriage, the couple must register in the offices of the Rabbinate. The marriage itself must be performed in front of ten people and the ceremony must include a *huppa*.
2. A woman may not marry before the age of sixteen.
3. Polygamy is forbidden (even for Sephardim who are not subject to the *herem DeRabbeinu Gershom*) without special permission from the Rabbinate.
4. *Yibbum* is forbidden; *halitza* must be performed.
5. Any rabbi who wishes to officiate at a wedding ceremony must be authorized by the Rabbinate.

Aside from these official *takkanot*, Rabbi Herzog adopted several practices for *battei din* that also amounted to changing halakha. We have already mentioned his practice of accepting testimony from gentiles. In some cases, he compelled husbands to make alimony payments to their divorced wives.[95] If the *beit din* had already decided that a husband should be forced to divorce his wife but lacked the apparatus to enforce its decision, he would threaten the husband with excessively high *mezonot* payments.

---

95. See Herzog, *Tehukka*, 2:168. See also Z. Warhaftig, "The Practice of Alimony Payments," *Sinai* 98, nos. 1–2 (5746): 57–67. See also his article in the previous footnote.

## Rabbi Yitzhak Herzog's Approach to Modernity

To summarize, it may be stated that Rabbi Herzog, especially when he was in office, highly regarded the status of the Chief Rabbinate and the Supreme Rabbinical Court and ascribed to them significant authority in legislating *takkanot* that became necessary in light of the establishment of the state. With regard to internal *takkanot* (such as marital affairs), which were subject to the sole authority of the Rabbinate, he was successful. Beyond this, regarding general matters pertaining to state law – such as inheritances and the status of invalid witnesses and judges – he was largely unsuccessful. This was due to a lack of interest in pursuing the project, both on the part of the secular legal establishment as well as on the part of his rabbinic colleagues.

### HALAKHIC APPROACH REGARDING OTHER MATTERS

Upon reading these summaries of Rabbi Herzog's rulings, one might come to the conclusion that Rabbi Herzog was a liberal, open-minded *posek* who was always willing to exercise a *heter*. Closer inspection, however, indicates that in matters which did not pertain to reconciling halakha and democracy, he would not be considered lenient.

In several responsa, Rabbi Herzog hesitated and raised a number of considerations, some which would dictate stringency and others that would warrant leniency. It is possible that although he felt sympathy for innovation, he became wary of changing convention and was concerned that too many changes based on lenient interpretations would destroy the system. The following are some examples of this tendency.

### A

Rabbi Herzog penned a response to a rabbi in Uruguay who wished to build a monument in the local cemetery to memorialize the victims of the Holocaust. In his responsa, he analyzed the question from several different angles, in particular considering the prohibition of *uvḥukkoteihem lo telekhu*, which might render a general prohibition against monuments. He concluded:

> If they decide to build the monument, we cannot classify them as *avaryanim* (sinners); however, since our ancestors did not employ monuments to honor the dead, if they would heed my

opinion I would say.... My brothers, it is best not to innovate such things.... Instead, establish in their memory a school, a charity fund, or a synagogue.... If, however, they insist, build the monument in the cemetery.[96]

**B**

In another responsum, Rabbi Herzog addressed the proper protocol for President Chaim Weizmann's funeral:

> It is the custom in Israel to bury without a casket, based upon the verse *"vekhipper admato ammo"* (the earth of Israel will provide atonement). This custom is hundreds of years old and was certainly instituted by great masters of Kabbala, and we cannot change it. Religious officials should inform the government of this. If, however, the government position cannot be changed, he should at least be buried in a wood coffin with holes underneath.[97]

**C**

In the Brit Hashmona'im Society of Jerusalem, someone proposed that during the memorial for Jabotinsky, a picture of Jabotinsky in a blackened frame should be placed on top of a black table, with two candles on either side. The assembly would then circle the table and remain silent. Rabbi Herzog outlawed this because it was an imitation of gentile customs.[98]

**D**

Rabbi Herzog related that when he was appointed chief rabbi in Belfast, Ireland, he discovered that their practice was to hold the *huppa* in a synagogue. He realized that he did not have the power to change this custom, and only managed to eliminate the playing of an organ during the ceremony. He continues:

---

96. Herzog, *Pesakim UKtavim*, *Yoreh De'ah* 158.
97. Ibid., *Yoreh De'ah* 115.
98. Ibid., *Yoreh De'ah* 116.

However, in our country [Israel], we do not have this custom [of holding a *ḥuppa* in a synagogue], and whoever changes this norm *yado al hataḥtona* (he does not have the upper hand). This is certainly true for Ashkenazim, whose custom it is to conduct the ceremony under the open sky. However, even Sephardim, who conduct their ceremonies indoors, should certainly oppose any change, such as holding a *ḥuppa* in a *beit mikdash me'at* (synagogue). The Diaspora should model itself after Israel; we should not learn from their innovations that were adopted in Western societies. These practices [of Jewish communities in the West] created much heartache and were, unfortunately, unavoidable.[99]

**E**

Rabbi Herzog was quite strict in disallowing the burial of non-Jewish wives next to their Jewish husbands, and even in a separate section of a Jewish cemetery. In opposing this practice, he assails intermarriage:

> Our many sins have caused this great tragedy to emerge in our birthplace of Germany.... In that country, the terrible Reform movement has removed all the divisions that our tradition – both the *Torah Shebikhtav* and *Torah Shebe'al Peh* – had imposed between Jew and gentile....[100] Many Jews were drawn; once the walls were removed, these Jews were easily led astray.... It is an established principle that in each generation, the *beit din* must

---

99. Yitzhak Herzog, *Heikhal Yitzḥak, Even HaEzer* 2:27. See also ibid., 1:1 and Z. Warhaftig, "The Practice of Alimony Payments."

100. Rabbi Herzog repeatedly denounced the Reform movement and viewed it as being extremely dangerous. In *Heikhal Yitzḥak, Yoreh De'ah* 77, he invalidates the appointment of a rabbi because he had served as a rabbi in a Reform congregation in the Diaspora. In *Teḥukka*, 1:74, he writes that a man who wed a woman who had only divorced through a civil divorce (the ceremony having been performed by a Reform rabbi) should not be accepted as a synagogue member. See also pp. 13, 92, and 94. Along with his colleague Rabbi Yitzḥak Nissim, Rabbi Herzog also assails the Conservative movement, warning against accepting the Conservative suggestions regarding divorce laws.

act vigilantly.... When they discern that a sin is being committed, they must enact a *seyag* and other protective *takkanot*.... Since this snare of intermarriage is especially prevalent in Israel, where a gentile spouse enjoys equal privileges to resident Jews, it is our responsibility to fine, punish, and institute extra-legal measures to protect the actual law. If we lack the authority to demand the divorce of gentile wives, at least after death it becomes our responsibility to [separate them].[101]

## F

Rabbi Herzog supported the decision of many Diaspora *battei din* to impose strict conditions upon candidates for conversion.[102] In addition, he challenged the validity of conversions that were motivated by marriage (*leshem ishut*). In a response to a Swiss rabbi, he reiterates his decision not to accept a teacher whose wife was a convert under such circumstances:

> Even though we maintain that *bediavad* such conversions are legitimate, I still have a very sound reason that in our generation this no longer is true. In earlier times, every Jew who did not adhere to the mitzvot was ostracized and embarrassed, and this created an underlying assumption that a convert had indeed seriously determined to fulfill mitzvot. Otherwise, he would be divorced from his previous gentile community [by dint of his conversion] and severed from the Jewish community [by dint of his lack of observance], and this would be a highly undesirable condition. However, in present times, the situation has changed to the point that one can be a highly regarded Jewish leader and still be a Shabbat violator. We no longer have a guarantee that the gentile has indeed resolved – even at the time of his conversion – to fulfill the mitzvot.[103]

---

101. Herzog, *Heikhal Yitzḥak*, *Yoreh De'ah* 125.
102. See ibid., *Yoreh De'ah* 86 (Ireland); 87 (Argentina); 90 (South Africa); 99 (Colombia).
103. Ibid., *Yoreh De'ah* 99. See also ibid., 92, 93.

**G**

In another instance, Rabbi Herzog addressed the obligation of a father to support a child born to his gentile wife. Someone voiced the opinion that this support was necessary for moral reasons. Rabbi Herzog responded:

> Regarding that which you raised, that support is mandated upon moral grounds since the child "begs" for pity – in fact, one who is a true *raḥaman* (sensitive to another's calls for pity) will avoid such a situation altogether. In any event, efforts should be made that the separation [between father and son] should be performed in a manner that no party will be insulted. Especially if the children are transferred to the father for conversion, one should seriously consider [beforehand] what would be in the best interest of the children. We cannot state that Torah law requires the father to support his child...and even to impose some form of informal pressure to encourage this support [is inadvisable] since this might mislead the public into believing, God forbid, that intermarriage has halakhic validity. This will lead to great danger, particularly in enlightened countries where the Jews are in direct contact with gentiles and are greatly influenced by them.[104]

**H**

Despite this tendency to fight innovation, Rabbi Herzog certainly did not forbid every innovation. For example, Rabbi Herzog argued with the *Ḥazon Ish*, who prohibited an ox from India simply because it was different from a standard ox. In response, Rabbi Herzog wrote that it is forbidden to be stringent simply because something is novel; in general, one should not apply the principle of *ḥadash asur min HaTorah*.[105]

In conclusion, when it came to vital issues, such as democracy of the Jewish state, Rabbi Herzog stretched leniencies to their limit. In other areas, however, he addressed the issue itself, as well as general Torah values, such as the preservation of *minhagim* (customs) and

---

104. Ibid., *Even HaEzer* 1:22.
105. Ibid., *Yoreh De'ah* 2.

concern about the danger of intermarriage. He appreciated the proper time and place for stringencies.[106]

## PRIVATE LIFE AND PUBLIC STANDING

Did Rabbi Herzog's unique approach to modernity express itself in his private life? In general, the answer is no. Even though Rabbi Herzog studied the sciences and was fluent in three languages, he was, at heart, a man of halakha, and he did not often interrupt his learning. Aside from his responsibilities as chief rabbi and, at times, his obligations in other official governmental capacities, he was fully immersed in learning Gemara and *posekim*.

Rabbi Herzog was a Zionist who loved, helped, and supported *benei Torah* from all walks of life. He served as the president of the *Vaad HaYeshivot* and maintained close ties with all the *gedolim*. His standing in ḥaredi circles declined only after the controversy surrounding the drafting of women and *sherut le'umi* (national service) in 1953, in which Rabbi Herzog disagreed with the rigid position adopted by the ḥaredi camp led by the Ḥazon Ish. This dispute reached the point that members of the ḥaredi community once embarrassed him, which very much disappointed him.

In general, in his private life, aside from a few particular customs, Rabbi Herzog behaved as any normal rabbi. In his political outlook, he was a moderate who disapproved of terror organizations, since they victimized innocent people. He was very sensitive to any murder, including that of gentiles. He also supported the law banning capital punishment.[107]

In one matter, it appears that he did take public perception into account. The question at hand had to do with the pronunciation of God's name of *Adnut*, which, according to Askenazic dialect, has a

---

106. See Herzog, *Pesakim UKtavim, Oraḥ Ḥayim* 44, in which he prohibits cooking on Shabbat through a gentile in order to prevent *hillul Shabbat* by a Jew. After considering all the factors, he reasons that such practices would lead to leniencies being adopted even when the situation was not dire. See also *Oraḥ Ḥayim* 47, regarding writing in foreign languages on Shabbat and *Oraḥ Ḥayim* 67 regarding use of electricity on Shabbat. However, in *Yoreh De'ah* 55, he is lenient regarding a woman who does not want to cut her nails prior to going to the *mikve*.
107. Herzog, *Teḥukka*, 3:93.

*kamatz* under the *nun*, while it has a *pataḥ* according to Sephardic dialect. Rabbi Herzog responded that it is permissible even for an Ashkenazi to pronounce the name with a *pataḥ*. He concludes:

> In practice, I have not changed my pronunciation, and in the beit midrash of my house, there is no change. However, I do not scold one who reads in Sephardic pronunciation, even when he leads the *tefilla*, since this is his familiar way of reading. When I pray in Yeshurun [Synagogue] on *ḥaggim* and receive an *aliya*, I do not change the dialect of the synagogue, in which everybody prays.[108]

In Rabbi Herzog's capacity as chief rabbi, he achieved a special status. He sensed the weighty responsibilities that had been placed upon him, and he responded by suggesting the *takkanot* discussed above. Many times in his rulings, he requested others to join him in his decision instead of authoring the position alone.

By nature, he was an easygoing person who had a distaste for arguments. Thus, although he outlined his approach in print, he was wary of enforcing his position. This is true, for example, regarding the issue of restoring the Sanhedrin,[109] as well as his proposals regarding the distribution of inheritances. He writes:

> I set down the most extreme positions that are tolerable…the most flexibility which can be implemented in making *takkanot*…. A vote was never held, but it is clear that most of the *rabbanim* would not have opted to make any *takkanot*…still, it is appropriate that future generations should know of my efforts and that they were taken with the purest of intentions.[110]

Indeed, most of Rabbi Herzog's suggestions were not accepted. However, his fundamental position regarding the possibility of reconciling halakha and democracy has made a lasting impact; the National

---

108. Herzog, *Pesakim UKtavim, Oraḥ Ḥayim* 1.
109. Herzog, *Teḥukka*, 2:250.
110. Introduction to his book about inheritances, Herzog, *Teḥukka*, 2:1.

Religious community has embraced both values. I do not know what Rabbi Herzog would have said regarding the present-day questions of Torah and state, but there is no doubt that the Religious Zionist community, which has chosen to integrate itself within the overall structure of the state, has been greatly inspired by Rabbi Herzog. From this standpoint, it seems that the Nationalist Religious community has not sufficiently appreciated his personality and his contribution to its own ideology.

# "Founding Brothers": The Rav, Rav Ahron, and the American Idea

### Rabbi Dr. Meir Soloveichik

**BROTHERS IN TORAH AND THE MODERN WORLD**

Several decades ago, Rav Ahron Soloveichik sat at his Shabbat table in his Chicago home, surrounded by family and students. In his hands he held a copy of a letter that he had received many years before, when he was a ten-year-old boy in Eastern Europe. The letter had been written by his older brother, Yosef Dov, who was studying philosophy at the University of Berlin, as a response to a *devar Torah* that young Ahron – or Ahrele, as he was known – had sent to his older sibling. In the letter, Yosef Dov extols the brilliance that the little boy was already exhibiting. Rav Ahron, now grown to an elderly rabbi, read his brother's words aloud to those assembled in his home that Shabbat afternoon:

> Yesterday evening, I received your enclosed letter. I simply could not believe my eyes – little Ahrele has become an adult! Until now, you have only sent me questions; you have been the one asking the questions (*makshan*). But now – suddenly – you have transformed into someone who answers them (*tartzan*) as an adroit,

learned person (*lamdan*) who depends not on others, who sits and writes Torah insights with comprehensive knowledge. Just recently, around Pesaḥ time, you were still far from reaching this level; it never occurred to me that I would receive goodly and beautiful *ḥiddushei Torah* from you this very year, and that you would already be able to perambulate the orchard of Torah and halakha, tread the Rambam's paths, and generate fresh and pleasant insights. I wholeheartedly pray that you will rise ever higher as a source of joy for us all.[1]

At this point, Rav Ahron looked up from the letter, surveyed those sitting around him, and said ruefully, "He then proceeds to destroy my *peshat*."

This story captures all at once the Torah world in which these brothers grew up, the deep emotional bond that bound them, and the difference in age and experiences between the two. Rabbi Joseph B. (Yosef Dov) Soloveitchik – or the Rav, as he was called – spent several years at the University of Berlin, where he first began his project of approaching the world of philosophy from the perspective of the Torah. Rav Ahron, by contrast, arrived in the United States at the age of thirteen, and continued his Torah studies and attended law school there. While he too sought to bridge the world of Torah and the West, his interest lay in American constitutionalism and in the democratic vision on which it was founded. Unlike those of the Rav, Rav Ahron's *divrei Torah* and philosophical lectures seldom made mention of Kant, Kierkegaard, and Rudolph Otto, but frequently made mention of Jefferson, Madison, and Lincoln. One would not be unjustified in suggesting that the Rav's academic interests were philosophical and Continental, whereas Rav Ahron's were political and American.

At the same time, we would be remiss if, in examining the Rav's magnificent oeuvre, we did not take note of one profound reflection on American democracy. The Rav's essay "Confrontation," an address delivered to the Rabbinical Council of America (RCA) and later published in the journal *Tradition*, is most famous for the strictures it set out for Orthodox inter-faith engagement, a subject that I have addressed at

---

1. Joseph B. Soloveitchik, *Iggerot HaGrid HaLevi* (Riverdale, NY, 2001), 273b.

length elsewhere.[2] Yet what is often missed is that the Rav addressed the issue of inter-faith relations by presenting an exegesis of Genesis, and thereby an account of human nature and religious difference, and founded on this account an argument for how a democratic, multi-faith society should work.

With this in mind, it is worthwhile to ponder together the writings of these two Brisker brothers. George Will has noted that the two polar values of the Founders' idea of America are liberty and equality;[3] these two notions are eternally in tension, but they can also be complementary. This insight allows us to appreciate how the reflections on democracy of the Rav and Rav Ahron complement one another as well. It is the Rav who made a theological case for religious liberty in America, and it was his brother Rav Ahron who made a case for the concept of equality based on the Torah, insisting that the vision articulated in the Declaration of Independence can and should be understood through the vision of religious Judaism. This essay will attempt to sketch out how these two brothers, born in Khislavichi, Russia, together embody worldviews that, when taken in tandem, give a uniquely Jewish expression to the American idea.

I will begin by elucidating the Rav's vision of religious liberty, and I will then address his brother's reconciliation of Jeffersonian equality with the Torah. In so doing, I hope to illustrate why the Rav and Rav Ahron ought to be seen by Orthodoxy in the United States as the "Founding Brothers" of a distinctly American, and yet still unwaveringly Orthodox, vision of democratic society.

## GER, TOSHAV, AND RELIGIOUS LIBERTY

What, for Rabbi Joseph B. Soloveitchik, is the religious liberty that Jews seek? The answer lies in Abraham's introduction to the sons of Ḥet: "*Ger vetoshav anokhi immakhem*" (I am a stranger and neighbor among you)

---

2. Meir Soloveichik, "A Nation Under God: Jews, Christians, and the American Public Square," in *Yirat Shamayim: The Awe, Reverence, and Fear of God*, ed. Marc D. Stern (Jersey City, NJ, 2008), 321–47.
3. Mr. Will made these remarks in a speech at the 2010 Conservative Political Action Conference (CPAC), which can be viewed at http://www.c-span.org/video/?292148-21/george-will-remarks.

(Gen. 23:4). This, in his interpretation, reflects more than a demand to be left alone, to practice unhindered the tenets of one's faith, to live a shtetl-like life free of pogroms, unattached to the larger gentile world. Such a situation, for the Rav, would allow for the fulfillment of one's covenantal duties but not the Jewish fulfillment of another duty, also divine in origin, which is universal rather than covenantal: the obligation to stand side by side with the rest of humanity in addressing the issues facing society at large. In addressing the RCA in 1964, the Rav gave voice to this vision:

> We think of ourselves as human beings, sharing the destiny of Adam in his general encounter with nature, and as members of a covenantal community which has preserved its identity under most unfavorable conditions, confronted by another faith community. We believe we are the bearers of a double charismatic load, that of the dignity of man and that of the sanctity of the covenantal community. In this difficult role, we are summoned by God, who revealed Himself at both the level of universal creation and that of the private covenant, to undertake a double mission – the universal human and the exclusive covenantal confrontation.[4]

We must pause to ponder how audacious a vision this is, for what the Rav seeks here was not offered to the Jews throughout centuries of persecution, nor was it really offered in the freedom of the European Emancipation. In the Europe of the Emancipation, Jews were tantalized by the vision of full integration into German or French society, but they had to be willing to sacrifice their public Jewishness on the altar of integration. Some Jews capitulated to these demands, embodying thereby their own version of Judah Leib Gordon's "be a Jew in your tent and a human being in the street."[5] But as Rabbi Soloveitchik noted, the very same Bible that demands absolute devotion to the divine simultaneously

---

4. Joseph B. Soloveitchik, "Confrontation," *Tradition* 6, no. 2 (Spring–Summer 1964): 17.
5. See Paul Mendes-Flohr and Jehuda Reinharz, eds., *The Jew in the Modern World: A Documentary History*, 2nd ed. (New York, 1995), 384.

obligates us to engage the world; we do not cease to be religious when we enter the public square. On the contrary; as he argues in *The Lonely Man of Faith*, we are simultaneously commanded to be a part of and apart from the world:

> On the one hand, the Bible commands man, "And thou shalt love the Lord thy God with all thy heart and with all thy soul, and with all thy might." On the other hand, the same Bible which just enjoined man to withdraw from the periphery to the center commands him to return to the majestic community which... builds, plants, harvests, regulates rivers, heals the sick, participates in state affairs, is imaginative in dreaming, bold in planning, daring in undertaking and is out to "conquer" the world. With what simplicity, not paying the least attention to the staggering dialectic implied in such an approach, the Bible speaks of an existence this-worldly centered...yet theo-oriented and unqualifiedly committed to an eternal purpose!... The task of covenantal man is to be engaged...in uniting the two...where man is both the creative, free agent, and the obedient servant of God.[6]

Religious freedom, for Rabbi Soloveitchik, is the ability to actualize both of these tasks in the modern age; true liberty is the ability to be loyal to your beliefs and customs even when they are unpopular with the neighbors and, more importantly, even when one is engaging with those neighbors while "participating in state affairs." This, as we shall see, is a deeply American idea; but first we must analyze the philosophical foundation of religious liberty that lies at the heart of the Rav's vision.

### GENESIS AND A THEOLOGY OF RELIGIOUS LIBERTY

What is the foundation of religious liberty? Why ought a society allow its inhabitants to profess theological beliefs that are counter to the opinions of the majority? Why is a religiously diverse society not something to be

---

6. Joseph B. Soloveitchik, "The Lonely Man of Faith," *Tradition* 7, no. 2 (Summer 1965): 50–51.

feared? The argument that Rabbi Soloveitchik puts forward is slightly different from that put forward by Anglo-American political thinkers such as Locke, Jefferson, and Madison, even as we note profound similarities between his arguments and those that are an essential part of the Founders' vision of America. Thomas Jefferson's discussions of the matter focused on human freedom; witness his eloquent Virginia Statute for Religious Freedom of which he was so proud: "Whereas, Almighty God hath created the mind free."[7] For Rabbi Soloveitchik in "Confrontation," an argument for a religious, free society would begin, "Whereas, Almighty God hath created every mind different." It is in human difference that the Rav grounds his arguments in "Confrontation," and he does so by focusing on the creation of the first man and woman in Genesis.

The title of the essay refers essentially to two different confrontations. One is man as an intelligent, divinely commanded being confronting the world in fulfillment of the duty to "fill the earth and subdue it" (Gen. 1:28). The second confrontation is derived from the first meeting of two individuals in human history. Adam is introduced to his wife with the dialectical description *"ezer kenegdo"* (2:18), which the Rav translates literally as "a helper against him." The very phrase indicates that human beings are suited to be a helpmeet to one another even as they find it impossible to bridge the existential gap between them:

> In fact, the closer two individuals get to know each other, the more aware they become of the metaphysical distance separating them. Each one exists in a singular manner, completely absorbed in his individual awareness, which is egocentric and exclusive. The sun of existence rises with the birth of one's self-awareness and sets with its termination. It is beyond the experiential power of an individual to visualize an existence preceding or following his. It is paradoxical yet nonetheless true that each human being lives both in an existential community, surrounded by friends, and in a state of existential loneliness and tension, confronted by strangers. In each to whom I relate as a human being, I find a friend, for

---

7. Available on the website of the Virginia Historical Society: http://www.vahistorical.org/collections-and-resources/virginia-history-explorer/thomas-jefferson.

we have many things in common, as well as a stranger, for each of us is unique and wholly other. This otherness stands in the way of complete mutual understanding. The gap of uniqueness is too wide to be bridged.[8]

Utilizing this notion of *ezer kenegdo*, the Rav argues that human difference is made manifest first and foremost in the development of different views of the divine. "Each faith community is engaged in a singular normative gesture reflecting the numinous nature of the act of faith itself, and it is futile to try to find common denominators."[9]

**THE NATURE OF FAITH**

Here Rabbi Soloveitchik is proposing an approach to religious faith that is profoundly modern, even as it remains staunchly Orthodox. The medieval philosophers had defined belief as a purely cognitive property, founding faith on a series of propositions and arguments. Anselm sought an ontological argument to establish God's existence; Aquinas proved the Almighty's existence through cosmology. For Maimonides, it seems, the verse stating "I am the Lord your God" (Ex. 20:2) is not, as it ostensibly appears to be, an introduction by God to His beloved people; rather, it is the first commandment, an obligation to philosophically know the existence of God. This knowledge is achieved through exposure to Aristotle's proof of the Unmoved Mover. For the Rav, however, the notion that this can be the foundation of faith – that it can be the *"yesod hayesodot ve'ammud haḥokhmot"* (the foundation of all foundations and the pillar of all wisdom) – is unthinkable. In a famous footnote to his essay "The Lonely Man of Faith," Rabbi Soloveitchik sides with Kierkegaard in ridiculing the medieval philosophers' obsession with logic instead of the numinous:

> Does the loving bride in the embrace of her beloved ask for proof that he is alive and real? Must the prayerful soul clinging in passionate love and ecstasy to her Beloved demonstrate that He

---
8. Soloveitchik, "Confrontation," 15.
9. Ibid., 18–19.

exists? So asked Soren Kierkegaard sarcastically when told that Anselm of Canterbury, the father of the very abstract and complex ontological proof, spent many days in prayer and supplication that he be presented with rational evidence of the existence of God.[10]

Rabbi Soloveitchik further argues that the foundation of Judaism, belief, cannot be purely cognitive in nature. After all, "the intellect does not chart the course of the man of faith; its role is an a posteriori one. It attempts, ex post facto, to retrace the footsteps of the man of faith, and even in this modest attempt, the intellect is not completely successful."[11] It is for this reason, the Rav continues in "Confrontation," that religious difference is inevitable:

> The logos, the word, in which the multifarious religious experience is expressed does not lend itself to standardization or universalization. The word of faith reflects the intimate, the private, the paradoxically inexpressible cravings of the individual for and his linking up with his Maker. It reflects the numinous character and the strangeness of the act of faith of a particular community which is totally incomprehensible to the man of a different faith community.[12]

Faith is not merely a matter of reason, but of the heart and of the soul, and therefore disagreements between religions – the confrontation of *ezer kenegdo* – is inevitable. Religious difference is, for the Rav, part of the warp and woof of human nature, and his right to religious difference stems directly from this. While Rabbi Soloveitchik does not utilize the terms "endowed by their Creator" and "inalienable rights," he comes close to them in stating his own interpretation of Creation:

> When God created man and endowed him with individual dignity, He decreed that the ontological legitimacy and relevance of

---

10. Soloveitchik, "The Lonely Man of Faith," 32n. Rabbi Soloveitchik argues there that this approach can be applied to Maimonides as well.
11. Ibid., 60–61.
12. Soloveitchik, "Confrontation," 23–24.

the individual human being is to be discovered not without, but within the individual. He was created because God approved of him as an autonomous human being and not as an auxiliary being in the service of someone else. The ontological purposiveness of his existence is immanent in him. The same is true of a religious community, whose worth is not to be measured by external standards.... The small community has as much right to profess its faith in the ultimate certitude concerning the doctrinal worth of its world formula and to behold its own eschatological vision as does the community of the many.[13]

## MADISONIAN MAN

The arguments advanced by Rabbi Soloveitchik bear a striking resemblance to another great thinker who pondered the possibility of a variety of faith communities coexisting together in one nation – James Madison. In a series of essays that, together with those of Hamilton and Jay, made up *The Federalist Papers*, Madison took upon himself the task of convincing America that the thirteen colonies that had fought a revolution together could become one nation. It is difficult today to grasp just how challenging and daunting this task truly was. We tend to see the thirteen original states as a small sliver of what America would ultimately be, often forgetting that in proposing the Constitution, Madison was suggesting that those thirteen states taken together would constitute by far the largest republic in the history of the world. It had always been taken for granted that only an empire could govern a large territory effectively and that democracy was for small republics, for city-states. Madison, by contrast, insisted that a religiously diverse democracy could endure.

Like Rabbi Soloveitchik, Madison argues in a famous passage that those who believe religious differences – like political differences – will disappear fundamentally misunderstand how difference is part and parcel of human nature:

> As long as the reason of man continues fallible and he is at liberty to exercise it, different opinions will be formed. As long as

---

13. Ibid., 23.

the connection subsists between his reason and his self-love, his opinions and his passions will have a reciprocal influence on each other; and the former will be objects to which the latter will attach themselves. The diversity in the faculties of men, from which the rights of property originate, is not less an insuperable obstacle to a uniformity of interests.[14]

Madison's great concern about democracy was the ability of the majority to tyrannize the minority factions through popular vote. He therefore endorses a constitution in which the powers of the national government are few and defined, giving smaller states and faith communities the space to carve out their own existence. Rabbi Soloveitchik similarly stresses that the true test of a democratic society lies in the ability of smaller faith communities to maintain their own identity and integrity:

> Therefore, any intimation, overt or covert, on the part of the community of the many that it is expected of the community of the few that it shed its uniqueness and cease existing because it has fulfilled its mission by paving the way for the community of the many must be rejected as undemocratic and contravening the very idea of religious freedom. The small community has as much right to profess its faith in the ultimate certitude concerning the doctrinal worth of its world formula and to behold its own eschatological vision as does the community of the many.[15]

In the inevitability of religious difference lies the definition of a truly democratic society – one which makes a place for all faiths without demanding that each change its covenantal vision.

### THE PROFOUND ORTHODOXY OF CONFRONTATION

Yet even as the Rav insists that religious differences lie in the numinous experience of the divine, he stresses another corollary of religious faith:

---

14. James Madison, "The Utility of the Union as a Safeguard Against Domestic Faction and Insurrection (continued)," *Daily Advertiser*, November 22, 1787.
15. Soloveitchik, "Confrontation," 23.

the exclusivity of religious truth claims. Indeed, it is clear that part of what worried Rabbi Soloveitchik is that those most enthusiastic about the inter-faith encounter often argued precisely the opposite, that the existential nature of faith means that religions must abandon the exclusivity of their truth claims. Thus argued Rabbi Abraham Joshua Heschel in his passionate inter-faith manifesto "No Religion Is an Island":

> The ultimate truth is not capable of being fully and adequately expressed in concepts and words. The ultimate truth is about the situation that pertains between God and man. "The Torah speaks in the language of man." Revelation is always an accommodation to the capacity of man. No two minds are alike, just as no two faces are alike. The voice of God reaches the spirit of man in a variety of ways, in a multiplicity of languages. One truth comes to expression in many ways of understanding.[16]

Heschel's answer seems to be that cordiality between Christians and Jews can be premised on the fact that it need not be said that Judaism is true and Christianity false or vice versa; rather, both are valid expressions of a larger truth.

The problem with this idea is that for any faith purporting to be the fullest expression of God's will on this earth, including Roman Catholicism and Orthodox Judaism, the proposal is a non-starter. As York University's Randi Rashkover notes, "Heschel's theological position is untenable" for traditional Jews and Christians, because "his assertion that the Jewish and Christian revelations are both equally valid, but only partial expressions of a single truth, sponsors a relativism that Orthodox Jews (and traditionalist Christians) cannot accept." In other words, Heschel is asking each faith to purge itself of its most defining feature – its claim to be truer than any other faith. Traditional Jews and Christians, writes Rashkover, "want to be able to maintain claims

---

16. Abraham Joshua Heschel, "No Religion Is an Island," in *No Religion Is an Island: Abraham Joshua Heschel and Interreligious Dialogue*, eds. Harold Kasimow and Byron L. Sherwin (Maryknoll, NY, 1991), 15.

to exclusivity."[17] From the perspective of Orthodox Jews and Christians, Heschel's solution to tensions between faiths is akin to asking them to cease to exist.

Indeed, this is exactly the argument advanced by the Rav in "Confrontation." In his RCA address, he warned that those who seek to break down divisions between faiths in the name of dialogue all too often fail to recognize that the "axiological awareness of each faith community is an exclusive one," for each believes "that its system of dogmas, doctrines, and values is best fitted for the attainment of the ultimate good."[18] For Rabbi Soloveitchik, dispensing with the exclusivity of religious truth claims, far from building bridges between Judaism and Christianity, actually destroys both Judaism and Christianity: "Standardization of practices, equalization of dogmatic certitudes, and the waiving of eschatological claims spell the end of the vibrant and great faith experience of any religious community."[19] For the author of "Confrontation," traditional Jews and Christians have deep disagreements, but they agree on their disagreement, and in this they find their ultimate commonality. To put it another way, even as Jews and Christians are divided as to what exactly is the religious truth, it is their old-fashioned belief in the very notion of truth that unites them.

We are now able to summarize the Rav's approach to religious freedom. The inherent fact of human difference, of *ezer kenegdo*, results inevitably in religious disagreement. This itself is the ground for respecting the fact of religious differences and respecting the rights of diverse religious communities. At the same time, exclusive truth claims are an essential part of any true religious experience. Because members of all faiths are obligated to stand side by side in addressing the needs of society, true religious freedom involves integrating minority faiths into these endeavors even as they proudly proclaim their disagreement with the religious truth claims made by the majority.

---

17. Randi Rashkover, "How Have Jews Responded to Christian Efforts to Transform Anti-Jewish Positions?" *Cross Currents* 50, nos. 1–2 (Spring–Summer 2000): 213.
18. Soloveitchik, "Confrontation," 19.
19. Ibid.

In order to see how truly American Rabbi Soloveitchik's vision is, let us ponder momentarily the tale of Jonas Phillips, perhaps the first genuinely American Jew.

## CONFRONTATION, RELIGIOUS FREEDOM, AND THE AMERICAN IDEA

Jonas Phillips arrived in America from Germany as the indentured servant of another Jew. By the Revolutionary War's end, he was one of the wealthiest Jews in America and a friend to several of the Founding Fathers. When the Constitutional Convention met in Philadelphia in 1787, Phillips wrote a passionate letter to the gathering's president, George Washington. The source of Phillips' ire was a law obligating all those taking part in the Pennsylvania legislature to first take an oath of office proclaiming that both the Old and New Testaments were given by "devine inspiration." He complained to Washington:

> [Such an oath] is absolutely against the Religious principle of a Jew, and is against his Conscience to take any such oath—By the above law a Jew is deprived of holding any publick office or place of Government which is a Contridectory to the bill of Right Sect 2. viz
>
> That all men have a natural and unalienable Right To worship almighty God according to the dictates of their own Conscience and understanding, and that no man aught or of Right can be Compelled to attend any Religious Worship or Erect or support any place of worship or Maintain any minister contrary to or against his own free will and Consent....
>
> *It is well known among all the Citizens of the 13 united states that the Jews have been true and faithfull whigs, and during the late Contest with England they have been foremost in aiding and assisting the States with their lifes and fortunes, they have supported the cause, have bravely fought and bleed for Liberty which they can not Enjoy*—[20]

---

20. United States State Department, *The Documentary History of the Constitution of the United States of America, 1786–1870*, vol. 1 (Washington, DC, 1901), 281–82. Emphasis added.

Here we have a man who practiced his faith in the freedom of Philadelphia, in the prosperity of the New World. The comforts of his life, spiritual and material, were unimaginable to his coreligionists overseas. Yet, strikingly, Phillips is unsatisfied, because he is still unable to serve in the state legislature even as he proudly proclaims his disagreement with the majority religion of the country. Perhaps even more remarkably, he argues that until he has this right, he is not truly free.

It is often assumed that the most important part of the Constitution for ensuring religious freedom in America is the First Amendment. This is incorrect; in fact, the Establishment and Free Exercise clauses of the Bill of Rights were meant originally to limit congressional power over the states, which were free to establish any religious establishment they wished. Jews in America enjoyed the ability to practice their religion freely while prospering economically. Nevertheless, countless states prohibited non-Christians from serving in their legislatures. The Constitution's banning of any religious test for federal office was a true sign of Jews being welcomed in America, because it recognized the right of all faiths to join in serving society without having to amputate their religious identity.

During a parade in Philadelphia on July 4, 1787, a rabbi walked arm in arm with the ministers of that city, leading Dr. Benjamin Rush – a close acquaintance of Phillips – to remark that this was "a most delightful sight. There could not have been a more happy emblem contrived, of that section of the new constitution, which opens all its power and offices alike, not only to every sect of Christians, but to worthy men of *every* religion."[21] Jonas Phillips understood this to be the very essence of American liberty, and he was perhaps the first American Jew to argue that integral to his country's vision was being both a *ger* and *toshav*. It was only two hundred years later that a rabbi, himself an immigrant to this country, would present a theological vision that would give voice to Phillips' dream.

---

21. Benjamin Rush, "Observations on the Fourth of July Procession in Philadelphia," in *The Documentary History of the Ratification of the Constitution, Digital Edition*, eds. John P. Kaminski et al. (Charlottesville, VA, 2009), http://csac.history.wisc.edu/benjamin_rush7.15.pdf.

## "Founding Brothers"

### RAV AHRON SOLOVEICHIK

Having elucidated the Rav's understanding of religious liberty and the distinct similarities between his vision and that of America's Founding Fathers, we turn now to Rav Ahron's articulation of the other value at the heart of the Declaration: equality. Rav Ahron noted often that R. Akiva's dictum "beloved is man who was created in the image of God" implies that "every human being, regardless of religion, race, origin, or creed, is endowed with divine dignity. Consequently, all people are to be treated with equal respect and dignity."[22] If Jews revere the ideals upon which America was founded, it is because the idea of equality that the Declaration proudly proclaimed is itself a biblical idea:

> This key concept of *kavod habriyot*, the dignity of all human beings, constitutes the basis of human rights. The maxim of "man was endowed by his Creator with certain inalienable rights" was not an innovation of the founders of the American republic. These men were impressed with the doctrine of human rights which flows naturally from the concept of "the dignity of man" and the "image of God in which He created man," as they knew from their biblical background.[23]

Rav Ahron further stresses that whereas the Lockean doctrine of "equal rights" implies first and foremost what one *cannot* do to another, the doctrine that "all men are created equal" entails a positive duty for Jews to act toward everyone with what the Bible terms *tzedek*. For Rav Ahron, the foundation of democratic values lies in the command "Righteousness, righteousness, you shall pursue" (Deut. 16:20), a mitzva that he sees as universalistic in scope:

> Torah law is distinct and unique in that, whereas modern jurisprudence is completely and exclusively grounded in human

---

22. Ahron Soloveichik, "Civil Rights and the Dignity of Man," in *Logic of the Heart, Logic of the Mind* (Jerusalem, 1991), 62.
23. Ibid., 63.

rights, Torah jurisprudence is additionally founded upon the pillar of duties.[24]

The Torah states, "*Tzedek, tzedek* you shall pursue" (Deut. 16:20). Why should the Torah repeat the term *tzedek*? Rabbeinu Baḥya, the student of Ramban, in his work *Kad HaKemaḥ*, interprets that the Torah intimates how the same standard of justice and righteousness that is applied toward our Jewish brothers is also to be applied toward all gentiles. When one delves into the halakha, one can readily see that the Torah does not make a distinction between Jews and non-Jews within the realms of *mishpat* and *tzedek*.[25]

Equality, in other words, implies not only equal inviolability; it leads normatively to a common obligation to one another.

It is with this in mind that we are fully able to appreciate the philosophical conundrum that one with such a worldview – one that takes for granted not only human equality, but also positive obligations stemming from that fact – might discover in Jewish law. In the realm of ethics, traditional Judaism seems to obligate a host of moral obligations that halakha expressly limits to Jews. Thus, Tractate Bava Metzia insists that the obligation of *hashavat aveda* (returning a lost object) applies only to fellow members of the covenant, noting that the lost objects included in the mitzva are limited in the verse to *avedat aḥikha* (the lost item of your brother). Similarly, one of the most celebrated commandments of the Torah, "love *re'akha* as yourself" (Lev. 19:18), is translated by Jewish tradition to refer not to a neighbor, but to a fellow Jew. Thus, Maimonides explicitly states, "It is a mitzva upon every person to love every single member of Israel like his own self, as it is written, 'and you shall love *re'akha* as yourself.'"[26] Not only obligations, but prohibitions like bearing a grudge are also limited to members of the Jewish people. For Rav Ahron, who embraced the American idea of equality not despite the Torah but precisely because of it, the exclusionary nature of these obligations demands an explanation.

---

24. Ibid.
25. Ibid., 65.
26. *Mishneh Torah, Laws of Moral Dispositions* 6:3.

## SHIMON BEN SHETAḤ AND THE AMERICAN IDEA

Rav Ahron's approach to Jewish ethics in general – and to the above laws in particular – can best be understood through his explanation of a well-known tale in the Jerusalem Talmud:

> Shimon ben Shetaḥ worked in the flax business. His disciples said to him, "Rabbi, relax; we will buy you a donkey so you will not have to work so much." They went and bought a donkey from an Arab [pagan]. A pearl was hanging on it. They came to him saying, "From now on, you will not have to work anymore."
> He said to them, "Why?"
> They told him, "We bought you a donkey from an Arab and a pearl was hanging on it."
> He said to them, "Did its owner know about it?"
> They said to him, "No."
> He said to them, "Go return it."

Shimon ben Shetaḥ's students then argue that their approach is in accordance with every jot and tittle of talmudic law:

> [They retorted:] "Did not R. Huna Bivi bar Gozlon state in the name of Rav, 'They replied in front of Rabbi [Yehuda HaNasi]: Even in accord with the one who has said stealing from an idolater is prohibited, all parties concur that his lost object is permitted [to be kept]'"?
> [Shimon ben Shetaḥ] replied, "Do you think that Shimon ben Shetaḥ is a barbarian? Shimon ben Shetaḥ wants to hear [the Arab say], "Blessed be the God of the Jews" more than all the money in the world.[27]

The sage then returns the precious pearl and sanctifies God's name in the process. And yet, from Shimon ben Shetaḥ's initial dismay with his students' argument, it does not seem to be sanctification that he stresses; he communicates apprehensions that appear far more fundamental

---

27. Y. Bava Metzia 2:5.

than concerns relating to sanctifying God's name. For this sage, returning it is not merely a matter of clever public policy, but demanded by his very humanity.

In a nearby passage, the Talmud seems to indicate that returning a gentile's lost object is not only a humanitarian obligation, but a halakhic one as well:

> Abba Oshaaya of Tiriah [was a laundryman in a bathhouse. The queen came to wash there and lost her jewels and gold pieces. He found them and returned them to her].[28]
>
> She said, "They are yours. As for me, what are they worth? I have more and better."
>
> He said to her, "The Torah has decreed that we return [lost objects]."
>
> She said, "Blessed be the God of the Jews."

This talmudic tale formed the cornerstone of Rav Ahron's own paean to the American idea, which he titled "Civil Rights and the Dignity of Man." The obvious lesson of the story, he argues, is that for the *Tanna*, "anyone who fails to apply a uniform standard of *mishpat*, justice, and *tzedek*, righteousness, to all human beings regardless of origin, color, or creed is deemed barbaric." The Talmud, he continues, teaches us that "people who refuse to grant any human being the same degree of respect that they offer to their own race or nationality are adopting a barbaric attitude."[29]

Rabbi Moshe of Coucy, known as *Semag* (the acronym of his magnum opus, *Sefer Mitzvot Gadol*), takes note of this tale to excoriate members of his own community who fail to follow Shimon ben Shetaḥ's

---

28. I have bracketed this essential background, which is necessary to make the Talmud's text intelligible, because it does not appear in the standard printed versions of the Jerusalem Talmud or the Leiden manuscript. It does appear in the Escorial manuscript, which was discovered in 1976, prior to which Rabbi Moshe Margoliot cited the background from "a midrash" (*Penei Moshe*, ad loc.) and Rabbi Ḥayim Yosef David Azulai adduced it in his glosses to the Talmud in his *Kikkar LaAden* (Livorno, 1801), 163b.
29. Ahron Soloveichik, "Civil Rights and the Dignity of Man," 66.

example. The *Tanna* clearly sensed that it was wrong – objectively immoral – not to return the lost object of one's fellow, his or her particular faith notwithstanding. This assumption, argues *Semag*, is absolutely accurate. While the specific command "you shall surely return it" (Ex. 23:4) is directed at Jews, there is nonetheless an additional, more general obligation that incorporates every member of humanity. *Semag*'s source is from Zephaniah 3:13: "*She'erit Yisrael lo yaasu avla*" (The remnant of Israel must not commit an injustice). Jews, to paraphrase Shimon ben Shetaḥ, are not allowed to be barbaric and are thus obligated to treat everyone ethically. Focusing on the narrow laws of *hashavat aveda* at the expense of the expansive *lo yaasu avla*, *Semag* admonishes, is what has caused the exile to last so long.

It emerges, said Rav Ahron of *Semag*'s interpretation of the Shimon ben Shetaḥ episode, that Jewish ethics encompasses two complementary sources of obligation: specific laws and general virtues. The former, such as *hashavat aveda*, are limited to Jews, whereas all humanity is included in the more universal moral virtues that lie at the core of the Torah.[30] Non-Jews may not be included in the law insisting upon *avedat aḥikha*, but they are nevertheless included in the general virtues, the positive exhortations, such as *tzedek tzedek tirdof*, and the negative ones, such as *lo yaasu avla*.

One can see another striking concern in *Semag*'s comments, a concern that Rav Ahron himself shared: the restriction of many laws to Jews may lead one to lose sight of the more expansive obligations found throughout Tanakh to act ethically. This statement by *Semag* is near and dear to students of Rav Ahron Soloveichik, who quoted it often in his lectures. We are left, however, with an obvious question: If the general virtues of *tzedek, imitatio Dei*, and *lo yaasu avla* demand an ethical consideration for all human beings, what is the purpose of a host of laws that obligate exclusive obligations among Jews? Why create

---

30. For the halakhic details of Rav Ahron's position set within the broader context of Jewish legal discourse, see his discussion of the prohibition *lo teḥannem* in *Paraḥ Mateh Aharon: Ḥiddushim al HaRambam Sefer Madda* (Jerusalem, 1997), *Laws of Idolatry* 9:16, pp. 138–53.

narrow obligations for members of a faith when the virtues delineated throughout Tanakh require us to be concerned for the welfare of all human beings?

## RAV AHRON'S TWO-TIERED SYSTEM OF JEWISH ETHICS

The answer lies in Rav Ahron's insistence that a reason-based commitment to the dignity of all mankind must be combined with a love of fellow Jews that defies all rational expectations. Anyone who knew Rav Ahron was struck by the fact that both of these beliefs – the universality of *tzedek* and the emotional identification with all Jews – lay at the core of his personality. In the 1960s, Rabbi David Luchins mentioned to Rabbi Mordechai Gifter that Rav Ahron was at that point very concerned about the suffering in the African region of Biafra. Rabbi Gifter responded in admiration, "It is not just that Rav Ahron is the only Rosh Yeshiva that speaks about Biafra, it's that he is the only Rosh Yeshiva who ever heard of Biafra."[31]

At the same time, Rav Ahron stressed to his students that if all members of the Jewish people are today known as *Yehudim*, it is because of the proud proclamation by Judah (Yehuda) to his father regarding Benjamin: "I will stand surety for him!" (Gen. 43:9) By its very name, "Judah-ism" proclaims that a Jew is bound to every other member of the Jewish people in a way that is even more profound than the ethical obligations binding humanity. We are members of mankind, but we are also members of a nation that is a family, in which every Jew stands surety for one another because all Jews are brothers and sisters. Reason dictates that every human being ethically obligates us; one might even say that it is a "self-evident truth." But halakha also insists on another truth that is not obvious at all, and yet nevertheless lies at the heart of Judaism: *Kol Yisrael arevim zeh bazeh*, all Jews stand surety for one another, because the children of Jacob are more than individuals obligated to one another – they are metaphysically one. They must therefore love one another as they love their very selves. It is, Rav Ahron argues, a love that "does not take cognizance

---

31. Luchins wrote this for Orthodox Union Israel Center's *Torah Tidbits* (Jerusalam) in 2002.

of the merits or failings of the person loved…must be applied toward all Jews indiscriminately – religious or non-observant, gentle or rude, pleasant or unpleasant, respectful or abusive." Is this, Rav Ahron asked, "in accordance with logic?" It is, he insisted, founded on "blind love," a familial love that must be limited to Jews. Throughout Jewish history, despite centuries of persecution at the hands of gentiles, Jews insisted that all human beings are created in the image of God. But that is not the same as blind love. "Blind love toward the entire world," he notes, "would be suicidal for the Jews themselves."[32]

Utilizing this dichotomy, Rav Ahron interprets the necessity of both biblical ethics and biblical law. The laws obligating Jews toward one another serve not to exclude ethical obligations to gentiles; on the contrary, they build upon ethical obligations by adding laws that establish all Jews as covenantal brothers and sisters. Law exists where ethics alone would be insufficient to obligate behavior. The laws binding Jew and Jew exist to demand kind acts even when such action may seem irrational. We can all imagine situations in which acts of kindness would seem uncalled for based purely upon reason. If one experienced terrible cruelty from another, and then was asked by that cruel man for a job or for financial assistance, a negative response would be justified. But if that person were one's brother, then we could understand that bearing a grudge might not be the proper response.

It is with this approach in mind that the story of Shimon ben Shetaḥ can be interpreted. The rabbi's students, having learned from their teacher that gentiles are excluded from the obligation of *hashavat aveda*, assumed it unnecessary to return the precious jewel to the pagan. Shimon ben Shetaḥ sternly replies that such an approach is not only halakhically wrong, but spiritually barbaric. *Hashavat aveda* as a law obligates Jews to return objects to other *Yehudim* even when such action may seem logically inadvisable, utterly undeserved, and an unreasonable expectation – when such a course of action would be logical only if we saw other Jews as our very selves. But reason and the universal ethical exhortations found throughout Tanakh in fact dictate that one *must*

---

32. Ahron Soloveichik, "Jew and Jew, Jew and Non-Jew," in *Logic of the Heart, Logic of the Mind*, 76–77.

return the precious jewel, for the gentile – however pagan – remains created in the image of God. The story, then, is a cautionary tale as to how legal exceptions can be misunderstood and how it can even cause us to lose sight of the democratic ethical vision that lies at the heart of the Torah.

## THE HEART AND HEAD: PREFERENTIAL LOVE AND UNIVERSAL CONCERN

As a metaphor for these two forms of obligation – the halakha-based obligations founded in familial love for all Jews, and the belief in self-evident equal dignity of all human beings – Rav Ahron coined a phrase with which he was forever associated, "Logic of the Heart and Logic of the Mind." To him, these two concepts are embodied by the two parts of the mitzva of donning *tefillin* (phylacteries): the *shel rosh* is placed on the head and is prominently visible, while the *shel yad* is laid near the heart and remains unseen by outsiders:

> The *tefillin* placed on the head corresponds to the commandments that are based upon logic of the mind. It represents something that can be perceived by everyone, by Jews and non-Jews alike. But the *tefillin* placed on the arm adjoining the heart is *mekhuseh*, a sign for *you*, peculiar to Israel…. Through the "reminder between your eyes," you articulate the Torah of God. You will represent the Torah before all the peoples of the world. But the *tefillin shel yad*, representing the obligations stemming from the logic of the heart, is "a sign to *you*, not a sign to others." Consequently, brotherly love that stems from the heart, emotional love, has application only to Jews.[33]

It is perhaps worth adding to Rav Ahron's example that it is only after the *shel yad* has been placed that the *shel rosh* follows. Adopting Rav Ahron's metaphor, we can therefore suggest that Jewish particularism and universalism go hand in hand, that a preferential love of those closest to us leads us to empathize with the sufferings of others.

---

33. Ibid., 75.

Prof. Ze'ev Maghen relates how he was once sitting in a restaurant in Tel Aviv when he heard that a plane crash in East Asia killed hundreds of people. Unperturbed, he continued with his meal. He then paused, thought to himself how he would feel if those killed were Israelis, and found himself without an appetite. It is preferential love for one's own nation, he realized, that can lead to compassion for others:

> Preferential love is the most powerful love there is, the only truly *motivating* love there is. It is by *means* of that love – the *special* love we harbor for those close to us – that we learn how to begin to love others, who are farther away. Genuine and galvanizing empathy for "the other" is acquired most effectively and lastingly through a process which involves, first and foremost, immersion in love of self, then of family, then of friends, then of community... and so on. It is via *emotional analogy* to these types of strong-bond affections that one becomes capable of executing a sort of "love leap," a transference of the strength and immediacy of the feelings one retains for his favorite people, smack onto those who have no direct claim on such sentiments.[34]

In pondering Rav Ahron's approaches to Jew and gentile, then, we realize that both are spiritually and ethically demanding, and we realize that love of one's people does not preclude helping those less close to us; on the contrary, it can serve as the very foundation for our concern with general society. This too, like the Rav's approach to religion, is distinctly American. When Alexis de Tocqueville visited the United States in the nineteenth century, he was struck by the diversity of communities and fellowships that existed throughout society, economic and religious organizations that simultaneously bound their own members to one another while serving as springboards toward serving society at large. As the scholar Yuval Levin has noted, it is this vision that is so desperately needed in America today, one which makes space for preferential relationships while seeing them as important building blocks of a nation:

---

34. Ze'ev Maghen, "Imagine: On Love and Lennon," *Azure* 7 (1999): 155.

In that space, in other words, we do more than provide for ourselves and others. We build our character and raise our children, we sustain and evolve our traditions and culture – we flourish and thrive. The various institutions and forces that act between the individual and the state do not all pull in the same direction, of course. There are disagreements and tensions, and different ideas of the common good and the individual good.... But the diversity (indeed, at times the incoherence) of our public square is not proof of its backwardness or uselessness, as progressives have suggested. It is often a source of its strength, and of ours. It is what a free society looks like.[35]

## THE "FOUNDING BROTHERS" AND OUR TASK TODAY

In the end, the ruminations of these two rabbinic brothers on democratic society are very different in style, content, and focus, reflecting their respective interests and personalities. Yet there is a profound similarity between the two worldviews discussed in this essay. Both stress that a truly free and flourishing democratic society must recognize the ability of its citizens to be bound to society at large while at the same time retaining a spiritual, emotional, and theological bond to the members of their own covenant.

The sad irony is that even as American Jewry has been furnished role models that attempted to illustrate this to the world, and precisely in an age when Jewish Americans have been free to embrace both the universality of their American identity and the particularity of their Jewishness, so many believe these two aspects of Jewish identity – *ger* and *toshav* – to be irreconcilable, and that true participation in the American experience necessitates a relinquishing of the obligations that keep us apart from society even as we work to be a part of it. This was noted by the Rav himself:

> The emancipated modern Jew, however, has been trying, for a long time, to do away with this twofold responsibility which weighs heavily upon him. The Westernized Jew maintains that it is

---

35. Yuval Levin, "The Real Debate," *The Weekly Standard* 18, no. 4 (October 8, 2012), http://www.weeklystandard.com/articles/real-debate_653224.html.

impossible to engage in both confrontations, the universal and the covenantal, which, in his opinion, are mutually exclusive. It is, he argues, absurd to stand shoulder to shoulder with mankind preoccupied with the cognitive-technological gesture for the welfare of all, implementing the mandate granted to us by the Creator, and to make an about-face the next instant in order to confront our comrades as a distinct and separate community. Hence, the Western Jew concludes, we have to choose between these two encounters.[36]

Meanwhile, Rav Ahron notes that all too often the Torah community fails to educate its members that liberty and equality, if properly understood, are Jewish values:

> Unfortunately, too many of our yeshiva youth labor under the erroneous notion that tolerance, democracy, and goodwill are concepts emanating from the writings of Thomas Jefferson and the other fathers of the American Revolution. While it is true that Jefferson and the propounders of the Bill of Rights were motivated by the concepts of justice, righteousness, and the equality of man, it is also true that they entertained these ideas because they were influenced by the Scriptures. Children in Jewish day schools should be taught instead that values like democracy, love, goodwill, tolerance, and equality are *Jewish* values. To the extent that the general society measures up to the godly, and therefore Jewish, concept of these ethical values, the values are sublime. To the extent that these concepts do not emanate from God's attributes, they are sources of profanity and vulgarity.[37]

To present an eloquent, Orthodox, democratic vision to the next generation of American Jews is without question one of the great challenges facing American Orthodoxy. Fortunately, these two "Founding Brothers" have helped show us the way.

---

36. Soloveitchik, "Confrontation," 17.
37. Ahron Soloveichik, "Jewish Education: The Fire of Sinai; Part 1: The Voice and the Fire," in *Logic of the Heart, Logic of the Mind*, 6.

# Prof. Nehama Leibowitz and the Revolution in Bible Interpretation

Yael Unterman

### INTRODUCTION[1]

The name Nehama Leibowitz is familiar to exponents of Modern Orthodoxy in both Israel and the Diaspora, but her fame does not end there. She is also beloved to an older generation of secular Israelis, although in her homeland she is often overshadowed by the reputation of her charismatic older brother, Yeshayahu Leibowitz. While she is less well known outside of these circles, individuals ranging from ultra-Orthodox Jews to Christians have also studied her work in depth.

---

1. This article represents to a large degree a summary of an extensive biography, *Nehama Leibowitz: Teacher and Bible Scholar* (Jerusalem: Urim, 2009), henceforth, Unterman, *Nehama*, with the focus on chapters 19–22 and 24. It is impossible to note the source for every sentence in the biography; instead, I will note sections so as to direct the interested reader to the location for further reading.

Prof. Leibowitz[2] (1905–97) had a tremendous impact upon thousands during her long life.[3] Her impact continues to this day through her books and articles, citations by rabbis and teachers, ongoing discussion and critique of her work, and the new schools of thought that arose from hers, using her methodology as a point of departure. She also had a profound influence on Tanakh studies within the Israeli National Religious educational system, although, as we will see, this is a mixed blessing.[4]

Prof. Leibowitz was many things to those who knew her. To some, she was the Torah teacher par excellence, the "Grande Dame of Torah Teaching"; to others, she was the author who popularized *parasha* study with its commentaries; and to yet others, she was the instigator of a correspondence course in Bible containing challenging questions. To some, she was a brilliant professor who drew crowds to her lectures; to others, a pioneering literary analyst of Bible; and to still others, the first widely recognized *talmidat ḥakhamim*.

Apropos the last, it is important from the outset to dispel any impression that it was as "the first woman to…" that she earned her place in the Jewish hall of fame. Her achievements stand on their own merit, as we shall see. Nonetheless, they do appear all the more striking in the context of her having been an Orthodox Jewish woman. Indeed, although she herself did not perceive it to be thus, her gender may in fact have played some role in shaping her life and work. This topic, though important, will not be discussed in this article due to space limitations.[5]

---

2. In my biographical work, mentioned in the previous footnote, I referred to this legendary teacher as "Nehama" throughout. This was due to her own preference to be addressed by her first name always, and it indeed achieved the effect of granting the readers a feeling of closeness and familiarity to her. However, in this volume, it is important and appropriate to give her the respect she deserves. Hence, like the other figures in this work, she will be referred to by her title, professor.
3. See further in Unterman, *Nehama*, ch. 9.
4. See the final section of this article and Unterman, *Nehama*, ch. 24.
5. See further in Unterman, *Nehama*, ch. 14.

## EARLY YEARS: LATVIA – GERMANY – PALESTINE[6]

Prof. Nehama Leibowitz was born on September 3, 1905 (3 Elul 5665), in Riga, Latvia, to Mordekhai Leibowitz and his wife Freyda, née Nimchevich. The language spoken in their home was Hebrew. The Torah-centered, Zionist, Jewish-humanistic, and cultured atmosphere of her upbringing was the foundry for her outlook and subsequent scholarship. Her father, a businessman, delighted in quizzing his daughter and her older brother, Yeshayahu, on Shakespeare and Tanakh. Yeshayahu subsequently became a prominent and controversial Israeli philosopher, and the two siblings maintained a relationship throughout their lives that was close but marked by much debate and disagreement. Their respective approaches to halakha and ethics exhibit some strong similarities and also significant divergences.[7]

Prof. Leibowitz was home-schooled until tenth grade. Then in 1919, due to political upheavals, the family moved to Berlin, where she attended the local gymnasium. Berlin, bustling with Jewish and academic activity, provided a remarkable platform for Prof. Leibowitz's intellectual development.[8] She spent the years 1925–30 at the Universities of Berlin, Heidelberg, and Marburg, studying Bible studies and English and German philology and literature with leading scholars. Her doctoral dissertation was on "Translation Techniques of Judeo-German Bible Translations in the Fifteenth and Sixteenth Centuries, as Exemplified by Translations of the Book of Psalms," examining Yiddish translations of

---

6. For more on her early years, see Unterman, *Nehama*, ch. 1.
7. For more on the siblings' relationship, as well as a brief comparison of their thought, see Unterman, *Nehama*, ch. 23. For more on Prof. Leibowitz's family background and early years in general, see ibid., ch. 1; see also Ḥayuta Deutsch, *Nehama: Sippur Ḥayehah shel Neḥama Leibowitz* (Tel Aviv, 2008), and Leah Abramowitz, *Tales of Nehama* (Jerusalem, 2003). Yeshayahu Leibowitz's reminiscences from his youth can be found in his book *Al Olam UMlo'o: Siḥot im Mikhael Shashar* (Jerusalem, 1987), 172–76.
8. For more on the influence of her German context on Prof. Leibowitz, see Alan T. Levenson, "Contextualizing a Master: Nehama Leibowitz, History and Exegesis," *Journal of Jewish Education* 77 (2011): 42–65; and Rivka Horwitz, "Neḥama Leibowitz VeHaparshanim HaYehudi'im BeGermania BaMe'a HaEsrim: Martin Buber, Franz Rosenzweig, UBenno Jacob," in M. Ahrend et al., eds., *Pirkei Neḥama* (Jerusalem, 2001), 207–20.

the Tanakh and utilizing manuscripts in the Parma and Berlin libraries. The period she chose allowed her to avoid issues relating to biblical criticism, which was predominant in the universities of the time. At the same time, she enrolled at the *Hochschule für die Wissenschaft des Judentums*, the Berlin college for the scientific study of Judaism. This resembled an academic department for Jewish studies, but was not located within any particular university. The *Hochschule* was the only institution where Prof. Leibowitz undertook any formal study of intellectual Jewish materials. Here she formed constructive connections with scholars, rabbis, and rabbinical students. For example, she learned philosophy from Leo Strauss, a young post-doctoral student and her classmate in Julius Guttmann's Maimonides seminar, while she in turn taught him Hebrew.

In addition to her studies, Prof. Leibowitz launched her teaching career in the *Ivrit Be'Ivrit* (teaching of Jewish studies in Hebrew) method in Jewish schools such as Adas Yisroel, belonging to Rabbi Azriel Hildesheimer's breakaway Orthodox congregation of the same name founded in 1869 in reaction to the Reform movement. Adas Yisroel espoused a philosophy akin to that of Rabbi Samson Raphael Hirsch. Hirsch's *Torah im derekh eretz* philosophy appealed to Prof. Leibowitz in combining Orthodox sensibilities, openness to German culture, and ethical sensitivity. However, she also felt distanced from the Hirschian camp, especially in her Zionism. By the time she left Germany, Prof. Leibowitz had given her first lectures on educational methodology and published her first articles.

Her marriage to Yedidyah Lipman Leibowitz, her father's brother who was twenty-nine years her elder, raised some eyebrows in her immediate circles. The fact that she went ahead with it is testimony to her determination and strong character. The two were happily married for forty years, until his passing.

In 1931, Prof. Leibowitz immigrated to Palestine with her husband. The couple's exit from Germany, although spurred by Zionism and not any sense of imminent threat, was nonetheless very timely, sparing them the horrors of the Nazi regime. Settling in the Kiryat Moshe neighborhood of Jerusalem, Prof. Leibowitz soon established her career, teaching at education seminaries and at Bar-Ilan, the Hebrew, and Tel Aviv Universities. She received a professorship in Bible education at the last.

Among several prizes awarded to her was the prestigious Israel Prize in the Field of Education (1957). A staunch Zionist, she remained in Israel until her death in 1997, refusing to leave its borders even for brief travel.

## IN THE CLASSROOM AND IN PRINT

Prof. Leibowitz was a master teacher, charismatic, brilliant, and humorous. Students flocked to hear her; in the course of her lifetime, she clocked many thousands of hours teaching Tanakh and commentary. She viewed herself a teacher, first and foremost, and indeed requested that upon her gravestone be engraved one word only: *mora* (teacher).

The purpose of this article, however, is not to survey her pedagogy or even various intellectual components of her classroom, although there is much to discuss.[9] Instead, the focus here will be on her published work and its contribution to Jewish thought.

Prof. Leibowitz's first major written enterprise, laying the groundwork for her later work in print, was spawned in the summer of 1942.[10] Two versions of the birth of that enterprise exist – her own recollection of the events and that of a colleague.[11] According to her own testimony, she "noticed that all sorts of subjects are taught by correspondence, from architecture to accounting, from advertising to stenography," and had the idea of applying the concept of a guided correspondence course to Torah, in order to boost adult education.[12] The other version is far more romantic. It claims that the said correspondence course had its roots in the weekly homework Prof. Leibowitz assigned a group of mature female students in Jerusalem's Mizrachi seminar. The homework consisted of a series of questions on various difficulties in biblical texts and

---

9. See further in Unterman, *Nehama*, chs. 7, 8, and 18, discussing Prof. Leibowitz's identity as a teacher, her pedagogical methods, and the "pluralism within limits" that characterized both her work and her classroom. See also Yael Unterman, "The Limits of the Orthodox Classroom," *Conversations* 4 (2009): 86–93 (http://www.jewishideas.org/articles/limits-orthodox-classroom).
10. For further reading on the development of Prof. Leibowitz's worksheets and books, see Unterman, *Nehama*, ch. 2.
11. Dov Rappel, "Horatam VeLeidatam," *Amudim* 609 (5757): 233.
12. Leibowitz, "Siḥa al Limmud Parashat HaShavua BeMikhtavim," in Ahrend et al., *Pirkei*, 458.

commentaries. So great was the students' enjoyment of these "Torah puzzles," which required intellectual exertion to unravel, that even after the school year's end they wrote to her from their kibbutzim to ask her to send more homework. Prof. Leibowitz acceded to the request and began sending out sheets on a weekly basis to her students during the summer, and they mailed their answers back to be checked. The sheets attracted other kibbutz members, who also wrote asking to receive them. Word spread, and increasing numbers of people, complete strangers to her, began contacting her and requesting inclusion in the mailings. Thus, Prof. Leibowitz found herself corresponding with dozens of laborers and farmers, city dwellers, teachers, and professors, who in their free time answered her questions on the *parasha* and returned them by mail. Her correspondents eventually numbered in the hundreds and came to include Diaspora Jews and even a number of non-Jews. She spent a good portion of her free time reading and returning these sheets – all without any remuneration. This colossal endeavor, which became known simply as the *gilyonot* (sheets), spanned from 1942 to 1972, and constitutes outstanding evidence of Prof. Leibowitz's devotion to the study of Tanakh and commentaries.

At some point, it was suggested to Prof. Leibowitz that she include answers along with her questions. A die-hard educator, she initially resisted such "spoon-feeding," but she eventually reluctantly consented, creating pamphlets with both questions and answers, organized by weekly portion. These were subsequently amalgamated and published, first as seven annuals known as *Studies in the Weekly Sidra* (*1954–1961*), and then, after being divided according to books of the Torah and re-edited, as her famous *Studies* series: *Studies in Bereshit, New Studies in Shemot, New Studies in Vayikra, Studies in Bamidbar,* and *Studies in Devarim* (published from 1966 through 1996).

The books were divided into essays by *parasha*. In each essay, Prof. Leibowitz expertly led the reader from the biblical text (vowelized and divided into phrases, with key words in bold), to the difficulty in the text, and on to various solutions. Along the way she quoted, often at length, from classic and modern commentators (mostly Jewish but with some exceptions, including a small number of Bible scholars, such as Driver and Gesenius), adding her own elucidations and comparisons. The essay built up to a climax, comprising either a recapitulation of a commentator's words or her own words bearing some ethical or spiritual message.

Nothing like this had ever been published. Proving extremely popular, the books were translated into English, French, Spanish, Dutch, German, and Russian. It is in these works, alongside a number of articles, that Prof. Leibowitz most concretely expressed her insights and scholarship, and introduced the analytical, comparative study of traditional (and some non-traditional) Jewish commentaries to the broader public. Her categorization and careful analysis of commentaries has been compared by some to the Brisker *derekh* in Talmud study, and was no less a revolution in its own way.

## BIBLE SCHOLARSHIP AND ACADEMIA[13]

Having completed this background section, we may begin the more in-depth discussion of Prof. Leibowitz's interpretative methodology and scholarly contributions. In order to place and categorize her work, a brief survey of relatively recent developments in academic Bible scholarship will be helpful.[14]

In the nineteenth and twentieth centuries, Jewish Bible scholarship underwent a revolution. The nineteenth century witnessed the reemergence of Tanakh as a subject of high-level study, reinstating it from its position as secondary to the Talmud. Both secular Zionist and traditional circles witnessed a return to a focus on Tanakh, and for the first time in a long while several monumental Orthodox biblical commentaries were produced by the likes of Luzzato, Hirsch, Mecklenburg, Malbim, Netziv, and Hoffmann.

As the twentieth century advanced, Diaspora and Israeli Orthodoxy developed somewhat different approaches to scholarly study of Tanakh.[15] Diaspora Orthodoxy tended for the most part to steer away from academic

---

13. The next four sections are based on Unterman, *Nehama*, ch. 19.
14. A helpful survey may be found in the introduction by Prof. Leibowitz's translator, Aryeh Newman, to her *Studies in Bereshit (Genesis)* (Jerusalem, 1993), xx–xxix.
15. B. Barry Levy, "The State and Directions of Orthodox Bible Study," in Shalom Carmy, ed., *Modern Scholarship in the Study of Torah* (Northvale, NJ, 1996), 53–58. For more on developments within Jewish academic Bible study, see S. David Sperling, ed., *Students of the Covenant: A History of Jewish Biblical Scholarship in North America*

scholarship. In Israel, by contrast, the rational-scientific approach gained a foothold among Orthodox Bible scholars, perhaps because scientific research of the Land was much more available and immediate.[16]

Where does Prof. Leibowitz fit into the above? Although she was educated in the Diaspora, we cannot place her with Jewish Bible scholars of the Diaspora, as she lived and worked in Israel, and her primary emphasis was on Hebrew language. Her approach was at least in part rational and academic. On the other hand, she did not join her Israeli peers in their interest in historical and geographical factors. Hence, she represents a middle path of sorts – a direct link in the chain of Jewish biblical exegesis, written in rabbinic Hebrew but flavored with academic methods and a rationalistic bent.

Prof. Leibowitz's closest peers tended to be those whose views of the Torah combined a fairly traditionalist approach (especially with regard to authorship) with an interest in text rather than realia. These included Israeli scholars hailing from strongly traditional backgrounds, such as Umberto Cassuto, Moshe Zvi Segal, Martin Buber, Yehezkel Kaufmann, and Meir Weiss. However, she also demonstrated an affinity for the commentaries of Benno Jacob, a Reform rabbi. She strongly preferred the literary approach espoused by Jacob, Cassuto, Buber, Rosenzweig, and Weiss over any biblical-critical approach. In fact, she had more in common with the non-Orthodox Buber than she did with her Orthodox colleague Rabbi Mordekhai Breuer. The latter reported that on the occasion of the first public presentation of his theory, Prof. Leibowitz was his fiercest opponent. His attempts to incorporate biblical-critical theories in ways consonant with Orthodox sensibilities was not at all to her liking; to his chagrin, she did not budge from this position throughout her lifetime.[17] Her years of immersion

---

(Atlanta, 1992), 38, 45–53, 69–107, 115–47; and B. Barry Levy, "On the Periphery: North American Orthodox Judaism and Contemporary Biblical Scholarship," in Sperling, op cit., 159–204.
16. Levy, "State," 61. He also suggests that this development is due to the fact that Israelis can specialize in more ways than North American scholars and are significantly enriched by non-Orthodox academia.
17. Mordekhai Breuer, "*Yaḥasah shel Neḥama Leibowitz el Madda HaMikra*," *Limmudim* 1 (2001): 12–14.

in Bible criticism in German universities had left her with the impression that such interpretations were frequently tendentious, driven by anti-Semitism, and erroneous, exhibiting a profound ignorance of Hebrew and of the only authentic context for reading the Bible: the moral-ethical one. Thus, for example, she writes:

> We shall decline to follow that non-Jewish commentator who endeavored to trace Jacob's limp, after the wrestling bout with the angel, to an attack of rheumatism, caused by sleeping in the open, all night, in the damp atmosphere of the brook. Such a mechanical approach to supernatural mystical events must be ruled out in favor of the primary demand of interpretation – response to the spirit, tone, and intention of the narrative.[18]

Prof. Leibowitz only rarely cited findings from historical scholarship, such as comparative Near East or philological research. When she did, it was generally in order to bolster the traditional viewpoint or to prove the uniqueness and superiority of the Tanakh. She was almost never interested in manuscripts, versions, and other tools of the scholarly trade. She avoided all mention of biblical emendation, feeling that it was speculative and not good methodology. On rare occasions in her writings, she even launched an explicit attack. By and large, however, her strategy was simply to ignore the theories of multiple authorship promoted by Graf and Wellhausen. Instead, when apparent inconsistencies arose, she adopted an approach to the text that suggested literary and educational meanings. These comprised the bulk of her work, as will be discussed below.

Prof. Leibowitz bore a dislike for the academic enterprise as a whole; teaching Jewish values seemed to her a more worthwhile way to spend one's time. This was most pronounced when it came to academic Bible scholarship, a realm that, for the most part, she chose to ignore altogether. She actively discouraged students from studying Bible in university, and she refused to go along with the predominant research directions or to compromise her beliefs for the sake of her career. She

---

18. Leibowitz, *Bereshit*, 366.

especially detested the prevalent assumption that traditionalists are prejudiced while others are not, declaring, "Everyone has prejudices, but I at least know that I have them!"

In general, for Prof. Leibowitz, academia did not offer a worldview to be adopted wholesale, but rather a set of tools and findings to be implemented selectively, with both rigor and caution. It was the academic way of thinking that she adopted, more than its conclusions, the "how" rather than the "what." She utilized academic devices, such as definition of terms, selection and categorization, comparing and contrasting, and more.[19] Her core methodology – evaluating commentaries for their faithfulness to the text – entailed keen probing and investigation; hers was a systematic approach. She rejected weak arguments and refused to bend the truth in order to reconcile commentaries; on the contrary, she delighted in highlighting their differences. Undoubtedly a modern thinker, she was interested in new scholarship when useful, and assimilated many of its terms and ways of thinking, yet she retained loyalty to traditional values and modes of thinking.

## STRADDLING WORLDS: CONTRIBUTIONS TO BIBLE STUDY

Instead of experiencing struggle and dissonance between her personal and professional life, as many Orthodox biblical scholars do,[20] Prof. Leibowitz made the most of straddling these two worlds. In fact, her traditional background granted her advantages. She was capable of reading the text very closely due to her profound familiarity with and fluency

---

19. See Erella Yedgar's two articles, "*Bein Megama Parshanit-Didaktit LeMegama Erkit-Ḥinnukhit*," *Limmudim* 1 (2001): 70, and "*HaIyyunim shel Neḥama Leibowitz KeDegem LeShiur Tanakh*," *Derekh Efrata* 9–10 (2001): 23–24.
20. For discussions of this phenomenon and some suggested solutions, see Unterman, *Nehama*, 422–23; Shalom Carmy, "A Room with a View but a Room of Our Own," in Carmy, *Modern*, 1–38; Levy, "State," 69, 74–75; Levy, "Periphery," 180–81; Erella Yedgar, "*Parashat Vayishlaḥ*: HaShipput HaMusari BeIyyunehah shel Neḥama Leibowitz; Maase HaAḥim BeShekhem KeMikre Mivḥan," in Naftali Rothenberg, ed., *Hogim BaParasha* [Meditations on the Parasha: The Weekly Torah Portion as an Inspiration for Jewish Thought and Creativity] (Tel Aviv, 2005), 109; and Moshe Z. Sokol, "How Do Modern Jewish Thinkers Interpret Religious Texts?" *Modern Judaism* 13, no. 1 (1993): 25–48.

in the range of Jewish interpretative literature, and her distance from prevalent academic theories granted her more leeway to accept or reject them as she saw fit. In this aspect, at least, she maintained more intellectual freedom than her non-Orthodox colleagues.

There were certainly those in the world of Bible scholarship who dismissed her approach. However, she also managed to earn the respect of many academics dedicated to biblical criticism; even some who would not count her as a Bible scholar per se nevertheless felt that her method complemented the academic approach.[21] One critic, for example, praised her for demonstrating that traditional exegesis explains textual difficulties better and more profoundly than biblical criticism does.[22] Her method challenged academics and kept them on their toes. Even those who rejected many of her assumptions confessed that they could not free themselves of the "Leibowitz" within:

> Every essay, every theory one tries to formulate demands serious consideration of the alternative – perchance the "Leibowitz method" is the more correct?[23]

Prof. Leibowitz's primary academic career took place in Tel Aviv University, the bastion of secular Israeli academia. The fact that her lessons were extremely popular attests to the contribution she was able to make at a time when classical Jewish commentaries had been deliberately sidelined as old-fashioned and of little interest. She was largely responsible for salvaging from obscurity this precious legacy of commentaries and reintroducing their insights into academic discourse. Yair Hoffman recalls:

> The fifties – the early days of Tel Aviv University. The first encounter with academic Torah study, enchanting the students with its

---

21. This section, discussing the attitude of Bible scholars toward Prof. Leibowitz's work, is based on Unterman, *Nehama*, 425–28.
22. Yosef Oren, quoted in Yair Sheleg, "*Kalat HaTanakh*," *Kol HaIr*, October 27, 1995, 70–73.
23. Yair Hoffman, "*Yoter MiḤokeret, Yoter MiMartza*," *Yediot Aḥaronot*, December 24, 1982, Culture supplement, 1–2.

iconoclasm and captivating them in its daring evaluation and dismissal of sacred cows. For a moment, it appears that we may now leave behind the traditional approach, which no longer has the power to satisfy anyone bitten by the bug of critical analysis in academic Tanakh study. But along Leibowitz comes, and in just one or two lessons, relights the flames of doubt, creates respect for the interpretations of the sages and medieval commentators, turns Rashi and Ibn Ezra into contenders with Wellhausen and Gunkel, contenders who regularly "win" – and not infrequently due to the force of Leibowitz's personality.[24]

Abba Oren, a teacher in secular Israeli circles, writes:

> At Oranim, I thought I had to make a choice between the obscurantism of the Uppsala School of Bible criticism, the latent anti-Semitism of Wellhausen, or the mean-spirited superiority of Martin Noth on the one hand and the ingenious but apologetic contributions of Cassuto. The latter was just too cerebral for me, and the first three plucked the Bible out of the bosom of Judaism, much as an instructor in medical school might plop the heart of a frog onto a dissecting table. It is very clear (a) that the instructor feels superior to the frog, (b) that the heart no longer belongs to the frog but to science, and (c) that the instructor, in the name of science, could overcome his disdain or squeamishness and is therefore to be applauded. Nehama Leibowitz was the one who put the heart of Judaism back into its rightful place for me.... The entire series really belongs in the home of every committedly curious and spiritually creative Jew.[25]

Prof. Israel Rozenson, although critical of many aspects of Prof. Leibowitz's approach, applauds her for not simply reintroducing the commentaries, but for imbuing their study with academic rigor:

---

24. Ibid.
25. Abba Oren, "That Thy Word Hath Quickened Me: Review of Studies in Bamidbar," *Forum* (WZO publication), 38 (Summer 1980): 157, 159.

She played a vital role in the battle to prevent the decline of traditional commentary into an assortment of random explanations often left to the mercies of various sermonizers, and in turning it into a "science" with stringent methodological requirements.[26]

For her own Modern Orthodox community, Prof. Leibowitz functioned as a beacon and scholarly standard-bearer for the Torah. Her ability to confront modern challenges with integrity saved others from being troubled by them.[27]

## REVOLUTION OF THE OLD

From all of the above, we learn that not all revolutions introduce the new; Prof. Leibowitz's revolution reintroduced the old, so to speak, while simultaneously updating it. Her action was somewhat akin, if we may draw an analogy, to restoring an old photograph or transferring a filing system from paper to computer. She went much further than simply defending the Tanakh from Bible critics. She rehabilitated it from its neglected status, analyzed it methodically, pinpointed gems of commentary, and explained and reworded them. All of this served to make its study accessible and popular.

We can argue that Prof. Leibowitz was aiming to be more than a modern academic student of Tanakh. She wished to remain loyal to the models of old, and these included both the traditional-rational models and the midrashic-homiletical models.[28] In terms of the former, she wished to follow in the footsteps of great medieval Jewish *pashtanim* such as Rashbam, Ibn Ezra, et al., and thinkers such as Maimonides. Like them, she drew insight from external sources and maintained a keen sense for the *peshat*

---

26. Israel Rozenson, "*HaParshanit, HaPerush, VeHaHistoria: He'arot al Tefisat HaParshanut shel Neḥama Leibowitz,*" *Al Derekh HaAvot* (2001): 434.
27. As Jay M. Harris observes, "People do not necessarily need to be able to articulate a response to challenge, so long as they have an authoritative source to which they can confidently refer for such a response"; Jay M. Harris, *How Do We Know This? Midrash and the Fragmentation of Modern Judaism* (Albany, 1995), 233.
28. This remark draws upon B. Barry Levy's categorization of Ashkenazic Tanakh interpreters of the nineteenth century as specializing in three main areas: the midrashic-kabbalistic; the talmudic-midrashic; and the anti-mystical rational-scientific, a school favoring philological accuracy and historical credibility. See Levy, "Periphery," 161–63, and Unterman, *Nehama*, 414, 430–31.

(the simple meaning); indeed, she did the Jewish world a great service in reclaiming the *peshat* and emphasizing rational-ethical understandings.[29] Her approach seems to have grown organically from the traditional models, while biblical criticism produced a thorough break with them. She proved that tradition and rational-critical thinking are not mutually exclusive.[30] In terms of the latter model, she took care to always read the verse within an ethical context, preferring psychologically attuned midrashic interpretations to overly literal interpretations deaf to the ethical tone of the text, even when offered by illustrious personalities such as Rashbam.[31]

Prof. Leibowitz persistently trod a careful line between "acceptable" rationalism and "dangerous" criticism, between academia and tradition. Her work was chiefly affirmative rather than defensive or polemical, replete with her own unique brand of insight and analysis.[32] We may suggest that in this, she restored the boundaries of normative traditional Torah scholarship to the former broad positions held by traditional Torah scholars before Orthodoxy retreated in the face of perceived attack during the Enlightenment period.

---

29. B. Barry Levy notes that among the rational traditionalists we find viewpoints contradicting certain axioms that have been incorporated into today's normative Orthodox view of Tanakh – for example, the understanding that the Patriarchs lived an Orthodox lifestyle. See Unterman, *Nehama*, 431–33, for a discussion of instances in which Prof. Leibowitz was likewise willing to contravene such axioms.
30. As B. Barry Levy notes, transforming into a Bible critic is not a prerequisite for every rational thinker; it is the archeological-historical perspective, not rational thinking, that primarily differentiates between modern writers and many of their premodern counterparts ("Periphery," 160).
31. Prof. Leibowitz had some biting things to say about "pursuers of *peshat*" who fail to ascertain the correct meaning of the text due to their "slavish adherence to the literal wording," which could "blind one to the real inner meaning." See *New Studies in Shemot (Exodus)* (Jerusalem, 1976), 488; and *Studies in Bamidbar (Numbers)* (Jerusalem, 1980), 209. For her, this was not *peshuto shel mikra*, the intended meaning of the text, but "*ivvut shel mikra*," a distortion of the text.
32. In this, she seems to have succeeded in beating out what Carmy ("Room," 37) described as a *derekh* – a path of study with positive insights. He notes that this is something difficult for Orthodox Bible scholars to achieve under the "hostile shadow of the academic establishment," with all one's energy squandered on defense, and only really an option for the rare Orthodox scholar whose attainments in this field permit bucking the consensus.

## EDUCATOR OR BIBLE SCHOLAR?[33]

Prof. Leibowitz did pay a price for keeping a foot in both worlds – she never officially became a fully fledged academic Bible scholar. Her professorship was in Tel Aviv University's Department of Education, not in the Bible Department, where she also taught. At the Hebrew University, despite her good relations with the faculty, she was never even hired to teach in the Bible Department. Ultimately, this left her freer to pursue her own agendas.

While she would not have been happy to have been termed a proponent of an "educational" approach to Tanakh (as the word smacks of tendentiousness), she also, on the other hand, never called herself a "Bible scholar." Rather, she saw herself as an objective teacher of *peshat* who demanded critical thinking while also maintaining loyalty to the ethical-spiritual messages of the text.

Is it then incorrect for us to term her a Bible scholar? A strong case can be made that Prof. Leibowitz did in fact make a tremendous contribution to modern Bible scholarship, and is hence worthy of that title. Although she was not a historical-critical Bible scholar, she did do important work in literary analysis of the Bible, and she ought to receive due credit for the influence of her pioneering work on this field.

## PROF. LEIBOWITZ'S LITERARY APPROACH[34]

In the second half of the twentieth century, a wind of change blew through the world of scholarly Bible study. A new literary direction had developed in reaction to the overload of the historical-critical approach in that field. While literary interpretation of the Bible had existed previously in various forms, in the 1950s it succeeded in making great inroads into the academic world, eventually becoming a significant subfield in biblical studies.

Prof. Leibowitz possessed a natural literary orientation. She studied and taught literature at university; she loved the skillful use of words to create atmosphere and meaning in texts. For her, the study of

---

33. This section is based on Unterman, *Nehama*, 428–30.
34. For a general discussion of the literary approach to studying Tanakh, as well as Prof. Leibowitz's role and place within that endeavor, see Unterman, *Nehama*, chs. 20–21.

literature, even on a high school level, constituted the in-depth scrutiny of philosophical reflections from the world's greatest thinkers. However, her attraction to the new literary direction in Bible studies was a matter of principle and not just preference, as it allowed her to navigate the world of analysis of the Tanakh in a way that would not compromise her beliefs.

Indeed, this new direction represented good news for Orthodox Jews engaged in modern biblical scholarship, enabling them to argue that biblical books were unified wholes. Now rabbinic corpora could be reclaimed from their exile, their primary assumptions at least partially acceptable to the academic mind. At last, the dialogue could shift to less defensive ground, and the gap between Orthodox and non-Orthodox might be transcended to some extent.

The new literary direction described could not have come at a better time for Prof. Leibowitz. She was delighted to be able to dismiss the documentary hypothesis by explaining textual irregularities as literary devices and to expend her energy on what the text said rather than who wrote it. Her discovery of the New Critics, a group of scholars who thought similarly about literature in general, was very exciting to her. If their approach could be applied to the Tanakh, it could preserve fundamental Jewish beliefs while still allowing for academic analysis.

Even more significantly (as Prof. Leibowitz's goal was not to find a way to take part in the academic enterprise, but rather to deepen the study of Torah), this new methodology might also reveal important dimensions in the Tanakh text through the art of close reading. Although for Prof. Leibowitz the act of close reading of the Torah derives from a fundamental theological postulate – that the Torah, being divine, is omni-significant – she also shared the New Critics' confidence that close reading applied to all literature, even without divine basis.

### INFLUENCES IN THE LITERARY DIRECTION

Prof. Leibowitz realized the potential for this new literary direction in Tanakh long before many of her colleagues, preempting its entry and subsequent popularity into mainstream academia by a good decade or two. A handful of other Jewish scholars, who also sensed the value of this approach early on, had a tremendous influence on her. Many of them are listed in the following passage from Prof. Leibowitz's pen:

Our sages have taught us the importance of every word in the text and to appreciate correspondences between similar phraseology and key words, recurring in different places. In our day, Buber and Rosenzweig, Benno Jacob, Cassuto, Meir Weiss, and others have paid careful attention to these repetitions and elicited their significance for us.[35]

This brief paragraph can be broken down into two important points:

First, we see Prof. Leibowitz contending here that a close reading of the text, a primary tool of the literary method, dates back over two millennia. The detailed attention paid by the sages of the Talmud and Midrash to Tanakh is evident to Prof. Leibowitz.[36] She presents modern close reading as a return to the midrashic close-reading method, believing that traditional sources read even more closely than modern ones. On a number of occasions, Prof. Leibowitz reports deriving a number of close-reading principles from the sages' rules and sayings, and remarks repeatedly on Rashi's close reading and sensitivity to context.[37] In "How to Read a Chapter of Tanakh," one of the few essays in which she reflects on her own methods, she notes that she learned to read Tanakh from Rashi, Nahmanides, Rashbam, Malbim, and Netziv, who shared the serious importance that they attached to every word.[38]

The second important point made here is that the traditional commentators' approach, its acuteness notwithstanding, was nonetheless able to benefit from an update by Buber, Rosenzweig, Jacob, Cassuto, and Weiss, who built upon the earlier work and also developed new methods of their own. It was from these scholars, along with Aryeh Ludwig Strauss (Buber's father-in-law and a professor of literature at

---

35. Leibowitz, *Shemot*, 474–75.
36. See examples in Leibowitz, *Bereshit*, 62; *Shemot*, 87, 380, 390, and 474; *New Studies in Vayikra* (*Leviticus*) (Jerusalem, 1980), 48; *Studies in Devarim* (*Deuteronomy*) (Jerusalem, 1980), 12. See also Gabriel H. Cohn, "HaParshanut HaMidrashit BeMifalah HaTorani shel Nehama," in Ahrend et al., *Pirkei*, 102, 105, 107.
37. See Unterman, *Nehama*, 451n1–2.
38. Leibowitz, *Torah Insights* (Jerusalem, 1995), 164. For more on the medieval commentators' close scrutiny of the text, see Unterman, *Nehama*, 442.

the Hebrew University), that Prof. Leibowitz learned the skill of literary analysis. While they were not as influential in their own lifetimes as they might have been, probably due to academic suspicion and the prevailing trends, over time ideas similar to theirs gained much ground within Bible scholarship. Nevertheless, their pioneering work is not always sufficiently credited in surveys of biblical scholarship, as is the case with Prof. Leibowitz's work as well, for reasons laid out below.

## USE OF LITERARY TOOLS

Prof. Leibowitz maintained a great interest in academic developments on the biblical-literary front and utilized modern literary terminology.[39] She adroitly developed the literary sensitivities in the Midrash and the medieval commentaries, using modern methodical and academic tools that, even if she did not invent most of them herself, she made accessible and familiar, popularizing them as none had before her. She wished to enhance students' appreciation for the rich, multilayered nature of the Torah – and she succeeded, as her work brought readers into a new relationship with Torah and restored their faith in it.

The act of closely reading the text, so important to the New Critics, was a thread running through her work from the early days. Prof. Leibowitz forced people to slow down and read what was actually written – every letter and word, the structures and patterns, keywords and repeated phrases. The questions on her worksheets compelled the reader to take a good look at the text and to keep returning to it. As she described it:

> And if previously he was like a person who sits in a car while the views fly past unseen, now he is like someone climbing a mountain with the view unfolding before him as he sweats and toils, increasingly with every new ascent.[40]

She was deeply interested in textual nuance and detail – not for their own sake (on the contrary, she actually condemned the act

---

39. Terminology scattered throughout her books includes such words as style, preamble, structure, poetics, chiasm, parallelism, and keywords. See Unterman, *Nehama*, 453.
40. Leibowitz, "*MiBereshit ad LeEinei Kol Yisrael: BiMlot Shana LaGilyonot*," in Ahrend et al., *Pirkei*, 451.

of drowning the student in a sea of meaningless minutiae), but rather as the medium for the Torah's message. Like the New Critics, she held that the form – the words used and their arrangement – was not random, but rather carried meaning. One small detail might contain an entire philosophy or a crucial moral point. Even the Torah's silence might be suffused with meaning.[41]

For Prof. Leibowitz, no repetition was insignificant, whether of words or entire passages. She very much enjoyed combing two similar texts, whether narrative or legal, for their similarities and differences in regard to each other. She was particularly fond of comparing the repeated account of the encounter between Abraham's servant and Rebecca (Gen. 24), and contrasting the words of Moses with those of the Reubenites and Gadites (Num. 32) in order to illustrate the differences in their outlooks. This activity of comparing repeated materials was particularly important in its inherent countering of biblical-critical claims that discrepant versions originated in different authors or schools. Prof. Leibowitz argued this point by citing the traditional hermeneutical rule that details missing from one story are frequently provided in another, and she taught that psychological and ethical messages are learned from the differences.[42]

Other elements important to both the New Critics and Prof. Leibowitz were context, rhythm, and tone. Tone, for example, is significant when Joseph's brothers throw him into a pit and then say, "And we will see what will become of his dreams" (Gen. 37:20). Nahmanides hears cynicism in these words, but Rashi takes them literally – they would indeed wait and see. Prof. Leibowitz explained that Rashi could not believe the brothers capable of such cruelty. It was one thing to plot to kill their brother, but it was quite another to do it so hard-heartedly. Only professional killers, such as those in Shakespeare's *Macbeth*, could so make light of the act of killing.[43]

Prof. Leibowitz's ability to detect the text's emotional tone owed much to the fact that she was a genuine student of human nature.

---

41. For some examples illustrating these points, see Leibowitz, *Bereshit*, 122; *Shemot*, 85; *Vaykira*, 52, 216; *Devarim* 7.
42. For examples, see Unterman, *Nehama*, 457.
43. Leibowitz, "*Limmud Parshanei HaTorah UDrakhim LeHoraatam: Sefer Bereshit*" (Jerusalem, 1978), 170 n9.

On the one hand, she believed that the Torah "is not a psychological novel and is not concerned with satisfying biographical curiosity": it does not characterize its protagonists through direct psychological analysis, but only indirectly, through their utterances, actions, and even lack of action.[44] They are literary figures, and we have no other details about them as individuals. Indeed, they often transcend their particular time and place, as archetypes whose actions represent historical movements.[45]

On the other hand, Prof. Leibowitz also saw the biblical figures as individuals, possessing ordinary psychological makeups,[46] and she loved to explore interpretations in this vein, with the proviso that they made textual sense.[47] She used psychological intuition in order to solve ambiguities of tone and intent in the text:

> Did Abimelech really wish to provoke [Abraham]? He is, after all, described as a righteous gentile, and Abraham will pray for him. If he speaks here ironically, that is tactless on his part.[48]

She also wrote about the psychological process behind the gradual enslavement in Egypt; human weakness, its excuses and rationalizations in avoiding responsibility; the outsider as leader; and the interpretation of dreams.[49] Her predilection for psychological explanations led Prof. Leibowitz to side fairly often with Nahmanides over

---

44. Leibowitz, *Shemot*, 39; *Bereshit* 131.
45. See, for example, her treatment of Potiphar's wife, who comes to represent manipulative and utilitarian behavior throughout the ages (Leibowitz, *Bereshit*, 419–20); see Unterman, *Nehama*, 275.
46. She insists that Esau be viewed not only as an archetype, but also as an individual, with positive and negative traits (Leibowitz, *Bereshit*, 283–84); see also Unterman, *Nehama*, 320.
47. In Leibowitz, *Shemot*, 315, she observes, "Psychologically true as is the commentator's observation, it hardly qualifies for a true reading of the text itself."
48. Ahrend et al., *Pirkei*, 677. See also her rejection of Nahmanides' explanation of Joseph's motives in advising Pharaoh to appoint a wise man; she did not believe that this fit Joseph's psychological-spiritual profile (*Bereshit*, 447).
49. See Unterman, *Nehama*, 39, 356–63; Leibowitz, *Shemot*, 40; *Bereshit*, 426.

Rashi. While Rashi's explanations contain some psychological elements, Nahmanides' generally possess deeper and more complex insights; when he cannot decide based on linguistic factors, he uses his intuitive understanding of human nature.[50] Prof. Leibowitz became correspondingly impatient with the "over-literalists," such as Kaspi, Ibn Ezra, Rashbam, and Radak, whose lack of close reading led them to misread the emotional atmosphere of the text. She believed that their ignorance of Tanakh's nuances led them to inferior interpretations and, at times, to completely trample the psychological layer of the text.[51] The seemingly far-fetched midrashic explanations are, in fact, sometimes more on target in their insight into human nature.[52]

## AN AHISTORICAL APPROACH

Prof. Leibowitz's approach was deliberately ahistorical. Like the New Critics, she remained committed to the text alone. The historical interpretation was too narrow and localized, explaining solely the Torah's external structure. She sought meaning, not fact; inspiration, not history. She writes, "Our Torah is not meant to be a saga of past glories, but a tale of truth and moral edification."[53]

In this, she followed midrashic methodology, as her citation from Yitzhak Heinemann indicates:

> The question historical science asks is: What were the factors (political, economic, religious) which motivated Egypt's persecution and enslavement of Israel? But the question the Midrash asks is: Why was Israel persecuted and enslaved more than the other nations of the world?[54]

---

50. Ruth Ben-Meir, "*LeDarkei Parshanuto shel HaRamban,*" in Ahrend et al., *Pirkei*, 125–42; Leibowitz, "*Limmud Parshanei,*" 38n2.
51. See her comments in Leibowitz, *Shemot*, 70, 85, 87, 102n4, 251, 382, 488, 495n4; *Devarim*, 293.
52. See, for example, Leibowitz, *Bamidbar*, 100–101.
53. Leibowitz, *Shemot*, 127.
54. Ibid., 1.

Prof. Leibowitz was almost entirely uninterested in biblical realia, the physical and cultural environment of the Tanakh.[55] She chose to adhere to Rashi's approach in turning geographical directions into theological concepts, rather than that of traditional commentators who were interested in historical explanations or biblical realia, such as Ralbag, Ibn Ezra, or Mendelssohn. In fact, at times she criticized commentators for an over-realistic rendering of the narratives.

No chapter in the Torah was written in order to teach us the trading laws of the Near East and ancient Canaan, which at best might be a footnote to the real interpretation. These realistic explanations cannot satisfy the mind that searches for ethical and intellectual inspiration. In a dramatic illustration of this principle, she told the story of the occasion when a student stood up in the middle of a class on Psalm 23 ("God is my shepherd") and declared that anyone who was not a shepherd like himself could not possibly understand the Psalm. He proceeded to explain it based on his profession. In the end, his speech lacked any meaningful insight for Prof. Leibowitz. In contrast, Prof. Leibowitz continued, a certain non-Jewish physicist who had requested to read this specific Psalm on his deathbed – *he* understood David's original intentions profoundly, as they were meant to be understood. Prof. Leibowitz unhesitatingly criticized teachers who focused on realia. Lessons based on reproducing the physical artifacts of the period, such as clothing, architecture, and furniture were in her eyes a misinterpretation of the concept of active learning, clearly "not a method of teaching history… but for teaching the history of objects and their manufacture."[56] True, familiarity with the language, history, and land of Israel are important, but they can never replace the act of finding meaning in the Torah.

Prof. Leibowitz was extreme in her ahistoricism. It was not Rashi's background, worldview, beliefs, or personal experiences that guided him in his exegetical work, but the Bible itself, its language and context. Information about his lifestyle – "what pants he wore" – would

---

55. For exceptions, see Unterman, *Nehama*, 464, 469.
56. Leibowitz, *Active Learning in the Teaching of History*, trans. Moshe Sokolow (New York, 1989), 5n2.

only distract from understanding what he said and why he said it from a textual standpoint. In this, Prof. Leibowitz was reading not only the Tanakh, but also Rashi's commentary in New Critical fashion. She assumed that in his intellectual honesty, he was capable of freeing himself of any outside influences, from events of his day. It was this standpoint that allowed her to seat commentators of different epochs "around the table together" in a dialogue transcending time and circumstances.

Sometimes, however, she applied this rule selectively:

> [Alterman's] words were written as all of Egypt's plagues descended upon Europe and filled them with blood, fire, and pillars of smoke. Rashi too saw with his own eyes the horrors of the massacres of 1096 and grieved over them; but when he approached the text, all that was important was the verses and context.[57]

Prof. Leibowitz was criticized for this highly ahistorical approach to Bible and commentary. There is some evidence that toward the end of her life, she became more amenable to the historical viewpoint.

## POST-MODERNISM, MIDRASH, AND *OMEK PESHUTO SHEL MIKRA*[58]

It is important to note that Prof. Leibowitz did not limit herself to a particular literary theory, or even to the literary approach in general. The text was only one of the factors in determining "the area of context" for Prof. Leibowitz's work.[59] Indeed, aspects of Prof. Leibowitz's work resemble very different literary approaches, including post-modern literary theory. In the importance she assumed for the individual reader's experience and for the multiplicity of possible interpretations, she

---

57. Leibowitz, *Iyyunim Ḥadashim BeSefer Shemot*, 126 n1.
58. This section is based on Unterman, *Nehama*, 473–76, ch. 22.
59. Marla Frankel, *"Iyyun VeHoraa: Havharat Shitatah shel Neḥama Leibowitz"* [A Clarification of Nehama Leibowitz's Approach to the Study and Teaching of Bible] (Jerusalem, 1997), 4, 130n15.

diverged from New Criticism and anticipated the post-modernists several decades before they became mainstream.[60]

Prof. Leibowitz's extensive and valuable work with midrashim distanced her from the New Critics and brought her closer to post-modernism. By dint of removing errors that had crept into some textual editions, and adding punctuation and vowels, with the help of Maharal, Maharsha, and her contemporary Yitzḥak Heinemann (a scholar of Midrash), as well as a great deal of inventiveness and insight on her part, she succeeded in opening up many cryptic midrashim to the average reader. She even developed a methodology of studying them. Although she focused chiefly on midrashim that furthered the text's primary meaning, at times she would introduce midrashic explanations that were in no way *peshat*. This was because she had other goals in mind, beyond text and context, namely that of getting the reader to identify with the text and teaching him relevant moral meanings.

The tension between Prof. Leibowitz's emphasis on *peshat* on the one hand and her embracing of non-*peshat*-based midrashim on the other is an interesting one, speaking to the contradictions, or at least complexities, in her intellectual makeup. While she viewed herself as ever questing for the *peshat*, and spared no commentator, however beloved, who deviated from this rule, she nonetheless felt that ascertaining the *peshat* was only half the job. The understanding of a particular verse is "only one brick in the edifice of what is [commonly referred to as] the Jewish worldview."[61]

She aimed at the edifying message and pedagogical payoff, and in order to attain this was willing to throw in her lot with lesser-known commentaries and even interpretations that fell short of the *peshat* but were inspiring in some way.[62]

---

60. Eliezer Greenstein, "*Parshanutah Rabbat HaPanim shel Neḥama Leibowitz VeHaParshanut HaPostmodernit*," *Limmudim* 1 (2001): 21–33. For more discussion on this topic, see Unterman, *Nehama*, 470–76.
61. Leibowitz, "*MiBereshit*," 452–53.
62. Scholars argue as to where Prof. Leibowitz's real love lay – with *peshat* or *derash*. Some even invent hybrid terms for her approach, such as "conscripted *peshat*." Some argue that she said one thing and did the other. (Interestingly, this tension is also to be found in Rashi's commentary.) See Unterman, *Nehama*, 498–501, for full discussion.

Historically, the modes of *peshat* and *derash* have been differentiated; the *pashtan* focuses on logic, form, and grammar, while the *darshan*, or homiletical preacher, inventively weaves together disparate texts to create imaginative interpretations and inspiring messages. In brief, the *pashtan* aims at elucidation, and the *darshan* at education. However, the lines between them are not always as clear as they might appear. Prof. Leibowitz herself was aware of the shifting nature of these two terms, often joking in her classes, "*Peshat* is what I say; *derash* is what you say!" (or, in another version, "My *peshat* is your *derash*!"). Indeed, we can state that one of Prof. Leibowitz's innovations was to argue that in fact the two are inseparable. The Torah's a priori intention, its very *peshat*, is to teach edifying lessons, and its primary meaning is geared toward that end. As she wrote:

> The Bible imparts its teachings not by direct indoctrination, by a moral tagged on the story, but through the medium of the narrative, its structure and style and the organization of the plot.[63]

In other words, for Prof. Leibowitz, one must discover the messages built into the text, not superimpose preconceived ideologies or value systems onto it. Educational messages must spring from nuanced philological and contextual clues implanted in the text. We must maintain the delicate balance between exegesis and eisegesis, between cheap actualization and genuine relevance-making. Hence, far from imposing a moral agenda on the text, Prof. Leibowitz believed that she was simply letting it speak in its naturally instructive tones.

It has already been noted that Prof. Leibowitz embraced non-*peshat*-based midrashim. In fact, she would argue with this very terminology, for she made the rather radical claim that the Midrash often expresses a form of *peshat*, even when it seems otherwise. She noted the "erroneous perception of *derash* as the opposite of *peshat*, instead of as a deeper level of the *peshat*," and taught that some interpretations that

---

63. Leibowitz, *Shemot*, 12.

are rejected as *derash* are in fact *omek peshuto shel mikra* – a genuine, in-depth *peshat*, going beyond the cursory reading of the words.[64]

This assertion represented a new way of looking at Midrash. Prof. Leibowitz suggested that, notwithstanding the widely held assumption that the Midrash contains only *derash* (i.e., non-*peshat*) material, in truth the midrashic corpus contains a vast mixture of materials, from straightforward interpretation to improbable tales, and more of it is *peshat* than it might seem at first. Her readers became used to seeing a midrashic opinion take its place in the discussion alongside Rashi and Ibn Ezra, with a demonstrably clear and rational point to make. In fact, the Midrash was sometimes shown to be the more careful reader of the text:

> Luzzato's interpretation…has not the slightest basis in the wording of the text. Accordingly the words of the Midrash…are to be preferred.[65]

Indeed, although this was a minority position for most of her life, she resolutely continued to declare that the Midrash is a commentary like any other. Some scholars objected to this definition, while others objected primarily to her divesting of the Midrash of its historical context.[66] Yet as today's scholars, influenced by post-modern trends, increasingly come around to her line of thinking, Prof. Leibowitz, who was in the minority for so long, has been vindicated.[67]

## Original Commentary[68]

As can be ascertained from the above discussion of her literary analysis, while Prof. Leibowitz's primary goal was to teach text with commentaries,

---

64. Leibowitz, *Iyyunim BeSefer Bereshit*, 290; *Studies in Bereshit*, 247 and 412. See also discussion in Cohn, "*HaParshanut*," 105–107.
65. Leibowitz, *Devarim*, 79.
66. Rozenson, "*HaParshanit*," 447; see also Breuer, "*Yaḥasah*," 19–20.
67. Examples of this approach are Boyarin (see Cohn, "*HaParshanut*," 96n11) and Kugel. See also Gabriel H. Cohn, "*HaMidrash KeParshan HaMidrash KePashtan*," *Maḥanayim* 7 (1994): 96n34, who lists several authors who compare the midrashic and literary approaches.
68. This section is based on Unterman, *Nehama*, 476–86.

there were also textual patterns and difficulties that she noticed on her own. We should not be too surprised to find her applying her keen literary sensibility, shaped by many years of exposure to the midrashic, medieval, and modern approaches, to the text she was reading. On the contrary, it would have been remarkable had a person of such creativity and skill failed to come up with new insights from time to time. Having developed theories for literary analysis (for example, concerning how to read dialogues that appear in the narrative),[69] it is only logical that she would apply these theories herself. Indeed, various original literary analyses and psychological and ethical insights are to be found scattered at irregular intervals throughout Prof. Leibowitz's *Studies*.

The material in the *Studies* series can be divided into three categories: citations of biblical texts and commentaries; Prof. Leibowitz's explanations of these citations; and original analyses and insights that stand alone. The first category needs no elaboration and contains no original content. The second category, however, contains some interpretations not attributed to any commentator. The ideas therein are most likely Prof. Leibowitz's own, but they are easily missed, for they are obscured and embedded in the other material or appear as bridges between citations. The superficial reader might easily mistake them for mere rewordings, and only a closer examination reveals their innovation.

The third category, which is both the most evident and the most interesting, is comprised of analyses and insights that appear with no commentators cited at all, for part or all of an essay. Several essays within the *Studies* series are almost entirely comprised of such presumably original interpretation, particularly those on the Joseph story. These essays display Prof. Leibowitz's proficiency with the literary technique. Having learned the literary technique from Buber and others, Prof. Leibowitz probably allowed herself to be at her most original in the literary area.[70]

Prof. Leibowitz made manifest her originality by developing certain traditional theological notions in unique ways. For example, her somewhat radical association between the concepts of *tzelem Elokim* (image of God) and *kedoshim tehiyu* (you shall be holy) are not found

---

69. Leibowitz, "*VaYomer.... VaYomer*," in Ahrend et al., *Pirkei*, 495–502.
70. Yedgar, "*HaIyyunim*," 22.

in any of her predecessors' writings, and her interpretation of the "idolatrous sinner" as someone who shirks responsibility is strikingly original.[71] As mentioned above, the midrashim she cites frequently lacked commentaries, forcing her to invent her own and become a *de facto* original commentator on Midrash.

A final realm in which Prof. Leibowitz also innovated was her moral message statements, which appear chiefly, although not solely, at the end of each of the articles in her *Studies*. These are not quite the simple summaries they appear to be. A closer look reveals careful selection and rewording of others' ideas, which also constitutes an act of originality and interpretation.

### THE OVERLOOKING OF PROF. LEIBOWITZ

Despite all of this, Prof. Leibowitz's contribution as an original scholar is often woefully overlooked in both traditional and academic circles. The *Studies* series is often considered a great work of collation, a skillful assembly of the interpretations of others, but one lacking any original content. Prof. Leibowitz is forgotten in surveys of the development of literary theory.[72] Robert Alter expresses astonishment in his book, published in 1981, that "at this late date, literary analysis of the Bible of the sort I have tried to illustrate here…is only in its infancy,"[73] but Prof. Leibowitz was in fact already doing this kind of work, albeit on a minor scale, decades earlier. She popularized these methods before they were in fashion, prefiguring later work. Prof. Yair Hoffman informs us:

> Before the principles [of the close-reading method, as established by Weiss] were even formulated systematically, Nehama Leibowitz paved the way for them. She cleared away the stumbling blocks of prejudice, uprooted weeds from the field of study, which all too quickly piled up "critical" solutions without first

---

71. Erella Yedgar, "Aḥrayut Ishit UBeinishit BiKhtavehah shel Neḥama Leibowitz – Iyun BeMegamatah HaErkit-Ḥinnukhit," in Ahrend et al, *Pirkei*, 377–406; Leibowitz, *Devarim*, 309; and see discussion in Unterman, *Nehama*, 358.
72. See Unterman, *Nehama*, 484n170.
73. Robert Alter, *The Art of Biblical Narrative* (New York, 1981), 14.

scrutinizing the text.... There are times when one reads a nice article about biblical prose and wonders, "Where did I read this already?" – and then remembers that it was in one of the *gilyonot*.

Professor Yairah Amit also calls Prof. Leibowitz "a pioneer in the literary-aesthetic approach to biblical interpretation."[74]

The responsibility for such undervaluation of Prof. Leibowitz must be laid partly at her own door. Her self-perception was overwhelmingly not as a commentator, but as a teacher of commentaries. She declared, "I teach only what the commentators have written. I do not innovate!" and, "My book [is] no more than a compilation of commentaries on the weekly Torah portion, of which there are many today." Such was the deference she granted to the classic biblical commentators, such as Rashi and Nahmanides, showing far more interest in promoting their words than her own and hiding her own words in the surrounding prose so that only the careful reader notices the tremendous insight and original analyses within. She did not make a clear distinction as to where others' readings stopped and hers began. She also had no desire to prove her own erudition, rarely saying, "This is my idea," and instead humbly stating, "I saw this somewhere...."[75]

Had she put her mind to it, Prof. Leibowitz might well have written an outstanding work of Torah interpretation. In fact, before the *Studies* came out, Prof. E. E. Urbach made a call for Prof. Leibowitz to write a complete and systematized commentary of her own, suitable for a traditional audience but updated for the times. Prof. Leibowitz never acceded to the request – perhaps due to her belief in the superiority of her predecessors' ideas, or perhaps due to her desire not to be involved in anything quite so revolutionary.[76] Thus, she left us to search for her original work ourselves.

Nevertheless, we should not desist from such effort or accept the pigeonholing of Prof. Leibowitz as "teacher, not Bible scholar," no matter what is carved on her gravestone. The above analysis has served

---

74. Yairah Amit, "Hebrew Bible – Some Thoughts on the Work of Nehama Leibowitz," *Immanuel* 20 (Spring 1986): 11.
75. Abramowitz, *Tales*, 60.
76. For further discussion of Prof. Leibowitz's habitual shying away from "revolutions" and from unnecessary emphasis on *ḥiddush* and publication, see Unterman, *Nehama*, 481–83.

to demonstrate that while not a biblical-critical scholar, Prof. Leibowitz was a probing, rationalistic analyst of the Tanakh who generated new literary analyses before this methodology entered the academic mainstream. Traditional Tanakh teachers (for example, Rabbi Elḥanan Samet) have drawn on the many literary techniques she utilized, including intertextuality, the *Leitwört*, and other tools, and she is on occasion recognized for her literary contribution by those who knew her work well enough to discern it.

In sum: With literary study today widespread in both the academic world and that of the modern sector of Orthodox Torah study, Prof. Leibowitz's contribution merits recognition. What she lacked in systematization, she made up for in the sheer scope of her impact, going well beyond academic circles. Hence, she should take her rightful place in surveys of twentieth-century Bible scholarship, and we may unabashedly call her a "Bible scholar."

## PROF. LEIBOWITZ'S TORAH IN THE TWENTY-FIRST CENTURY[77]

Our final discussion relates to the question of how Prof. Leibowitz's work fits with current trends in the world of Torah study that presage the future of Jewish education. The following remarks will attempt to answer this question critically, measuring it against two criteria: that of an emerging global zeitgeist and that of the Torah of the Land of Israel.

Let us begin with praise. On the one hand, Prof. Leibowitz's name is still widely known and respected. She functions as a role model for religious women and school girls, and articles and books have been written about her life. Her worksheets are available on the Internet, and her books continue to be purchased, studied, and used to prepare classes and sermons. She continues to be quoted in books, articles, and newspapers. In her Bible scholarship, she anticipated emerging modern and post-modern literary theories; in her educational outlook, she heralded

---

77. This section is based on the final chapter of Unterman, *Nehama*. Note that reference is also made there to components of Prof. Leibowitz's work not dealt with here, namely her pedagogical methods and the nature of her classroom. The interested reader will find information there concerning the evolved application of her pedagogy by her students, such as Erella Yedgar, Judy Klitsner, Dr. Marla Frankel, Rabbi Elḥanan Samet, and Dr. Gabriel H. Cohn.

current trends. She can be credited with bringing about a major enhancement to the status of Tanakh study, and the substantial expansion today of this area of study within modern yeshivas owes much to her work.

The truth is, however, that, while revolutionary at its outset, Prof. Leibowitz's Torah had become mainstream by the time of her death. It has been left to others to take the next steps in the evolving process of Torah teaching. In recent decades, some of the most important new directions that have sprung up depart considerably from Prof. Leibowitz's work. The nature of these departures may be best illustrated by pointing to two particular individuals who personify them in their work: Dr. Avivah Zornberg and Rabbi Yoel Bin-Nun.

A contrast between Dr. Zornberg and Prof. Leibowitz is particularly enlightening. Prof. Leibowitz's work may be scrutinized for its lack of correspondence to the twenty-first century zeitgeist, which, many would suggest, is a notable obsession in Western society with the self. Works of psychological complexity and awareness spring up constantly in order to meet the thirst for self-understanding and meaning. Prof. Leibowitz's Torah, it can be argued, lags behind that of those contemporary teachers such as Dr. Zornberg, who take on the search for meaning, wholeness, and belonging.

It is true that Prof. Leibowitz's books were ahead of their time; indeed, they are still capable of surprising with their freshness and contemporary tone. She was successful in creating meaning from ancient materials, pointing out the complexity of issues in the Torah, and providing her readers with a sense of belonging to a community of intelligent Torah learners – indeed, to a larger Jewish society responsible to each other and to the world. She had her finger on the pulse of her age and was said to have understood "the rupture of the modern world" and the internal struggles of the younger generation. She was interested in the individual, whom she encouraged to respond uniquely and personally to every reading of text:

> That "I" who speaks, weeps, expresses joy, offers thanks to God, cries for help, is the "I" of the reader at that very moment of reading.[78]

---

78. Leibowitz, *Leader's Guide to the Book of Psalms* (New York, 1971), 1.

She tended, however, to speak in general terms, relating for the most part to the reasons for the mitzvot rather than to their significance on a personal level for the student. While she liked to quote Nahmanides' psychological explanations, sometimes preferring them above all others, she did not approve of exaggerated self-analysis. Her Torah was primarily located on the axes of relationship of self to God and self to other; interest in the self qua self was not seen as a positive thing, but rather, in the vein of her generation of hardy Zionist pioneers, as self-indulgence. In fact, Prof. Leibowitz saw the emphasis on the self as a contemporary form of idolatry.

Yet the collectivist Israel that Prof. Leibowitz knew has dwindled in an age of post-modernism and post-Zionism. Within the Jewish religious world, there has been a tremendous growth in interest in Hasidism and Kabbala, in mystical and psycho-spiritual dimensions, and in ecstatic worship – precisely the topics Prof. Leibowitz disliked or avoided.

Here it is instructive to contrast Dr. Zornberg's work with that of Prof. Leibowitz. An internationally acclaimed lecturer and scholar, Dr. Zornberg is recognized by many as a – or, indeed, the – leading creative teacher and interpreter of Torah for the English-speaking world. Like Prof. Leibowitz, Dr. Zornberg is Jerusalem-based and much in demand, attracting large crowds of both men and women. She too espouses an approach that is intellectually broad and critically probing, yet at the same time steeped in the traditional commentaries, and her books incorporate diverse materials and open new vistas for the study of the weekly Torah portion.

The resemblance, however, ends at a certain point. As it has been aptly put:

> Leibowitz is rigorously rational, tightening thought; Zornberg is richly associative, loosening imagination. Leibowitz is the ultimate pedagogue, the master facilitator deftly enabling Torah and commentators to speak with their startling immediacy. Zornberg speaks for herself, the poet and philosopher, inviting us to "eavesdrop" on her exquisitely personal response to the dialogue of life and text.[79]

---

79. Ben and Judy Hollander, "Multi-Disciplined Thinkers," *Jerusalem Post Magazine*, July 21, 1995, 2.

Dr. Zornberg employs a greater range of sources than Prof. Leibowitz did, drawing heavily on contemporary psychology, literary theory, and philosophy, as well as hasidic sources. She works, in the words of Prof. Susan Handelman, "at the edge of the vulnerable, the unknown, dealing with the angst and the shadow."[80]

We can suggest that Prof. Leibowitz's Torah might be characterized as archetypically masculine in its analytical, rigorous, and linear form, while Dr. Zornberg's may be more archetypically feminine in its non-linear form and its emotional content. Prof. Leibowitz was ultimately a transitional figure between the modern and the post-modern era. What she intuited only in patches, Dr. Zornberg teaches in full force.

A different type of evolution in Torah study is manifest in Rabbi Yoel Bin-Nun's revolutionary method of Tanakh study, catalyzed by insights by Rabbi Zvi Yehuda Kook. Rabbi Bin-Nun's method diverges from that of Prof. Leibowitz in demanding a hearing for Tanakh at face value, without commentaries (at least initially); in examining broad strokes, structures, and processes throughout Tanakh, not just small units; and in emphasizing realia, namely the historical, archeological, anthropological, geographical, zoological, and botanical dimensions of Tanakh, incorporating them into traditional Tanakh learning.

Such approaches began to emerge in the late 1970s and marked, from its proponents' perspective, the emergence of a new religious Israeli identity predicated upon *Torat Eretz Yisrael* (the Torah of the Land of Israel). Rabbi Bin-Nun and others teaching in a similar vein (such as Rabbi Yaakov Medan) were embraced by Yeshivat Har Etzion and its teacher-training institution, Herzog College, where hundreds of students were exposed to the new way of thinking. Concurrently, other Orthodox scholars and teachers not directly influenced by Rabbi Bin-Nun were moving in the same direction, returning to direct engagement with the text, a historical approach, and the use of realia.

For almost her entire life, Prof. Leibowitz remained adamantly opposed to such methodologies. More regrettable still was that her followers actively impeded their entry into the National Religious high schools' curriculum for the *bagrut*, the Israeli matriculation exams. This

---

80. Private communication.

would not have been so disastrous had Prof. Leibowitz herself been teaching the pupils, but in the hands of the schoolteachers, her method was in practice reduced to a repetitive formula of "What does this commentator say and what does that commentator say?" This substandard imitation of her method, basically entailing mechanical repetition of what each commentator said, completely contravened Prof. Leibowitz's educational goals. She would have been appalled to discover that such tedious pedagogy, leading to the alienation of thousands of teenagers from Tanakh, was being perpetrated in her name.

Prof. Leibowitz's error lay in assuming that the relevant ideas and values would emerge naturally from the text and commentaries, while in fact, a capable guide and teacher is needed if any but the most astute students are to grasp this relevance. The sad truth is that contemporary Israeli high school teachers, crippled by the dry *bagrut* format and their own lack of imagination, overuse the analytical aspects of the Leibowitz method, comparing commentaries ad nauseum, and young teachers trained in newer approaches such as that of Rabbi Bin-Nun find themselves unable to introduce them into the high schools because of the pressure to complete the material in time.

This problem is not limited to the *bagrut* format or even to Israel alone. Rabbi Francis Nataf remarks:

> While, thanks to the efforts of Nehama Leibowitz, her students, and others like them, more and more classrooms are asking the question, What's bothering Rashi?, once we figure that out, we are content to get Rashi's (or Nahmanides' or Sforno's) answer to what was bothering him and to move on to the next problem. In other words, that which was once an exercise in literary analysis has become more akin to work on math problems.[81]

Fortunately, ways are also being found to bring Prof. Leibowitz's methods up to date. This is not the forum to discuss the new pedagogy, but, in brief, it is most successful when teachers avoid trying to imitate

---

81. Francis Nataf, "Learning Torah with Our Own Eyes: Initial Feedback to Redeeming Relevance," Cardozo Academy email list, *Ideas*, no. 86, November 23, 2006.

Prof. Leibowitz exactly, but rather make the material their own and place more value on originality of interpretation – both the teacher's and the student's. A number of her students are indeed updating her methods in their own teaching, sharing a belief that Prof. Leibowitz's method needs to be interpreted liberally, in terms of spirit and not only letter. Not only is change unavoidable, they believe that her system demanded such changes, being fundamentally dynamic.

In the critical debate as to the future of Prof. Leibowitz's work, scholars are not all of one mind. Some believe her work will endure and that interest in her project is still strong. Others, however, question to what extent her work will survive long-term. There is no one obvious successor to Prof. Leibowitz. She left behind a small band of scholars and teachers who are intimately involved with her work, researching it for articles, books, and doctorates, working to disseminate it, and viewing their teaching as a direct continuation of hers. Her work is considered "old school" by many scholars, their considerable respect for her achievements notwithstanding. Many of her potential reading audience has shifted too far left (for example, in struggling with the gap between contemporary moral sensibilities and the Tanakh's attitude toward slavery, killing, homosexuality, racial superiority, and the status of women) or have moved too far right to be comfortable with the pluralistic aspects of Prof. Leibowitz's work. Today's students are also not willing to work hard, but seek instant gratification, leaving Prof. Leibowitz's books outside of their purview.[82]

The truth is that every revolution eventually becomes standard practice and may stagnate if subsequent generations do not bring it up to date. Teachers with imagination may be needed to enable students' access to Prof. Leibowitz's work in a way that is relevant, but given that, it seems to me that if her method is taken up, intelligently adapted in line with twenty-first-century developments, and integrated alongside other Tanakh-teaching methods, it can continue to play a vital role in Jewish education. In many ways, her work is needed now more than ever.[83]

---

82. Erella Yedgar "*Parshanut Nashim Datiyot o Parshanut Nashit-Datit LaMikra?*" *Lihyot Isha Yehudiya* 1 (2001): 109–12.
83. See Unterman, *Nehama*, 584–85, for more detail.

# Rabbi Immanuel Jakobovits and the Birth of Jewish Medical Ethics

## Dr. Alan Jotkowitz

Moral autonomy or moral automation – between these alternatives lies the most fateful choice confronting mankind today. As long as the moral law reigns supreme, the spectacular advances in science and technology will be effectively controlled by the overriding claims of human life and dignity. Man will be safe from the menace of his own productions. But when the quest for knowledge and power is unhemmed by moral considerations, and the fundamental rights of man, as conferred and defined by his Creator, are swept aside in the blind march for mechanical perfection, the ramparts protecting mankind from self-destruction are bound to crumble. Today the contest between science and religion is no longer a competitive search for the truth as in former times. It is a struggle between excesses and controls, between the supremacy of man's creations and the supremacy of man himself. For many centuries, rabbis and physicians, often merging their professions into one, were intimate partners in a common effort for the betterment of life. The perplexities of our age challenge them to renew their association in the service of human life, health, and dignity. Indeed, they challenge Judaism itself to reassert its place as a potent force in the moral advancement of humanity.[1]

With these words, Lord Rabbi Immanuel Jakobovits not only began his magnum opus *Jewish Medical Ethics*, but through them pioneered the academic discipline of Jewish medical ethics (JME). The call for Judaism "to reassert its place as a potent force in the moral advancement of society" was a guiding principle of Rabbi Jakobovits' work. From the beginning of his illustrious career, he passionately argued for the universality of Jewish morality. Jewish ethics based on the revealed word of God as expressed in the halakha should guide not only Jews, but all of humanity as it faces such difficult modern moral quandaries as the permissibility of abortion, euthanasia, and artificial reproduction. This assertion led to his role, at the pinnacle of his career as chief rabbi of the United Kingdom, as perhaps the Western world's leading theological spokesman for conservative values. His adherence to these principles led to much personal criticism, particularly from the more liberal elements of British society.

In a post-modern world, this fervent belief in the universality of Jewish ethics is not at all self-evident. In fact, Rabbi Jakobovits' successor as chief rabbi, Lord Jonathan Sacks, has passionately argued that a belief in universalism is the most important modern theological mistake. In his own words:

> The truth at the beating heart of monotheism is that God transcends the particularities of culture and the limits of human understanding. He is my God, but also the God of all mankind, even of those whose customs and way of life are unlike mine.[2]

---

1. Immanuel Jakobovits, *Jewish Medical Ethics: A Comparative and Historical Study of the Jewish Religious Attitude to Medicine and Its Practice* (New York, 1975), vii–viii. Other important sources for the works of Rabbi Jakobovits related to medical ethics are his books *Journal of a Rabbi* (New York, 1966) and *The Timely and the Timeless: Jews, Judaism and Society in a Storm-tossed Decade* (London, 1977), and his numerous articles in *Tradition*, in which from 1961 to 1966 he edited the section entitled "Survey of Recent Halakhic Periodical Literature."
2. Jonathan Sacks, *The Dignity of Difference: How to Avoid the Clash of Civilizations* (London, 2003).

## Birth of Jewish Medical Ethics

From this perspective, it does not necessarily follow that Jewish morality based on halakha has universal applicability. Notwithstanding these reservations, a leading bioethicist, Daniel Callahan, has written:

> There are many benefits to an extensive exposure to the accumulated wisdom and knowledge that are the fruit of long-established religious traditions. I do not have to be Jewish to find it profitable and illuminating to see how the great rabbinical teachers have tried to understand moral problems over the centuries.[3]

Rabbi Jakobovits' *Jewish Medical Ethics* was the first, and remains the best, introduction to the world of rabbinic thought as it relates to medical ethics. In Rabbi Jakobovits' own words, the book "will be the first attempt at a comprehensive presentation of the Jewish medical legislation."[4]

It is interesting to note the topics covered and not covered in the book. The book begins with an overview of the generally positive attitude of Judaism toward scientific medicine and the supreme value it places on human life. Another chapter deals with the laws of Shabbat, the holidays, and the fast days as they relate to sickness and health. There is a chapter on the Jewish attitude toward pain and the duty to visit the sick. Another section of the book deals with treatment of the dead and the dying. There is extended discussion related to beginning-of-life issues, including contraception, abortion, artificial insemination, and circumcision. The book ends with four chapters on issues relating to physicians, including their responsibilities, payment for services, admissibility of their expert testimony as evidence in a Jewish court, and whether a priest (a *kohen*) can be a physician.

In the revised edition published in 1975, there is an additional chapter entitled "Recent Developments in Jewish Medical Ethics," which elaborates upon such issues as contraception, euthanasia, definition of death, autopsies, organ transplantation, and human experimentation.

---

3. Daniel Callahan, "Religion and the Secularization of Bioethics," *Hastings Center Report*, Special Supplement: "*Theology, Religious Traditions, and Bioethics*," 20, no. 4 (1990): 2–4.
4. Immanuel Jakobovits, *Jewish Medical Ethics*, xxxiv.

Some omissions in the book might be surprising to modern readers, and are probably due to the fact that the book was conceived in the 1940s and written in the 1950s. Curiously, the issue of truth-telling to patients takes up less than one page, and the Jewish perspective on the dying patient and euthanasia is discussed in fewer than five pages. Important issues such as the allocation of scarce resources, triage, care of the preterm infant, and care of the Alzheimer's disease patient are also absent.

Before we examine Rabbi Jakobovits' writings further, it is worthwhile to briefly sketch his biography.

**BIOGRAPHY**

Rabbi Jakobovits was born in Konigsberg in what was then East Prussia on February 8, 1921. He was given the Hebrew name Israel, but also the secular name Immanuel, after Immanuel Kant, whom his father greatly admired. He came from a long line of rabbis on both sides of his family, and his father, Rabbi Julius Jakobovits, served as the local rabbi. When he was seven, the family moved to Berlin, where his father had been invited to join the rabbinical court. As a result of the rise of Hitler, Immanuel was sent to London at the age of fifteen to a Jewish boarding school, and over the next three years the rest of his immediate family joined him.[5]

Rabbi Jakobovits frequently commented that his greatest teacher and most important influence was his father. The elder Rabbi Jakobovits, like his son after him, studied at both a traditional yeshiva (the Pressburg Yeshiva established by the Ḥatam Sofer) and a more modern yeshiva (the Berlin Rabbinical Seminary established by Rabbi Azriel Hildesheimer). He also received a doctorate from the University of Berlin. *Jewish Medical Ethics* is movingly dedicated: "To the memory of My Sainted Father, Rabbi Dr. Julius Jakobovits, as the first fruits of his firstborn."

Even though Rabbi Jakobovits left Germany as an adolescent, the values of German Jewry, particularly the philosophy of *Torah im derekh eretz*, stayed with him throughout his life. As Rabbi Jakobovits wrote:

---

5. Chaim Bermant, *Lord Jakobovits: The Authorized Biography of the Chief Rabbi* (London, 1990).

My close friends also influenced me. They were followers of the *Torah im derekh eretz* school, but not necessarily the Frankfurt version. They possessed wider horizons and sought values also in the general culture and its literature, and, of course, in the world of science.[6]

In London, he studied at the Etz Ḥayim yeshiva under Rabbi Eliyahu Lopian, at Jews' College under Prof. Isidore Epstein, and also at University College. He considered pursuing a career in science but, under his father's influence, decided instead to become a rabbi. After receiving ordination, he held three appointments as a rabbi in London. He then spent ten years as chief rabbi of Ireland (during which time he completed his doctorate in Jewish medical ethics), eight years in New York City as the founding rabbi of the Fifth Avenue Synagogue, and twenty-five years as chief rabbi of the United Hebrew Congregations of the British Commonwealth. He was knighted in 1981 and was created a life peer in 1988, as Baron Jakobovits of Regent's Park in Greater London. In 1991, he received the Templeton Prize for Progress in Religion. He died on October 31, 1999.

Rabbi Jakobovits' life and writings can be better appreciated by looking at the wider context of the field of medical ethics.

## THE BIRTH OF BIOETHICS

The second half of the twentieth century witnessed an explosion of progress in the medical sciences, fueled by new technologies and remarkable achievements in laboratories. Using mechanical ventilation and dialysis, physicians could keep alive patients who certainly would have died quickly in the past. Patients with failing hearts, kidneys, and lungs could be saved by transplanting organs from the recently deceased. For couples unable to conceive naturally, life could be created outside the body and inserted into the woman's uterus, mimicking a normal pregnancy and gestation. All these advances had been the pipedreams of visionary scientists just a few short decades before.

---

6. Michael Shashar, *Lord Jakobovits in Conversation* (London, 2000), 18.

Notwithstanding the amazing success of these new developments, it is imperative to address the ethical questions that arise in their wake. Should physicians in all instances strive to extend life with new technologies available to them? How about the terminal cancer patient racked with pain or the elderly Alzheimer's disease patient with pneumonia? Is it moral to create life by artificial means? How do we define death, in order to know when it is ethical to harvest the organs for the benefit of another human being who desperately needs them? Do we even have to wait until the patient is clinically dead? When, if ever, is it acceptable to abort a fetus? Whose rights should be paramount, those of the mother or those of the fetus? Questions previously thought of as purely theoretical have become relevant to the survival and death of patients in hospitals, clinics, and waiting rooms.

Partly in response to these burning questions, the field of medical ethics was born, and many theologians and philosophers as well as physicians turned their attention to these difficult issues. Daniel Callahan has noted that the field of bioethics was founded by religious thinkers who have been gradually replaced by more recent authorities writing from predominantly secular perspectives.[7]

Protestant theologians, such as Paul Ramsey and Joseph Fletcher, began searching for a methodology to answer these ethical questions. Based on a thoughtful analysis of the Scriptures, they developed a "covenantal theory" of ethics. Although each thinker formulated his own particular theology, they were all based on the existence of a covenant between man and God and posited that man's moral actions should reflect this holy partnership. The basic problem with this perspective is that there can be many, even contradictory, interpretations of this covenant. For example, Fletcher argues for a covenant based on almost limitless human freedom and autonomy, leading him to argue for the legalization of euthanasia and support for all methods of artificial reproduction. He asserts:

> We shall attempt, as reasonably as may be, to plead the ethical case for our human rights to use contraceptives, to seek insemination

---

7. Callahan, "Religion and the Secularization of Bioethics," 2–4.

anonymously from a donor, to be sterilized, and to receive a merciful death from a medically competent euthanasiast. We believe we can show, at the very least, that any absolute prohibition of these boons of medicine is morally unjustified, subversive of human dignity, and most serious of all, spiritually oppressive.[8]

For Fletcher, the overriding ethical principle is *agape*, or love, and what is moral is determined by how this principle is best served. In this consequentialist approach, which he labeled situational ethics, the ends always justify the means.

In contrast, Ramsey, also invoking the covenantal theory, maintains that human ethical relations should be modeled on the relationship of God to man, and that therefore there exists an unbreakable bond of covenantal loyalty between men.[9] This is interpreted to mean that man must always act with love and charity toward his fellow man. In most instances, this means using all of one's power to cure a patient's illness, but in the case of the suffering terminal patient, it means easing the pain of the dying process. For Ramsey, the emphasis is on relieving the suffering of the patient and on maintaining a human presence until the patient's last breath; active euthanasia is considered a violation of this covenant. Ramsey was also opposed to many forms of artificial reproduction because he viewed it as an intrusion on the power of God and as a violation of the holy covenant of marriage ordained by God.[10] In Ramsey's deontological approach, the covenant is expressed in rules and ethical principles that govern moral behavior.

In this fervent intellectual milieu, Rabbi Jakobovits was the first to develop and present a comprehensive Jewish approach to medical ethics, based on two guiding principles:

---

8. Joseph Fletcher, *Morals and Medicine* (Princeton, NJ, 1954). Rabbi Irving Greenberg developed a covenantal theory of medical ethics from a Jewish perspective; see his "Toward a Covenantal Ethic of Medicine in Jewish Values," in *Bioethics*, ed. Levi Meier (New York, 1986).
9. Paul Ramsey, *The Patient as Person* (New Haven, CT, 1970).
10. Paul Ramsey, "Preface to *The Patient as Person*," in *On Moral Medicine: Theological Perspectives in Medical Ethics*, ed. Stephen E. Lammers and Allen Verhey (Grand Rapids, MI, 1998).

1. "The decision on whether, and under what circumstances, it is right to destroy a germinating human life depends on the assessment and weighing of values, on determining the title to life in any given case. Such value judgments are entirely outside the province of medical science.... Such judgments pose essentially a moral, not a medical problem. Hence they call for the judgment of moral, not medical, specialists."[11]
2. "In the Jewish view, the human conscience is meant to enforce laws, not make them. Right and wrong, good and evil, are absolute values which transcend the capricious variations of time, place, and environment, just as they defy definition by relation to human intuition or expediency. These values, Judaism teaches, derive their validity from the divine Revelation at Mount Sinai, as expounded and developed by sages faithful to, and authorized by, its writ."[12]

Rabbi Jakobovits' work was not limited to the Jewish sources. As reflected in its full title, *Jewish Medical Ethics: A Comparative and Historical Study of the Jewish Religious Attitude to Medicine and Its Practice* is also a comparative study of other theological approaches to medical ethics. At the time of its writing, the most fully developed competing system was the approach of the Roman Catholic Church, grounded in natural law, and Rabbi Jakobovits frequently compared and contrasted that approach to the Jewish model. In his own words:

> I was in Ireland, and I saw that the Catholics had much to say about medical ethics, and I asked myself: What do we as Jews have to say about medical ethics?... If the Catholics have much material concerning this, Judaism – the mother of religious ethics in the world – must certainly have no fewer sources, and we should search for them and adapt and publish them.... I also sought to show that in this sphere as well Judaism has something to contribute to the moral life of humankind.[13]

---

11. Immanuel Jakobovits, *The Timely and the Timeless*, 248.
12. Ramsey, "Preface to *The Patient as Person*."
13. Shashar, *Lord Jakobovits in Conversation*, 49–51. In the view of Rabbi Jakobovits, the universal moral message of Judaism is not limited to issues relating to medical

He was also not hesitant about taking a historical approach; he frequently compares the Jewish system with ancient Greek and Roman law.

Rabbi Jakobovits' son Yoel, an accomplished scholar of JME in his own right, makes the important point that the choice of the word "ethics" in the title of *Jewish Medical Ethics*, rather than "halakha" or "law," was not arbitrary:

> By employing terminology akin to that which describes the prevailing discipline of general medical ethics, many who are more secularly inclined have also come to regard the Jewish enterprise with similar seriousness.... The term "ethics," though perhaps not entirely correct in the Jewish context, is the single crucial term that has made these parallel developments possible by bridging the halachic world with its outside counterpart.[14]

Rabbi Jakobovits wanted to demonstrate that JME, although sometimes couched in technical rabbinic language, shared universal ethical concerns and can contribute "to the solution of some of the most crucial moral and social problems of our day."

## BIOETHICS AND AUTONOMY

While modern bioethics was relatively late in accepting the value of personal autonomy in medical decision-making, it is now universally recognized as the dominant theme in Western medical ethics. For example, a large number of Western medical organizations recently ratified the Charter on Medical Professionalism, which states as one of its cardinal principles: "Physicians must be honest with their patients and empower them to make informed decisions about their treatment."[15]

---

ethics. In response to urban poverty, he relates the Jewish view that "cheap labor is more dignified than a free dole, and industriousness generates greater wealth than increased wages for decreased hours of work"; see Immanuel Jakobovits, *Doom to Hope* (London: Office of the Chief Rabbi, 1986), 10.

14. Yoel Jakobovits, "Lord Immanuel Jakobovits," in *Pioneers in Jewish Medical Ethics*, ed. Fred Rosner (New Jersey, 1997), 138–39.

15. ABIM Foundation, American Board of Internal Medicine et al., "A Physician Charter on Medical Professionalism," *Annals of Internal Medicine* 136, no. 3 (2002): 243. Notwithstanding its adoption by many physician organizations, the document may

This paradigm of bioethics based on autonomy and human rights was, from its onset, challenged by Rabbi Jakobovits and other theologians, particularly Roman Catholics. As Rabbi Jakobovits writes so eloquently:

> Now in Judaism, we know of no intrinsic rights. Indeed, there is no word for rights in the very language of the Hebrew Bible and of the classic sources of Jewish law. In the moral vocabulary of the Jewish discipline of life, we speak of human duties, not of human rights, of obligations, not entitlement. The Decalogue is a list of Ten Commandments, not a bill of Human Rights. In the charity legislation of the Bible, for instance, it is the rich man who is commanded to support the poor, not the poor man who has the right to demand support from the rich. In Jewish law, a doctor is obligated to come to the rescue of his stricken fellow-man and to perform any operation he considers essential for the life of the patient, even if the patient refuses his consent or prefers to die. Once again, the emphasis is on the physician's responsibility to heal, to offer service, more than on the patient's right to be treated.[16]

Following in Rabbi Jakobovits' footsteps, Benjamin Freedman has pointed out that what distinguishes a Jewish approach to moral dilemmas is its emphasis on a duty-based ethic, as opposed to a secular ethic based on rights.[17] The eminent legal scholar Robert Cover makes a similar point:

> Every legal culture has its fundamental words.... The word "rights" is a highly evocative one for those of us who have grown up in the post-Enlightenment secular society of the West.... Judaism

---

reflect a Western liberal bias in its approach to medical ethics. See Alan B. Jotkowitz, Shimon Glick, and Avi Porath, "A Physician Charter on Medical Professionalism: A Challenge for Medical Education," *European Journal of Internal Medicine* 15 (2004): 5–9.

16. Immanuel Jakobovits, *The Timely and the Timeless*, 128.
17. Benjamin Freedman, *Duty and Healing: Foundations of a Jewish Bioethic* (New York, 1999).

is, itself, a legal culture of great antiquity.... When I am asked to reflect upon Judaism and human rights, therefore, the first thought that comes to mind is that the categories are wrong. I do not mean, of course, that basic ideas of human dignity and worth are not powerfully expressed in the Jewish legal and literary traditions. Rather, I mean that because it is a legal tradition, Judaism has its own categories for expressing through law the worth and dignity of each human being.... The principal word in Jewish law, which occupies a place equivalent in evocative force to the American legal system's "rights," is the word "mitzva," which literally means commandment but has a general meaning closer to "incumbent obligation".... All law was given at Sinai, and therefore all law is related back to the ultimate heteronomous event.[18]

Rabbi Jakobovits' and Cover's formulations have the effect of taking medical decision-making away from the patient and placing it in the hands of the rabbis. This is most readily seen in Rabbi Jakobovits' discussion of the ethical principle of informed consent in medical ethics. As we have discussed, this stipulation, based on autonomy and human freedom, is the cornerstone of modern medical ethics, but it receives only scant mention in *Jewish Medical Ethics*. Consent is not mentioned at all in the first edition, published in 1959, and only mentioned in the revised edition, published in 1975, in the context of obtaining consent from the family before an autopsy or organ donation. In an article published in 1965, Rabbi Jakobovits expands on the issue in relation to obtaining patient consent before a surgical procedure:

> In Jewish law, the consent of a patient is not required for any operation medically deemed necessary for his health. Indeed, even if he wished to avoid the operation and submit to danger as a means to penitence through suffering, he should be forced to undergo the treatment "against his will if necessary."[19]

---

18. Robert Cover, "Obligation – A Jewish Jurisprudence of the Social Order," *Journal of Law and Religion* 5 (1987): 65–74.
19. Immanuel Jakobovits, *Journal of a Rabbi*, 158. He reiterated this position in a letter to a physician: "In strictly halakhic terms, I have little doubt that Jewish physicians

This approach, rooted in Rabbi Jakobovits' conception of human duties and responsibility, also explains his teaching that "the rabbis insisted on maintaining the patient's hopefulness not merely by withholding information of his imminent death, but by positive means to encourage his confidence in recovery.... [For in Judaism] we give preference to the good of the patient over everything else."[20] In Rabbi Jakobovits' conception of Jewish medical ethics, beneficence takes precedence over autonomy.

Rabbi Eliezer Waldenberg, one of the foremost modern decisors on questions relating to medical ethics, takes a similar position. Should a physician listen to the request of a terminal patient who does not want his or her life extended? Rabbi Waldenberg cites Rabbi Yaakov Emden, who discusses a case of a patient who prefers to die rather than live in suffering and requires the doctor to amputate a limb even against the patient's own will because it is not the patient's decision to make.[21] Rabbi Waldenberg explains Rabbi Emden's opinion based on the principle that a person's soul does not belong to him, but to God.[22] Rabbi Waldenberg says in similar situations that it is not the patient's or the family's decision to make whether to extend life; rather, the physician

---

should carry out life-saving procedures even against the wishes or religious convictions of the patient concerned, whether, Jewish or non-Jewish.... However, other considerations may also have to be taken into consideration, possibly modifying this norm. In particular, we are required to avoid a *ḥillul Hashem* (desecration of God's name) by causing 'enmity' between Jews and non-Jews." See Yoel Jakobovits, "Lord Immanuel Jakobovits," 158. This last requirement may have much practical significance in a modern healthcare setting, where it would be very difficult, if not impossible, for a doctor to treat against the wishes of the patient. Yoel Jakobovits comments (ibid., 139), "My father never attempted, however, to erect the bridge in the other direction, to bring secular ethical concepts into the language of Jewish conceptualization. Currently popular terms such as autonomy, beneficence, maleficence, or distributive justice never figure in his writings or speeches." However, from a Jewish ethical perspective Rabbi Jakobovits related to these concepts differently. He clearly accepted the principle of beneficence and did not accept the primacy of autonomy.

20. Immanuel Jakobovits, *Jewish Medical Ethics*, 120.
21. *Mor UKtzia, Oraḥ Ḥayim* 328.
22. *Tzitz Eliezer* 18:62.

is required to do everything in his or her power to compel the patient to extend his life.[23]

Rabbi Moshe Feinstein, the preeminent halakhic authority of the second half of the twentieth century, challenged this paradigm. In response to the question of whether one is required to treat a secondary illness in a terminal patient (for example, a patient with incurable cancer in great pain who develops pneumonia), he ruled that this depends on the wishes of the patient – whether he wants to continue to live in agony or not: "It is plausible that one is not required to cure this patient who does not want treatment that will only extend his life of pain."[24] In explaining Rabbi Feinstein's opinion, Rabbi Dr. Moshe Tendler comments, "It is a decision that the patient must make."[25] This decision of Rabbi Feinstein is consistent with a belief in the concept of autonomy. Rabbi Feinstein leaves the decision of whether a life in agony is preferable to death in the hands of the patient.

It is instructive to compare his position with that of Rabbi Shlomo Zalman Auerbach. In a similar situation, Rabbi Auerbach agrees with Rabbi Feinstein's *pesak* that the decision is the patient's to make, but adds, "If the patient is a God-fearing person and is competent, one should explain to the patient that one hour of repentance in this world is more valuable than life in the world to come."[26] This appeal to influence the decision of the patient is missing from Rabbi Feinstein's responsum. Additionally, Rabbi Feinstein also attempts to develop a halakhic rationale for why the choice should be the patient's to make. According to Rabbi Feinstein, the question of who should decide treatment is dependent on who has the primary obligation to care for the patient. When a patient is competent, it falls on the patient; when he is unable to fulfill the mitzva, it falls on the relatives.[27]

Benjamin Freedman develops a similar argument in advocating for informed consent from a Jewish perspective. He maintains that even

---

23. Ibid.
24. *Iggerot Moshe, Ḥoshen Mishpat* 2:74:2.
25. Moshe David Tendler, *Responsa of Rav Moshe Feinstein* (New York, 1996), 57.
26. *Minḥat Shlomo* 1:91.
27. *Iggerot Moshe, Ḥoshen Mishpat* 2:74:2.

though Judaism recognizes that the body belongs to God, a person is legally considered a *shomer* (watchman) over his or her body:

> Persons have duties with respect to the body, duties to act as prudent caretakers. Because of the nature of the relationship between a person and his or her body, nobody else can understand precisely what medical treatment will mean better than that same person. Hence, only the patient can truly fulfill the demands of bodily preservation and caretaking.[28]

## THE METHODOLOGY OF JEWISH MEDICAL ETHICS

Modern bioethics has been heavily influenced by the work of Tom L. Beauchump and James F. Childress, who argued that moral dilemmas should be analyzed from the perspective of the four major principles of bioethics: autonomy, beneficence, non-maleficence, and justice.[29] This approach, called principlism, applies the most appropriate of these four principles in each case to resolve ethical dilemmas. In contradistinction to this approach, halakhic decision-making has traditionally been based on the principles of casuistry, using analogical case analysis to render decisions, as opposed to reasoning from theoretically derived principles. Some modern bioethicists have also argued that casuistry is the optimal methodology to analyze modern bioethical dilemmas.[30]

Alfred R. Jonsen and Stephen Toulmin used this methodology extensively during their tenure as chairmen of the US National Commission for the Protection of Human Subjects of Biomedical and Behavioral

---

28. Benjamin Freedman, *Duty and Healing*, 176. For further discussion on Rabbi Feinstein's position on autonomy, see Alan Jotkowitz, "R. Moshe Feinstein and the Role of Autonomy in Medical Ethics Decision Making," *Modern Judaism* 30, no. 2 (2010): 196–208. For an enlightened discussion on autonomy and religion, see Moshe Sokol, "Personal Autonomy and Religious Authority," in *Rabbinic Authority and Personal Autonomy*, ed. Moshe Sokol (Northvale, NJ, 1992).
29. Tom L. Beauchamp and James F. Childress, *Principles of Biomedical Ethics* (Oxford, UK, 2008).
30. Albert R. Jonsen and Stephen Toulmin, *The Abuse of Casuistry: A History of Moral Reasoning* (Berkeley, CA, 1988).

Research. Instead of developing a set of principles that could then be applied to problematic cases, the commission started by analyzing the cases in order to reach a consensus on practical guidelines. Following in their footsteps, John D. Arras comments that "the new casuistry insists that our moral knowledge must develop incrementally through the analysis of concrete cases."[31] Bioethical principles emerge from the responses to individual cases. In fact, the commission's statement of principles was written only after it reached consensus on many of the difficult cases.

This approach seems very similar to Rabbi Joseph B. Soloveitchik's contention that a true Jewish theology can only come from a halakhic, legal perspective.[32] Marvin Fox explains Rabbi Soloveitchik's view:

> Religious and philosophical accounts of Jewish spirituality are sound and meaningful only to the extent that they derive from the halakha. The deepest religious emotion, the subtlest theological understanding, can only be Jewishly authentic to the extent that they arise from reflections on matters of halakha.[33]

---

31. John D. Arras, "Getting Down to Cases: The Revival of Casuistry in Bioethics," *The Journal of Medicine and Philosophy* 16 (1991): 29–51.
32. Joseph B. Soloveitchik, *The Halakhic Mind* (New York, 1986), 101.
33. Marvin Fox, "The Unity and Structure of Rabbi Joseph B. Soloveitchik's Thought," *Tradition* 24, no. 2 (1989): 49. In contrast to Fox, Prof. Shubert Spero has argued forcefully that even according to Rabbi Soloveitchik, Jewish ethics and philosophy cannot be derived solely from the halakha; see Shubert Spero, "Rabbi Joseph Dov Soloveitchik and the Philosophy of Halakha," *Tradition* 30 (1998): 2; see also Lawrence Kaplan, "From Cooperation to Conflict: Rabbi Prof. Emanuel Rackman, Rav Joseph B. Soloveitchik, and the Evolution of American Modern Orthodoxy," *Modern Judaism* 30, no. 1 (2010): 46–68. For a more general discussion of the relationship between ethics and halakha, see Rabbi Aharon Lichtenstein's now-classic article, "Does Jewish Tradition Recognize an Ethic Independent of Halakha?," in *Modern Jewish Ethics: Theory and Practice*, ed. M. Fox (Ohio, 1975), 62–88. That article has spawned a large secondary literature, most recently an online symposium available at http://www.theapj.com/symposium-on-aharon-lichtensteins-paper-does-jewish-tradition-an-ethic-independent-of-halakha/.

Rabbi Jakobovits also champions this view:

> Secular medical ethics is the effort to turn ethical guidelines or rules of conscience into law, i.e., into legislation. Attempts are made constantly to choose ethical insights and then to gradually distill these into legislative laws adopted by different legislatures. Jewish medical ethics does the reverse. We determine law or legislation, distill it, and then come to the conclusion that it contains certain ethical guidelines. Thus, Jewish medical ethics derives from legislation. It does not lead to legislation. We look at legislation as rulings of law that have been given, i.e., halakha, which means law or legislation, and then try to extrapolate ethical rules from the legislation. Therefore, the Jewish concept of medical ethics is the very reverse of that commonly accepted in civilized countries of the world.[34]

## END-OF-LIFE CARE

An example of how this proposed methodology works can be found in the Jewish attitude toward euthanasia. The law codified by Maimonides, based on the Talmud, is "that anyone who kills a dying person is liable to the death penalty as a common murderer."[35] However, at the same time, the halakha sanctions the withdrawal of any factor that may artificially delay death. Rabbi Jakobovits summarized the Jewish position on end-of-life care as follows:

> We, too, would make a fundamental distinction between a deliberate hastening of death, whether with or without the patient's consent, on the one hand, and the withdrawal of artificial means to sustain a lingering life in its terminal stages on the other hand, particularly when the recourse to such "heroic" methods would serve only to prolong the patient's agony.[36]

---

34. Immanuel Jakobovits, "The Role of Jewish Medical Ethics in Shaping Legislation," in *Medicine and Jewish Law*, ed. Fred Rosner (Northvale, NJ, 1990), 1–18. For further discussion, see Alan Jotkowitz, "On the Methodology of JME," *Tradition* 43, no. 1 (2010): 38–55.
35. *Mishneh Torah, Laws of the Murderer and the Preservation of Life* 2:7.
36. Immanuel Jakobovits, *The Timely and the Timeless*, 384.

In formulating the Jewish position, Rabbi Jakobovits also makes use of aggadic sources:

> This uncompromising opposition to any deliberate acceleration of the final release is well exemplified by the martyred sage Ḥanina ben Teradyon, who, whilst the Romans burnt him at the stake, refused to follow his disciples' advice to open his mouth to the flames [in order to speed his death] with the defiant exclamation: "It is better that my soul shall be taken by Him who gave it than that I should do any harm to it on my own."[37]

The use of aggadic sources in the development of a Jewish position is not at all self-evident, as halakha is usually based on the legal sections of the Talmud. Regarding end-of-life care, Rabbi Jakobovits was simply using the talmudic narrative to illustrate the normative halakha. However, the use of the story does demonstrate the importance of these narratives, particularly in areas where the halakha is not fully developed, and attests to the importance of stories in the legal tradition, as argued by the legal theorist Robert Cover:

> We inhabit a *nomos* – a normative universe. We constantly create and maintain a world of right and wrong, of lawful and unlawful, of valid and void. The student of the law may come to identify the normative world with the professional paraphernalia of social control. The rules and principles of justice, the formal institutions of the law, and the conventions of a social order are, indeed, important to that world; they are, however, but a small part of the normative universe that ought to claim our attention. No set of legal institutions or prescriptions exists apart from the narratives that locate it and give it meaning.[38]

---

37. Immanuel Jakobovits, *Jewish Medical Ethics*, 122–23.
38. Robert Cover, "Nomos and Narrative," *Harvard Law Review* 97 (1983): 4. Notwithstanding the above quotation relating to the death of Ḥanina ben Teradyon, Rabbi Jakobovits rarely discusses talmudic narratives in *Jewish Medical Ethics*. It is interesting to note that Rabbi Feinstein developed his end-of-life ethic primarily from a talmudic story, that of the death of R. Yehuda HaNasi; see *Iggerot Moshe*, Ḥoshen

The Jewish opposition to active euthanasia rooted in the halakhic sources enables Rabbi Jakobovits to develop an ethic of end-of-life care based on the sanctity of life:

> Judaism regards every human life as being of infinitive value. Infinity, by definition, is indivisible, so that any fraction of life, whether ten years or a minute, whether healthy, crippled, or even unconscious, remains equally infinite in value. By attacking the ebbing life of a terminal patient because it is deemed worthless, we would rob all human beings of their absolute claim to life.[39]

The ethical principle of the "sanctity of life" follows from the legal prohibition of euthanasia.

## ABORTION

Interestingly, it is within the context of abortion that Rabbi Jakbovits employs the "sanctity of human life" as a moral imperative prohibiting certain actions even absent violation of a specific biblical prohibition

---

*Mishpat* 2:73:1. For further discussion, see Alan Jotkowitz, "Nomos and Narrative in Jewish Law: The Care of the Dying Patient and the Prayer of the Handmaid," *Modern Judaism* 33, no. 1 (2013): 56–74. This reliance upon an aggadic source on the part of Rabbi Feinstein may be due to the fact that there is a paucity of talmudic sources dealing with end-of-life care, as the issue was much less relevant before the advent of modern medicine. The aggadic literature may be more prominent in developing a Jewish ethical response in areas where there is no halakhic precedent, such as artificial reproduction, surrogacy, and cloning. See Ezra Bick, "Ovum Donations: A Rabbinic Conceptual Model of Maternity," *Tradition* 28 (1993): 28–45; and the response by Rabbi J. D. Bleich, "Maternal Identity Revisited," in *Jewish Law and the New Reproductive Technologies*, ed. Emanuel Feldman and Joel B. Wolowelsky (Hoboken, NJ, 1997), 113–14. For further discussion of the relationship of Cover to Jewish Law, see Samuel J. Levine, "Halacha and Aggada: Translating Robert Cover's Nomos and Narrative," *Utah Law Review* 465 (1998): 497–98; Barry Scott Wimpfheimer, *Narrating the Law* (Philadelphia, 2011), 13–24; and Moshe Simon-Shoshan, *Stories of the Law: Narrative Discourse and the Construction of Authority in the Mishnah* (Oxford, 2012). There is much literature on the relationship of halakha and Aggada; see, for example, Yair Lorberbaum, *Image of God* (Tel Aviv, 2004) (Hebrew), especially ch. 3 and the references therein.

39. Immanuel Jakobovits, *The Timely and the Timeless*, 334.

(*lav*). Ethical issues related to abortion are, of course, a major concern of many bioethicists, and Rabbi Jakobovits addresses abortion frequently in his writings. He first discusses it in *Jewish Medical Ethics,* and his treatment of the topic is a good example of his mastery of secular and Jewish thought. His discussion opens with a description of the traditional Buddhist opposition to abortion and the condemnation of the act in the ancient Indian law books of the *Aryas* and the *Manava Dharma-Sastra*. He then moves to Western cultures, particularly classical Greek and Roman society, where abortion was widely practiced, while at the same time its morality was debated among the philosophers. He then addresses the development of the vehement Catholic opposition to abortion and proceeds with a discussion of the question of ensoulment, with attention to the writings of Cangiamila, Aristotle, Tertullian, Augustine, Fulgentius, and Aquinas. He provides a historical review of the question of abortion in civil law, focusing on German, Austrian, Prussian, French, and English law. He then moves on to the Jewish sources, beginning with the discussions of Philo and Josephus, and then proceeds to the classic Jewish sources.

Rabbi Jakobovits makes a telling point:

> Criminal abortion is not treated in Jewish religious literature before the twelfth century, when it received a casual mention. There is no reference to the subject in the codes, and even the responsa do not discuss it until the seventeenth century. This omission seems all the more glaring in view of the extraordinary attention given to abortion by Christian authors and other legislators at all times.

He concludes from this that abortion "was virtually non-existent in Jewish society at any time."[40]

In his review of the Jewish sources, Rabbi Jakobovits notes the opinion of R. Yishmael cited in the Talmud (Sanhedrin 57b) and codified by Maimonides that abortion is considered murder when performed by a non-Jew. The focus of his discussion is the enigmatic position of Maimonides regarding abortion performed by a Jew. The Mishna states,

---

40. Immanuel Jakobovits, *Jewish Medical Ethics*, 181.

> If a woman is having difficulty giving birth [and it is feared that she might die], one may abort the infant in the womb and remove it limb by limb, because her life comes before the life of the fetus. If most of the fetus has emerged, one does not touch it, because one does not put aside one life [the fetus'] for another life [the mother's].[41]

Rashi comments:

> As long as the fetus has not been born, he is not a *nefesh* (living person) and one may kill him to save the mother, but once his head has emerged, one may not touch him to kill him because it is as if he has been born, and one does not put aside one life for another life.[42]

Maimonides, in codifying this law, engendered great controversy and debate among later authorities. He writes:

> If a pregnant woman is having difficulty giving birth, one may abort the fetus in the womb with a medication or by one's hand, because he [the fetus] is like a *rodef* [a pursuer] trying to kill her. But if his head has emerged, one does not touch him, because one does not put aside one life for another, and this is the way of the world.[43]

Maimonides does not offer Rashi's explanation that the fetus is not considered a person to explain why one is allowed to kill the fetus in the womb, but instead suggests that the reason is based on the principle of *rodef*. Does Maimonides maintain that the only reason one is allowed to abort the fetus in the first case is because he considers the fetus a *rodef*, whereas otherwise it would be murder? Or does he think that abortion is not murder, and the principle of *rodef* is introduced for another reason, not necessarily to overcome the prohibition of murder?

---

41. Mishna Oholot 7:6.
42. Rashi to Sanhedrin 72b, s.v. *yatza rosho*.
43. *Mishneh Torah, Laws of the Murderer and the Preservation of Life* 1:9.

In answering this question, Rabbi Jakobovits writes:

> There may be a further reason which prompted Maimonides to introduce the factor of "pursuit" into the first case treated in the mishna. When an expectant mother is sentenced to death, the mishna rules that her execution must be deferred until after the child's birth only if "she already sat on the birth stool" at the time the verdict was announced. The Talmud explains this by arguing that the fetus is regarded as a separate body, whose life must not be sacrificed, as soon as it has "torn itself loose" from its normal uterine position. But before the process of birth has set in, the child, as an organic part of the mother, is liable to share her fate so as to spare the mother the agony of suspense. Once the mother sits on the "birth stool," then the unborn child enjoys an intermediate status. It is not yet "a man," making its destruction a capital offense; at the same time, it is no longer "a part of the mother," when its dismemberment can be treated like the excision of any other organ which may endanger her life. It is during this stage, when the mother is already "in hard travail," that the threat to the mother's life is not by itself a sufficiently good cause for the child's destruction; only the additional "pursuit" element can justify the operation.[44]

Based on this distinction, Rabbi Jakobovits suggests that until labor begins, the fetus is considered part of the mother, and therefore "its life is not protected by any definitive legal provisions." Nevertheless, he insists that "the artificial termination of pregnancy is strongly condemned on moral grounds unless it can be justified for medical or possibly other grave reasons."

---

44. Immanuel Jakobovits, *Jewish Medical Ethics*, 185–86. This is an elegant explanation in that it ties together the uncontested talmudic position that one is allowed to execute a pregnant woman prior to her "sitting on the birth stool" with the ruling of Maimonides. A similar distinction is made by *Aḥiezer* (3:72), quoted by Rabbi Jakobovits in footnote 167. There are numerous other possibilities offered to explain the enigmatic statement of Maimonides; see Avraham Steinberg, "Abortion," in *Encyclopedia of Jewish Medical Ethics* (Jerusalem, 2003), and David Feldman, *Birth Control in Jewish Law* (Northvale, NJ, 1998).

Rabbi Jakobovits summarizes the traditional Jewish position as follows:

> The consensus of present-day rabbis is to condemn abortion, feticide, or infanticide to eliminate a crippled being, before or after birth, as an unconscionable attack on the sanctity of life.[45]

This summary does not necessarily follow from the learned discussion he presented in *Jewish Medical Ethics* written eight years previously, where he wrote regarding a fetus before the onset of labor that "its life is not protected by any definitive legal provisions." Perhaps recognizing this inconsistency, the bulk of his later essay is devoted to moral, philosophical, and social reasons for condemning abortion. These include the necessity to enforce moral standards in society, the cost in children who otherwise would have been born, the obligation for society to care for handicapped children, the deterrent effect on preventing adulterous relationships, and the importance of parental responsibility.

Rabbi Jakobovits thus occupies a middle ground in the spectrum of twentieth-century Orthodox decisors who wrote about abortion. His position on abortion is consistent with the thought of Rabbi Moshe Feinstein, who limits its permissibility to cases of definite threat to the life of the mother. At same time, Rabbi Feinstein clearly insists that abortion is the halakhic equivalent of homicide, a position Rabbi Jakobovits does not adopt. The Orthodox decisor who takes the most liberal approach to the question of abortion, Rabbi Eliezer Waldenberg, limits his discussion to the technical halakhic issues found in the Talmud and responsa, and does not rely on broad moral principles in

---

45. Immanuel Jakobovits, *The Timely and the Timeless*, 334; see *Iggerot Moshe, Ḥoshen Mishpat* 2:69. Rabbi Jakobovits himself points out the fact that Rabbi Feinstein was very lenient on issues pertaining to end-of-life care but very stringent regarding abortion; see Shashar, *Lord Jakobovits in Conversation*, 176. In a review of Rabbi Jakobovits' contribution to medical ethics, Marc Gellman takes issue with many of the principles espoused by Rabbi Jakobovits in his article on abortion. Notwithstanding the importance of many of these principles from both halakhic and moral standpoints, I have chosen to focus on the methodological difficulties with Rabbi Jakobovits' approach.

rendering his decision permitting abortion to prevent the birth of a severely handicapped child. In contrast, Rabbi Jakobovits condemns such abortion on moral grounds. Indeed, it is revealing that he groups together abortion and infanticide in his summary statement, clearly revealing how disdainful the procedure is to him.

## ARTIFICIAL REPRODUCTION

Rabbi Jakobovits was also wary of new forms of artificial reproduction. As we have seen previously regarding abortion, his discussion of artificial insemination (AI) in *Jewish Medical Ethics* begins with a survey of the historical and legal sources relating to the subject and the opinions of the major religions regarding AI. He demonstrates through a deft analysis of the halakhic sources that

> the considerations involved, though complex, may appear to warrant rather liberal conclusions on the legitimacy of the practice.... If Jewish law nevertheless opposes AI without reservation as utterly evil, it is mainly for moral reasons, not because of the intrinsic illegality of the act itself.[46]

The moral revulsion is due to the reduction of human procreation to stud-farming: the breaking of the link between childbearing and marriage; the empowering of women to have children without husbands; the potential increase in promiscuity from enabling an adulterous woman to claim her pregnancy; the destruction of the mystical partnership between God and man in the creation of life; and the threat against the integrity and sanctity of the traditional family.

These sentiments echo the feelings of other theologians and bio-conservatives. Prominent conservative ethicist Leon Kass writes regarding artificial reproduction:

---

46. Immanuel Jakobovits, *Jewish Medical Ethics*, 248. This position is consistent with the thought of Rabbi Waldenberg, who strongly opposed AI, primarily on theological grounds. See *Tzitz Eliezer* 9:51; 4:5, 1; and Alan Jotkowitz, "The Role of Theology in Contemporary Jewish Ethical Decision Making: The Case of Artificial Insemination," *Journal of Contemporary Religion* (forthcoming).

1. Man is defined partly by his origins and his lineage; to be bound up with his parents, siblings, ancestors, and descendants is part of what we mean by human. By tampering with and confounding these origins and linkages, we are involved in nothing less than creating a new conception of what it means to be human.
2. The new procedures for making babies all involve a new partner: the scientist-physician. The obstetrician is no longer just the midwife, but also the sower of seed. Even in the treatment of intra-marital infertility, the scientist-physician who employs in vitro fertilization and laboratory culture of human embryos has acquired far greater power over human life than his colleague who simply repairs the obstructed oviduct. He presides over many creations in many patients.
3. How and why dehumanizing? Because human procreation is not simply an activity of our rational will.... Is there possibly some wisdom in the mystery of nature that joins the pleasure of sex, the inarticulate longing for union, the communication of love, and the deep and partly articulate desire for children in the very activity by which we continue the chain of human existence?
4. The notion of man as a creature who is free to create himself... is problematic to say the least.... Moreover, the freedom to change one's nature includes the freedom to destroy (by genetic manipulation or brain modification) one's nature, and thereby the capacity and desire for freedom itself. It is literally a freedom that can end all freedom.
5. Properly understood, the largely universal taboo against incest, and also the prohibitions against adultery, defend the integrity of marriage, kinship, and especially the lines of origin and descent. These time-honored restraints implicitly teach that clarity about who your parents are, clarity in the lines of generation, clarity about who is whose, are the indispensable foundations of a sound family life, itself the sound foundation of civilized community.[47]

---

47. Leon R. Kass, *Toward a More Natural Science* (New York, 1985), 43–79.

Paul Ramsey was also bothered by the separation of the sexual act from conception and felt that AI from a non-husband donor "puts completely asunder what God joined together."[48]

But one is again perplexed by the impact of moral principles on halakhic decision-making. It is not clear why the relatively liberal halakhic attitude led to such moral condemnation by Rabbi Jakobovits.

## COSMETIC SURGERY

Rabbi Jakobovits' discussion of the halakhic permissibility of cosmetic surgery, originally delivered in 1962 at a symposium on "Religious Views on Cosmetic Surgery" before the American Society of Facial Plastic Surgery, is different than his usual writings. As he himself points out in his presentation, he could not find any direct reference to the topic in the rabbinic literature; he therefore had to develop his own analysis of the issue. He notes three possible objections to the procedures: the prohibition against putting oneself at risk (as every operation has an inherent risk), the prohibition against injuring oneself, and a problem of a more theological nature:

> We believe, of course, that our world is governed by divine providence. God is not only our creator, but the ultimate authority for all lawful human activities, especially when these may involve changing the order of things as He created them. The question therefore is: By trying to improve on God's work and create a human being other than He had created or intended, do we not attack the scheme of providence?... This permission [to practice medicine] may well be restricted to healing, so that the physicians' therapeutic work, since it enjoys divine sanction, would thus not be regarded as an unauthorized interference with providence. But whether such sanction goes beyond healing to include also acts of surgery dictated by purely cosmetic

---

48. Paul Ramsey, "Moral and Religious Implications of Genetic Control," in *On Moral Medicine: Theological Perspectives in Medical Ethics*, ed. Stephen E. Lammers and Allen Verhey (Grand Rapids, MI, 1987), 336.

considerations, is a question which would still require a great deal of careful thought.⁴⁹

He concludes that these objections can be set aside in only two instances: if the deformity is serious enough to interfere with a woman's ability to marry or it prevents a person from playing a constructive role in society. Once again, the theological component plays a dominant role in his thinking.

Rabbi Jakobovits anticipates the opinion of Rabbi Waldenberg, who prohibits plastic surgery because he feels that it does not fall under the general dispensation that is learned from the biblical imperative "he shall surely be healed," which gives a physician permission to heal. Rabbi Waldenberg rules:

> One should know and believe that there is no creator like God and He created each person in a unique way and one should not add or detract from this creation.⁵⁰

Rabbi Waldenberg further maintained that an operation done for aesthetic purposes would not be considered an act of "loving your neighbor" and would be "prohibited on the basis of assault."⁵¹

This concern of the doctor playing the role of creator did not enter at all into the thinking of another halakhic decisor, Rabbi Feinstein, who maintained that cosmetic surgery is allowed.⁵² For him, the halakhic question was simply whether one is permitted to injure oneself for a favorable purpose. In other words, is one allowed to undergo the trauma of surgery for the potential benefits of plastic surgery? Rabbi Feinstein quotes Maimonides, who defines assault as an action done with the intent of demeaning the victim.⁵³ This obviously would not apply in the case of an operation; therefore, cosmetic surgery should

---

49. Immanuel Jakobovits, *Journal of a Rabbi*, 196–97.
50. *Tzitz Eliezer* 11:41.
51. Ibid.
52. *Iggerot Moshe, Ḥoshen Mishpat* 2:66.
53. *Mishneh Torah, Laws of Injury and Damages* 5:1.

be permitted. He further argues that even those who disagree with Maimonides' definition of assault would not prohibit plastic surgery because of the commandment to "love your neighbor like yourself," which would override the principle of assault in this case because of the benefit of the surgery to the patient.

## AUTOPSIES

The halakhic and moral issues involved in autopsies were a major concern of JME in the 1950s and 1960s, and Rabbi Jakobovits wrote extensively on the issue throughout his career. In the first issue of *Tradition*, published in 1958, Rabbi Jakobovits provides a masterful presentation of the topic. He not only summarizes the multitude of rabbinic responsa on autopsies and dissection, but discusses at length the history of the subject from antiquity to the modern era, presenting religious, secular, and legal perspectives. The traditional Jewish disdain for autopsies teaches:

> Their bodies are not our property... and to reduce the human corpse to the utilitarian function of a textbook from which the pages are torn out one by one and to ransack the body by wanton raids on its scientific treasures is as irreverent to the dead as it is degrading and spiritually hebetating to the living.[54]

The Jewish legal prohibition on disfigurement of the dead leads to the ethical principle of respect for a corpse and the moral sensitivity that one should develop toward a dead body.

The consensus of rabbinic opinion, following the landmark ruling of Rabbi Yeḥezkel Landau (*Noda BiYehuda*), is that any disfigurement of the dead is strictly prohibited unless there is a reasonable and immediate prospect of saving a human life.[55] This dispensation is known in rabbinic parlance as "at hand"; there has to be an identifiable person "at hand" who can immediately benefit from the medical knowledge obtained from the autopsy. In a presentation delivered in Jerusalem in 1963 before the Sixth Congress on the Oral Law, Rabbi Jakobovits

---

54. Immanuel Jakobovits, *Journal of a Rabbi*, 191–92.
55. *Noda BiYehuda* 2:210.

maintained that one had to take into account new circumstances in applying the principle of "at hand":

1. Due to modern communication, patients all over the world can be considered "at hand."
2. "The need for autopsies to conquer some of the worst scourges, such as cancer and heart disease, is, according to medical opinion, incontestable. Indeed, any autopsy nowadays, however routine, is more likely to help in the saving of life than in any 'at hand' case permitted two hundred years ago, when medical science was primitive by comparison and the prospect of any meaningful results yielded by an autopsy was negligible."
3. Autopsies are needed to test for the safety of new drugs.
4. On the other hand, the frequency of autopsies now performed has the potential to make them routine without any concern for the potential lifesaving benefits.
5. Some religious patients are afraid to go to the hospital because of the fear of autopsies.[56]

Based on these principles, Rabbi Jakobovits suggests:

1. The sanction for autopsies should be broadened to include tests for new drugs and cases in which there is reasonable suspicion that a diagnosis was missed.
2. An autopsy board should be established consisting of two physicians and one rabbi.
3. The autopsy should be reduced to a minimum, with assurance that all body parts are returned for burial.
4. Rabbis should advocate for autopsies in situations in which lives can be expected to be saved.[57]

These principles demonstrate Rabbi Jakobovits' confidence in scientific medicine and demonstrate his affinity for modern medicine and

---

56. Immanuel Jakobovits, *Jewish Medical Ethics*, 282–83.
57. Ibid.

technology. He is willing to accept new technologies and acknowledges that halakha must change in response to them as long as they are not used to upset the God-driven natural order. One can certainly argue with his expansive definition of "at hand" and his contention that "the need for autopsies to conquer some of the worst scourges, such as cancer and heart disease, is, according to medical opinion incontestable." But these principles demonstrate his ability to understand the long-term consequences of halakhic positions. Rabbi Jakobovits felt that in addition to advocating for universal moral principles, Jews should be at the forefront of the fight against human diseases, and rabbis should encourage these efforts.

## RABBIS AND RASHEI YESHIVA

If the fundamental nature of the debate regarding some issues in bioethics is theological as opposed to legal, who then is qualified to make judgments? Traditionally, Orthodox Jews have looked to the legal masters to guide their behavior, but does their mastery extend to theological issues as well? I would argue that it should, with one caveat.

In resolving ethical dilemmas, Rabbi Walter Wurzburger maintained:

> [One should] accord special weight to the views of eminent Torah scholars even in matters where no formal halakhic ruling is feasible. Implicit in both positions is the belief that the residual exposure to halakhic categories of thought makes itself felt in areas where the law itself cannot be applied.[58]

Rabbi Wurzburger believed that recognized halakhic masters should also be the court of last resort for ethical disputes grounded in theology.

While agreeing with this position, Rabbi Jakobovits pointed out that in the previous fifty years there had been a shift in Jewish legal authority from the community rabbi, who by necessity was intimately involved in all aspects of daily life, to the yeshiva dean, who spent most of his time in the company of serious scholars. In his own words:

---

58. Walter S. Wurzberger, *Ethics of Responsibility* (Philadelphia, 1994), 33.

*Dr. Alan Jotkowitz*

> With the decline of the professional rabbinate and the ascendancy of rabbinical deans as the principal arbiters of Jewish law and religious policies, the present tendency is increasingly in favor of the latter group. This development is not without considerable consequence to current trends on halakha. Practicing rabbis are of necessity exposed to the problems, thinking, and pressures of the often religiously alienated masses in the communities they serve, much more than scholars and teachers ensconced in the rarified atmosphere of learning together with disciples, who, these days, frequently exceed the zeal of their masters. This factor naturally contributes to the distinctly conservative orientation in the rabbinic law-making process today.[59]

This observation of Rabbi Jakobovits, himself considered a conservative decisor, reflects a similar phenomenon to that described by Haym Soloveitchik. He comments on the shift in contemporary Orthodoxy from a mimetic tradition, in which religious practice was learned from observation of family and friends, to a text-based one, in which correct behavior is learned from the study of books.[60] In this new environment, authority has shifted from the community rabbi to the master of the books, the Rosh Yeshiva. These sociological changes have the potential to heavily influence halakhic decisions based on theological principles. For example, community rabbis who minister directly to couples unable to conceive naturally might be more inclined to search for leniencies than yeshiva heads who have no direct contact with the unfortunate couples.

Rabbi Aharon Lichtenstein creates an intellectual framework for this position:

> *Horaa* (halakhic decision-making) is comprised of two elements: *pesak* and *pesika*, respectively. The former refers to codification, the formulation of the law pertinent to a given area,

---

59. Immanuel Jakobovits, *Jewish Medical Ethics*, 259.
60. Haym Soloveitchik, "Rupture and Reconstruction: The Transformation of Contemporary Orthodoxy," *Tradition* 24, no. 4 (1994): 64–131.

and it is most characteristically manifested in the adoption, on textual or logical grounds, of one position in preference to others. As such, it is, essentially, the concluding phase of the learning process proper, whether on a grand or a narrow scale, and its locus is the beit midrash. *Pesika*, by contrast, denominates implementation. It bespeaks the application of what has already been forged in the crucible of the learning experience to a particular situation. It does not entail the definitive postulation of the law governing a delimited area or its detail, but rather the concurrent and coordinate meshing of all aspects, possibly drawn from widely divergent spheres, obtained in a concrete situation. Its venue is, publicly, the *beit din* or, privately, the meeting of the inquirer and respondent. It does not necessarily demand of the *posek* that he take a stand or break fresh ground. Its challenge lies in the need to harness knowledge and responsibility at the interface of reality and halakha. The halakhic tools that a *posek* can use in rendering a differential *pesika*, the principle that divergent answers may be given to identical questions depending on the human and social conditions, is the principle of "Rabbi So-and-So is worthy of being relied upon in difficult circumstances." The principle teaches that opinions rejected in the world of *pesak* can be relied upon in extenuating circumstances in the world of *pesika*.[61]

In his own writings, Rabbi Jakobovits advocated for a return to the primacy of community rabbis, as opposed to Rashei Yeshiva, in adjudicating halakhic quandaries through the judicious use of *pesika*.

---

61. Aharon Lichtenstein, "The Human and Social Factor in Halakha," in *Leaves of Faith*, vol. 2 (Jersey City, NJ, 2004), 2:162–63. It is interesting to note that the two most influential *posekim* of the second half of the twentieth century, Rabbi Moshe Feinstein and Rabbi Ovadia Yosef, started their careers as community rabbis. Some scholars have argued that there is a difference between the Sephardic and Ashkenazic approaches to *pesak*; see Zvi Zohar, *He'iru Penei HaMizraḥ: Halakha VeHagut etzel Ḥakhmei HaMizraḥ BaMizraḥ HaTikhon* (Tel Aviv, 2000). For a critique, see B. Brown, "Ḥakhmei HaMizraḥ VeHaKana'ut HaDatit," *Akdamot* 10 (2001): 289–324.

## KIDDUSH HASHEM

Miri Freud-Kandel is certainly right that a dominant element of Rabbi Jakobovits' thought is imbuing Judaism with a sense of mission to the nations of the world.[62] In his own words:

> *Torah im derekh eretz*, Hirsch's synthesis of Judaism with Western secular culture... [is] like the philosophy of Reform Judaism... albeit along very different lines, [in that both] held that the ultimate Jewish national purpose is the mission to the nations.[63]

This mission is primarily reflected in the charge to be a "light unto the nations," particularly in the moral sphere. As Rabbi Jakobovits writes:

> My intent is to a Jewish contribution that will influence all of humankind, in terms of how one looks upon life and its meaning.... The mission of the People of Israel is to function as a signpost for the whole world.[64]

---

62. Miri Freud-Kandel, "Immanuel Jakobovits: A Coherent Theology of Apparent Contradiction," *Journal of Modern Jewish Studies* 10, no. 1 (2011): 43–64. In her article, Freud-Kandel explains the contradiction in Rabbi Jakobovits' thought between his conservative social values and his support for territorial compromise with the Palestinians based on the concept of *kiddush Hashem*. While I agree with her conclusions, I do not think there is necessarily a contradiction between those two principles.
63. Immanuel Jakobovits, *"Torah im Derekh Eretz,"* in *Jewish Legacy and the German Conscience: Essays in Memory of Rabbi Joseph Asher*, ed. Moses Rischin (Berkeley, CA, 1991), 158. For more on Rabbi Jakobovits' appreciation for Rabbi Samson Raphael Hirsch and *Torah im derekh eretz*, see his study on Rabbi Hirsch in *The Timely and the Timeless*, 251–58.
64. Shashar, *Lord Jakobovits in Conversation*, 51. Another modern thinker who based much of his outlook on the principle of *kiddush Hashem* was Rabbi Yehuda Amital, and there are other areas where his and Rabbi Jakobovits' thoughts coincide. Rav Amital also regretted the loss of authority of the community rabbi to the yeshiva heads and was the leading religious Zionist rabbi advocating for territorial compromise. Rabbi Jakobovits expressed his regard for Rav Amital:

> Here was a development for which I had long waited: the emergence from within the *Gush Emunim–hesder* yeshivas heartland of a purely religious challenge to the whole "Greater Israel" concept, which had hitherto been its main plank....

Not surprisingly, this is a primary reason for his interest in Jewish medical ethics:

> I was interested not only in opening a new chapter in Judaism. I also sought to show that in this sphere as well Judaism has something to contribute to the moral life of humankind. This is *kiddush Hashem* before the non-Jewish peoples.[65]

*Jewish Medical Ethics* is not only a survey of the thousands of years of rabbinic scholarship or an academic approach to the topic, but a call to action in the spirit of the prophets:

> It is our task, as spiritual leaders who have assumed the heritage of the Prophets, to become interpreters of our history.... The time has perhaps also come when we should again address ourselves to the nations of the world as the authentic spokesmen of God's will on universal issues.[66]

---

Immediately after the publication of Rabbi Amital's article, I wrote to him to express my admiration." (Immanuel Jakobovits, *If Only My People...* [London: Vallentine Mitchell Publishers, 1984], 96–98).

For more on Rav Amital's thought, see the essay by Reuven Ziegler and Yehudah Mirsky in this volume.

65. Shashar, *Lord Jakobovits in Conversation*, 51.
66. Immanuel Jakobovits, *Journal of a Rabbi*, 39–40. Notwithstanding these sentiments, Rabbi Jakobovits "always opposed the idea of seeking to enforce halakhic discipline in Israel by way of Knesset legislation, thus subjecting the majority of Israel's citizens – secularists as they sadly are – to 'religious coercion.'" See Jakobovits, "The Role of Jewish Medical Ethics," 1–18. In December 2005, a law was passed in the Knesset by an overwhelming majority regulating the attitude toward and the treatment of dying patients. The law was framed by a fifty-nine-member public advisory body representing many components of Israeli society. The law was criticized for its reliance on Jewish law in reaching some of its conclusions, particularly in limiting its scope to patients with less than six months to live and in not allowing withdrawal of therapy. See Anat Assiag, "On Withdrawing Care from the Dying Patient in Israel," *Journal of Health Law and Bioethics* 1 (2008): 160–86 [Hebrew]. It is not clear to me if Rabbi Jakobovits would agree with this critique, even though he generally opposed religious legislation, given the fact that the law was drawn up by a large public committee and passed by an overwhelming majority in the Knesset.

This is a bold and courageous statement. Unfortunately, in the years since it was written there has been less interest in the Orthodox community in fulfilling its charge. Works on JME from the ultra-Orthodox community tend to focus on technical halakhic issues and are geared toward the insular Jewish community, and many segments of Modern Orthodoxy influenced by post-modernism are reluctant to apply Orthodox Jewish standards to universal moral problems.

Did Rabbi Jakobovits fulfill his mandate to show the world "that Judaism has something to contribute to the moral life of humankind"? The answer is, probably, yes and no. Under his tutelage, JME has grown into a respected academic discipline with hundreds of articles published every year in both academic and religious journals. There are even journals, in both Hebrew and English, solely dedicated to JME. The multivolume *Encyclopedia of Jewish Medical Ethics*, by Prof. Avraham Steinberg, has been written in Hebrew and translated into English. Interest in the field is demonstrated by both secular and religious scholars, and the subject is taught in many universities and medical schools. However, its impact on the moral life of humankind has been less measureable. Rabbi Jakobovits himself was a powerful advocate for his vision of Jewish morality and had a strong following in the United Kingdom, but he was less successful in his ability to translate his moral values into practical accomplishments. Abortion is still widely available in almost all Western countries and passive euthanasia is freely practiced. As opposed to his vision of medical ethics based on responsibilities and duties, autonomy and unlimited human freedom are the dominant themes in modern medical ethics. In addition, there is increased skepticism regarding religion in the modern world and less desire to listen to a universal moral message.

Notwithstanding these sentiments, the sense of mission that defined the life and works of Rabbi Jakobovits should inspire the Jewish community to become "a light unto the nations."

# Torah and Humanity in a Time of Rebirth: Rav Yehuda Amital as Educator and Thinker

Rabbi Reuven Ziegler and Dr. Yehudah Mirsky

Religious virtuosi, the figures who powerfully transmit and reshape their traditions and whose life stories become their own teaching, come in many forms, but they have something in common: a combination of faithfulness and daring that is at once uniquely personal and yet at one with all they received from their own teachers. In the Jewish context, this central, defining paradox of great religious figures means faithfulness to God, Torah, mitzvot, and the Jewish people, combined with audacity in exegesis, and the willingness to engage in probing personal and communal self-criticism and to examine commonly held notions again and again in a new light.

Great religious figures also undertake distinctive quests of their own, and in the case of Rabbi Yehuda Amital (1924–2010) this quest was guided by two overriding values: truth and a bedrock humanity. He grappled as honestly as he could with God, Torah, and Israel, in all their complexity, while being as faithful as he could to the tradition, his historical moment, and himself.

One can "explain" the emergence of such figures only with great difficulty, if at all, let alone parse their complex personalities into discrete parts. One can, however, try to trace their origins and life histories, and to mark the stations and crossroads that shaped them on their way.

Rav Amital's teachings are not easily summarized for two reasons. The first is the sheer complexity of the man, who lived and taught a fundamental simplicity while at the same time wrapping his hands around complicated questions with no hope for easy answers – and encouraging others to do the same. The second is the fact that he did not write much, certainly not systematically.[1] The latter reason seems in part related to the existential immediacy of his life and ideas, his fully inhabiting the moments and encounters in which he found himself, and the fusion of thought and action in his engagements. As he put it to one of the authors, "There are those whose Torah is in their books, and those whose Torah is in their lives."[2] Therefore, parts of this essay will interweave discussions of his life with his thought.[3]

---

1. The primary sources for a study of Rav Amital's thought are his books *HaMaalot MiMaamakim* (Alon Shevut, 1974); *Jewish Values in a Changing World*, ed. Amnon Bazak, trans. David Strauss (Jersey City, NJ, 2005); *Commitment and Complexity*, ed. Aviad Hacohen, trans. Kaeren Fish (Jersey City, NJ, 2008); and *When God Is Near: On the High Holidays*, ed. Yoel Amital, trans. Kaeren Fish (Jerusalem, 2015). All of his essays and books were originally written in Hebrew; wherever possible, we will refer to English translations. Dozens more essays and *siḥot* appear in the various publications of Yeshivat Har Etzion and on its Israel Koschitzky Virtual Beit Midrash. For a sampling of material translated into English, see http://etzion.org.il/en/seminal-articles-harav-yehuda-amital-ztl. (This webpage also contains links to most of the articles cited below.) Rav Amital wrote little himself, but encouraged his students to transcribe and adapt his oral discourses. Some of the fruits of his talmudic and halakhic scholarship are collected in his book *Resisei Tal*, ed. Yoel Amital (Alon Shevut, 2005), as well as in the journals of Yeshivat Har Etzion: *Alon Shevut*, *Daf Kesher*, and *Alei Etzion*.
2. This is reminiscent of the comment of Akiva Ernst Simon that there are two kinds of religious thinkers: those for whom God has a system, and those for whom God has truth. See Akiva Ernst Simon, *Ye'adim, Tzematim, Netivim: Haguto shel Mordekhai Martin Buber* (Tel Aviv, 1985), 164–65.
3. Regarding Rav Amital's life, see Elyashiv Reichner, *By Faith Alone: The Story of Rabbi Yehuda Amital*, trans. Elli Fischer (Jerusalem, 2011). Regarding his educational and

## Torah and Humanity in a Time of Rebirth

**BACKGROUND AND INFLUENCES**

Central as the teachings of Rav Avraham Yitzhak HaKohen Kook and the internal dynamics of Religious Zionism were to Rav Amital's life and thought, as we shall see, the Hungarian-Jewish landscape of his early years was also deeply significant. This is true not only in personal terms, but, it seems fair to say, in spiritual, intellectual, and even ideological terms as well.

Rav Amital was born Yehuda Klein in 1924, in the Transylvanian city of Grosswardein (Oradea).[4] Its Jewish community was, as were those in much of Hungary, far more internally diverse than is generally thought. It was home to Hasidim, acculturated and assimilated Jews, Jewish-Hungarian nationalists, and a large concentration of Hungary's Religious Zionists.[5]

One figure from that milieu to whom Rav Amital often referred was Rabbi Moshe Shmuel Glasner. Born in Pressburg in 1856 and a great-grandson of the Ḥatam Sofer (hence the title of his major work and eponym, *Dor Revi'i*), Rabbi Glasner served as rabbi of Cluj-Klausenberg from 1877 until his death in 1924. Although he passed away shortly before Rav Amital's birth, Rabbi Glasner remained a living presence. He was also the grandfather of Rav Amital's own beloved teacher, Rabbi Ḥayim Yehuda Levi, himself a Hungarian alumnus of great Lithuanian yeshivas who brought their hallmark conceptual methods of study back to his native milieu.[6]

Rabbi Glasner's approach appealed to Rav Amital in several ways. In the lengthy introduction to his commentary on Tractate Ḥullin, he laid out a theory of the Oral Law, placing great emphasis on the need for rabbinic authorities to exercise their own independent judgment in adjudication, out of steady dialogue with their times and with the needs

---

    public impact, see Reuven Ziegler and Reuven Gafni, eds., *LeOvdekha BeEmet: LiDemuto ULeDarko shel HaRav Yehuda Amital* (Jerusalem, 2011).

4. Though at the time of his birth Grosswardein was part of Romania, it soon thereafter transferred back to Hungarian sovereignty.
5. On Grosswardein, see, briefly, www.yivoencyclopedia.org/article.aspx/Oradea. The Grosswardein memorial book can be read online at yizkor.nypl.org.
6. Regarding Rabbi Ḥayim Yehuda Levi, see the biographical sketch written by Rav Amital in *Resisei Tal*, 335–36.

of their communities.[7] He also presented the notion that there are actions that – although not explicitly prohibited in the Torah – are nonetheless forbidden because they contradict human dignity and diminish one's *tzelem Elokim*, a proscription with broad ramifications that Rav Amital frequently cited when discussing ethical obligations that precede and complement formal Torah.[8] In his talmudic exegesis, Rabbi Glasner's method, reminiscent of the Brisker method but without its elaborate and specialized terminology, synthesized conceptual analysis with great emphasis on a close reading of Maimonides' *Mishneh Torah*, a combination which, inter alia, retained the flavor of more traditional Talmud interpretation.

Rabbi Glasner was also one of the early supporters in Hungary of Religious Zionism, for which he faced strong opposition by his peers. In addition, while most of the rabbis affiliated with the Mizrachi movement argued that Zionism could serve only as a vessel for improving Jews' political and social situation, but nothing more, Rabbi Glasner argued – as did Rav Kook – that it could serve as a vehicle of religious and spiritual renewal.[9]

Although, as mentioned, Rabbi Glasner passed away shortly before Rav Amital was born, it seems that his teaching and public image were a source of inspiration for Rav Amital in several areas: his emphasis on intellectual independence, his ethical concern, and his commitment to Zionism. Rabbi Glasner's approaches in these realms were all in a somewhat different key than those of Rav Kook, whose riveting teaching and persona were soaked in longing, pathos, and not a little contradiction. It is unclear whether Rabbi Glasner was a culture hero and role model for Rav Amital throughout his life or if, in the course of his development and his working to meet the practical, moral, and spiritual leadership challenges he faced, he found himself drawn back to and learning from this prominent figure from his youth.

---

7. Rabbi Moshe Shmuel Glasner, *Sefer Dor Revi'i: Biur Raḥav al Masekhet Ḥullin* (Cluj-Kolozsvar, 1921).
8. See, for example, *Jewish Values in a Changing World* (henceforth: *Jewish Values*), 38–43. Unless specified otherwise, all books and articles cited below are by Rav Amital.
9. A great deal of material on Rabbi Glasner may be found at www.dorrevii.org. A very interesting discussion of his life and ideas is found in Netanel Katzburg, "LeShitato HaToranit VeHaLeumit shel HaRav S. M. Glasner," in *Sefer HaZikkaron LeYahadut Cluj-Kluzhvar*, ed. Moshe Carmilly (New York, 1970), 48–60. See also Avraham Fuchs, *Yeshivot Hungarya BiGdulatan UVḤurbanan* (Jerusalem, 1987), 2:273–77.

In addition to the complex legacy of the *Dor Revi'i*, Rav Amital inherited multiple traditions during his formative years – the traditional Hungarian modes of study with their emphasis on responsa literature and the practical application of halakha, the Lithuanian conceptualism of his Rosh Yeshiva, echoes of Hungarian Hasidism, and the simple piety of the Jewish masses and of his family.

## HOLOCAUST AND *ALIYA*

After rudimentary schooling, young Yehuda Klein spent his childhood and adolescence in yeshiva, more specifically under the tutelage of the aforementioned Rabbi Hayim Yehuda Levi. Rav Amital's father was a bookkeeper, and Rav Amital might well have gone into his father's profession had he not been forced to witness his culture's murder. In May 1944, he was taken away to a Nazi forced labor camp, and shortly afterwards the rest of his family was deported to Auschwitz. He managed to sneak an anthology of Rav Kook's writings into the labor camp, as he later testified:

> I was seventeen when the Germans came, and I was summoned to be transported to a labor camp in an unknown location – the Siberian plains or the Carpathian mountains. I had to take leave from my parents, and our feeling was that this was to be a final farewell (for what had happened to our Jewish brethren in Poland was no secret to us). I didn't know what awaited me. I took a few small books in a bag: a Pentateuch, Prophets, Mishna, and I thought there would be a need for something else, something that would perhaps maintain the necessary morale in hard times. And so I took *Mishnat HaRav*[10] as well. Indeed, I received encouragement and strength from that book. The ideas and words influenced me to such a degree that I attributed to them my steadfast endurance in the labor camp, not contaminating myself with forbidden foods even when this involved great hunger.[11]

---

10. This anthology, compiled by Rabbi Moshe Zvi Neriah, was first published in 1936.
11. Appendix to Rabbi Avraham Yitzhak Kook, *Mishnat HaRav*, 3rd ed. (Beit El, 1992), 147–48.

Rav Amital had first encountered Rav Kook's thought incidentally, when he read a quotation from Rav Kook in Rabbi Ḥayim Hirschensohn's *Motza'ei Mayim*.[12] He was electrified by the ideas of Rav Kook, whose mix of passionate religious experience, Jewish nationalism, messianic fervor, and ethical universalism would set the terms for his later engagements. Although Rav Amital was deeply influenced by Rav Kook and, as we saw, testified that Rav Kook's thought gave him strength during the *Shoah*, it was precisely the fact that Rav Kook's vision of redemption had not grappled with the Holocaust that later led Rav Amital to question some of its premises and conclusions.[13] Furthermore, as we shall see, Rav Amital's interpretation of Rav Kook differed from that espoused by Rav Kook's son Rabbi Zvi Yehuda and the latter's disciples.

After his liberation by the Red Army on *Simḥat Torah* in 1944, Rav Amital headed for the Land of Israel, arriving on the second night of Ḥanukka, the sole survivor of his immediate family. Having twice sworn during his time in the camp that if he survived he would study Torah in Jerusalem, he made his way there and found a place in Yeshivat Ḥevron, a leading *ḥaredi* institution.[14] He threw himself into his studies, acquiring a reputation for his fervent and independent-minded spirituality and for his mastery of halakhic responsa literature. He and several other students also joined the Haganah, despite the fact that Zionism

---

12. *Motza'ei Mayim* (Budapest, 1924) is a commentary on the seafaring *aggadot* of Rabba bar bar Ḥana. Rabbi Hirschensohn cites Rav Kook therein at p. 120, in particular the tenth section of *Orot HaTeḥiya*, on how the quintessence of Israel's striving is rooted not in socio-economics, but in a sense of spiritual mission and longing for God.
13. Rav Kook died in 1935, four years before the outbreak of World War II.
14. Although a student at Yeshivat Ḥevron, he also studied privately with Rabbi Yaakov Moshe Ḥarlap, a close associate of Rav Avraham Yitzhak Kook, who succeeded Rav Kook as Rosh Yeshiva of Merkaz HaRav. For Rav Amital's reflections on Rabbi Ḥarlap and correspondence from the latter to him, see *Alon Shevut* 20 (Adar 5734): 18–21, and *Meimad* 3 (Tevet 5755): 23; both items have been reprinted in Aryeh Strikovsky, ed., *Daf LeTarbut Yehudit* 271 (Tishrei 5767), available online at http://meyda.education.gov.il/files/tarbut/pirsumeagaf/kitveet/271pdf.pdf.

While at Yeshivat Ḥevron, Rav Amital also formed a close lifelong friendship with his fellow student Rabbi Mordekhai Breuer. They later taught together at Yeshivat HaDarom in Rehovot, and when Rav Amital became Rosh Yeshiva of Har Etzion, he invited Rabbi Breuer to teach Tanakh there – a pivotal move in the "Tanakh study revolution" spearheaded by Har Etzion and its affiliated Herzog College.

was not encouraged at the yeshiva. Though a penniless, orphaned survivor from an undistinguished family, he married, by dint of his learning, piety, and personality, into one of the most prominent rabbinic families of the time, that of Rabbi Isser Zalman Meltzer.

The day after Israel's declaration of independence, a Shabbat, he enlisted in the Israel Defense Forces (IDF). During the War of Independence he fought in Latrun and the Galilee, and founded a journal in which he published perhaps the first programmatic essay ever written on being a Jewish soldier in a Jewish army.[15] While savoring Jewish national self-defense in the wake of the Holocaust, he also projected Jewish law and values as a defense against the dehumanization and brutalization of wartime: "Recognition of the value of the individual within the military is in great danger if the erroneous notion that each soldier is only a number, and therefore expendable, has taken root."[16] He called upon religious soldiers to band together in order to help shape the image and traditions of the fledgling army, to imprint Jewish values on the army's conduct, and to sanctify God's name by upright behavior.[17] In the Israeli assumption of Jewish responsibility for all realms of society, which he characterized as the move from narrowly defined *religion* to the fullness of *Torah*, he saw the restoration of the primal force of biblical religion. His essay closed with Joshua's call to the people, "Make yourselves holy, for tomorrow God will work wonders with you" (Josh. 3:5). The farsighted words of the twenty-four-year-old soldier broached themes that he would develop and bring to fruition years later, as a founder of the IDF's *hesder* program and as a Rosh Yeshiva.[18]

---

15. This essay, "*LeDarko shel HeHayal HaDati BeMilḥemet HaKomemiyut*" (On the Path of the Religious Soldier During the War of Independence), originally appeared in the journal *Moreshet* (published by the synagogue of the 79th Battalion) in Tevet 5709 (1949) and was reprinted in Rav Amital's *HaMaalot MiMaamakim*, 96–107.
16. *HaMaalot MiMaamakim*, 106.
17. In the essay's penultimate paragraph, Rav Amital called for religious soldiers to engage in soul-searching: "We do not pretend that everything is all right with us, and far be it from us to ignore our own faults." As Reichner points out (*By Faith Alone*, p. 146), "This call for constant soul-searching and introspection became one of the lessons most closely identified" with Rav Amital.
18. Regarding Rav Amital's views on and contribution to the Israel Defense Forces, see Aharon Ahrend, "*Sherut BeTzahal BeMishnato shel HaRav Amital*," in Ziegler and Gafni, *LeOvdekha BeEmet*, 345–52.

This early essay, writes Rav Amital's biographer, became a manifesto:

> It was the first programmatic-halakhic essay to examine the IDF as a Jewish army, and it made a huge impression on the yeshiva world and religious community at the time. Most instructive in this regard is a single reaction, that of [Rav Amital's wife's grandfather,] Rabbi Isser Zalman Meltzer, who wept when he read it. When his confidants asked him why he was crying, he pointed to the article and said, "Until now, we have had *Orah Hayim* for the halakhot of daily life and *The Laws of Kings* for the Messianic Era. Then our Yudl comes along and tells us that *The Laws of Kings* have now also become part of *Orah Hayim*!" These words were spoken by the Rosh Yeshiva of Etz Hayim, a leading sage of the *haredi* community at the time.[19]

It was at this point that the passionate Religious Zionist Yehuda Klein hebraized his name to Amital, based on Micah 5:6: "And the remnant of Jacob will be among many nations (*ammim*) like dew (*tal*) from God, like droplets on the grass, that does not wait for any man nor place its hope in mortals."

Through the 1950s, Rav Amital taught in the Rehovot yeshiva of his father-in-law, Rabbi Zvi Yehuda Meltzer. In those years, he developed a rich, and in some ways rare, network of deep connections with many figures in both the ultra-Orthodox and Religious Zionist worlds.[20] In 1959, Rabbi Meltzer and Rav Amital secured from the army the first *hesder*, literally, "arrangement," whereby yeshiva students could alternate between their studies and military service. Ever sensitive to societal needs and anticipating future developments, he foresaw the need to strengthen the Religious Zionist community with a broad cadre of

---

19. Reichner, *By Faith Alone*, 146.
20. For instance, he developed warm ties with both Rabbi Elazar Menachem Mann Shach and Rabbi Ovadia Yosef; he mentored another eventual *Rishon LeTziyon*, Rabbi Eliyahu Bakshi-Doron, as well as the future Rosh Yeshiva of Har HaMor, Rabbi Zvi Tau.

*talmidei ḥakhamim* and simultaneously to prevent alienation between yeshiva students and the state. The *hesder* yeshivas eventually grew into a network that decisively shaped Religious Zionist society and whose contribution to Israeli society and to the IDF was collectively acknowledged by the state's highest honor, the Israel Prize.

After the Six-Day War, Rav Amital was asked to become the head of a new *hesder* yeshiva being established in Gush Etzion, the Etzion Bloc, in the Judean hills near Bethlehem. The site of a number of kibbutzim (three religious and one secular) in the years preceding Israel's independence and of bitter fighting and massacres in 1948,[21] the area loomed large not only in biblical history but in Israeli memory as well. After 1967, the children of the victims of the 1948 massacre – now adults and demobilized soldiers – returned, and Yeshivat Har Etzion was established in abandoned Jordanian army barracks in Kfar Etzion.[22] It was through Rav Amital's four decades of leadership of Yeshivat Har Etzion, soon to become a flagship institution of Religious Zionism and a counterweight to the dominance of Yeshivat Merkaz HaRav, that he made his greatest mark.

## BUILDING AN INNOVATIVE INSTITUTION

Early on, Rav Amital told his students at Yeshivat Har Etzion that while intensive and rigorous Torah study was the heart of their enterprise, the yeshiva would also remain attentive to the outside world and especially to the needs of the Jewish people. As was his wont, he conveyed this by means of a story:

> When the first group of students came to the yeshiva, they asked me, "What's special about this yeshiva?" I told them the hasidic story about the Baal HaTanya, who was sitting and studying in the inner room of the house. His grandson, the *Tzemaḥ Tzedek*, sat in the middle room. In the outer room there was a baby in a cradle.

---

21. These included the massacre of the *Lamed Heh*, thirty-five soldiers on their way to reinforce the defenders of Gush Etzion, and culminated in the massacre of the vastly outnumbered residents and defenders of Gush Etzion after their surrender on the day before Israel's declaration of statehood.
22. The yeshiva moved in 1970 to a nearby site and founded the town of Alon Shevut.

> The baby suddenly awoke from his sleep and began to cry. The *Tzemaḥ Tzedek* was so immersed in his study that he did not hear the baby crying, but the Baal HaTanya, whose room was further away, did hear. He stopped learning and emerged from the room to calm the baby. On his way back, he passed the room where the *Tzemaḥ Tzedek* sat and told him, "When a person studies Torah and does not hear a cry for help, something is deficient in his learning."[23]

In an interview years later, he elaborated:

> Every generation has its own cry, sometimes open, sometimes hidden; sometimes the baby himself doesn't know that he's crying, and hence we have to try to be attentive to the hidden cries as well.[24]

Related to this, as well as to his appreciation of the new historical reality presented by the State of Israel, was his articulation of *hesder* as an ideal. Even within the Religious Zionist world, many yeshivas regarded military service with ambivalence and preferred that their students not serve at all. Rav Amital declared that the IDF is not the Czarist army, but rather something that had not been seen since the time of R. Akiva: a Jewish army. He further cited the talmudic passage: "For a yeshiva, there is none better than an old man (*zakein*); for war, there is none better than a young man (*baḥur*)."[25] If so, the term *"yeshiva baḥur"* would seem to be an oxymoron; one should speak only of a *zekan yeshiva* (elder of the yeshiva) or *baḥur milḥama* (young man of war). As opposed to those who viewed *hesder* as second best, an option for those who aren't studious, Rav Amital stated that, in light of the teaching of the Gemara, only *hesder* students are worthy of the title *yeshiva baḥur*.[26]

---

23. "Lishmo'a Kol Bikhyo shel Tinok," *Alon Shevut Bogrim* 1 (5754): 83.
24. This interview was conducted for a film marking Rav Amital's eightieth birthday. Portions of the interview can be viewed online: "A Tribute to Rav Yehuda Amital," http://www.youtube.com/watch?v=JPxq_p8L-MM (the above quote is at 12:40).
25. Ḥagiga 14a.
26. Rabbi Yoel Bin-Nun, "Ma Zeh Baḥur Yeshiva?" in Ziegler and Gafni, *LeOvdekha BeEmet*, 33–37.

## Torah and Humanity in a Time of Rebirth

This declaration had deeper roots in Rav Amital's philosophy. Torah, he insisted, is not meant to cut one off from life and desensitize a person to his historical and social surroundings, but rather to guide him in engaging his milieu and uplifting it. It can be said that not only did he advocate "*hesder lekhatehilla*" – the union of army and yeshiva study not as a concession, but as the preferable option from the start – he also advocated "life *lekhatehilla*," an engagement of the world by the student of Torah. This approach may seem obvious to many today, but at the time it was bold and surprising. The yeshivas viewed themselves as "Noah's ark." Parents, especially in the Religious Zionist world, feared sending their sons to yeshiva, lest they remove themselves from life, ignore the surrounding world, and remain in yeshiva forever. Rav Amital believed that the Torah is a Torah of life, and that it is meant to be lived and not to remove one from the world.[27] This relates to his belief in naturalness, which will be explored later, as well as to his belief – articulated as early as the 1950s – that especially after the Shoah, we should strive to follow a *lekhatehilla* path in all our activities.[28]

While some yeshivas were headed by figures who served mainly as spiritual guides, administrators, and fundraisers, Rav Amital viewed the foremost task of a Rosh Yeshiva as delivering in-depth lectures on Talmud and halakha, and especially the weekly *shiur kelali* to the entire student body. His talmudic methodology reflected his capacious personality, synthesizing a foundation of Lithuanian-style analysis with traditional *lomdus*, grounded in wide-ranging *bekiyut* (erudition), and mixing conceptual analysis with more harmonistic interpretation and very close reading of texts, as well as a classic Hungarian approach to grasping the *sugya* (subject under study) as a whole. His conceptualization

---

27. Rabbi Uziel Friedlich, "Hayim Lekhatehila," in Ziegler and Gafni, *LeOvdekha BeEmet*, 65–68; see also Rabbi Aharon Lichtenstein, "Ahi, Ahi," in *LeOvdekha BeEmet*, 247–49.
28. The context of this declaration is noteworthy. When some parents complained that his father-in-law's yeshiva in Rehovot accepted too many students of Sephardic background, Rav Amital replied that the equal treatment and admission of Sephardic students (uncommon in those days) was not a concession but *lekhatehilla*, that in Israel after the Shoah everything should be done *lekhatehilla*, and that great things would come of the yeshiva's Sephardic students. Many indeed did go on to become distinguished figures in Israeli public life; see the tribute by Rav Amital's student Prof. Moshe Bar-Asher, the president of the Academy of the Hebrew Language (Ziegler and Gafni, *LeOvdekha BeEmet*, esp. 286–87).

was thus guided by fidelity to the text and to straightforward thinking, never becoming overly abstract. His scholarship was enriched by great erudition, both in the responsa literature and in the writings of latter-day halakhic decisors and commentators – the former reflecting his aforementioned belief in the necessity of linking Torah to life, and the latter reflecting his deep sense of tradition. Especially noteworthy was his willingness, inherited from Rav Kook, to incorporate theological ideas into talmudic and halakhic discussions.

As a *posek*, he was called upon to answer not only conventional questions, but to deal with many issues arising for the first time in military, state, and societal contexts. His approach to *pesak* was characteristically non-doctrinaire, but rather attentive to the factual and moral specifics of each situation, within a framework of overall commitment to halakha, to the Jewish people, and to basic ethical and spiritual principles.[29]

Rav Amital made clear to his students that he was there to challenge and be challenged, that he expected his students to forge their own religious paths, and that he had no intention of creating "little Amitals."[30] He invited discussion, dissent, and independent thought, decrying the frequently authoritarian spirituality of the yeshiva world and declaring to his students that he was "not a hasidic rebbe" who would make their decisions for them. He was, though, richly charismatic, a warm and fatherly presence to his students, and possessed of exuberant humor and joie de vivre.

Rav Amital imparted lessons not just through his teachings but, even more powerfully, through his actions. In 1968, in a mix of humility and self-confidence practically unheard of in yeshiva circles (and most elsewhere too), he invited Rabbi Aharon Lichtenstein, an outstanding talmudist at New York's Yeshiva University (and holder of a doctorate in English

---

29. For a brief survey of Rav Amital as talmudist and halakhist, see the articles in *LeOvdekha BeEmet* by Rabbis Mosheh Lichtenstein, Shmuel David, Yosef Zvi Rimon, Shmuel Reiner, Yitzhak Brand, and Yoel Bin-Nun. A full study of Rav Amital's *pesak*, drawing on the many *teshuvot* and writings contained in the Torah journals of Yeshivat Har Etzion over the decades, is a worthy desideratum, as is an oral history of the many military commanders and public officials with whom he came into contact over the years.

30. For more on the quest for authenticity, see the next section of this essay.

literature), nine years his junior and different from him in most every way, to head the yeshiva in his place, offering to serve beneath the newcomer as *mashgiaḥ*, spiritual tutor. Rabbi Lichtenstein accepted in 1971 – on the condition that Rav Amital continue alongside him as co-head of the yeshiva.

The harmonious and deeply respectful collaboration of such wildly different figures – an astonishing partnership that spanned nearly four decades – was perhaps the most powerful lesson their yeshiva ever imparted. The two shared not only ardent religious and moral commitments, but the conviction, rare in the yeshiva world, that it was their job not only to transmit the tradition, but to teach their students to think for themselves. By bringing in a Rosh Yeshiva so different from himself, Rav Amital ensured that his students would learn to see the merits of differing positions, and to think broadly and with complexity. This is also the reason he declared that although the writings of Chabad, Rabbi Nachman of Breslov, and Rav Kook would be taught in his yeshiva, they would not be taught by "hasidim" of these approaches, since the latter tended to believe that their way is the exclusive truth and all other approaches are less legitimate.

Upon nearing eighty, Rav Amital proved his unconventionality once again, announcing his intention to step aside and letting a search committee appoint his successor before his retirement. In the end, two rabbis were needed to replace him, and they served alongside him until his full retirement in 2008. In a yeshiva world regularly wracked by bitter succession struggles, often waged among sons and sons-in-law, this was truly a final instance of "his sober and realistic vision,"[31] as well as one last, resounding lesson for his students in the moral power of humility.

## HUMANITY, NATURALNESS, AND MORALITY

Two fundamental principles in Rav Amital's approach are humanity (*enoshiyut*), and the striving for truth and authenticity. In a sense, these are two sides of the same coin. In elaborating the principles of his religious-educational outlook in his book *Jewish Values in a Changing World*, Rav Amital points to four dimensions of what he means by *enoshiyut*:[32]

---

31. Reichner, *By Faith Alone*, 316.
32. The original Hebrew title of this work translates as *And the Earth He Has Given to Humanity*, which points to the centrality of *enoshiyut* in Rav Amital's religious, educational, and moral worldview.

(a) "The worship of God, in whatever form, cannot wipe out simple human feeling."[33] As an example, he cites the obligation of a *kohen* to defile himself and mourn for close relatives, despite his calling to serve in the Temple.[34] Even Aaron the High Priest, who was not permitted to desist from his service, received Moses' approval when he asserted that he still mourned his sons in his heart (Lev. 10:16–20).

(b) *Enoshiyut* further entails the recognition of fundamental human traits – human weakness and frailty prominently among them. This applies even to great individuals and extends to our revered canonical figures, as we find them depicted both by the Tanakh and by the sages:

> There has been a tendency in recent years to idealize great rabbis, to the point of total disregard of their human feelings and weaknesses. The Torah presents the opposite approach: Every person has a human side, which must not be denied. Even the prophets had doubts and difficulties. The Torah recognizes that man lives in this world, and has no expectation that he behave as if he were living in an ideal and unreal universe.[35]

(c) A further dimension is accepting the inevitability of prosaic motivations in our ethical and religious lives. In turn, this means that we cannot expect widespread adoption of asceticism and detached equanimity.[36]

---

33. *Jewish Values*, 193.
34. See Zevaḥim 100a.
35. *Jewish Values*, 195.
36. This realism extended to many realms, including prayer. Despite his high estimation of the power of prayer, he also taught that there is value even to rote prayer, and that *kavana* (intention) is elusive. He liked to recount that when the students of the Baal Shem Tov asked him how they could know whether a certain person was a true *tzaddik* or a charlatan, the Besht answered, "Ask him whether he has a *segula* against foreign thoughts intruding on prayer. If he says yes, you can be sure he is a charlatan." Nevertheless, even though Rav Amital opposed *segulot*, shortcuts, and magical solutions, he advocated the hasidic technique of "raising" foreign thoughts: "You must translate the problem which occupies your thoughts into the language of

(d) A final expression is the assertion in the *piyut* recited on Yom Kippur, *Asher Eimatekha*, that God longs precisely for the prayers not of angels, but of human beings, with all their weaknesses and limitations. In this vein, Rav Amital frequently cited the Kotzker Rebbe's comment on the verse, "And you shall be to Me holy people" (Ex. 22:30) – God, as it were, is saying, "Angels I have in sufficient quantity; I seek *human beings* who will be holy *people*."

This set of ideas is connected to another in that same volume – the importance of "naturalness" in the life of mitzvot. Rav Amital's favorite song was "and purify our hearts to serve You in truth." In explaining this prayer, he writes:

> A person's performance of mitzvot should correspond to his internal state of loving God, fearing Him, and seeking His closeness. There should be no disproportion between the quantity of his actions and his internal values.[37]

The acceptance of human frailty does not dictate sufficing with low levels of spiritual achievement; rather, it means that one should not deceive oneself about one's level and should make sure that actions (especially stringencies, *ḥumrot*) are consonant with inner levels of spirituality.[38] Inauthentic forms of *ḥitzoniyut* (externality), he said, are akin to writing checks without sufficient funds to cover them.

---

prayer. Whether you are thinking about business or family or anything else, God is certainly able to help you in solving the problem. Don't banish this 'foreign thought' from your mind; on the contrary – keep it with you, and turn that very thought into a prayer" (*Jewish Values*, 127).

37. Ibid., 88.
38. "I was once asked by one of my students why I do not observe a particular stringency, which the *Mishna Berura* recommends that a God-fearing person should practice. I replied, 'When you read a section in the *Mishna Berura* that is directed at a "God-fearing person," you are convinced that he is referring to you. I have no such presumptions.' It should also be noted that the *Mishna Berura* says that it befits one who fears Heaven to practice stringency, but he does not say that such stringency leads a person to fear of Heaven!" (Ibid., 94).

A further consequence of naturalness is the avoidance of "religious anxiety." On the one hand, the human ideal according to Judaism is not, as in some Eastern teachings, the attainment of tranquility, but rather perpetual aspiration, activity, and growth. Yet, on the other hand, excessive tension and anxiety in the worship of God is abnormal and counterproductive, often leading to paralysis.[39] Fear of God should be natural, like fear of one's parents.[40] Similarly, prayer should be natural, a "conversation" with God.[41] What is natural is not necessarily holy, but what is holy should be natural.

Thus, throughout Rav Amital's teachings one finds fundamentally positive outlooks on the world and on people as they are. He not only sees value in the naturalness emerging from the human tapestry, but sees it as a source, a quarry, for values and norms in and of themselves.

It is natural, then, that Rav Amital's views on *enoshiyut* affirm natural morality. This stance is of a piece with a central theme in the teachings of Rav Kook. A well-known passage in Rav Kook's *Orot HaKodesh* states:

> Piety must not displace man's natural morality, for such piety is impure. The sign of pure piety is when natural morality, implanted in man's naturally just nature, ascends at piety's direction to greater heights than it would otherwise have attained.[42]

Rav Kook wrote this around 1910 – and indeed the biblical verse cited perhaps most often in his writings in that time is "God has made man upright, but they sought many reckonings" (Eccl. 7:29). In those years Rav Kook was striving to make sense of the flood of thoughts and feelings – regularly contradictory – sweeping over his generation and himself. In this effort, the idea of the fundamental goodness of God's creation and humanity's God-given nature emerged for him both as a means of making sense of the fundamental rightness of the moral

---

39. Ibid., 107–13.
40. Ibid., 14–15.
41. This follows from the rabbinic interpretation of Gen. 24:63, according to which *lasuaḥ basade* refers to prayer, from the root s-y-ḥ, meaning "to converse" (Berakhot 26b).
42. *Orot HaKodesh* 3:11, p. 27; *Shemona Kevatzim* 1:75.

intuitions of his time and as an assertion of faith that, indeed, "the earth is full of His glory" (Is. 6:3), or, in the classic words of the Zohar, "There is no space that is empty of Him."[43] This recognition, in turn, yields a fundamentally positive outlook toward the natural world, the body, and human sentiments, which, in Maimonidean philosophy as understood by Rav Kook, are the bridge between the physical body and the ethereal mind.[44] As a result, the role of natural morality, of fundamental human moral intuitions, as a vital foundation for divine ethics is rooted in the very structure, physical and metaphysical, of the world.

A related idea with roots in the teachings of Rav Kook and the *Dor Revi'i*, and with antecedents going back to the Maharal,[45] is the need to fulfill ethical obligations out of desire and not merely due to a command. This speaks not only to motivation, but also to the scope of ethical demands. Many moral duties are not mentioned explicitly in the Torah but are nevertheless obligatory. Nahmanides famously wrote that since the Torah could not possibly spell out every contingency, it established general directives such as "You shall be holy" and "You shall do the right and the good."[46] Rav Kook, however, offers a different reason: Many moral duties are not included in formal halakha because the individual and the nation should perform them out of inner desire and as an expression of *ḥesed*.[47] The animating ideal of moral self-cultivation is thus to keep Torah as the Patriarchs kept it – out of inner cognition, not command. Ethics is a natural capacity of the soul and not merely a derivative of halakha.[48]

---

43. *Tikkunei Zohar* 57, p. 91b.
44. For a lengthier discussion of the roots of Rav Kook's mature thought on these matters, see Yehudah Mirsky, *An Intellectual and Spiritual Biography of Rabbi Avraham Yitzhaq Ha-Cohen Kook from 1865 to 1904* (PhD diss., Harvard University, 2007), esp. chs. 3–4.
45. *Gur Arye* to Ex. 20:21, cited in *Jewish Values*, 47–48.
46. Nahmanides to Lev. 19:2.
47. See *Iggerot HaRe'aya*, vol. 1, no. 89, 92–101.
48. See Rav Amital's seminal essay, "The Ethical Foundations of Rav Kook's Nationalist Views," trans. Bernard Caspar and Reuven Ziegler, *Alei Etzion* 2 (5755): esp. 22–27; *Jewish Values*, 95–106. See also Moshe Maya, *A World Built, Destroyed and Rebuilt: Rabbi Yehudah Amital's Confrontation with the Memory of the Holocaust*, trans. Kaeren

Thus, *enoshiyut*, as conceptualized and put into practice by Rav Amital, cuts deeper and reaches farther than good counsel and pedagogy. It is a theological assertion about God's goodness, reflected in the goodness of creation, and, above all, in human beings. The affirmation of *enoshiyut* is, in other words, an affirmation of faith.

Moreover, one can perhaps read this affirmation as the closest one can come to a post-Holocaust theology – not as a matter of post-Holocaust theodicy (an enterprise Rav Amital rejected as an insult to the memory of the victims), but rather as a way of asserting the faith that remains after the Holocaust. In response to the *Shoah*, we must heighten our sense of natural morality, a morality that reflects faith. To go on believing in God is to believe in the fundamental goodness of creation, irrational or a-rational as that may be – which is to say, to believe in *enoshiyut*.

Yet Rav Amital's belief in humanity is not that of secular humanism, some resemblances and points of contact notwithstanding. Secular humanism attempts to enshrine human dignity without recourse to God. This attempt may be said to have run entirely and desperately aground in the Holocaust. Once again, Rav Amital resolutely opposed any attempt to "explain" the Holocaust by way of one theological formula or other, be it that of Satmar or of Rabbi Zvi Yehuda Kook.[49] To the contrary,

---

Fish (Jersey City, 2004), 121–29, and the valuable discussion in Alan Brill, "Worlds Destroyed, Worlds Rebuilt: The Religious Thought of Rabbi Yehudah Amital," *The Edah Journal* 5, no. 2 (2006): esp. 4–9.

49. The proximity of two overwhelming events – the Holocaust, in which six million Jews were systematically murdered, and the birth of the State of Israel, in which Jewish sovereignty was restored in the Land of Israel following nearly two thousand years of exile – almost begged one to connect them. At the extremes, some saw the connection in terms of strict causality. For example, the Satmar Rebbe believed that the Holocaust was a divine punishment for the sin of attempting to establish Jewish sovereignty before the coming of the Messiah, and the success of the Zionists in establishing the State of Israel was to be attributed to the *sitra aḥara*, the metaphysical forces of evil; see Rabbi Yoel Teitelbaum, *VaYoel Moshe*, 2nd ed. (New York, 1961), 122–25. At the opposite end, Rabbi Zvi Yehuda Kook believed that the Holocaust was divine "surgery" necessary to sever the Jews' connection to the Diaspora and bring them to the Land of Israel as part of an inexorable process of national revival and messianic redemption; see Rabbi Zvi Yehuda Kook, *Siḥot HaRav Zvi Yehuda al HaMo'adim*, ed. Rabbi Shlomo Aviner (Jerusalem, 2006), 2:230–49; in English, see *Torat Eretz Yisrael: The Teachings of HaRav Tzvi Yehuda HaCohen Kook*, ed. Rabbi

the Holocaust placed an eternal question mark over any claims that one could read God's mind. Yet this epistemological humility, this religious submission before the unknowable, accompanied by acceptance of God's ethical charge and spiritual demands on us, is precisely that which can give us the strength and guidance to go on living after the Holocaust. By contrast, humanism, lacking such a foundation, cannot endure, its good intentions notwithstanding.

Thus, Rav Amital's ethics were not a function of the procrustean bed of one abstract theory or other; they emerged from his fundamental humanity, intuition, and existential stance. While avoiding the extreme dialectical tendencies of Rav Kook or Rabbi Joseph B. Soloveitchik, he embraced complexity as a reflection of reality. Though he often expressed his ideas with profound conviction and primal, prophetic force, he sought to engage a wide range of experiences and people, in all their complexity, exaltations, and tragedies. His profound *enoshiyut* was intertwined with his search for authenticity, leading him to embrace people who strove for truth – his students above all.

## COMMUNITY AND COMMITMENT

Rav Amital's striving for truth was far from solipsistic, but rather anchored in deep interpersonal commitment, which stood at the base of his educational argument with the neo-hasidic trends of the 1990s and early twenty-first century. Rav Amital was ahead of his time in introducing these currents – *devekut* (cleaving to God), joyous worship, fraternity – into Religious Zionist education, and ahead of his time in grasping their excesses.[50]

It is worth noting that his own interpretation of hasidic teachings – about *devekut*, the raising of sparks, and *avoda begashmiyut* (worship through corporeality) – was removed from mysticism, magic, and

---

David Samson (Jerusalem, 1991), 259–74. For penetrating discussions of both, as well as other thinkers in these veins, see Aviezer Ravitzky, *Messianism, Zionism, and Jewish Religious Radicalism*, trans. Jonathan Chipman (Chicago, 1996), and the numerous studies of Orthodox responses to the Holocaust by Prof. Gershon Greenberg.

50. Regarding his dispute with neo-Hasidism, see his *Between Religious Experience and Religious Commitment: Five Addresses on Youth in Crisis*, ed. Reuven Ziegler (Alon Shevut, 5763). These essays can be found on the website referenced above in n. 1.

personality cult, and rather conveyed as events occurring within dialogic frameworks between people, and between them and God. He once remarked to a student that he diminished his study of Kabbala when he realized that it often espoused a mechanical approach to the influence of man's actions on the upper realms.[51]

Although he acknowledged that neo-Hasidism expressed a legitimate critique of the dryness of much contemporary religiosity and that it was driven by a desire for authenticity, he also felt that it manifested several problems: too much emotion and too little reason, impatience in seeking results, and turning to wonder-working. Most seriously, he felt that it often devolved into a form of spiritual thrill-seeking that ignored the needs of society and lacked a firm commitment to mitzvot.[52] Rav Amital's own understanding of Polish Hasidism was that it advocated individualism only *after* immersion in community and that it did not forfeit intellect in the quest for experience. Rav Amital wanted to cultivate the individual, but only within the context of commitment to the community and with reason ascendant.[53]

Rav Amital's grounding in reality made him acutely sensitive to all forms of self-deception, including escapist mysticism. Religious experience is only occasional and can often be artificial and external. He objected to forms of religiosity that remove one from reality, constricting life and closing one to the world and to broader society. Although halakha untethered from reality can become "autistic" and lead to widespread alienation among religious youth,[54] the solution is not to be found

---

51. Rabbi Elyakim Krumbein, "HaHitraḥashut HaRuḥanit SheBiVrakhot," *Alon Shevut* 160 (5762): 132n5.
52. His educational disagreement with Religious Zionist neo-Hasidism is in a sense rooted in differing inheritances – that of Polish Hasidism à la Przysucha-Kotzk-Izbica-Gur, for whom the encounter between the lone individual and God is at the center; and that of Maimonides and Rabbi Moshe Ḥayim Luzzato (Ramḥal), as mediated by Rav Avraham Yitzhak Kook, for whom the search for *devekut* must always entail deep communal and societal responsibility, without which *devekut* simply cannot take place.
53. See Brill, "Worlds Destroyed," 11–13. Two additional influences on contemporary neo-Hasidism are Breslov and New Age, but a discussion of their interplay with other influences lies beyond the scope of this article.
54. "*Lo HaKol Halakha*," *Alon Shevut Bogrim* 13 (5759): esp. 97–98.

*Torah and Humanity in a Time of Rebirth*

in self-absorbed enthusiasm that is, to his mind, equally disconnected from reality.

In this context and in others, Rav Amital frequently quoted a lost midrash cited in the introduction to the *Ein Yaakov*, according to which the Torah's most encompassing principle, the cornerstone of Judaism, is neither *Shema Yisrael* nor "You shall love your neighbor as yourself," but rather, "You shall bring one lamb in the morning and one lamb in the evening" (Num. 28:4). The daily sacrifice, the routine of commandments, normal life: these – rather than peak experiences – are the foundations of religious existence.

This emphasis on daily sacrifice introduces one of his best-known aphorisms: *ein patentim* – there are no shortcuts, no tricks, and no magic solutions in religious existence, in education, or in any other area of life. There is just hard work and commitment to slow, gradual improvement. He decried what he called *akhshavism*, the desire to attain everything immediately: "Peace Now," "*Mashiaḥ* Now," and so on. Nothing is that simple: change is a process, issues are multifaceted, and reality can be recalcitrant. He had nothing but disdain for quick, easy, black-and-white solutions to complex problems.

Yet, although he emphasized the importance of routine and of incremental change, he nevertheless sought and found the poetry within the prose, the beauty and freshness that suffuse Torah study and observance of mitzvot.

## ISRAEL, THE *SHOAH*, AND UNDERSTANDING HISTORY

Rav Amital's attitude to the State of Israel rests on two foundations of his thought. The first is the ethical: Jewish nationalism has a universalistic moral orientation. Maimonides writes that Abraham's goal was "to found a nation that would know God and serve Him."[55] This goal derives from Abraham's trait of *ḥesed*, from the desire to do good to all, for this nation would convey to mankind "the way of God, to do righteousness and justice" (Gen. 18:19). However, explains Rav Kook, in order to redeem humanity from its suffering, it is necessary for this nation to possess a state and all the accoutrements of government and

---

55. *Guide of the Perplexed* III:51.

culture. The Jewish polity will thereby demonstrate that not only pious individuals, but whole nations as well, can live by the light of the divine idea. Rav Kook feared that were the Zionist idea to be divorced from a universal moral purpose, it would lead to moral breakdown and to reliance solely on strength. Even on those occasions (later in life) when his realism prevented him from making such a high-flown assessment of the State of Israel, Rav Amital viewed the state as a vehicle for sanctifying God's name in the world; hence his sensitivity to anything involving the state that smacked of ḥillul Hashem, desecration of God's name.

A second foundation of Rav Amital's philosophy is the need for perspective and proportion, especially with regard to the realms of values and history.[56] Regarding historical perspective, he marveled at what he had witnessed:

> My beard has not turned white with age, and yet during the course of my life I have seen, as our sages have said, "a world built, destroyed, and rebuilt."[57] I have seen Jews being led to Auschwitz; I have seen Jews dance at the establishment of the State of Israel; I have seen the great victories of the Six-Day War; I have traveled with soldiers to the Suez Canal. I have lived through an epoch, in the shortest span of time. It is hard to believe that in such a short lifetime one could witness so many changes.[58]

This perspective offers insight into the famous words of the prophet:

> "Old men and old women shall yet again dwell in the streets of Jerusalem, and every man with his staff in his hand because of his old age; and the streets of the city shall be full of boys and girls playing in its streets" (Zech. 8:4–5). This describes simple, normal life. Only someone with a deep historical awareness can

---

56. We will discuss below the question of proportion and perspective regarding values in the context of his views on *Eretz Yisrael*.
57. *Midrash Lekaḥ Tov* to Gen. 6:9 uses this phrase in connection with Noah.
58. "Forty Years Later: A Personal Recollection," appendix to *A World Built*, 139–40. (This talk was given in 1985.)

understand the significance of such a scene. Miracles are one-time events. But Jews living a normal life in *Eretz Yisrael* after seventy years [of the Babylonian exile] during which the country was empty and desolate – someone looking with historical perspective can only be astonished. Of him the prophet says, "If it will be wondrous in the eyes of the remnant of this nation in those days, it will also be wondrous in My eyes, says the Lord of hosts" (v. 6).... After two thousand years, children play in the streets of Israel and old people sit in the squares of Jerusalem! Can this be a natural phenomenon?[59]

As one who was a "remnant of this nation," Rav Amital tried to convey to his students the enormity and wonder of seeing old people and children living a normal life in the streets of Jerusalem. While a historical perspective on the sweep of Jewish history highlighted the enormity of apparently small things, it also put seemingly large obstacles and problems into proper proportion, calming his students' fears and giving them hope.

Rav Amital's senses of ethics and of perspective, combined with a Kookian reading of the workings of divine providence within history, led to sensitivity to the charge of the hour:

> Today, the State of Israel stands at the focal point of world history. It is clear that we are living in a period of great change and, as such, it demands of us great deeds. It necessitates sacrifice; it hungers for creativity; it requires accomplishment; it compels us to take action.

---

59. "This Day God Has Made – Let Us Rejoice and Be Glad in It" (Yom HaAtzma'ut 1994), http://etzion.org.il/en/topics/yom-haatzmaut; reprinted in *The Koren Maḥzor for Yom HaAtzma'ut and Yom Yerushalayim* (Jerusalem, 2015), 111–20. It is worth noting that one of Rav Amital's educational innovations was his insistence that Tanakh be studied in the beit midrash, as an integral part of the yeshiva's course of study. This was due to a number of factors, not least among them the fact that he saw a biblical dimension to his own times. In his writing and speaking, he regularly expressed himself in simple biblical cadences, to stunning effect.

> From day to day, from year to year, changes take place. To live in such a period, to really and truly live it; to see and understand the dynamics and intensity of Jewish history as it unfolds before us; to gaze upon the great events – upon each one, in and of itself, and upon all of them combined – while we maintain the correct perspective, knowing that it is just a part of the whole; to sense the process of redemption as it unfolds before our very eyes; to know our responsibility in this world, at this time and in this place; to perceive what it is that God demands of us, here and now – all this creates a grave responsibility which one can neither escape nor ignore.[60]

The attempt to discern and interpret God's hand in history has deep roots in the thought of Rav Avraham Yitzhak Kook.[61] It exerted a strong impact on Rav Amital, as it did on many other Religious Zionist thinkers:

> A Jew who believes that events touching on the life of *Am Yisrael* are guided by divine providence will naturally inquire as to their meaning and significance. The Torah and the prophets command us unceasingly to pay attention. It is also a natural intellectual inquiry for one based in faith. If events pass one by without one attempting to penetrate the depth of their true meaning, the sages consider such a person dead. "A wicked person is considered dead even during his lifetime, since he sees the sun rise but does not recite the blessing 'who creates the lights'; he sees it setting, but does not recite the blessing 'who brings evenings'" (*Tanhuma, VeZot HaBerakha* 12). Clearly, we do not have the tools to know the secrets of God and to know the considerations,

---

60. "Forty Years Later," 140.
61. See, for example, *Iggerot HaRe'aya*, vol. 2, no. 737, p. 334: "We are a nation that knows the letters in the Book of God...like the book of Creation and the history of the world and of mankind; we also know how to read – through select individuals and their light that lives among us – that blurred script of the causes of these events.... In our heart of hearts there is not the slightest doubt concerning the wondrous precision of the Supreme Wisdom in the processes of the evolution of history."

motives, and intentions of divine providence, "for My thoughts are not your thoughts" (Is. 55:8). However, this does not exempt us from our obligation to observe and to delve. It is Torah, and we must study it.[62]

For Rav Kook, the hand of God revealed within history, and especially within the Zionist enterprise, pointed in the direction of "the revealed end." Influenced by Rav Kook and by his own experience of ascending from the pit of the *Shoah* to the birth of an independent Jewish state, Rav Amital also saw current events in light of redemption.

The Six-Day War of 1967 elicited in Israelis, and especially in Religious Zionists, not only euphoria, but also a sense of the biblical magnitude of the victory and a feeling of messianic imminence. But this was followed by the tragedy of the Yom Kippur War of 1973. Eight students of Yeshivat Har Etzion fell in battle, and Rav Amital was torn between personal anguish and the need to strengthen and give hope to his students, as well as to understand the meaning of this seeming reversal in the process of redemption. His grief and his commitment to his students found expression in action, as he took a hiatus from his duties as Rosh Yeshiva and spent months visiting military bases, field hospitals, and outposts.[63]

His theological response to the war appeared in a slim volume, *HaMaalot MiMaamakim* (The Ascents from the Depths), which became a chief theological text of the settler movement due to its argument that Israel's triumphs and travails are both part of the process of redemption. His redemptive reading of events was darkened, but unshaken. The fact that the war had almost resulted in a US-Soviet nuclear confrontation was further proof that Israel was at the center of God's inscrutable plan for world history. At the same time, he noted, the war called for new

---

62. "LeMashma'utah shel Milḥemet Yom HaKippurim," in Rav Amital, *HaMaalot MiMaamakim*, 11.
63. Regarding Rav Amital's actions and reactions in this period, see Rabbi Aharon Lichtenstein, "Mishan UMivtaḥ LaShakulim," in Ziegler and Gafni, *LeOvdekha BeEmet*, 331–36, and "Azut VeAnava," *Daf Kesher* 1316 (*Parashat Devarim* 5772): 2–4, http://etzion.org.il/he/download/file/fid/7127.

introspection, and the Holocaust was, as ever, a standing caution against too confident a reading of God's workings in history.

"It is clear that we are in the process of redemption through the path of suffering," he wrote, adding that "this obligates us in the mitzva of crying out, of introspection, of contemplating our actions, so that we know that God awaits our repentance."[64] Rather than point a finger outward, he said, the soul-searching must begin within the yeshivas themselves, and especially as regards ethics: "The necessary conclusion is to search for identity with no preconceptions. Not 'who is a Jew?' but 'what is a Jew?'… to ask questions bravely, with the bravery of the battlefield."[65]

The war quickened the messianic energies of the settler movement, which crystallized into *Gush Emunim* (the Bloc of the Faithful), many of whose leaders and activists had been Rav Amital's early students at Har Etzion. *HaMaalot MiMaamakim*, by framing the disastrous Yom Kippur War in eschatological terms, seemed to offer a way forward from the despair of the war, onto the hilltops of Judea and Samaria.

And yet, sympathetic though he was to the settlement movement and to *Gush Emunim*, Rav Amital never actually joined the latter, arguing that while his Zionism was "redemptive," it was not meant to be "messianic." The distinction was subtle at first, but became clearer over time. What was certainly clear was his refusal to accept the authority of *Gush Emunim*'s unchallenged leader, Rabbi Zvi Yehuda Kook (who had succeeded his father as head of Merkaz HaRav), because of what Rav Amital perceived as Rabbi Zvi Yehuda's prioritizing of the Land of Israel above almost every other religious value, draining his father's teachings of their universalistic elements, and his functioning as a spiritual and halakhic authority when it came to politics – a realm, in Rav Amital's view, where things are meant to be decided not by charisma or halakhic writ, but through deliberation and debate.

One of the strongest points of disagreement between Rabbi Zvi Yehuda Kook and Rav Amital concerned the understanding of history. While both of them discerned a redemptive process at work in the founding of the State of Israel and in the Six-Day War, Rabbi Zvi Yehuda also

---

64. "*LeMashma'utah shel Milḥemet Yom HaKippurim*," 13.
65. "*Al Tira Yisrael Ki Itekha Ani*," in *HaMaalot MiMaamakim*, 39.

saw the Holocaust as part of God's plan, at last excising Israel from exile and bringing about the creation of the state. Rav Amital refused to view those horrors the same way.

The Holocaust certainly deepened Rav Amital's sense of awe at the times through which he was living. While the *Shoah* did not shake his faith in God, it eventually came to place an unanswerable question mark on any attempt to read His mind. Rav Amital steadfastly refused to interpret the *Shoah* as part of any divine plan, let alone as justification for anything, even for the Jewish state. But he also did not attribute the Holocaust to *hester panim*, the "hiding of [God's] face."

> I clearly experienced the hand of God during the Holocaust – only I did not understand its meaning. It was so clear – so abnormal, so unnatural, so illogical. I was not in Auschwitz, but I saw Jews being taken there. I saw regiments of Germans who were not going to the Russian front, but rather guarding the trainloads of Jews headed to the death camps. It went against all military logic and interests. Can one possibly begin to understand such madness? I saw the hand of God in everything. It was not natural; it was not human. I saw the hand of God, but I did not understand its significance.[66]

Moshe Maya, author of an important monograph on Rav Amital's perspective on the Holocaust, writes that Rav Amital came to realize that our inability to understand the meaning of such an overwhelming event undermines our ability to understand God's communication through history in general.[67] Even when we perceive God's hand acting in history, this does not mean that we can understand His plan. Therefore, beginning in the 1980s, Rav Amital began to retreat from a redemptive interpretation of Zionist history. Rav Avraham Yitzhak Kook and others before him had spoken of "the beginning of the flowering of our redemption," he said, but even R. Akiva – the greatest of *Tanna'im*, and someone with a profound understanding of the intricacies of Jewish

---

66. "Forty Years Later," 138–39.
67. Maya, *A World Built*, 36–45.

history (as indicated by the famous story in Makkot 24a–b) – had been mistaken when he declared Bar Kokhba to be the messiah.[68] Rav Kook never had to grapple with the *Shoah*.

But even as Rav Amital diminished his talk of the redemptive dimension of the State of Israel, he highlighted the sheer value of Jewish sovereignty, of Jews ruling themselves and having a homeland. He frequently cited Maimonides' introduction to the laws of Ḥanukka, which emphasizes that the events of that festival are worthy of celebration because "Jewish sovereignty was restored for over two hundred years."[69] Sovereignty itself was significant even though many members of the Hasmonean dynasty were unworthy – and all the more so is self-determination valuable when it serves as a basis for morality practiced at a national scale.[70]

While Moshe Maya understands Rav Amital's retreat from a redemptive understanding of history as a delayed reaction to the *Shoah*, perhaps precipitated by the tragedy of the Yom Kippur War, Rabbi Elyakim Krumbein suggests a different factor. It is not so much that Rav Amital changed his position on redemptive history; rather, the moral valence of this position changed over time such that he could no longer identify with it. Immediately after the *Shoah*, a redemptive reading of the birth of Israel gave the Jewish people hope that they had not been abandoned by God. The return of Jewish sovereignty after two thousand years was a massive sanctification of God's name after the inconceivable desecration of His name brought about by the *Shoah*. Seeing God's hand in the creation of the state was both heroic for the survivors, as well as therapeutic. However, for the next generation, raised in dramatically easier conditions, belief in "the beginning of redemption" was

---

68. "Sing to Him, Praise Him, Speak of All His Wonders" (1996), trans. Kaeren Fish, http://etzion.org.il/en/topics/yom-haatzmaut. Rav Amital relies here on Maimonides' understanding of R. Akiva's attitude to Bar Kokhba (*Mishneh Torah, Laws of Kings* 11:3).
69. *Mishneh Torah, Laws of Ḥanukka* 3:1.
70. See, for example, "What is the Meaning of *Reishit Tzemiḥat Geulatenu*?" trans. Kaeren Fish, *Tradition* 39, no. 3 (2006): 7–14; "The Religious Significance of the State of Israel," trans. David Silverberg and Reuven Ziegler, *Alei Etzion* 14 (5766): 9–19. Both articles can also be found at http://etzion.org.il/en/topics/yom-yerushalayim.

comfortable and undemanding. They could maintain the illusion of an idyll by ignoring the *Shoah*, explaining that it was part of pre-redemptive reality or was necessary for redemption to come. Rav Amital refused to countenance all those who claimed to condone, explain, or understand the *Shoah*, for he insisted that *avodat Hashem* (divine service) flow from human morality and integrity, and that these reflect the ways of divine providence.[71] Thus, the moral cost of the certainty of redemption was now too high, and it was perhaps the moral criterion more than the actual historical-theological question that forced Rav Amital to abandon his certainty of redemption.[72]

## DIVINE SERVICE AND JEWISH IDENTITY AFTER THE *SHOAH*

Confronting the *Shoah* affected Rav Amital's thinking in a number of other areas as well, some of them very fundamental, such as the foundations of divine service and the halakhic attitude to those who lack belief in God.

Regarding the former, Rabbeinu Bahya ibn Pekuda, in his *Duties of the Heart*, developed the notion that service of God is based on gratitude to Him. Despite the moral and religious importance of the quality of gratitude, asked Rav Amital, can it still serve as the basis of *avodat Hashem* after the Holocaust?

---

71. Hence his impatience with facile assumptions about *reishit tzemihat geulatenu*, which so easily forgives inhumanity because it supposedly brought (or bought) redemption.

72. Rabbi Elyakim Krumbein, "HaEnoshiyut BeMaavakah im HaShoah," in *Ma Ahavti Toratekha: MiToratah UmiDarkah shel Yeshivat Har Etzion BiMelot Mem Heh Shanim LeHivasdah*, ed. Shaul Barth, Yitzhak Recanati, and Reuven Ziegler (Alon Shevut, 2014), 283–301. As Rav Amital once put it, with characteristic verve, "Nothing in the world can justify the hundreds of thousands of children who were killed, burned, nothing in the world – not the State of Israel, not the Messiah, not all the Jewish people doing *teshuva*, nothing in the world...and yet Jews have faith" (viewable in the video mentioned above, n. 24, at 3:20). A substantial discussion of Rav Amital's views appeared shortly after the present essay was completed; see Motti Inbari, *Messianic Religious Zionism Confronts Israeli Territorial Compromises* (Cambridge, United Kingdom, 2012), 72–80; see also, briefly, Yehudah Mirsky, *Rav Kook: Mystic in an Age of Revolution* (New Haven, CT, 2014), 229.

> On my first Yom Kippur after being liberated from a Nazi labor camp, I prayed with other survivors in a cramped cellar. I cannot fully describe the storm of emotion that I felt then, but I will try to reconstruct some of that feeling.
>
> I was young then. I had no children. My parents had been murdered, along with most of the population of our town. Among the survivors in that small room, there were people who had lost their children, parents, spouses, and siblings. They prayed, and I with them. Was their worship of God based on gratitude? Can a Jew who has lost his wife and children possibly serve God on the basis of recognition of His kindness? Can a Jew whose job was the removal of the charred remains of corpses from the crematoria of Auschwitz be capable of serving God on the basis of gratitude? No, not in any way, shape, or form! But where, then, does that leave us?[73]

Rav Amital cites the talmudic statement that in the wake of the destruction of the Temple, Jeremiah and Daniel could no longer address God as "awesome" and "mighty," for "since they knew that God is truthful, they would not lie to Him."[74] The Jerusalem Talmud words this even more strongly: "Since they knew God is truthful, they would not fawningly flatter Him."[75] Divine service, Rav Amital concludes, "must be built on truth, not on falsehood or fawning flattery (ḥanifa)." Hence, "within the era that saw the greatest destruction in the history of the Jewish people, it is impossible to base our divine worship" on the foundation of gratitude alone:

> Of course, we must always remain aware of God's daily acts of kindness, and must sincerely pray, "We are grateful to You".... But, while gratitude should certainly constitute one component

---

73. "Confronting the Holocaust as a Religious and a Historical Phenomenon," appendix to Maya, *A World Built*, 146; also at http://etzion.org.il/en/topics/jewish-tragedy.
74. Yoma 69b.
75. Y. Megilla 3:7.

of our divine service, it cannot serve as the entire foundation of our worship.[76]

Rav Amital finds an alternative path of divine service at the end of Rabbenu Baḥya's *Duties of the Heart*, one based not on gratitude but on love and faith, as expressed by the verse, "Even if He kills me, I will still trust in Him" (Job 13:15),[77] and in the talmudic passage, "'A bundle of myrrh (*tzeror hamor*) is my beloved to me, and he will sleep between my breasts' (Song 1:13) – our sages said, by way of derivation: Though He constricts and embitters me (*meitzer li umeimer li*), He will sleep between my breasts."[78] "In the wake of the *Shoah*," asks Rav Amital, "to whom can we still flee? To where can we flee? The answer is clear: 'We have fled from You to You.'" He concludes:

> The verse "Were Your Torah not my delight, I would have perished in my misery" (Ps. 119:92) has a broader meaning. *Knesset Yisrael* wonders, "How could I ever have persevered without God?" How can anyone survive without God? Without God, one simply could not cope with all the problems besetting him. It is not in spite of undergoing a test of this magnitude, but rather because of it, that we need our faith in order to survive.[79]

Rav Amital likewise asserts that both the *Shoah* and the widespread secularization of the modern era compel a reassessment of our attitude toward Jews who do not accept the Torah.[80] He concedes that in principle halakha's approach toward those who violate it is harsh (though this is often more a matter of principle than practice). However, before applying the sages' harsh statements regarding sinners and heretics to

---

76. "Confronting the Holocaust as a Religious and a Historical Phenomenon," 147–148.
77. See *Duties of the Heart* 10:1.
78. Shabbat 88b.
79. "Confronting the Holocaust as a Religious and a Historical Phenomenon," 149.
80. See esp. "A Torah Perspective on the Status of Secular Jews Today," trans. Moshe Kohn, *Tradition* 23, no. 4 (1988): 1–13; reprinted in *Alei Etzion* 2 (5755): 29–45; see also "Rebuking a Fellow Jew: Theory and Practice," trans. Michael Berger, *Alei Etzion* 2 (5755): 47–64; *Jewish Values*, 173–89.

secular Jews today, we must ask ourselves if those pronouncements are still pertinent in light of our vastly different circumstances. He marshals halakhic sources to distinguish between deniers and skeptics, and argues that according to contemporary epistemology, disbelief is not warranted and skepticism is the most that is possible. More powerfully, he says that after the Holocaust, we cannot blame people for having difficulty with faith. If the Ḥazon Ish and Rav Kook spoke before the *Shoah* of secularists as being "coerced" by the zeitgeist, what are we to say after?

However, although he was a disciple of Rav Kook, Rav Amital was not satisfied with finding categories by which to understand contemporary secularists, whether by classifying them as wicked, as "coerced innocents," as "whole in their *nefesh* but lacking in their *ruaḥ*," or any other category.[81] Rather, as in so many other areas, he sought a natural and human connection to them.[82] He offers four considerations for loving even those who are not observant, despite the fact that halakha seems to mandate love only for "your brother in mitzvot."

First, "the mere fact that so many Jews have forsaken God calls for a more lenient attitude to them and a special effort to find their good points and plead in their defense."[83] Second, in the past, people who were suspect of Shabbat desecration were also suspect of immorality; today, many irreligious people have high ethical standards.[84] Third, just

---

81. See, respectively, "Al Bamoteinu Ḥalalim," in *Maamarei HaRe'aya*, 1:89–93; *Iggerot HaRe'aya*, vol. 1, no. 138, p. 171; *Orot*, 84.
82. Indeed, over the years he developed warm friendships with a number of leading Israeli thinkers and educators outside the ambit of Orthodoxy, such as Eliezer Schweid and Zvi Zameret, with literary figures such as Abba Kovner and Ḥayim Gouri, as well as with less-known secular Jews and the many secular military commanders with whom he came in contact. He also had mutually respectful relationships with a number of leading political figures, most notably Yitzhak Rabin.
83. "A Torah Perspective on the Status of Secular Jews Today," 42–43.
84. For this reason, Rav Amital objected to the idea of *ahavat ḥinnam*:

> After the assassination of the prime minister [Yitzhak Rabin], we hear many people quoting Rav Kook *zt"l*, who said that just as the Second Temple was destroyed because of *sinat ḥinam*, baseless hatred (Yoma 9b), so will the Third Temple be built because of *ahavat ḥinam*, baseless love. But why call it *ahavat ḥinam*? Are there not many others – yes, even among the non-religious – who have earned our love? There are many dedicated members of our society who

as anti-Semitism is directed at Jews today not because of their beliefs but because of their identity, so too should we love any Jew, regardless of beliefs or practices: "In Auschwitz, they did not check people's tzitzit before sending them to the gas chambers; should we check tzitzit before regarding someone as a brother?"[85] Finally, the State of Israel is a haven for Jews, a *kiddush Hashem* and a gift from God; if we want it to survive, all Jews have to treat each other as brothers: "The State of Israel is not going to endure if cordial relations do not prevail between all sectors of the nation.... Otherwise, we live under a threat of destruction."[86] While Rav Amital cites halakhic and aggadic sources to support many arguments in his essay, he highlights the natural sense of fraternity and the value of straightforward thinking by concluding:

> I do not have to adduce any source texts to support these latter two considerations. Concerning such instances, the sages have already said,[87] "Why do I need a quotation from Scripture? It stands to reason."[88]

## POLITICAL INVOLVEMENT

Alone among the thinkers discussed in this volume, Rav Amital was also a participant in national politics and state affairs, although it must be admitted that his involvement, as befitting his personality (though not his role as the head of a party), was more educational than political. His political positions, although surprising to many in the Religious Zionist community and even to many of his students, actually flowed from his educational and ideological guidelines as set forth above.

---

certainly fall into that category: members of the security services who vigilantly protect us, boys who give three years to the army, doctors who work for meager wages rather than seek their fortunes overseas, and many others. If someone does not share our religious commitment, it does not mean he has no values, and it does not mean that he has no just claim to our love. ("On the Assassination of Prime Minister Rabin," *Alei Etzion* 4 [5756]: 16)

85. *Jewish Values*, 188.
86. "A Torah Perspective on the Status of Secular Jews Today," 45.
87. Ketubot 22a.
88. "A Torah Perspective on the Status of Secular Jews Today," 45.

> As long as I feel that I am able to say something that will be to the benefit of the Torah, to the benefit of *Am Yisrael* or of *Eretz Yisrael*, I will not refrain from speaking out. As long as I believe that I am able to diminish the desecration of God's name, to increase the glory of Heaven, to bring individuals closer, to save Jews from bloodshed, or to save something of *Eretz Yisrael* – I have not refrained from speaking out, for I too was taught that one must listen to the sound of a baby's cry.[89]

Before reluctantly entering the political fray, his political involvement began with public pronouncements widely reported in the press. He posited that there is a hierarchy in the scale of Jewish values, with the proper order being: the People of Israel, the Torah of Israel, and the Land of Israel: "Anyone who fails to distinguish *bein kodesh lekodesh* (between one level of holiness and another) will end up unable to distinguish *bein kodesh leḥol* (between the holy and the profane)."[90] Thus, despite his great love for and attachment to the Land of Israel, he regarded it as subordinate to the first two values. This statement had educational significance, but its operative conclusion was that if lives could be saved and the state preserved, parts of the land could be sacrificed.

> The importance of *Eretz Yisrael* is not dependent on any outline of its borders, but rather in its being a platform for sovereignty, for kingship, for a state – a platform for the realization of the personality of the individual and of the collective. Our people's destiny is to be "a light to the nations" (Is. 49:6), not as singular individuals, but as a "singular nation" (Deut. 7:6). Beyond the day-to-day social, economic, and military problems, we must be an ethical example, a moral example. *Eretz Yisrael* is meant to be the land of an exemplary Jewish society.[91]

In 1982, his anguish over his students again going to war flared into outrage with his discovery, first, of Ariel Sharon's lying to the government

---

89. "Lishmo'a Kol Bekhyo shel Tinok," *Alon Shevut Bogrim* 1 (5754): 83.
90. "Meser Politi o Meser Ḥinnukhi," *Alon Shevut* 100 (5743): 42.
91. "Am Yisrael Lifnei Eretz Yisrael," *Sevivot* 22 (5749).

about the war's aims and prosecution – Rav Amital publicly opposed the IDF's assault on Beirut – and then the IDF's inaction in face of the massacres at Sabra and Shatila. He issued a public statement:

> We now stand four days before Yom Kippur. My entire being quakes and trembles out of fear for the Day of Judgment, for, as is known, Yom Kippur does not atone for the sin of the desecration of God's name.

He and Rabbi Lichtenstein, along with Rabbi Joseph B. Soloveitchik in America, were practically the only rabbis to call for the inquiry that eventually arose as the Kahan Commission. Although Religious Zionists, especially the rabbinic establishment dominated by the school of Merkaz HaRav, increasingly viewed Rav Amital as a renegade, he could not remain silent in the face of what he saw as a desecration of God's name:

> I believe that we merited a Jewish state only because of God's desire to sanctify His name in the aftermath of the terrible desecration of His name during the Holocaust. The establishment of the state and its victories in war against the Arab armies that rose up against it constitute a response of sanctification of God's name. Precisely for this reason, the obligation to sanctify God's name has special significance in our time for those of us who live in the State of Israel, the entire establishment of which stemmed from this principle. This is why, on various occasions over the years, I have felt obligated to protest against instances of the desecration of God's name. This was the only cause for which I felt a need to speak out publicly.[92]

While Rav Amital's move from the right to the left perplexed many, his close associates countered that the same mix of prophetic intuition and lucid realism that had led him up to then was still guiding him. His universalistic vision and hierarchy of values, they asserted, had been consistent throughout; now, his sensitivity to a changing social

---

92. *Jewish Values*, 155.

and historical reality had dictated new practical conclusions.[93] The explanations for this shift have been many, reflecting his multifaceted and non-doctrinaire character: his discomfort at the Religious Zionist community's coming to be seen as forbiddingly monolithic; its increasing disconnection from Israeli society and its growing inclination to support the use of force; his deep grief at the loss of his students in combat and his hope that future wars could be avoided; and more. His shift also expressed a deep moral sense that without a bona fide attempt to make peace – with the painful sacrifices that would entail – Israel would not only run the risk of further war, but also do an injustice to Arab populations, also created in God's image, and thus disfigure their own *tzelem Elokim*.

On the left he was as unconventional, unpredictable, and free of clichés as he had been on the right. In December 1982, he addressed the founding meeting of *Netivot Shalom*, a religious peace movement, and inveighed against what he said were the three false messianisms stalking the land – *Gush Emunim*, Peace Now, and Ariel Sharon. All, he said, presume to solve complex questions with simple answers – faith, good intentions, and force, respectively. None by itself provides the answer. We need all three, he said, and the wisdom of balance.

In 1985, at a conference marking Rav Kook's fiftieth *yahrzeit*, he laid out the theological foundations of his position. Like Rav Kook's, Rav Amital's Zionism was not a response to anti-Semitism:

> It is not [the Jewish people's] terrible suffering that is the source of its longing for redemption, but rather its striving to do good to mankind, for this is the essence of its soul.[94]

This, from a Holocaust survivor, was astounding. Promoting a universal ethical vision must be of the essence of Zionism, he said, not only to save it from the moral hazards of violent chauvinism, but precisely because the ethical message is itself the divine word that Israel is

---

93. See the thorough analysis of Rabbi Daniel Tropper, "*Mishnato HaTzibburit shel HaRav Amital*," in Ziegler and Gafni, *LeOvdekha BeEmet*, 273–84.
94. "The Ethical Foundations of Rav Kook's Nationalist Views," 19.

charged with spreading in the world. As he later explained in an interview, the difference between his conception and Ben-Gurion's vision of Israel as "a light unto the nations" was that, to his mind, without a divine foundation, ethical universalism will not survive.[95]

In 1988, at the urging of supporters, Rav Amital founded a party, Meimad, offering a centrist religious voice on both political-diplomatic issues and relations between religious and secular Israelis. Everything that made the party appealing to well-wishers and observers – its non-dogmatic stance, the manifest absence of political ambitions on the part of its leaders, its mix of religious conviction with political liberalism – made it an electoral disaster in the rough-and-tumble of Israeli politics, and it failed to receive even one Knesset seat. Rav Amital returned to his yeshiva and abandoned political life – until late 1995 when, in the wake of the Rabin assassination, he was asked to join Shimon Peres' short-lived government as a minister without portfolio.[96] This he did, hoping that his presence would ease, even a little, the terrible fissures then rocking Israeli society and ease the desecration of God's name wrought by the *kippa*-wearing assassin. He pursued various initiatives in public health, education, Israel-Diaspora relations, and the ever-elusive goal of fostering dialogue within Israeli society. When the Peres administration was over, he returned to Yeshivat Har Etzion. His leftward moves cost him many supporters, and his natural role as the premier leader of Religious Zionism. But he was at peace with the course he had taken.

## THE RIGHTEOUS MAN WILL LIVE BY HIS FAITH

The essential faith and piety of Rav Amital's Hungarian childhood never left him. Many of the questions bedeviling and thus defining modern Jewish thought simply did not preoccupy him. God's existence and providence, the divine origin of the Written and Oral Torah, the binding

---

95. See the interview with him published as "*Am Yisrael Lifnei Eretz Yisrael*" in *Sevivot* 22 (1989): 6–14. (*Sevivot* was the journal of Midreshet Sdeh Boker.) The interview is worth reading in full for its focused exposition of Rav Amital's ideas on a number of crucial issues.
96. Shimon Peres explained, "Every government needs inspiration. I believe that Rav Amital provides the inspiration necessary to maintain the nation's unity, diversity, and internal dialogue" (Reichner, *By Faith Alone*, 269).

power of rabbinic tradition and law, and the Jews' unique role and destiny were all for him simply axiomatic. It was perhaps this unaffected, almost guileless faith and deep identification with what he called "simple Jews" that freed him to embrace complexity, even as he expressed his ideas with powerful conviction.

A deep sense of God's presence, expressed so powerfully in his natural and flowing prayer, led him to discern God's hand not only in the restoration of Jewish sovereignty after two thousand years, but also in the unfathomable depths of the Holocaust. Yet the absolute human inability to fathom the meaning of the Holocaust ultimately led him to a position of epistemic humility. Another part of his response to the Holocaust was, almost paradoxically, redoubled commitment to a universalistic ethics. Rav Amital, following Rav Kook, saw "natural morality," an innate sense of justice and mercy, as the very foundation of religious life. If after the Holocaust one can no longer believe in humanism, our acting on our ethical impulses is the deepest assertion of faith, if not in man, then in God and His world. Thus, a central category for him, and one which he said motivated many of his more controversial stances, was *ḥillul Hashem*, the need to avoid the desecration of God's name and, conversely, to instantiate God in this world through Torah and especially its social message – ethics.

It was this twinned commitment to epistemic humility and to ethics that drove the deepest wedge between Rav Amital and *Gush Emunim* and therefore disqualified him for leadership in the eyes of some members of his own Religious Zionist community. Yet it was these same qualities, along with his deep piety, scholarship, and charisma, that acquired for him many devoted students who brought his message and values to all corners of Israeli society and even to many communities in the Diaspora. Perhaps the deepest impact that the Holocaust made on him was to engender and fortify his sense of personal mission, the burden of fulfilling the dreams and hopes of his many peers who did not survive – a sense that, as he testified, gave him the strength and drive to initiate, to lead, and to accomplish things beyond his natural abilities.[97]

---

97. "A Sense of Mission" (1995), http://etzion.org.il/en/sense-mission. For Rav Amital's last public reflections on the Holocaust, see the interview with him conducted by Yair Sheleg, "BeInyan HaShoah Ani Omed Bifnei Kir," *Eretz Aḥeret* 50 (March–April 2009): 46–48.

Alan Brill, a scholar of Modern Orthodoxy and of contemporary religiosity, summarizes Rav Amital's contribution as follows:

> No other Modern Orthodox theologian in our age has written with the emotion, imagination, and depth of character that Rav Amital has. His writings are a complex body of ingrained reactions, memories, hopes, and visions. He has had less influence in the United States than in Israel, primarily because his Modern Orthodoxy consists of state-building, army service, the creation of a liberal democracy, and the writings of Rav Kook combined with Torah study. It also does not tackle the American concerns of secular studies, particularism, ritualism, suburbanization, and professionalism. Rav Amital's thought is particularly valuable in our world of education, textuality, and programmatic ideologies, for it allows us to return to a natural sense of morals, piety, and sovereignty.[98]

Indeed, Rav Amital did not leave behind him a system or set of doctrines, but rather a cluster of powerful, provocative ideas, and an example from which we can learn as we each go about building our moral and spiritual lives.[99]

---

98. Brill, "Worlds Destroyed," 18–19.
99. Parts of this essay are excerpted from Yehudah Mirsky, "The Audacity of Faith," *The Jewish Review of Books* 2, no. 3 (Fall 2011): 29–31, as well as from the authors' essays in *LeOvdekha BeEmet*. We thank the publishers for their permission to use the material.

# Rabbi Dr. Norman Lamm on the Role of Talmud Torah in a Torah Umadda Framework

## Rabbi Dr. David Shatz

In 1966, Rabbi Norman Lamm, then serving in the pulpit of the Jewish Center in New York City, earned his doctorate in Jewish philosophy from the Bernard Revel Graduate School of Jewish Studies at Yeshiva University. His dissertation carries a unique distinction: it was the only doctoral thesis ever sponsored by Rabbi Joseph B. Soloveitchik (known as the Rav). The subject was one infinitely precious to the Rav, and utterly central to his life and thought. In particular, the work explored the concept of *talmud Torah*, focusing on the notion of *Torah lishmah* (Torah for Torah's sake) in the writings of Rabbi Ḥayim of Volozhin (1749–1821), one of the most illustrious disciples of the Vilna Gaon (1720–97).

The topic of the dissertation and the fact that the Rav agreed to sponsor it reveals a great deal about Rabbi Lamm, and not just that the Rav held him in high esteem. On the one hand, Rabbi Lamm's writings on *Torah Umadda*, especially his book of that name, are widely known for advocating the study of *madda* (defined by the book's subtitle as "worldly knowledge") and integrating such study with the learning and teaching of Torah.[1] On the other hand, for all that Rabbi Lamm vigorously advocates secular education, Torah study for him – as he repeats countless times – has axiological primacy; that is, it is the highest of Judaism's values: "Torah remains the unchallenged and preeminent center of our lives, our community, our value system."[2] As Ḥazal teach, "*vetalmud Torah keneged kullam*" – the study of Torah outweighs all other mitzvot.[3] Although Ḥazal say "*keneged kullam*" about several mitzvot, "clearly Torah study has the greatest place of eminence in the hierarchy of Jewish values."[4] Indeed, Rabbi Ḥayim of Volozhin understands the statement "*vetalmud Torah keneged kullam*" to mean that Torah study is "the entity from which all others radiate" and "the origin of all mitzvot."[5]

In a sermon that he delivered on Shavuot in 1956, Rabbi Lamm points to Ḥazal's understanding of the phrase "*peloni almoni*," the biblical equivalent of "John Doe," which the Bible uses to designate the anonymous character in the Book of Ruth with whom Boaz conducts critical business during the book's climax. The sages say that the man was called "*almoni*" because he was "*illem bedivrei Torah*," mute as regards Torah.[6] Rabbi Lamm homiletically develops this comment into a symbolic statement

---

1. Originally published by Jason Aronson in 1990, *Torah Umadda: The Encounter of Religious Learning and Worldly Knowledge in the Jewish Tradition* was republished in 2011 by Maggid Books and Yeshiva University Press with a new preface, as well as a review by Rabbi Lord Jonathan Sacks originally published in *L'Eylah* in 1990. Page references to *Torah Umadda* refer to the 2011 edition. Notwithstanding the phrase "worldly knowledge" in the subtitle, Rabbi Lamm discusses other definitions of *madda*, such as Maimonides' term *ḥokhma* (wisdom) and "worldly wisdom." See *Torah Umadda*, 8–12.
2. Norman Lamm, *Seventy Faces: Articles of Faith* (Hoboken, NJ, 2002), 1:46. This book is a collection of essays and addresses spanning many years.
3. Shabbat 127a; see also Mishna Pe'ah 1:1.
4. "Knowing vs. Learning: Which Takes Precedence?," in *Wisdom from All My Teachers: Challenges and Initiatives in Traditional Jewish Education*, ed. Jeffrey Saks (Jerusalem, 2003), 15n1. In that footnote, Rabbi Lamm avers that even Ḥasidim agreed with this view.
5. Ibid. See *Nefesh HaḤayyim* 4:29.
6. Ruth Rabba 7:7.

that a Jew's very identity depends on having Torah – so that, if a person is *illem bedivrei Torah*, speechless about Torah, then he or she lacks an identity, and hence a name. That individual can be called only *"peloni almoni."*[7]

The centrality of Torah study in Judaism[8] does not conflict with the ideal of *Torah Umadda*, because "centrality is not the same as exclusivity. It does not imply the rejection of all other forms or sources of knowledge."[9] Nonetheless,

> for *Torah Umadda* to be religiously meaningful, it is imperative that Torah be acknowledged as possessing central value and primacy over all else. Only when such centrality is affirmed does the enterprise of *Torah Umadda* become pregnant with meaning and the promise of sanctity. Writing of the righteous, the psalmist says (Ps. 92:14), "Those who are planted in the house of God shall flourish in the courts of our God." Indeed, only if one is firmly planted within, in the inner precincts of Torah, will he or she spiritually flourish in the outer courtyards of *madda* as well.[10]

As his works on *Torah lishmah* indicate – his dissertation, his 1972 book in Hebrew based on it, the 1989 English edition of the book, and additional articles – Rabbi Lamm believes that not only must we study Torah, and not only should we analyze the requirement halakhically, but we should develop a theory, a philosophy, of what we are doing when we study. Torah study is, in short, a vibrant subject for philosophical analysis and exploration.[11]

---

7. Norman Lamm, "The Torah's Mystery Man," in *Festivals of Faith: Reflections on the Jewish Holidays*, ed. David Shatz, associate ed. Simon Posner (New York, 2011), 303–8. Of course, as noted, the interpretation is homiletic (after all, many nefarious biblical characters are identified by name), but it nicely encapsulates Rabbi Lamm's axiology.
8. Generally, I will be using the term *talmud Torah* to include both the study and the teaching of Torah, even though Rabbi Lamm's work on Rabbi Ḥayim of Volozhin deals with study. He discusses the teaching of Torah in many of his addresses on education and on the rabbinate.
9. Lamm, *Seventy Faces*, 1:46.
10. Lamm, *Torah Umadda*, 171–72.
11. Rabbi Lamm's major Hebrew book on *talmud Torah* is *Torah Lishmah BeMishnat Rabbi Ḥayim MiVolozhin UVMaḥashevet HaDor* (Jerusalem, 1972); the English edition

By the term "*talmud Torah,*" Rabbi Lamm of course often means talmudic or halakhic learning and teaching. But his concept of *talmud Torah* is capacious and broad, and his oeuvre accordingly includes a treasure house of halakhic discourses, reflections on the Bible and methods of studying it, analyses of kabbalistic and philosophical texts in the framework of scholarly articles, and more.[12] In fact, he notes that ironically the very authors who affirm the privileged status of halakha draw from non-halakhic works like *Nefesh HaḤayyim* and the Rav's *Ish HaHalakha* (*Halakhic Man*) in order to establish their thesis! This, he argues, refutes their own pan-halakhism, the thesis that law is all there is to Judaism.[13] His stress on *talmud Torah* does not mean that Judaism is a purely intellectualist religion. Rabbi Lamm devotes much attention to the emotional and experiential demands that Judaism imposes, and recognizes the costs of excessive intellectualism.[14]

No less than his writings and speeches, Rabbi Lamm's actions as president of Yeshiva University vividly reflect his commitment to Torah study and teaching. During his administration, he quickly established a variety of *kollelim*, appointed numerous new Rashei Yeshiva to endowed chairs, and in his first year as president introduced Talmud study for women, with the Rav giving the first *shiur*. Funding was

 is *Torah Lishmah: Torah for Torah's Sake in the Works of Rabbi Hayyim of Volozhin and His Contemporaries* (New York, 1989). Rabbi Lamm devotes a halakhic essay to numerous issues in the mitzva of *talmud Torah*. See "*Iyyun BeMitzvat Talmud Torah,*" in *Halakhot VaHalikhot* (Jerusalem, 1990), 53–67. See also *Torah Umadda*, ch. 3.
12. As we shall see later, Rabbi Lamm posits a hierarchy of texts. On method in Bible study, see Rabbi Lamm's essay, "How to Read the Torah," in *Mitokh Ha-Ohel*, ed. Daniel Z. Feldman and Stuart W. Halpern (Jerusalem, 2010), 3–10 (adapted from a 1971 sermon).
13. See Norman Lamm, "Notes of an Unrepentant *Darshan,*" in Lamm, *Seventy Faces*, 2:94–107.
14. Many of Rabbi Lamm's sermons call for a particular emotional and experiential orientation. Rabbi Lamm says that Judaism's response to the intellect versus emotion question is "not either/or, but both/and." He leaves it up to the individual which to make primary. See the Shabbat *Shuva* discourse (1975), "Heart and Mind," http://brussels.mc.yu.edu/gsdl/collect/lammserm/index/assoc/HASH0144/7bee5808.dir/doc.pdf. On the dangers of excessive intellectualism, see, for example, "Be Not Overwise: The Haggadah's Third Son in a New Light" (1964), in Lamm, *Festivals of Faith*, 228–32.

provided to publish *sefarim* by Rashei Yeshiva, student-edited volumes of essays by teachers and students thrived, and new prizes were instituted for students who excelled in Torah scholarship. Rabbi Lamm continued the tradition of his predecessor, Rabbi Dr. Samuel Belkin, in delivering an annual Talmud *shiur* to rabbinic alumni, along with many other *shiurim*. He also has published numerous halakhic articles (twenty-seven of which are collected in his *Halakhot VaHalikhot*, discussed below). His commitment to *talmud Torah*, then, is hardly theoretical; his actions as president spoke as loudly as his words. At the same time, he dramatically enhanced the integration of Torah and *madda* by founding the Torah Umadda Project, convening the annual Orthodox Forum, and crafting countless speeches and many writings that articulate the ideology, including the capstone book already referenced.

How, though, in Rabbi Lamm's outlook, does *talmud Torah* relate to general culture? There is more to the answer than the familiar proposition that *madda* study enhances understanding of Torah, although that is a part of it. Rabbi Lamm's linkages between Torah study and teaching, and *madda* are numerous and varied. For example, as we will see, not only do the substance of Torah and the substance of *madda* impact upon each other, but a *philosophy* of *talmud Torah* impacts upon a *philosophy* of university study. The present essay does not discuss at length Rabbi Lamm's rationales for *Torah Umadda*, nor his analyses of *talmud Torah* per se. Rather, it addresses where *talmud Torah*, both study and teaching, fits into his *Torah Umadda* framework.

## TORAH SPEAKS TO THE MODERN WORLD

Rabbi Lamm was born in 1927. After graduating Mesivta Torah Vodaath in 1944, he continued to learn at the yeshiva each day until 3:00 PM, at which point he would, in his words, "wander through" the library of his grandfather, Rabbi Yehoshua Baumol, where he would "learn...the wonders of responsa literature."[15] He spent a period learning with Rabbi

---

15. "There Is Only One Yeshiva College: A Memoir," in *My Yeshiva College: 75 Years of Memories*, ed. Menachem Butler and Zev Nagel (New York, 2006), 220. Much of this paragraph is based on that brief autobiographical essay.

Baumol, while reading at night Freud, Adler, Schopenhauer, Meade, and Durant. Then, with his grandfather's approbation, he entered Yeshiva College at the age of eighteen, a decision that met with disapproval from some in his former yeshiva. He then began "a lifelong romance" with Yeshiva University's ideal,[16] which in those days was known as "synthesis" or integration.[17] He became a top student of the Rav, majored in chemistry, and graduated as valedictorian of his class in 1949. Torn between accepting a four-year scholarship in chemistry at the Hebrew University and entering the rabbinate, Rabbi Lamm followed the counsel of Dr. Belkin to do the latter, though he did pursue graduate work in chemistry at Brooklyn Polytechnic Institute. After receiving *semikha* from the Rabbi Isaac Elchanan Theological Seminary (RIETS), he took a position as assistant rabbi to Rabbi Dr. Joseph Lookstein at Congregation Kehilath Jeshurun in New York City in 1951. In 1954, he was named rabbi of Kodimah Congregation in Springfield, Massachusetts, and in 1958 he came to the Jewish Center, one of the most prominent American synagogues, serving with the senior rabbi, Rabbi Dr. Leo Jung. He remained in the Jewish Center pulpit for eighteen years before assuming the presidency of Yeshiva University.

Rabbi Lamm's twenty-seven-year tenure as president was remarkably lengthy for a university leader. Upon assuming the position, he also succeeded Dr. Belkin as Rosh HaYeshiva of RIETS. One extraordinary feature of his presidency was that his scholarly productivity continued unabated even while he held the major office in American Orthodox life and in that capacity was called upon to generate innumerable speeches and writings on matters of institutional and communal policy. He remained Rosh HaYeshiva after leaving the presidency and becoming chancellor of the university. He retired from the university in 2013.

During his twenty-five years in the rabbinate and beyond, Rabbi Lamm acquired a worldwide reputation as a fabulous *darshan*, a speaker who combined linguistic artistry, homiletic imagination, philosophical depth, and inspirational power, along with a magnificent delivery. In

---

16. See Lamm, *Torah Umadda*, xii.
17. Dr. Bernard Revel called it "harmony." See Will Lee, "Revel's Harmony: Both 'The Yeshiva' and 'Yeshiva College,'" in Butler and Nagel, *My Yeshiva College*, 68–75.

all, he preached approximately eight hundred sermons. In the sermons, we encounter one mode of interaction between Torah and the world at large.[18] Very simply, for Rabbi Lamm, Torah has something to say to the world, and one of the principal benefits of a secular education is the acquisition of a language that can articulate its message.

Thus, in a 1966 address to the Orthodox Union, "The Voice of Torah in the Battle of Ideas,"[19] Rabbi Lamm stresses that Torah must be made relevant to Jews. This does not mean compromising the validity of halakha, but it does entail expressing Judaism's teachings in "the problematica and vocabulary of modern man." In a 1969 essay, he asserts in a similar vein:

> It is our *religious* duty, our *sacred* responsibility, to live the whole Torah tradition in the world, instead of retreating.... We must engage the world right now and, speaking in a cultural idiom it understands, say that we are dissatisfied with it.... We must speak about covenant and halakhic living.[20]

Effective sermons are excellent examples of the sort of communication that Rabbi Lamm calls for. They illustrate, moreover, an important facet of Rabbi Lamm's approach to studying and teaching Torah: an insistence on appreciating and developing *derush* – an often deprecated genre – as a legitimate and in fact vital means of interpreting and imparting Torah. Feebly translated as "homiletics," *derush* is an exciting, imaginative, inspirational mode of expounding a traditional text, one that, usually going considerably beyond what the text actually states, relates to people of the *darshan's* time and place and yet often carries

---

18. The sermons, along with some eulogies and speeches, are available on the website of the Yeshiva University library, at http://brussels.mc.yu.edu/gsdl/cgi-bin/library.exe?site=localhost&a=p&p=about&c=lammserm. The project was conceived by Pearl Berger, dean of libraries at Yeshiva University. There are now two collections of the sermons in print: *Festivals of Faith* (cited in n. 7 above) and the *Derashot LeDorot* series ed. Stuart W. Halpern (New York, 2012–2014).
19. See Lamm, *Seventy Faces*, 1:23–34.
20. "Modern Orthodoxy's Identity Crisis," in Lamm, *Seventy Faces*, 1:36.

perennial import.[21] In a widely read essay, "Notes of an Unrepentant *Darshan*,"[22] Rabbi Lamm bemoans the waning of *derush* as part of the rabbinic repertoire; halakhic discourses have taken its place. Despite the centrality of halakha in the Jewish value system and the ready availability of *peshat*-oriented elucidations of Tanakh, Rabbi Lamm argues that *derush* is an essential mode of religious expression.

Even halakhic texts may be expounded homiletically. Rabbi Lamm prefaces a sermon on the laws of Sukkot as follows:

> Moral instruction is available to Jews not only in the *Ḥummash*, not only in Aggada and Midrash, but sometimes in halakha. If we look closely and carefully enough, we will discover the grand themes of human destiny even in legal technicalities, profound human wisdom even in halakhic discourses. All it requires is imagination, a sense of allegory, some homiletic license, and a readiness to find beautiful insights in unlikely places.[23]

To a large degree, it is through the *derush* mode of expounding Torah that rabbis address and meet the challenges of their day.[24] Rabbi Lamm quotes the story of R. Shimon bar Yoḥai, who together with his son stayed in a cave twelve years learning Torah.[25] When the pair finally

---

21. Avraham Kariv laments the fact that "there is no branch of the tree of Jewish culture that the 'enlightened' among us belittle as much as *derush*." He continues, "This attitude is really a desperate blindness to a powerful source of emotional and spiritual experience in Israel, and a gross ingratitude toward those many and varied preachers who graced our people with this gift called *derush*.... *Derush* is a legitimate field of creativity in Judaism, a broad field, fruitful and thriving, as well as a powerful channel of influence upon the life of our people, vital and indispensable." See Kariv, *Shabbat UMoed BaDerush UVḤasidut* (Tel Aviv, 1966), 5. See also Pinchas Peli, "Hermeneutics in the Thought of Rabbi Soloveitchik – Medium or Message?" *Tradition* 23, no. 3 (Spring 1988): 9–31. I have used Peli's translation of the Kariv passage.
22. Lamm, *Seventy Faces*, 2:94–107 (first published in 1986).
23. "Man Is More than *Sekhakh*," in Lamm, *Festivals of Faith*, 140.
24. Some of Rabbi Soloveitchik's great works, such as *The Lonely Man of Faith*, "Confrontation," and various addresses on Zionism, are built on *derush*. See Peli, "Hermeneutics."
25. Shabbat 33b.

emerged, their eyes burned everything to cinders, until God Himself told them to return to the cave because they were destroying His world. Saying to the world "we are dissatisfied with you" is no reason to destroy it. Jews must not aspire to live in caves.[26] Of course, a collective Orthodox commitment to making Judaism relevant to modern problems makes knowledge of culture necessary.

Rabbi Lamm's arguments, then, advocate for an important component of *Torah Umadda*. In his address at the dedication of the Hebrew University in 1925, Rabbi Avraham Yitzhak HaKohen Kook proclaimed that there have been two opposite movements in Jewish history, a movement inward into the world of the yeshivas and an outward movement – engagement with the world. To use Rabbi Lamm's language, these are, respectively, the "centripetal" and the "centrifugal" movements of the sacred.[27] Judaism absorbs ideas from the outside, but, having absorbed them, it transforms the ideas and brings a new product to the outside world. In language that Rav Kook borrows from the laws of Shabbat, the integration of Judaism with the world requires both *hakhnasa* (bringing into one's domain) and *hotzaa* (exporting to another domain).[28] A Jewish renaissance requires, for Rav Kook, that "we must translate our entire holy house of treasures into the idiom of the times."[29]

It is common to associate *Torah Umadda* with absorbing ideas from the outside, but bringing ideas to the world is an integral part of the ideology as well. Accordingly, Rabbi Lamm's addresses confront the issues of their day: the dramatic expansion of science and technology; the civil rights movement; the "New Morality"; the moon landing; the Eichmann trial; the maturation of the Jewish state; Jewish-Christian dialogue; and perennially relevant themes like parenting, marriage, aging,

---

26. "Caves and Enclaves," in Lamm, *Seventy Faces* 2:163–69.
27. See "Two Versions of '*Torah Umadda*,'" in Norman Lamm, *Faith and Doubt: Studies in Traditional Jewish Thought*, 3rd Augmented Edition, (Jersey City, NJ, 2006), 73. The article was originally published in 1962 with the title "Two Versions of Synthesis," reflecting the predecessor term for *Torah Umadda*.
28. The original Hebrew of the address is found in *Maamarei HaRe'aya*, 306–8. An English translation by Shnayer Z. Leiman appeared in *Tradition* 29, no. 1 (1994): 87–92.
29. *Iggerot HaRe'aya* 2:226.

and Jewish identity, to name but a few.[30] The sermons illustrate *hotzaa*. Moreover, although framed in a modern idiom, these speeches amply illustrate as well that *Torah Umadda* involves not a blanket, uncritical embrace of *madda* but, on the contrary, a process of sorting out the good and the objectionable using Torah as a touchstone – and criticizing society accordingly.

There is unmistakable irony in the fact that the man most associated with *Torah Umadda* in our time so sharply rebuked the ideas and values of modern society. It is important to recognize, however, that whereas as president of Yeshiva University, Rabbi Lamm was responding to elements in Orthodoxy that attacked the very idea of secular education for Jews, as a rabbi he served congregations that, especially on the High Holy Days, were populated by a large number of Jews who were not observant and who were more enamored of modernity than of mitzvot. He had to inspire those Jews to lead lives of Torah learning and observance, and accordingly sought to loosen the grip of modernity and its values. The result was some strong and strenuous critiques of the modern world, crystallized in one sermon title, "The Arrogance of Modernism." He even criticized the term "Modern Orthodoxy" because it could imply that everything modern is good and worthy of our pride,[31] and he excoriated what Jacques Maritain called "chronolatry" – the worship of the new, the fascination with novelty as distinct from inner renewal.[32]

The Torah gives no date for Shavuot, Rabbi Lamm suggests, because Torah is beyond time.[33] In this spirit, Rabbi Lamm cries out in his sermons against, for example, the "New Morality" of the

---

30. Besides showing that the themes and messages of Torah are perennially resonant, Rabbi Lamm's sermons illustrate the many places from which Torah speaks. Indeed, the range of motifs and sources is remarkable. As noted in the editor's preface to *Festivals of Faith* (p. xix), of the nearly 320 sources cited in the fifty-five sermons, only eighteen appear in more than one sermon, usually for different purposes and with different interpretations. Only one quoted text appears in more than two sermons.
31. See "The Arrogance of Modernism," in Norman Lamm, *The Royal Reach: Discourses on Jewish Tradition and the World Today* (New York, 1970), 36–42.
32. See the 1965 sermon "Novelty and Renewal" at http://brussels.mc.yu.edu/gsdl/collect/lammserm/index/assoc/HASHb2b1.dir/doc.pdf.
33. Lamm, "The Arrogance of Modernism," 40.

1960s – sexual permissiveness, drugs, and pornography. Needless to say, there is no wholesale condemnation of modernity. The word "modern" "confers neither distinction nor opprobrium."[34] Rabbi Lamm's target was rather the view that "modern" *always* or *automatically* is a mark of distinction. In truth, each modern value, each phenomenon, must be considered in itself.[35]

Let's look at a specific example. Science and technology are central components of modernity and a vital part of *Torah Umadda*. It was not uncommon, however, for Orthodox thinkers in the second half of the twentieth century to advocate the pursuit of science while simultaneously bemoaning its consequences, such as depersonalization and the dominance of science in human life at the expense of religion.[36] Rabbi Lamm, too, decried not science and technology per se, but rather their excesses, which inflict psychological damage and contribute to secularization.

The criticism was at times quite sharp. Consider a sermon delivered on Shabbat Ḥazon in 1964. Ḥazal teach that "all that happened to Adam happened [as well] to Israel."[37] Rabbi Lamm applies this midrash as follows:

---

34. Ibid., 41.
35. Ibid. We have already noted that as president, Rabbi Lamm shifted focus from applying Torah to the world and criticizing aspects of modernity to the other half of *Torah Umadda*, viz., integrating general culture into a life of Torah. Even so, in his advocacy of *Torah Umadda*, he continued to recognize that modernity champions values that Judaism refuses to recognize as absolutes, or even as valid at all: "The substitution of experience for tradition as the touchstone of its worldview; a rejection of authority…; a radical individualism… and thus a preoccupation with the self; a repudiation of the past and an orientation to the future, and thus a fascination with the new…; and secularism, not as a denial of religion as much as an insistence upon its privatization…; and a rejection of particularisms of all sorts" (Lamm, *Torah Umadda*, 10). Rabbi Lamm adds that there are countercurrents to these tendencies.
36. Note, for example, the contrast between Rabbi Eliezer Berkovits' essay, "An Integrated Jewish World View," *Tradition* 5, no. 1 (Fall 1962): 5–17, which urges Jews to pursue the sciences, and his sharp criticism of science in *Crisis and Faith* (New York, 1976), 6–22. See my "Berkovits and the Priority of the Ethical," *Shofar* 31, no. 4 (Summer 2013): 87–88.
37. *Yalkut Shimoni* 11:1001.

Adam, having eaten of the Tree of Knowledge and supposedly grown more sophisticated, now flees to the cluster of trees in the midst of the Garden – and attempts to hide from God! His illegitimate grasp for knowledge has gained for him the idiotic illusion that he can set boundaries for God, keeping Him away from his own areas, and that he can erect impenetrable barriers between the domains of God and man. Adam thus invites the response of the Almighty, in syllables of searing sarcasm, "*ayyekah* – where art thou?" Adam, where do you think you are that you can hide from Me? What makes you think that you can declare any place in the world out-of-bounds for God?...

Modern man repeats the same syndrome – with even more tragic results. We have eaten of the Tree of Knowledge like no generation before us – and we have found the fruits bitter, for such is the taste of radioactive ash. We have developed science and technology at an incredible pace. Yet we have become what in Jewish literature is known as ḥakham lehareia, wise for our own hurt.... With our increase in knowledge has come a shrinkage of wisdom; with the conquest of the universe, we have discovered that we have let our own lives lie fallow; learning to make a living, we have forgotten how to live; exploring outer space, we have ignored the thunderous silence of our inner space and inner void.

For what has all this learning and sophistication led us to? To an ever stricter seclusion of God from life. Like Adam and like our ancestors two thousand years ago and more, we have determined to incarcerate God in His reverent jail and we have declared the rest of the world forbidden to Him. What is to God is to God, but all the rest is to Caesar.

What is the name of this ideology which "respects" religion so long as it does not venture out of its prescribed sphere? It is the theory and practice of secularism. Secularism is not atheism.... It accepts God – but equally as much accepts that one can hide from Him, that in some little clump of trees one can surround himself with cool shade and be free from the searing gaze of the Deity who has clumsily been permitted to escape from His House of Worship. Modern secularist man gets even with God;

once He expelled us from Paradise, now we shall build ourselves a little Paradise and keep *Him* out![38]

Torah – especially when explained in a manner accessible to "modern man" – has the power to defeat such secularization and remedy modernity's deficiencies.

Another intriguing feature of Rabbi Lamm's application of Jewish texts to modern problems, one that typifies his broad conception of Torah study and teaching, is his substantial use of kabbalistic ideas, especially hasidic ones. Rabbi Lamm's immersion in kabbalistic and hasidic texts and ideas has deep roots. His paternal grandfather was a follower of the Belzer Rebbe, and his maternal grandfather identified with the Sanzer dynasty, admiring its founder, Rabbi Ḥayim of Sanz. Rabbi Lamm's anthology-cum-commentary on Hasidism, which received a National Jewish Book Award in 2000, is dedicated in memory of the Skolier and Kozhnitzer Rebbes, in whose *shtieblakh* he prayed as a youth.[39] His adult fascination with Kabbala and Hasidism is richly evident in his philosophical writing; and, in his use of *derush*, he frequently adduces *vertlakh* (homiletic bon mots) of hasidic masters.

Kabbalistic texts, it must be noted, are parts of the *masora* that typically are used far more heavily by the Orthodox right than by the Modern Orthodox community, notwithstanding Rabbi Soloveitchik's occasional use of them.[40] In part, this asymmetry exists because a mystical worldview sits uneasily with a Modern Orthodox Jew's acceptance, or at least qualified acceptance, of a scientific outlook. Moreover, hasidic leaders, while often theologically bold, were and are fiercely critical of secular study and even Jewish philosophy. For that reason, it no doubt will surprise readers that, as we will see later,

---

38. Norman Lamm, "When We Try to Keep God in His Place," in Lamm, *Festivals of Faith*, 322–23.
39. See Norman Lamm, *The Religious Thought of Hasidism: Text and Commentary*, with contributions by Alan Brill and Shalom Carmy (New York, 1999).
40. On how Rabbi Soloveitchik used Kabbala in his writings, see Lawrence J. Kaplan, "*Motivim Kabbaliyyim BeHaguto shel HaRav Soloveitchik: Mashma'utiyyim o Itturiyyim?*," in Avi Sagi, ed., *Emuna BiZemannim Mishtannim: Al Mishnato shel HaRav Y. D. Soloveitchik* (Jerusalem, 1996), 75–86.

Rabbi Lamm recruits concepts of Hasidism in his argumentation for *Torah Umadda*. Further, Rabbi Lamm sees the themes of Kabbala and Hasidism as vital and relevant to Jewry and to humanity.[41] In this regard, he is again reminiscent of Rav Kook, who regarded Kabbala as the right idiom, imagery, and constellation of ideas with which to address his generation. Indeed, Rav Kook is the featured thinker in some of Rabbi Lamm's discussions, and Rabbi Lamm authored a book about him along with several articles.[42]

How, specifically, does Kabbala bear on modern problems? In a 1961 essay, "The Unity Theme and Its Implications for Moderns,"[43] Rabbi Lamm argues that the kabbalistic theme of unity or monism provides an antidote to the disintegration and fragmentation characteristic of modern society. Rav Kook believed that all phenomena are manifestations of the divine, and all that exists is therefore harmonious and unified. This unity, however, is not apparent to humanity. Its becoming manifest is a step in improving the world – including ours today.

Fragmentation and disintegration – the kabbalist's *alma diperuda*, the world of separation (the opposite of *alma diyeḥuda*, the world of unification) – is evident in our society, says Rabbi Lamm, in motley ways: specialization and divisions of labor; the shift from extended family to nuclear family; the prevalence of divorce; the documentary hypothesis; and the splitting of the atom, which relates to fragmentation of the self: "A fragmented world is merely fragmented man writ large."[44] Rav Kook's vision of unity overcomes fragmentation. The unity theme moves us from an atomistic view of personality to a holistic one. Most significantly for the enterprise of *Torah Umadda*,

---

41. Because Hasidism often goes along with rejection of general culture, and, in addition, Hasidim often live in socially separate communities, many Modern Orthodox Jews experience hasidic culture as another world, depriving themselves of its treasures.
42. See Norman Lamm, *Rav Kook: Man of Faith and Vision* (New York, 1965); see also, for example, Norman Lamm, "Harmonism, Novelty, and the Sacred in the Teachings of Rav Kook," in *Rabbi Abraham Isaac Kook and Jewish Spirituality*, ed. Lawrence J. Kaplan and David Shatz (New York, 1994), 159–77.
43. See Lamm, *Faith and Doubt*, 42–67, where it is retitled "The Unity Theme: Monism for Moderns."
44. Ibid., 53.

in a monistic view, there is no absolute distinction between holy and profane. Religion and science can be united, and the various branches of wisdom integrated.[45]

In short, *Torah Shebikhtav* and *Torah Shebe'al Peh*, the Written Law and the Oral Law, as well as kabbalistic texts, speak to modern society. They can be formulated in contemporary language and categories so as to effectively communicate tradition's ideas and values, which is an outer-directed element of *Torah Umadda*. To attain this end, a serious, sustained employment of *derush* as an element of Torah and *talmud Torah* is needed. True, opponents of *Torah Umadda* likewise homiletically contrast and compare Torah to modern culture, and like Rabbi Lamm, they often denounce it. But the differences are clear: Unlike *darshanim* of the "Torah only" school, Rabbi Lamm frequently calls

---

45. The essay on monism stimulated a rejoinder by another prominent Orthodox thinker, Rabbi Dr. Walter Wurzburger. See Wurzburger, "Pluralism and the Halakha," *Tradition* 4, no. 2 (Spring 1962): 221–40. Rabbi Wurzburger championed the cause of a pluralistic rather than monistic metaphysics precisely by appealing to the need to make distinctions in halakha between holy and profane, pure and impure. Blurring such distinctions through a monistic theology, Rabbi Wurzburger maintained, leads to antinomianism (undermining of law). As Rabbi Lamm himself points out, acosmism and "ontological nihilism" (the doctrine that the world does not exist) lurk in a monistic outlook; so, we may add, does pantheism. Rabbi Ḥayim of Volozhin pointed to certain behaviors of Hasidim to substantiate the charge of antinomianism – for example, their reading sacred literature in unclean places and, more famously, praying at halakhically problematic times.

In the revised versions of the article, published in the various editions of *Faith and Doubt*, Rabbi Lamm responds to Rabbi Wurzburger's critique. Essentially, Rabbi Lamm argues that "even the most ardent monists took great pains to keep it within bounds" and avoid antinomianism (Lamm, "The Unity Theme," 51–54). The details of the monists' strategies need not be elucidated here; they rest on the crucial kabbalistic distinction between "from His side" and "from our side," which was mined in opposite ways by Hasidim and *mitnaggdim*.

The relevance of Kabbala is again affirmed in a 1994 interview conducted for Joshua Haberman, *The God I Believe In* (New York, 1994), 95–111, which is reprinted in Lamm, *Seventy Faces* 1:104–19. There Rabbi Lamm describes God as "beyond personality," which is to say, in accord with Kabbala, that He has both an impersonal aspect, the *Ein Sof* (Infinite), and a revelational aspect, the ten *sefirot*. Human beings can relate only to the personal aspect, though they can assert the existence of the impersonal one. See Norman Lamm, "The God I Believe In," in *Seventy Faces*, 1: 107–8.

upon secular culture, its teachings and vocabulary, to explicate Torah, and, while not allowing "modern" to invariably serve as an encomium, he affirms modern doctrines and values where appropriate, contrary to those who push them all away.

We turn now to other ways in which *talmud Torah* and *madda* are related in Rabbi Lamm's works.

## PARALLELS BETWEEN TORAH STUDY AND UNIVERSITY STUDY

As president of Yeshiva University, Rabbi Lamm was impelled to think through many of the same issues about higher education that presidents of other colleges face. Should knowledge be pursued for its own sake, or should it be pursued with practical applications in mind? Should universities teach values, or instead remain neutral on value questions? We find several instances in which Rabbi Lamm's conception of *talmud Torah* helps generate a particular model for university study, by dint of his seeing parallels between methods and goals of studying Torah, and methods and goals of studying *madda*.

In his address at his investiture in 1976, Rabbi Lamm initially stressed that not only must Torah study be pursued for its own sake, but likewise must worldly wisdom, which has inherent value, be pursued for its own sake.[46] Even so, he went on to state that learning must be applied to life. According to the Zohar, the Tree of Knowledge (*etz hadaat*) possessed within it a "Tree of Death." When one combines knowledge and life, Rabbi Lamm suggests, one can suppress death; by

---

46. The address is published as "A Vision for Yeshiva University," in Lamm, *Seventy Faces*, 1:203–13. In a private communication, Rabbi Lamm explained, by way of clarification, that in attributing inherent value to worldly wisdom he is adopting the schema of Rabbi Ḥayim of Volozhin, who declared that *Torah lishmah* means studying Torah for its own sake, for cognitive purposes, and not for the spiritual purposes proposed by the Hasidim – that of *devekut*. But ultimately, *Torah lishmah* is based upon religious commitment to the Creator. Thus, studying *lishmah* in the manner of Rabbi Ḥayim but with no intent to live by the Torah's teachings is considered unacceptable. Hence, just as *Torah lishmah* is "for its own sake" yet ultimately rests upon another, more fundamental basis, so *ḥokhma* (wisdom) or secular *madda* studies may likewise be indulged in *lishmah* and yet rest firmly on the unstated but clearly maintained religious principle of *yirat Shamayim* (fear of Heaven).

contrast, the pursuit of knowledge alone without application to life leads to death. Both Torah and *madda* must be practically applied.

The theme of study and practice also appears in an article by Rabbi Lamm titled "Scholarship and Piety." He focuses on how the two values named in the title are ranked and related by Rabbi Ḥayim of Volozhin and suggests, albeit briefly and allusively, that his discussion is relevant to contemporary times.[47] Even while teaching that *yira* (piety) is a precondition for learning, Rabbi Ḥayim "dissociated" halakhic scholarship from charismatic experience, from the study of Kabbala, from the experience of *devekut*, from fear of sin, from the study of devotional literature, and from *musar*. He opposed introducing *musar* into yeshiva curricula.

In a preface to the article as reprinted in *Faith and Doubt*, Rabbi Lamm notes that the scholarship versus piety distinction has a parallel in the modern university. He writes that the rebellion of youth in the 1960s is primarily directed against the campus, the university:

> [The rebellion] rejected the antiseptic disinterestedness of much of the irrelevant and pedantic academic exercises that substitute for scholarship. In the last decades of the twentieth century and even to the present, it was repelled by that part of the academic community that has subordinated its goals to those of the military-industrial complex.

He then asks:

> However, if pure scholarship is dismissed as irrelevant, and industry or defense work is a case of "selling out," must the university necessarily commit its scholarly resources to those social and political causes that the most radical and vocal students demand?
>
> The role of scholarship in contemporary society has not yet been defined with any finality.... However, until then it is worth taking the trouble to learn how scholarship was viewed

---

47. See Lamm, *Faith and Doubt*, 208–41. The article was first published in 1968. Chapter 9 of Lamm, *Torah Lishmah*, presents a reworked version of this material.

in another age and in another culture in its interaction with other values. [This examination] will at least give us the reassurance that similar problems, mutatis mutandis, have engaged the most creative minds of the past. At least we are not alone in our vexation.[48]

The essay does not draw explicit comparisons between past and present, nor does Rabbi Lamm advocate a secular analogue to Rabbi Ḥayim's Dissociation Principle, nor does he endorse that principle itself even in a purely Torah context. But it is of interest that Rabbi Lamm sees parallels between religious and secular modes of study with respect to core questions that they confront. The theoretician of Torah and the university president must ponder the same issues.

Still another example of a parallel between *talmud Torah* and university study emerges – albeit only implicitly – in a 1986 *New York Times* op-ed article. Rabbi Lamm argues that values and moral instruction ought to be part of a college education.[49] In this article, Rabbi Lamm was swimming against a tide; many in higher education preached keeping university education free of the imparting of values. Rabbi Lamm points out, however, that universities themselves must and *do* promote values:

> If the university does not teach the moral superiority of education as opposed to ignorance, of reason over impulse, of discipline over slovenliness, of integrity as against cheating – then its very foundations begin to crumble.[50]

Given this point, the issue cannot be *whether* values should be taught – after all, universities do teach the value of education, reason, discipline, and integrity[51] – but rather *which ones*. As one philosopher has put it, "every university expresses a number of positive value

---

48. Ibid., 208–9.
49. "A Moral Mission for Colleges," in Lamm, *Seventy Faces*, 1:214–16.
50. Ibid., 1:215.
51. Despite their claims of neutrality, many educators maintain that universities and other types of schools must cultivate autonomy and affirm it as a value.

commitments through the character of its faculty, of its library, even through the buildings it chooses to build."⁵² Rabbi Lamm emphasizes teachings that impart dignity – spiritual dignity – and morality:

> A modern university should not be "spooked" by the specter of sectarianism. It should encourage a moral climate that elicits respect for the human spirit, for honor, for law, for the pursuit of knowledge and love of learning, for the human capacity for self-transcendence.⁵³

Although Rabbi Lamm does not say so explicitly in the op-ed piece, there is little question that in his opinion, value-centered university education resembles Torah education. The values that universities *should* teach, furthermore, are the very same ones that Torah imparts.

## TORAH AND NATURE AS PARALLEL PHENOMENA

An entirely different sort of parallel between Torah study and *madda* study draws upon a motif from medieval writing and beyond. In this image, God wrote two books, the Bible and the Book of Nature.⁵⁴ On the page of epigrams at the front of *Torah Umadda*, Rabbi Lamm cites a variant of this idea expressed by Rabbi Tzaddok HaKohen of Lublin (1823–1900): "I heard it said that God wrote a book – the world; and He wrote a commentary on that book – the Torah."

---

52. Robert Paul Wolff, "The Myth of the Neutral University," which appears among a group of readings at the end of a lengthy defense by Robert Simon of neutrality in the university. See Simon, *Neutrality and the Academic Ethic* (Lanham, MD, 1994). Simon's essay is on pp. 3–99, and the quotation from Wolff's essay is on p. 106. That Wolff holds highly controversial, even notorious, political views (he wrote a book defending anarchism) does not impugn his point in our context.
53. Lamm, "A Moral Mission for Colleges," 216.
54. Galileo used this model in defending himself against the charge that believing the sun is at the center of the planetary system (heliocentrism) constitutes heresy. He argued that the Bible cannot contradict the book of nature; that is, it cannot contradict science. See, for example, Maurice A. Finocciaro, ed., *The Galileo Affair: A Documentary History* (Berkeley, 1989), 50, 93. Maimonides (*Guide of the Perplexed* III:25–26) maintains that the laws of nature and the laws of God (mitzvot) are parallel because both reflect divine wisdom.

Several pages of *Torah Umadda* invoke a parallel between Torah and nature, developing it as follows: Torah reflects God as teacher, while nature reflects God as creator. Thus, to study both Torah and nature is to study God more comprehensively than to study Him by means of one of these alone. The psalmist describes God as both creator and teacher. Still, the revelation of Torah is a *direct* disclosure of God's will; the revelation of the created world is not. Hence the former's axiological primacy.[55]

## USING *MADDA* TO EXAMINE PHILOSOPHICAL ISSUES ABOUT *TALMUD TORAH* AND HALAKHA

At times, Rabbi Lamm conceptualizes and analyzes *talmud Torah* using philosophical and historical categories, methods, and principles. The most obvious example of this procedure is his already-referenced scholarly works on *Torah lishmah*, but there are other illustrations. Rabbi Lamm asks, for example: Which is greater in Torah study, process or product – the process of learning and study (*limmud*), or knowledge of Torah (*yedia*)? He replies by introducing the famous philosophical distinction between being and becoming.

Plato's philosophy, Rabbi Lamm explains, values being – a state of static perfection – over becoming; knowledge is the ultimate goal in Plato's thought "because it is in a state of being."[56] Rabbi Lamm discerns the Greek assignment of supremacy to "being" in a claim of philosophers that Maimonides reports in his famous sixth chapter of *Shemona Perakim*. The philosophers, Maimonides explains, value the ḥasid, one who is born perfect or is in a permanent state of virtue through repeated actions, over one who struggles against inclination but consistently does the right thing. The sages, by contrast, rank the successful struggle against inclination and the conquest of temptation higher than the possession and exercise of natural or acquired virtues. Maimonides reconciles the two opinions by applying them to different groups of mitzvot. Rabbi Lamm uses the *Shemona Perakim* text to illustrate his generalization

---

55. See Lamm, *Torah Umadda*, 123–26. Rabbi Lamm, of course, makes clear that Rabbi Ḥayim of Volozhin did not endorse the ideal of *Torah Umadda*.
56. Lamm, "Knowing vs. Learning," 17.

that for the Greeks the static state is best, while for the sages a dynamic state ranks higher.

Mobilizing other examples as well, Rabbi Lamm argues that Judaism "adopts a worldview diametrically opposed to that of the Greeks and holds that becoming takes precedence over being."[57] Thus, studying is becoming, growing, moving toward a goal; a talmudic scholar is called a *talmid ḥakham* (a student of the wise), not a *ḥakham*. Further, *Ḥazal* teach that "according to the pain is the reward"[58] — "the pain of studying, the pain of researching, the pain of thinking, the pain of solving conflicts, the pain of being confronted by one's own ignorance and struggling to overcome it." Struggle, effort, *yegia*, is itself an achievement.[59] Judaism's stress on teaching children, whose minds are in the process of "becoming," further supports the primacy of studying over knowing. Consider, argues Rabbi Lamm, implanting a microchip of the Bar-Ilan Responsa Project (a massive electronic database of Torah sources) in someone's brain. That would provide Torah knowledge, but would that erudite state be preferable to the process of learning?

Applying this ranking of values, Rabbi Lamm offers encouragement to educators who become frustrated by not achieving the results they desire: "The very act of teaching, the struggle of challenging the students, is worthwhile even if it does not succeed in the way the teacher would like, and even if it appears to fall on deaf ears."[60]

Not all of Greek philosophy elevates being over becoming. Heraclitus taught that all is in flux, and Aristotle, even while endorsing the idea that ultimate perfection is static, focuses on the dynamic processes in nature that lead to that (static) goal. But historical nuances aside, what we have in the essay on knowing versus learning is a way of elucidating the mitzva of *talmud Torah* by using categories drawn from the world of *madda*.

---

57. Ibid., 18.
58. Mishna Avot 5:26.
59. Megilla 6b.
60. Lamm, "Knowing vs. Learning," 22. Rabbi Lamm frequently offers such encouragement to educators and rabbis. See, for example, Lamm, *Seventy Faces*, 1:226–27, 237–39, 241–46, and the Chag HaSemichah addresses assembled in *The Spirit of The Rabbinate* (New York, 2010).

*Rabbi Dr. David Shatz*

## THE USE OF *MADDA* IN HALAKHIC ANALYSIS

Alongside his many writings on theology and community, Rabbi Lamm, as mentioned, has published numerous halakhic essays and discourses, primarily in Hebrew. *Halakhot VaHalikhot* (1990) collects twenty-seven of these articles. All are written in the literary style and dialectical, analytical mode characteristic of traditional rabbinic halakhic discourses. In a word, they are works of *lomdut*.

In the introduction to the book, Rabbi Lamm stakes out, with great passion, one aspect of his philosophy of halakha. Nearly half the essays, he notes, reflect the integration of halakha and Aggada, in the sense of Jewish thought, including both philosophical and kabbalistic ideas. Hence, the book's title: *Halakhot* – legal analyses – are "gateways" to *Halikhot*, the world of religious thought, which he argues must be attached to the halakha.[61]

In *Halakhot VaHalikhot*, halakha is primarily tied to *Jewish* thought. Thus, certain analyses call upon hasidic metaphysics or Maimonides' concept of free will and divine foreknowledge to explain disputes and clarify laws. In English halakhic writings, however, Rabbi Lamm presents halakhic analyses of contemporary moral issues that reflect the integration of Torah and *secular* thought. For example, during the 1950s, in the pages of the periodical *Judaism*, Rabbi Lamm addressed two issues in American constitutional law, self-incrimination and privacy.[62] The essay on self-incrimination was composed during the McCarthy era, when "pleading the Fifth" was often construed as a presumption of guilt. The work was cited by United States Supreme Court Chief Justice Earl Warren in the landmark *Miranda* decision in 1966 and by Associate Justice William O. Douglas in *Garrity v. New Jersey* in 1967.

The essay on privacy originated in testimony at hearings of the US Senate Judiciary Committee before "the right to privacy" became a vexed concept in matters like abortion and homosexuality; the issue in those earlier days was the use of surveillance technology. Both essays reflect the interpenetration of *maḥashava* and halakha of which he spoke in *Halakhot VaHalikhot*.

---

61. The *halakhot-halikhot* word association is talmudic (Megilla 28b).
62. See the material reprinted in Lamm, *Faith and Doubt*, chs. 10–11.

In his essay on self-incrimination, Rabbi Lamm writes that whereas the Fifth Amendment of the United States Constitution states that a person may not be *compelled* to testify against himself, halakha's principle of *"ein adam meisim atzmo rasha"* (literally, an individual does not make himself into a wicked person) dictates that a person is *not even permitted* to testify against himself in criminal cases (although confessions are accepted in monetary cases). Furthermore, one cannot confess to a sin that would disqualify him as a witness. Rabbi Lamm offers a halakhic and psychological analysis. He explores the rationales for the halakhic positions that were offered by Maimonides and Radbaz and then suggests that the difference between these two authorities may be captured by reference to the difference between Sigmund Freud and his disciple Karl Meninger as regards the death wish. An explanation of the laws governing confessions in terms of the death wish extends, he believes, to self-disparagement and hence to cases in which the confession would result only in disqualification as a witness; in addition, guilt feelings may play out in producing a confession. The essay concludes with a discussion of self-incrimination in Noahide law and the bearing of Noahide rules (which do accept confessions) on the comparison between halakha and secular law.

In his essay on privacy, Rabbi Lamm shows that the halakhic discussion as to whether *hezek re'iya* (damage caused by viewing) constitutes actionable damage analogous to physical intrusion has parallels in conflicting Supreme Court decisions. The essay goes on to consider other forms of invasion of privacy – disclosure, protection of mail, polygraphs, and (in an updated version of the essay) DNA testing and a national data center. Rabbi Lamm provides a theological rationale for a dialectical balance between privacy and communication. Affronts to privacy in contemporary society, he asserts, grow out of a trend of depersonalization. In Judaism, by contrast, there is "an inviolate core of personality" that translates into privacy laws, although God observes us with a "seeing eye" and "hearing ear."[63]

Secular materials may be used not only in explaining halakhot, as in the previous examples, but also in halakhic decision-making. In

---

63. Mishna Avot 2:1.

an article coauthored with Tel Aviv law professor Aaron Kirschenbaum about the balance of freedom and constraint in the halakhic process,[64] the authors apply to halakha an account given by former US Supreme Court Associate Justice Benjamin Cardozo of four methods in the judicial process (logic, history, custom, and sociology). They thus oppose a purely formalistic approach to *pesak halakha* and advocate introducing general knowledge into *pesak*. By contrast, another *madda*-based approach to Jewish law, the "academic" study of Talmud, is said not to affect halakhic decision-making.[65] The academic approach views the composition of the Talmud in a way that challenges traditional sensibilities. Apart from stressing the checking of textual variants and, moreover, dividing the text chronologically into strata, the academic method at times attributes misunderstandings to the *stamma'im* (the anonymous redactors who pose questions, answers and comments). Rabbi Lamm argues that the challenge to halakha from academic methods is not great, for if there are misunderstandings on the part of the *stamma*, these do not affect practical halakha – mitzvot are "non-ontic." So the method carries no danger of antinomianism.[66]

Furthermore, there is no one methodology or *derekh* that is inherently superior to others; it is all a matter of intellectual conviction, taste, orientation, and personal choice. Hence, "everyone is entitled to use whatever satisfies him in attempting to understand *devar Hashem zo halakha* (the word of God – this is halakha)."[67] Since "academic assistance in learning is a form of *madda*," therefore, "*Torah Umadda* can be exemplified in talmudic study."[68]

---

64. Norman Lamm and Aaron Kirschenbaum, "Freedom and Constraint in the Jewish Judicial Process," *Cardozo Law Review* 1, no. 1 (Spring 1979): 99–133.
65. The discussion appears as an appendix to the 3rd edition of Lamm, *Torah Umadda*, 227–31.
66. Ibid., 229.
67. Shabbat 138b.
68. Lamm, *Torah Umadda*, 230. On occasion, the academic study of Talmud has been the subject of papers at the Orthodox Forum, convened annually by Rabbi Lamm. See the articles by Daniel Sperber and Yaakov Elman in *Modern Scholarship in the Study of Torah: Contributions and Limitations*, ed. Shalom Carmy (Northvale, NJ, 1996), and those by David Flatto and Yaakov Nagen in *The Next Generation of Modern Orthodoxy*, ed. Shmuel Hain (New York, 2012). Nagen examines a variety

# Role of Talmud Torah in a Torah Umadda Framework

## MODELS OF *TORAH UMADDA* AND THE
## IDEA OF TEXTLESS TORAH

The book *Torah Umadda* formulates and appraises six models for grounding that philosophy. These include the rationalist model of Maimonides; the cultural model of Rabbi Samson Raphael Hirsch; the mystical model of Rabbi Avraham Yitzhak Kook; the instrumentalist model of the Vilna Gaon; the "textless Torah model," which is built by combining concepts in the thought of Rabbi Ḥayim of Volozhin with some in the writings of Maimonides; and the hasidic model of *madda* study as a form of worship, which involves an extension of hasidic concepts of worship. (As noted earlier, hasidic thinkers themselves generally opposed *madda* study.)

After carefully comparing the models, Rabbi Lamm favors the hasidic one and draws out its implications for education. The book concludes, however, with a pluralistic perspective that sees the *Torah Umadda* ideology and the "Torah only" position as complementary. Both have validity; both contribute to "the totality of Jewish life."[69]

The dynamics of Rabbi Lamm's arguments need not concern us here, but certain of the book's discussions are relevant to us because they address components of *talmud Torah*. Consider, for example, the notion of *yeridat hadorot*, the decline of the generations.[70] Defenders of a "Torah only" approach sometimes explain the orientation of figures like Maimonides by saying that, whereas in earlier times there were great Jews who could engage in both Torah and *madda* without damaging themselves spiritually, nowadays we are "too inadequate, too weak, too vulnerable" to take such risks.[71] (I find this to be an

---

of approaches to talmudic study. See also, however, the Orthodox Forum volume *Lomdus: The Conceptual Approach to Jewish Learning*, ed. Yosef Blau (New York, 2006), which deals with the traditional conceptual approach.

69. Notwithstanding these concluding thoughts, the book *Torah Umadda*, as expected, elicited a highly critical reaction from the Orthodox right. Rabbi Mayer Schiller responded to certain of these criticisms in his "*Torah Umadda* and *The Jewish Observer* Critique: Towards a Clarification of the Issues," *Torah u-Madda Journal* 6 (1996): 58–90.

70. The topic is explored in Lamm, *Torah Umadda*, 75–90.

71. Ibid., 75.

odd position for "Torah only" proponents to take, since it implies that Torah plus *madda* is superior for those on the highest spiritual level – a huge concession!) Rabbi Lamm rejects the contention about *yeridat hadorot* and concomitantly affirms the value of and potential for *ḥiddush* (innovation). This theme of *ḥiddush* in *talmud Torah* appears elsewhere in his writings, where he laments the contemporary "animus against originality." He tells about giving a certain original explanation in the course of a *shiur* in *Ḥumash*, at which point someone objected solely on the grounds that the explanation had not been proposed by any previous interpreter.[72]

Let us now look at the concept of "textless Torah." Noting Rabbi Ḥayim of Volozhin's judgment that Bible study is not as valuable as the study of halakha, Rabbi Lamm proposes that, for Rabbi Ḥayim, there is a hierarchy in Torah study. He then suggests that studying *madda*, too, is a form of Torah study, albeit one on a lower level. He extracts this principle from Maimonides' interpretation of a talmudic passage pertaining to allocating time for Torah study. According to the passage, a person should divide his Torah study into three parts: one-third *Mikra* (Bible), one-third Mishna, one-third Gemara.[73] Prior to Maimonides, and post-Talmud, commentators understood these components in their straightforward sense: Bible, the Mishna of R. Yehuda HaNasi, and the Gemara texts in the tractates of *Shas*. Maimonides, however, understood Mishna to encompass all of *Torah Shebe'al Peh*, leaving the category of Gemara to denote a different activity: roughly speaking, reasoning about what the texts say. Maimonides then adds one sentence: "The subjects called *Pardes* [physics and metaphysics] are included in Talmud."[74] This sentence seems to have rankled the sensibilities of later authorities. Rabbi Yosef Karo, in his *Shulḥan Arukh* code, borrows almost verbatim Maimonides' ruling about how to divide daily Torah study into three – but omits the sentence about

---

72. See "The Future of Creativity in Jewish Law and Thought," in Lamm, *Seventy Faces*, 2:3–16.
73. Kiddushin 30a.
74. *Mishneh Torah, Laws of Torah Study* 1:11–12.

*Pardes*.[75] Earlier post-Maimonidean authorities likewise avoided Maimonides' wording.[76]

Rabbi Lamm underscores that Maimonides has very explicitly imported *Pardes* into the mitzva of *talmud Torah*. Yet, he points out, there is no specific Torah text from which *Pardes* is learned. It therefore can be called "textless Torah." Using Rabbi Ḥayim of Volozhin's notion that there is a hierarchy in Torah study, we may say that *madda* study counts as Torah study but only as *textless* Torah study. By introducing this concept, Rabbi Lamm says that he can answer two questions: Must one recite *Birkat HaTorah* when studying a *madda* field, such as chemistry? And does one fulfill his obligation of *talmud Torah* by studying calculus all day? *Birkat HaTorah*, he argues, applies only to Torah texts, not textless Torah, and the mitzva of *talmud Torah* can be fulfilled only by means of a text.

Rabbi Lamm freely admits that the model of textless Torah, while in his opinion faithful to Maimonides, runs contrary to Rabbi Ḥayim's stance on secular studies. Likewise, he admits that Hasidim who advocated *avoda begashmiyut* (worship through corporeality), his favored model of *Torah Umadda*, strongly opposed secular studies.

## THE ROLE OF TORAH STUDY IN RESTORING FAITH

In the title essay of *Faith and Doubt*, Rabbi Lamm asks, how can we retain faith in an age of doubt?[77] He distinguishes three types of faith – cognitive, affective, and functional (behavioral) – along with three corresponding types of doubt. Rabbi Lamm maintains that cognitive doubt can actually broaden and deepen cognitive faith, and he even proposes a halakhic legitimation for cognitive doubt (but not for affective or functional doubt). Affective faith can be restored through

---

75. *Yoreh De'ah* 246:4 (note the gloss of the Rema).
76. See Isadore Twersky, "Some Non-Halakhic Aspects of the *Mishneh Torah*," in *Jewish Medieval and Renaissance Studies*, ed. Alexander Altmann (Cambridge, MA, 1967), 118: "The post-Maimonidean writers either ignored this formulation, camouflaged it, or blunted its edges." The article contains an invaluable discussion of Maimonides' tripartite division.
77. Lamm, *Faith and Doubt*, 1–40.

prayer and study, and in turn affective faith restores cognitive faith. Thus, *talmud Torah* has the potential to restore a faith that has been challenged and weakened – and often the challenge will have come from the world of *madda*.

## TORAH LISHMAH

My emphasis above on how *talmud Torah* functions in a *Torah Umadda* framework should not obscure the fact that Rabbi Lamm also considers the topic of *talmud Torah*, one might say, *lishmah* – as worthy of study in its own right, independent of ideological associations and import. Through the prism of Rabbi Ḥayim of Volozhin, Rabbi Lamm explores a variety of issues concerning *talmud Torah* and explains his protagonist's stance and contribution. His topics include study and practice (*limmud* and *maase*); study and piety; and of course *Torah lishmah*, along with its opposite, *Torah shelo lishmah*. Prior to Rabbi Ḥayim, *Torah lishmah* was explicated as either functional (for the sake of mitzvot) or devotional (for the sake of the commandment to study and as a response to the Commander). Rabbi Ḥayim's definition is cognitive: for the sake of Torah itself – that is, for the cognitive act per se, not an external *telos*. To be sure, Rabbi Ḥayim saw the functional approach – study for the sake of practice – and the devotional as elements in Torah study, but they are subordinate to the intellectual and must be "dissociated" from it. Study itself is for Rabbi Ḥayim an act of *devekut*, or communion with the Creator. As noted earlier, the historical and philosophical tools which Rabbi Lamm brings to this entire topic illustrate the value of *madda* in deepening our understanding of *talmud Torah*.[78] Much more could be said by way of examining the philosophy of *talmud Torah* per se, but that is a different task than the one undertaken in this essay.

## SUMMATION

In Rabbi Lamm's thought, Torah study interacts with *madda* in a rich variety of ways:

---

78. See also Norman Lamm, "Pukhovitzer's Concept of *Torah Lishmah*," *Jewish Social Studies* 30, no. 3 (1968): 149–56.

- Torah speaks to the modern world, often through the medium of *derush*, which is a legitimate and essential mode of Torah study and teaching.
- *Talmud Torah* provides instructive parallels to university study with respect to the question of studying for its own sake versus studying for practical application, and with respect to imparting values in a university education.
- Torah and nature are both written by God.
- Philosophical and historical categories, methods, and principles can illuminate issues in *talmud Torah*, such as how to rank the value of process versus the value of product.
- *Madda* sheds light on halakhic questions.
- *Madda* study falls under the heading of "textless Torah."
- *Talmud Torah* can restore faith.

In embracing *Torah Umadda*, it is important to demonstrate concrete ways in which the domains interact. Few thinkers have created as many diverse opportunities for such interaction as has Rabbi Norman Lamm in his immensely creative and rewarding work on *talmud Torah*.[79]

---

79. Some material in this article is adapted from my "The Writings of Rabbi Norman Lamm: A Bibliographic Essay," *Torah u-Madda Journal* 15 (2008–2009): 209–36.

# Halakha and History, Intellectualism and Spirituality: Professor Isadore (Yitzhak) Twersky's Academic-Religious Profile[*]

### Rabbi Dr. Carmi Horowitz

**BIOGRAPHY**

Rabbi Dr. Isadore (Yitzhak) Twersky (1930–97) was as unique a figure in academic circles as he was unusual in rabbinic circles.[1] He was

---

[*] I want to express my profound thanks to Rabbi Dovid Shapiro for the extremely thorough reading of this article, which resulted in major improvements in its style and precision. Dr. Michael Shmidman of Touro College and Jonathan Dubitzky carefully read the manuscript and suggested a number of important corrections and additions. I take sole and full responsibility for everything written here.

[1.] For other biographical material on his life and scholarship, see Joseph Hacker, "Isadore Twersky: Historian of Jewish Culture," in *Be'erot Yitzḥak: Studies in Memory of Isadore Twersky*, ed. Jay Harris (Cambridge, MA, 2005), 1–15, and Bernard Septimus, "Isadore Twersky as a Scholar of Medieval Jewish History," in Harris, *Be'erot Yitzḥak*, 15–24. See Carmi Horowitz, "Professor Yitzhak Twersky – The

universally recognized and acclaimed as one of the preeminent scholars of his time in academic Jewish studies, with particular emphasis on medieval Jewish culture.[2] He spent his academic career at Harvard University, first as a student and then as a teacher, and maintained close ties with scholars at the Hebrew University of Jerusalem. He published extensively in English and in Hebrew on themes in medieval Jewish intellectual history generally, paying special attention to halakhic literature, and on a wide range of topics in Maimonidean thought.[3]

Rabbi Twersky grew up in the home of a hasidic rabbi, Rabbi Meshulam Zusha Twersky (1893–1972), a descendant of the Chernobyl hasidic dynasty and a great-grandson of Rabbi David of Talne, who was a major figure in the hasidic movement in the Ukraine in the second half of the nineteenth century.[4] Rabbi M. Z. Twersky immigrated to the United States in 1925, settled in Boston, and established the Talner Beit Midrash, first in Roxbury and later in Brighton.[5] His wife, Rebbetzin Rivka née Bronstein, was a learned and insightful woman in her own

---

Talner Rebbe z"l: A Brief Biography," *Torah u-Madda Journal* 8 (1998–1999): 43–58. I have utilized material from that article and incorporated insights from my two colleagues as well. See also the Hebrew booklet, *LeZikhro shel Yitzhak Twersky: Devarim SheNe'emru BiMlot Sheloshim LeMoto* (Jerusalem, 5798 [1997]), particularly the very sensitive portrait painted by his very close friend, the late Prof. Ezra Fleisher (pp. 7–13).

2. See the flyer "Convocation: The Hebrew University of Jerusalem," Sunday, June 2, 1996, issued upon his being awarded an honorary doctorate from the Hebrew University: "Professor Isadore Twersky...is the senior scholar of Jewish studies in this generation in the US and the renowned and expert authority in the study of Jewish culture in the Middle Ages."
3. For a full bibliography of Prof. Twersky's writing, see my "A Bibliography of the Works of Professor Isadore Twersky," in *Me'ah She'arim: Studies in Medieval Jewish Spiritual Life in Memory of Isadore Twersky*, ed. Ezra Fleischer et al. (Jerusalem, 2001), English section 1–10.
4. For a full scholarly biography of Rabbi David of Talne, see Paul Ira Radensky, "Hasidism in the Age of Reform: A Biography of Rabbi Duvid ben Mordkhe Twersky of Tal'noye" (PhD diss., Jewish Theological Seminary of America, 2001).
5. See Shlomo Zalman Weinberg, *Nezaḥ SheBeNezaḥ: Toledot Ḥayav UFaolo shel HaRav Dovid MiTalne* (Jerusalem, 1994), which contains a biography of Rabbi David of Talne and his descendants, and includes, on pp. 247–50, a brief outline of Rabbi M. Z. Twersky's life, written by Prof. Twersky.

right who stood beside her husband, assisting him in all aspects of the Talner Beit Midrash.[6]

Prof. Twersky's Torah education was attained through private teachers, *melammdim*, with whom he studied in his youth in early mornings and late evenings while attending public elementary school and Boston Latin School. He attended Hebrew Teachers College, founded in 1921 by educators committed to the Zionist and Hebraist movements as part of their attempt to create a vital Hebrew culture in America.[7] He then went on to Harvard University, where he studied with Harry A. Wolfson, preeminent scholar of medieval religious philosophy with particular emphasis on Jewish philosophy. Prof. Twersky wrote several necrologies of his teacher, which reveal his closeness with Wolfson and the extensive influence that the teacher had on the student.[8] There were other important scholars at Harvard at the time, such as Charles H. Taylor and Werner Jaeger, who may have had an influence on Prof. Twersky's intellectual development.[9]

He interrupted his studies at Harvard in 1949–50 for a year at the Hebrew University, where he studied under the major Judaic studies scholars of the time, including Yitzhak Baer, Ben-Zion Dinur, Simḥa Assaf, Y. N. Epstein, Ḥanokh Albeck, Hugo Bergman, Gedalia Alon, and Gershom Scholem.[10] Outside of the university, he found time to spend with author S. Y. Agnon as well as with the Rachmastrivker Rebbe, who was his cousin.

Upon his return to Harvard, Prof. Twersky completed his undergraduate degree with a senior thesis on medieval Christian historiography and continued in his graduate studies, ultimately writing his doctoral dissertation on Rabad. A major halakhic scholar and critic of

---

6. See Joseph B. Soloveitchik, "A Tribute to the Rebbetzin of Talne," *Tradition* 17, no. 2 (Spring 1978): 73–83.
7. Prof. Twersky's rich and elegant Hebrew style probably had its roots in his exposure to Hebrew culture in his youth.
8. See, for example, Isadore Twersky, "Harry Austryn Wolfson (1887–1974)," in *American Jewish Yearbook 1976* (New York and Philadelphia, 1975), 99–111.
9. Correct Septimus, "Isadore Twersky" (above note 1) 18 accordingly.
10. See Hacker, "Isadore Twersky," 7.

Maimonides, Rabad lived in Provence during the twelfth century. Prof. Twersky's decision to write his dissertation on Rabad constituted a bold move on his part, as Bernard Septimus has pointed out,[11] and reflected the centrality that he attributed to halakhic literature in the study of Jewish culture and Jewish history. It also pointed to his independence as a scholar and as a trailblazer in new ways of understanding Jewish history and Jewish thought.

His marriage to Atarah Soloveitchik during his graduate years was a major turning point in his life, and not only on a personal level. His very deep and close association with his father-in-law, Rabbi Joseph B. Soloveitchik, or the Rav, as he was honorably called, to whom we will return below, brought him into the home of the preeminent Orthodox rabbinic leader and Torah scholar of the twentieth century. He studied Talmud with his father-in-law on a regular basis for the next thirty years, and while the son-in-law was independent in his scholarly pursuits, the impact on him by this towering figure was great. This is true concerning his talmudic knowledge and methodology, but it is also true concerning themes such as the interaction of law and spirituality in Judaism. Rabbi Twersky dwelt extensively on this theme in the course of his works of Jewish intellectual history from a historical perspective, and that emphasis interconnected with his father-in-law's elaboration of the notion of inwardness and the spiritual meanings that lie behind many of the practical mitzvot.[12] Prof. Twersky's broad and detailed knowledge of Western humanistic culture, and his use of it in his scholarship, paralleled the Rav's extensive use of Western philosophy, from its early Greek origins until the twentieth century, in his own philosophical insights and analyses. In his enthusiastic, even passionate, eulogy for his father-in-law, Prof. Twersky put special emphasis on the Rav's "sovereign mastery of... general culture – philosophy, science, literature," which he used "selectively, creatively and imaginatively, with great philosophic

---

11. Septimus, "Isadore Twersky," 19.
12. In his *shiurim*, which were less historically and more conceptually oriented, Prof. Twersky was even closer to the Rav by virtue of the emphasis he placed on the inwardness and spirituality that accompany the fulfillment of mitzvot. See his "Make a Fence Around the Torah," *Torah u-Madda Journal* 8 (1989–1990): 25–42.

## Halakha and History, Intellectualism and Spirituality

acumen and originality." The entire *hesed* shimmers with his personal identification with the Rav.[13]

Upon the completion of his doctorate in 1956, Prof. Twersky was appointed as lecturer at Harvard University. In 1965, upon the retirement of Harry A. Wolfson, he succeeded to the Nathan Littauer Chair in Hebrew Literature and Philosophy. For the next thirty-two years, Harvard University became a unique center for the study and research of Jewish intellectual history. Students of a high caliber who came with a substantial knowledge of Jewish studies were attracted to Harvard,[14] and many of them subsequently produced important pieces of scholarship that carried the stamp of their teacher's scholarly methodology. He was a demanding teacher who was never satisfied with mediocrity, but the result of the high standards that he demanded was success in educating a generation of young scholars who acquired both breadth and depth in Jewish intellectual history and were inspired by their teacher's method and approach.

Some of the figures and topics they studied include Rabbi Shmuel ben Ḥofni Gaon; Rabbi Meir HaLevi Abulafia; Radak; the thirteenth-century aggadic commentator Rabbi Yitzḥak ben Yedaya; the fourteenth-century preacher Rabbi Yehoshua ibn Shu'eib; the talmudic commentator and rationalist Rabbi Menaḥem HaMeiri; Rabbi Shem Tov ibn Falaqera; Rabbi Yosef ibn Shoshan and his Mishna Avot

---

13. Yitzhak Twersky, "The Rov," *Tradition* 30, no. 4 (Summer 1996): 30. See also p. 16: "His extraordinary Torah erudition together with his wide-ranging general knowledge, his dazzling brilliance, lucid, compelling analysis, phenomenal originality (which did not tolerate the shallow or the commonplace), astonishing intuition, almost legendary preoccupation with Torah, uncompromising honesty, unfailing eloquence, deep-seated sensitivity and lyricism, carefully crafted philosophy (or *hashkafa*), and overpowering charisma – all combined to shape a remarkable Torah personality, unlike others whom we knew." See below, n. 65.
14. Prof. Twersky writes in his *Mada'ei HaYahadut BeArtzot HaBrit* (Jerusalem, 1970), 32, that it is necessary to reconsider the relationship between yeshivas and universities. To paraphrase, the advantage of scientific training in Jewish studies can be realized only if there are resources of *benei Torah*. For students who come to the academy lacking expertise in primary Jewish sources, closing the gap between their lack of knowledge and serious academic analysis will be difficult if not impossible: "Scientific tools cannot replace fundamental knowledge of Judaism; philosophic and pseudo-philosophic views cannot cover up ignorance."

commentaries; the biblical exegete Rabbi Avraham Sava; Don Yitzḥak Abarbanel; the halakhic scholar Rabbi Yosef Kolon; Rabbi Mordekhai Yaffe and his halakhic and philosophic writings; the historian and humanist Rabbi Azarya de Rossi; Rabbi Yehuda Aryeh of Modena and his *Kol Sakhal*; Rabbi Yaakov Emden; and the Jewish communities of Venice, Livorno, and Trieste. Almost forty graduates went on to scholarly careers in the United States, Israel, and England, and many other "ABDs" (students who completed "all but dissertation") carried the training they received at Harvard into other areas, particularly into Jewish education.

## LEADERSHIP: ACADEMIC, RELIGIOUS, EDUCATIONAL, AND COMMUNAL

Prof. Twersky's activities at Harvard were not limited to instruction in his department and to guiding his students. He was also active within the university in preserving high academic standards, particularly during the student upheavals of the late 1960s and early 1970s. He maintained close ties with Harvard's presidents and deans, and served twice as chairman of the Department of Near Eastern Languages and Civilizations, which housed the program in Jewish history. In 1978, he founded the Center for Jewish Studies, which he headed until 1993. He nursed the center through critical times, raised money for it, and withstood tremendous pressure from the powers in the university to create programs more in tune with contemporary trends. It was a model of academic integrity and a major factor in the professional advancement of dozens of young Israeli scholars whose careers were nurtured by their stay at Harvard. He initiated many conferences at the center that produced important scholarly volumes. A number of doctoral dissertations, recast as scholarly monographs, were published by the center as well.

While teaching Jewish studies at Harvard, Rabbi Twersky's role in the Talner Beit Midrash, which had moved from the declining Roxbury section of Boston to the developing Brookline-Brighton section in the early 1960s, grew slowly but inexorably. During his father's lifetime, and particularly after his father suffered a debilitating stroke, Rabbi Twersky began giving *shiurim* in Talmud and speaking regularly at *Seuda Shelishit*. After his father and his mother passed away (in 1972 and 1976 respectively), he accepted upon himself the full leadership of the Talner Beit Midrash, and in 1982 he agreed, despite a deep and genuine modesty and an antipathy to ceremonials, to be officially known as the "Talner Rebbe."

Rabbi Twersky also gradually took on more responsibilities in the leadership of the Maimonides School, founded by his father-in-law.[15] He was a member of the executive committee of the school, which was responsible for policy decisions, and was actively involved whenever a particularly sensitive issue of educational or religious philosophy was to be discussed. As Rabbi Soloveitchik's advancing age and illness prompted his withdrawal from active engagement with the curriculum and its implementation, Rabbi Twersky began to visit Judaic studies classes at the school periodically. He attended faculty meetings on occasion and provided guidance for specific educational initiatives. He made himself available at all hours to both the professional and the lay leaders of the school; no issue was too small for his attention. Leaders of the wider Jewish community of Boston also consulted with him on matters of public policy.

His involvement in Jewish education was motivated not only by concern for the local Jewish community and its educational institutions. His was a concern for *Klal Yisrael*, for the entire Jewish community, and its level of Jewish knowledge. He invested years of active work and cooperation with the Mandel Foundation, which launched a project whose goal was "to stimulate the philosophical considerations of Jewish existence in our time as reflected in alternative visions of Jewish education, its purposes and instrumentalities, the values it should serve, and the personal and social character it ought to foster."[16]

---

15. Rabbi Soloveitchik's wife, Dr. Tonya Levitt Soloveitchik, chaired the school committee until her death in 1967. She was succeeded by her daughter, Dr. Atarah Twersky. Thus, beyond Rabbi Twersky's sense of communal responsibility, it was natural for him to be involved in the school that his family had founded and nurtured.
16. Seymour Fox, Israel Scheffler, and Daniel Marom, eds., *Visions of Jewish Education* (Cambridge, United Kingdom, 2003), 1. Prof. Twersky passed away before the publication of the book, which presented the results of the collaborative effort. Daniel Marom edited Prof. Twersky's contribution that was published in the volume (pp. 46–94).

Prof. Twersky had a deep concern for the future of the Jewish people, a keen awareness of the historical crisis that Judaism faced in the twentieth century as religion and secularity wrestled with each other, and a heartfelt solicitude for the widespread ignorance of Judaism and Jewish sources that prevailed among much of the Jewish people. He emphasized the pressing need to articulate an educational vision that explicated the centrality of and commitment to halakha that any vital and viable version of Judaism must encompass and at the same time pointed to Judaism's broad and expansive compass. His own vision of Judaism drew on Maimonides' notion that philosophy is an integral part of the mitzva of *talmud Torah*.[17] He firmly adhered to Maimonides' maxim, "One should accept the truth from whatever source it proceeds."[18] Indeed, he was in the midst of formulating "various halakhic perspectives on the study of such areas as the natural sciences, arts and literature, history, and physical education – including the question of their relative priority,"[19] and just before his untimely death he was preparing to share the results with educators.

This deep concern for the future of Judaism operated not only on an educational level, but also on an existential-religious level, and encompassed the future of the Jewish people, Zionism, and the State of Israel. In an article titled "Survival, Normalcy, Modernity,"[20] he critiques secular Zionism for its attempt to break the continuity of Jewish history, for its emphasis on the political and not on the spiritual, and for the lack of Jewish character of the State of Israel. His arguments are not couched in the language of a Religious Zionist preacher, but rather in that of an objective historian. Despite his critique of the Zionist movement, he was a passionate lover of the Land of Israel and the State of Israel. He wrote a detailed and extensive article on Maimonides' attitude toward

---

17. See Isadore Twersky, "Some Non-Halakic Aspects of the *Mishneh Torah*," in *Jewish Medieval and Renaissance Studies*, ed. Alexander Altmann (Cambridge, MA, 1967), 95–118, esp. 111–16. The theme is repeated in his other writings.
18. Conclusion of the introduction to the *Shemona Perakim*, cited in Isadore Twersky, *A Maimonides Reader* (New York, 1972), 363. See also his cross-reference to *Mishneh Torah, Laws of the Sanctification of the New Moon* 17:24.
19. "Supplement: Isadore Twersky," in Fox, Scheffler, and Marom, *Visions of Jewish Education*, 91.
20. Moshe Davis, ed., *Zionism in Transition* (New York, 1980), 347–66.

the Land of Israel,[21] and he was a frequent visitor there. Shortly before he died, he was beginning to make concrete plans to establish a beit midrash in Jerusalem for a Talner *minyan*.[22]

## FROM TORAH STUDY TO ACADEMIC RESEARCH

The contrasts and the potential for conflict between the many aspects of Rabbi Twersky's activities, in the varied personae that he represented – professor of Jewish history, hasidic rabbi, and son-in-law and disciple of the leading talmudic-halakhic scholar of the generation – invite the question: Did Rabbi Twersky harmonize the disparate elements in his life and thought? Was there an explicit resolution of some seemingly conflicting positions? Or did they exist in a creative tension? I will describe what was apparent to this observer, and let the reader draw his own conclusions.

Rabbi Twersky was unquestionably and totally committed to halakha and a halakhic way of life.[23] This commitment was transparent on a personal level through the daily rigor of public prayer (he would bear almost any inconvenience to be present three times daily at communal prayer), blessings, Shabbat observance, and the myriad details of halakhic practice. He was particularly careful in preserving hasidic customs, which he performed rigorously. Reading Psalms was a regular part of his worship, and spending time at the Western Wall was usually the first thing he did upon arrival in Israel.

---

21. See Isadore Twersky, "Maimonides on *Eretz Yisrael*: Halakhic, Philosophic, and Historical Perspectives," in *Perspectives on Maimonides: Philosophical and Historical Studies*, ed. Joel Kramer (Oxford, 1991), 257–92. See also Horowitz, "Professor Yitzhak Twersky" (n. 1 above), 54.
22. The prayer for the State of Israel was recited every Shabbat in the Talner Beit Midrash in Boston; Hallel was recited on Yom HaAtzma'ut (Israeli Independence Day) and on Yom Yerushalayim (Jerusalem Day).
23. Take, for example, this sentence from *divrei Torah* delivered at *Seuda Shelishit* at the Talner Beit Midrash: "We, too, in our generation of religious relativism, must do whatever we can not to be *mahazik bemahaloket* (sustain controversy) – while maintaining an unwavering commitment to authentic halakha. *Mahaloket* can be destructive, but this does not mean that one compromises principle, or that one fails to take a stand" (from a transcript of a *shiur* written down by Rabbi Dovid Shapiro after Shabbat *Parashat Korah* 1992).

His silent prayer, with barely perceptible bodily movements, communicated a profoundly deep concentration. His expression of joy on Simḥat Torah was similarly externally restrained, but exuded an intensity that clearly communicated his celebration of the joyous holiday. He carried out his rabbinic duties with a deep sense of responsibility, performing innumerable acts of *ḥesed*[24] (which he generally tried to conceal); his *kibbud av va'em*, the honor and respect he accorded his parents, knew no bounds. In short, he saw himself as a link in the chain of continuity of the Jewish tradition.

Paramount was his commitment to study, to the study of Torah as a religious obligation, as well as his commitment to the ethical and moral underpinnings of halakha. His *shiur* in Talmud in his beit midrash was a classical Talmud *shiur* in which he utilized the conceptual tools that he learned from the Rav. His *divrei Torah* during *Seuda Shelishit*, as well as his more extensive thematic *shiurim* (such as his eulogies for the Rav),[25] were not dispassionate academic expositions, but fully engaged Torah instruction that sought out the moral, ethical, and deeply spiritual lessons inherent in Torah and halakha. Some of the recurring themes in his *divrei Torah* were moral and ethical consistency; modesty and inwardness in religious life; going beyond the letter of the law; the need for constant effort to avoid falling into religious routine; sanctity as a product of human activity; the dignity of man in theory and in practice; constancy in the study of Torah; centrality of prayer in religious life; mitzva observance as a joyous privilege, rather than a burden; and the awareness of and sensitivity to God's immanence. Although they were not academic expositions, many of the same themes that Rabbi Twersky dealt with in his scholarly analyses of Maimonidean thought appear in various forms in his *divrei Torah* as well.[26]

His professional career – professor of Jewish history at Harvard – was combined with the study of and commitment to Talmud

---

24. I am not sure that the English translation for the word *ḥesed* – loving-kindness – captures the passionate, emotional, and religious depth from which these actions flow.
25. For one of the eulogies, see Twersky, "Make a Fence" (n. 12 above).
26. Rabbi Dovid Shapiro, formerly of Boston, who provided me with the list of themes, is now editing and preparing for publication more than twenty years of Rabbi Twersky's *divrei Torah* delivered at the Talner Beit Midrash.

and halakha. His childhood study of Talmud in the early mornings and evenings was the beginning of a life-long commitment to Torah study, study which he viewed not only as a religious fulfillment, but as fully congruent with his professional, academic activities as a Jewish historian. Once, during my first or second year at Harvard, I asked him, at the urging of one my friends, "Does not the study of Jewish history border on *bittul Torah* (i.e., a failure to maximize all of one's time in the study of Torah)?" He answered me immediately, "Whatever we are doing here in the seminar room is a fulfillment of *talmud Torah* (the study of Torah)." There was a seamless connection in his eyes between his scholarly endeavors and the religious obligation to study Torah.

At the same time, however, his graduate seminars were not exactly classic exercises in *talmud Torah*. In fact, they were academic investigations into a wide array of issues and questions of Jewish intellectual history. Yet the fact remains that he called this engagement "*talmud Torah*." In order to understand this, let us examine Prof. Twersky's self-perception as a historian, define his historical methodology, and try to understand how he not only saw no conflict between his scholarly pursuits and his beliefs, but defined his scholarly subject matter as *talmud Torah* itself. We will start with a quick survey of the rise of the historical-scientific study of Judaism and view Prof. Twersky's scholarship from that perspective.

Ever since the canonization of the Tanakh, Jewish tradition by and large has failed to produce historiographical works.[27] While, as Prof. Twersky often emphasized, Jewish thought retained its historical orientation, its awareness of divisions in history, its appreciation of the religious dimensions of history, and of the implications – halakhic and otherwise – of differences between different periods of history, Jews did not expend time and effort in the writing of works of history or of critical historical investigations.[28]

---

27. See, for example, Yosef Hayim Yerushalmi, *Zakhor: Jewish History and Jewish Memory* (Seattle, 1982).
28. See Isadore Twersky, *Introduction to the Code of Maimonides (Mishneh Torah)* (New Haven, CT, 1980), 220–28, for a sensitive and insightful analysis of the historical dimension of *Mishneh Torah*; see also Yitzhak Twersky and Michael Shmidman, *Halakha VeHagut: Kavei Yesod BeMishnato shel HaRambam* (Tel Aviv, 1995), 2:211–13.

The critical historical study of Judaism had its origins in the late-eighteenth-century Haskala movement, but took shape in nineteenth-century *Wissenschaft des Judentums*, when the critical historical study of Judaism and its sources began in earnest. It represented a major change in how Jewish sources were studied and understood, for it insisted on viewing Judaism as composed of historical layers that have changed and developed as a natural process over the centuries. *Wissenschaft* demanded that one's understanding of Judaism should no longer be dogmatic, rejecting the assumption that its essence lay in a divinely revealed tradition that was handed down through the generations. The tools of free and objective inquiry would be used to see how Judaism had changed its shape and form over the centuries. The practitioners of *Wissenschaft* insisted that Judaism as it was known and practiced in their time was not identical with the Judaism of previous centuries.[29] The historical approach of these scholars saw the foundation and development of Judaism as the result of human activity operating in nature, without any divine intervention.

Historical scholarship, it should be noted, is concerned not only with the "truth of history" – that is, arriving at a true account of the facts of history. It is a way of looking at the totality of human activity, viewing its development, and attributing its consequences to human causality. This historicism has been variously defined as "the theory that each period of history has its own unique beliefs and values and can only be understood in its historical context" or "a theory that all cultural phenomena are historically determined and that historians must study each period without imposing any personal or absolute value system."[30] The

---

29. For full discussions of the rise of historical studies among Jews in the nineteenth and twentieth centuries and its implications see Michael A. Meyer, "The Emergence of Modern Jewish Historiography Motive and Motifs," in *Judaism Within Modernity: Essays on Jewish History and Religion* (Detroit, 2001), 44–63 (the article first appeared in 1989); Ismar Schorsch, *From Text to Context: The Turn to History in Modern Judaism* (Hanover, NH, 1994); David N. Myers, *Re-Inventing the Jewish Past: European Jewish Intellectuals and the Zionist Return to History* (New York, 1995); Myers, *Resisting History: Historicism and Its Discontents in German-Jewish Thought* (Princeton, NJ, 2003); Shmuel Feiner, *Haskalah and History: The Emergence of a Modern Jewish Historical Consciousness* (Oxford, 2004); Michael Brenner, *Prophets of the Past: Interpreters of Jewish History*, trans. Steven Randall (Princeton, NJ, 2010).
30. "English Word Information" at http://wordinfo.info/unit/2881.

assumptions of objective historical research thus have the potential of challenging the very foundations upon which religion rests.

Despite the claim of objectivity, nineteenth-century *Wissenschaft* was not an ideologically pure venture. It was dominated by scholars who were not only committed to historical research for its own sake, but who also believed in the need to reform Judaism as it was practiced and as it was conceived. They believed that since classical Judaism was fashioned and formed by changing historical forces, new circumstances could, indeed should, generate corresponding changes in the nature of Jewish practice. The historicism of the *Wissenschaft* scholars was used purposively by them to undermine the legitimacy of the continuity of Jewish tradition.

Traditional Jewish scholars have not been sympathetic to critical historical thinking and research and to its application to classical Jewish sources. Orthodox Judaism has held fast to the belief in a supernatural revelation as the source of its sacred books, which included both the Bible as well as the Oral Law as it is presented in the Talmud and other works of rabbinic literature. The leadership within the traditional Jewish camp in the nineteenth century viewed the use of critical historical approaches with suspicion and distrust, at the very least, and with censure, contempt, and scorn at the worst.

There were, however, Orthodox scholars in Eastern Europe and northern Italy who participated in the scholarly programs of Ḥokhmat Yisrael, the more traditional branch of *Wissenschaft*. Scholars such as Shlomo Yehuda Rapoport and Shmuel David Luzzatto combined critical historical research with loyalty to traditional Judaism. As time went on, more Orthodox scholars began to utilize methods of historical research, although very few approached scholarly historical research in the manner that would meet the objective standards required in non-denominational universities.[31] Nonetheless, it was unquestionably a new way of studying Jewish sources and of looking at the totality of Jewish life.

In light of the ongoing opposition to the historical study of Judaism in Orthodox-fundamentalist circles, as well as exceptions

---

31. Jacob J. Schacter, "Facing the Truths of History: On Combining Historical Awareness and Secular Knowledge with Torah Scholarship," *Torah u-Madda Journal* 8 (1998): 200–276, esp. 206–9.

taken to historicism in moderate Orthodox circles, Prof. Twersky's engagement with Jewish history and with the historical study of Judaism is noteworthy. This self-identified hasidic rabbi who was a loyal son-in-law and disciple of Rabbi Soloveitchik saw himself capable of maintaining his Orthodox beliefs along with his scholarly and academic integrity.

Prof. Twersky clearly situated himself within the scholarly academic community, continuing the *Wissenschaft* methodology that used a literary-historical-philological approach.[32] In his essay on Jewish studies in American universities,[33] he describes the development of Jewish studies in the United States (including the chair at Harvard that he then occupied) within that context, and he evaluates the place of Jewish studies within the provenance of the non-denominational university. His own historical research was firmly and extensively built upon the results of *Wissenschaft* scholarship. That is not to say that in accepting the tools of scientific research, he agreed with the entire agenda of *Wissenschaft*. When discussing the centrality of halakha and halakhic literature in Jewish tradition, he is severely critical of "the hatred and lack of understanding" of rabbinic literature displayed by previous scholars of Jewish studies, and the "burden of the maskilic [pertaining to the Enlightenment] legacy that saw the study of the Talmud as something sterile and onanistic... and halakhic matters as creating a depressing and constricted routine of mechanical fulfillment of ritual, empty of any religious experience and divorced from spiritual aspiration."[34] Although he worked from within the community of historically trained scholars, he used his critical facilities to correct misperceptions and to forge a new agenda in the writing of history.

## PROFESSOR TWERSKY AS A HISTORIAN

One of the major duties of the historian is to chart the flow of change and continuity over the course of history. The historian studies the past in order to examine what is different and what is the same in human

---

32. Twersky, *Introduction*, xi (n. 28 above).
33. Twersky, *Mada'ei HaYahadut* (n. 14 above).
34. Ibid., 24, and Yitzchak Twersky, "HaRav Yosef Karo Ba'al HaShulḥan Arukh," *Asufot: Annual for Jewish Studies* 3 (1989): 246.

society. Prof. Twersky fulfilled that obligation thoroughly, comprehensively, precisely, insightfully, and responsibly.

As noted above, his tools were historical, philological, literary, and conceptual analysis. First and foremost were close readings of the text, assumptions of its integrity, and analysis of these fundamental blocks of human communication. He read all of his texts with great precision, paying attention to the meanings and nuances of words in their context, as well as their use in respective time periods. The literary qualities of the text were also of great importance, as were the interconnecting webs of meaning and ideas that were represented in the text; its broader historical context rounded out his analysis. While he did not ignore manuscripts and variant readings, he would emphasize that there is still much to be done with the printed texts as they exist.

His vision focused on major issues in Jewish intellectual history, particularly those of the medieval period. He chose to deal with topics that resonated over many generations and in many different Jewish cultural configurations. His methodology was to look at issues and ideas from both a diachronic and a synchronic perspective. A diachronic perspective would have the historian look at the shaping of ideas and attitudes, and their subsequent changes over the course of generations and ask what the causes and circumstances of those changes were, and how they differed in the final analysis from the earlier expressions of those ideas. Simultaneously, ideas and attitudes should be viewed from a synchronic or contemporary perspective, analyzing their presence in different geographical locations and in the writings of different personalities and in different circumstances during the same historical period. He was aware of the danger that intellectual history "might become ensnared in Zeitgeist theories and exaggerated sociologizing, presumptions of excessive homogeneity or uniqueness of periods," and therefore sought to complement it with the "history of ideas, which uncovers continuity, identity, or similarity of basic attitudes and intellectual postures in various periods."[35] He noted that this approach uncovered continuities,

---

35. The quotations are from Isadore Twersky, "Joseph Ibn Kaspi: Portrait of a Medieval Jewish Intellectual," in *Studies in Medieval Jewish History and Literature* (Cambridge, MA, 1979), 234.

but, it should be added, that it also uncovered discontinuities and breaks in intellectual postures.

Thus, for example, in his study of Provençal Jewry,[36] he discusses the dynamics of tradition and change in various aspects of Jewish culture. Some of the changes he notes are in the way Talmud and halakha were studied, the way in which the study of philosophy influenced Jews and Judaism, and the significance of the entrance of Kabbala into Jewish society. He observes:

> The confrontation of conventional cultural preoccupations with new secular learning, the relationship or integration of apparently disparate cultural disciplines, the role of charismatic and rationalistic forces within the framework of traditional communal institutions, personality clashes, and polemics. Furthermore, the interaction of Jewish and general cultural developments... is significant and, finally, the measured influence of relatively favorable social, political, and economic circumstances upon cultural creativity is noteworthy. Provence in this period thus provides a case study for the analysis of the rise and fall of Jewish culture in a foreign environment.[37]

There is a clearly formulated sense of dynamic change in this programmatic statement. Judaism is not static and unchanging; it has changed and it continues to change. What interested Prof. Twersky was tracing issues and attitudes that emerged from halakhic, philosophic, or kabbalistic texts and culture, or from the practitioners of these disciplines. Thus, for example, when characterizing Jewish cultural activity in medieval Provence, he points to

> students of philosophy and philosophers and devotees of philosophy, as well as patrons and protagonists, who are responsible for preserving and transmitting the accumulated philosophic and

---

36. See Isadore Twersky, "Aspects of the Social and Cultural History of Provençal Jewry," *Journal of World History* 11 (1968): 185–207.
37. Ibid., 187–88.

scientific learning of Arabic-speaking Jewry as well as for interpreting it, disseminating it, and extending its frontiers.[38]

His focus was the various ways in which philosophic ideas were received and studied, rather than the actual technical philosophic, kabbalistic, or exegetical positions taken by their respective adherents.

Prof. Twersky's concluding remarks in the introductory chapter to *Introduction to the Code of Maimonides* add insight into his historical methodology.[39] He stresses the importance of clearly identifying Maimonides' uniqueness and avoiding bland homogenizing statements about him that would blur his individuality. He believes that one must bring to bear all that one can glean from Maimonides' own writings as well as what can be learned from contemporary materials. Not only have Jewish traditional characterizations blurred Maimonides' individuality, but at times modern scholarship has also used uniform categories to describe him without addressing his uniqueness. A true, objective, unbiased account must be presented, and all the available material must be used, refraining from ahistorical, abstract categories that tend to impose preconceptions on Maimonides. Knowledge of Maimonides' medical career can often clarify aspects of his biography, as well as his halakhic writings. The need for a comprehensive study of Maimonides that will take into account everything that we know about him and everything that he himself said is explicitly asserted. There are no dogmatic assumptions.

One of the tools of intellectual history is the intellectual biography or profile. Prof. Twersky used this method creatively, writing a book-length intellectual portrait of Rabad of Posquières, which was, as he himself noted, "the first such monograph on one of the leading *Rishonim*."[40] His book on the *Mishneh Torah* of Maimonides, while not intended to be an intellectual biography of the author but rather an analysis of the work, possesses some of the elements of an intellectual

---

38. Ibid. 186–87.
39. Twersky, *Introduction*, 92–96.
40. Isadore Twersky, *Rabad of Posquières: A Twelfth-Century Talmudist*, revised ed. (Philadelphia, 1980), xvii.

biography.[41] Prof. Twersky stressed the importance of seeing the uniqueness of each scholar, and rejected out of hand fundamentalist attempts to homogenize all great scholarly figures and to have them "ensconced in a rigid, unchanging mold fashioned to suit every halakhist."[42]

It is worthwhile to add that while Prof. Twersky studied each scholar, each *talmid ḥakham*, in his own uniqueness, with his strengths and weaknesses, it was always with the humility and respect that Jewish tradition mandates when confronting outstanding Torah scholars. There is no reason, he claimed, why only rabbis cannot be referred to as such while Christian saints are accorded their religious titles.[43] Objective analysis need not engender disrespect. He implemented in his own writing the concept of *melekhet shamayim*, an approach that he claimed characterized the methodology of the *Rishonim*. The notion of *melekhet shamayim* requires one to express himself independently and creatively, without fear of articulating critical comments, and yet at the same time with deference, caution, and restraint.[44] This stance of humility, of caution and restraint vis-à-vis outstanding Torah scholars, has its source in the halakhic requirement to respect *talmidei ḥakhamim*, and it is reflected in Prof. Twersky's biographical essays.

Prof. Twersky held a very broad view of Judaism with a profound understanding of the importance not only of halakha (in all of its various literary forms: talmudic texts, codes of law, responsa, and halakhic essays), but of all other aspects of Jewish cultural creativity, including philosophy, Kabbala, biblical and aggadic exegesis, sermons, ethical works, poetry, linguistics, interreligious polemics, and travelogues. He examined these additional sources, which are not frequently studied in the beit midrash, and looked for the answers to new questions that were never asked before of traditional Jewish texts. This fact alone confirms a different way of looking at and conceiving of Jewish tradition than the

---

41. Some other figures that he wrote about were Rabbi Yedaya Bedersi and Rabbi Yosef ibn Kaspi. Prof. Twersky lectured on a number of other figures, such as Rabbi Menaḥem HaMeiri, Rashba, Ritva, and Ḥatam Sofer, but these works were not published.
42. Twersky, *Rabad*, xx.
43. Twersky, *Mada'ei HaYahadut*, 28.
44. Twersky, *Rabad*, xxi; Twersky, *Introduction*, 170–75.

way Prof. Twersky's father and grandfather did, and ultimately different from that of the Rav and his immediate ancestors as well.

## HALAKHA AND HISTORY

Notwithstanding this broad vision of Jewish culture, Rabbi Twersky viewed halakha as central to Jewish tradition and Jewish cultural creativity:

> There is no doubt whatsoever that my conviction about the centrality of halakha and halakhic literature in Jewish history as well as Jewish historiography needs to be firmly and boldly underscored; its centrality in Judaism, which is halakho-centric, and hence in any religious phenomenology, is obvious and need not be belabored.[45]

Halakha has been the linchpin of Jewish civilization through the ages, Prof. Twersky taught, and there was hardly a concentration of Jews anywhere in premodern times that did not study halakha, practice halakha, pose halakhic queries, or produce halakhic literature.

How does the historian treat halakhic literature? What are the criteria one should use to characterize and evaluate it? What makes one commentary to the Talmud different than others and one code of law unique in light of an abundance of similar codes? Prof. Twersky proposed the following criteria: (1) halakhic novelties in theory or practice; (2) methodological advances; (3) reflection of social and historical realities; (4) questions of authority and independence; and (5) integration of meta-halakhic material such as Aggada, philosophy, philology, and exegesis.[46]

Prof. Twersky's analyses of halakhic works did not deal with *pesak halakha*, or halakhic praxis, and there were those who saw this as avoiding historicistic inquiries into the development of halakha. However, in

---

45. Twersky, *Rabad*, xx. See also Twersky, *Mada'ei HaYahadut*, 24; Twersky, "*Karo*" (n. 34 above), 245.
46. The list is a collation from Twersky, "Provençal Jewry" (n. 36 above), 192, and Twersky, "*Karo*," 245.

his capacity as historian of ideas and intellectual historian, he asked a wide variety of questions, such as biographical, bibliographical, cultural, and literary questions, as well as ones regarding the place of halakha vis-à-vis other disciplines in the Jewish curriculum. These are questions which had not been asked of halakhic sources in the past. His innovative treatment of halakhic scholars is evident in his treatment of Rabad, and particularly in his work on Maimonides.

## MAIMONIDES AND MAIMONIDEAN STUDIES

Prof. Twersky characterized his study of Maimonides as "a literary-historical study of the *Mishneh Torah*…organized around five characteristics repeatedly emphasized by Maimonides himself: codificatory form, scope, classification, language and style, and philosophy and law."[47] All of these aspects were, of course, put into a historical perspective; however, it is not the normative halakha that is historicized, but its literary forms and expression, the intellectual context of many of the Maimonidean innovations in *Mishneh Torah*, as well as the interaction of halakha with philosophy.

Prof. Twersky's *Introduction to the Code of Maimonides* places the *Mishneh Torah* at the center of his vision of Maimonides' intellectual universe, and it is with respect to this work that he constructs his understanding of Maimonides.[48] The *Mishneh Torah* belongs at the center not only because of the centrality of halakha in Maimonides' system, but also because Prof. Twersky did not accept the bifurcated Maimonides – Maimonides the halakhist and Maimonides the philosopher – who commonly appears in earlier scholarly literature. *Mishneh Torah* reflects his philosophic as well as his halakhic stature.

As mentioned above, Prof. Twersky was critical of the attitude of earlier scholars, which he claimed was influenced by the maskilic

---

47. Twersky, *Introduction*, xi. The preface to the Hebrew translation of the book is structured differently from the English and differs in nuances and emphases. In the Hebrew there is no mention of a "literary-historical study," and in its place he characterizes his approach as an "analytic description of *Mishneh Torah*." See also Twersky, "*Karo*," 245, where he discusses a "topical-systematic" treatment of halakhic works. The change in language may be significant.
48. Twersky, *Mada'ei HaYahadut*, 24. See Twersky, *A Maimonides Reader*, xv–xvi.

## Halakha and History, Intellectualism and Spirituality

antagonism to halakha.[49] This brought about an imbalanced view of halakhic creativity and a lack of clear criteria for evaluating the uniqueness of halakhic scholars.

The use of literary-historical categories to analyze the *Mishneh Torah* provided Prof. Twersky with finely honed tools with which to analyze Maimonides' intellectual posture, his ideational and conceptual accomplishments, and their stand within the diachronic progression of Jewish culture. Maimonides' motivation for writing the *Mishneh Torah* is carefully assessed based on his own testimony and not on the basis of speculation. Then, in order, Prof. Twersky analyzes (1) the codificatory form of the *Mishneh Torah* – bare-boned and undocumented; (2) its scope – the most comprehensive code of Jewish law ever written; (3) its system of classifying the law – he rearranged and reclassified, and thereby redefined, the halakhic system; and (4) its language – Hebrew, and style – succinct. All of these are unique categories of analysis that were never before systematically applied to *Mishneh Torah* in a comprehensive manner utilizing all the tools of historical, philological, and literary analysis. The issues are placed in a historical perspective, while the questions are correlated throughout with Maimonides' own awareness of the innovative elements of the Code. Thus, the broader issues of intellectual and literary history, the dynamic and innovative features of the Code, are the focus of his attention.[50]

The fifth and final category, and one of the most significant, that characterizes the *Mishneh Torah* is the relationship between law and spirituality, which is one of the major themes throughout Prof. Twersky's scholarly writings, as well as in his personal Torah study and teaching. The last chapter of *Introduction to the Code of Maimonides* is dedicated to explicating the spiritual-intellectual underpinnings of the *Mishneh Torah*. Prof. Twersky shows in great detail how Maimonides' intellectual and spiritual principles are clearly and forcefully articulated throughout the *Mishneh Torah*, despite the fact that the book is primarily a book of halakhic decisions:

---

49. Twersky, *Mada'ei HaYahadut*, 24.
50. Cf. his discussion of the *Shulḥan Arukh* in his Hebrew article on the topic, "Karo," 245–62.

> It contains many philosophical comments, theological principles, and rationalistic directives, comments on the history of religion and prophecy, science and medicine, and a full ethical system.... Maimonides' systematization of the halakha included a good measure of ethicization and rationalization.... The thread of intellectualization and spiritualization, which is woven uninterruptedly and unabashedly from Maimonides' earliest writings... is thus especially discernible in the texture of the *Mishneh Torah*.... This comprehensive code takes within its purview, in other words, not only the laws, but the theological stimuli and ethical underpinnings which suffuse the legal details with significance and spirituality.[51]

Prof. Twersky goes on to demonstrate how central the study of philosophy was for Maimonides as a source for a spiritually informed halakhic performance. Not only is Maimonides' *Guide of the Perplexed* a source for understanding his philosophical positions, but his halakhic works, such as his Mishna commentary and the *Mishneh Torah*, are of comparable importance. A linchpin of this argument is the demonstration that for Maimonides, the study of philosophy was an integral part of the mitzva of *talmud Torah* and its ultimate culmination.[52] Of similar importance was the considerable attention that Maimonides paid to "reasons for the commandments" – *taamei hamitzvot* – with his emphasis on their spiritual and intellectual value. Again, this theme appears not only in the *Guide*, but prominently in *Mishneh Torah* as well.

Prof. Twersky's presentation of Maimonides is clearly appreciative if not admiring, while adhering to strict scholarly standards. In truth, it is beyond admiring; and one could argue that there was a definite existential identification with Maimonidean positions – philosophic, spiritual, and, of course, halakhic – on the part of Prof. Twersky.[53] A copy of the *Mishneh Torah* was always on his table beside him, and he would often remark that every time he looked at Maimonides, he found something new.

---

51. Twersky, *Introduction*, 371.
52. Ibid., 488–500. See also n. 17.
53. I remember his telling me that I should study carefully Maimonides' explanations of the reasons for the mitzvot, and generally reflect carefully on his works, for they continue

## META-HALAKHA AND SPIRITUALITY

It should be noted with particular emphasis that Prof. Twersky's admiration and appreciation for rationalism and the rationalist school in the Middle Ages meshed with his appreciation of the deep religious spirituality that he saw as an integral part of medieval rationalism generally, and of Maimonidean rationalism specifically. In a footnote that appears in his article "Religion and Law," he writes:

> It should be stated unequivocally that there is here no natural alliance between spirituality and anti-intellectualism, as is often the case in the history of religion.
>
> One way to achieve spirituality is by study, understanding, rationalization; emotionalism or "sensuousness" are not the exclusive, not even the preferred, means toward heightened sensitivity and spirituality. Rationalism and spirituality are congenial; the cognitive gesture is not only not antagonistic, but is conducive to sensitivity, subjectivity, and spontaneity.[54]

Prof. Twersky's concern with the broader theme of law and spirituality became a major focus of his scholarship after the publication of his book on Maimonides. His focus was the relationship between halakha and its spiritual-ideational underpinnings. Specifically, he dedicated much effort to exploring the relationship between the study of Talmud and other areas of study that would provide a spiritual underpinning for a halakhic life. With passion and with compressed, precise elegance, Prof. Twersky writes:

> A tense, dialectical relationship between religion in essence and religion in manifestation is at the core of the Jewish religious consciousness – its legal configuration and its historical experience. Halakha is the indispensable manifestation and prescribed

---

to be relevant and robust. On Prof. Twersky's close identification with Maimonides, see my "Brief Biography," 43, and Septimus, "Isadore Twersky," end of article.

54. Isadore Twersky, "Religion and Law," in *Religion in a Religious Age*, ed. S. D. Goitein (Cambridge, MA, 1974), 78 n6.

concretization of an underlying and overriding spiritual essence, a volatile, magnetic, and incompressible religious force designated as Judaism. The tension flows from the painful awareness that manifestation and essence sometimes drift apart, from the sober recognition that a carefully constructed, finely chiseled normative system cannot regularly reflect, refract, or energize interior, fluid spiritual forces and motives. Yet, if the system is to remain vibrant, it must. If halakha is a means for the actualization and celebration of ethical norms, historical experiences, and theological postulates, then external conformity must be nurtured by internal sensibility and spirituality. This *concordia discordantium* – prophecy and law, charisma and institution, mood and medium, image and reality, normative action and individual perception, objective determinacy and subjective ecstasy – is the true essence of halakha and its ultimate consummation, but this harmonious, mutually fructifying relationship between law and experience is not always attainable.... When the spiritualizing speculative quest, in philosophic, mystical, or pietistic terms, is overshadowed, then the incidence of atrophied patterns of behavior sets off attempts to restore the ideal equilibrium: to see that action is reflective and deliberate, that the religious performance is both an expression of as well as stimulus to experience, deep and rich, full and fresh.[55]

Accordingly, halakha – its performance and its study – cannot exist by itself, but must be sustained by a spiritually informed meta-halakhic system that provides its underpinning and that endows it with significance and meaning beyond the actual physical act.

Maimonides is not alone; a procession of major Jewish thinkers and halakhists after him agreed in principle, although they did not always identify the content of the meta-halakhic material as he did. Thus, there were kabbalists who insisted that those who have the capabilities are required to attain knowledge of Kabbala after mastering halakha. In articles dealing with the "trialogue between talmudists, philosophers,

---

55. Ibid., 69–70.

and kabbalists,"[56] Prof. Twersky documents the wide range of extra-halakhic and meta-halakhic works written from the fifteenth through seventeenth centuries that deal with this relationship between Talmud study and meta-halakhic disciplines:

> We have here an intriguing, polychromatic array of authors who appear as learned expositors, skillful controversialists, erudite and versatile commentators, polemicists defending Judaism against external defamation while presenting their own vision of religious vitality and virtuosity, forceful proponents of a rabbinic culture free of adventitious elements, assiduous students of Bible and Aggada, ethicists, determined defenders of a waning philosophy or optimistic proponents of a revitalized philosophy, inspired protagonists of Kabbala, indeed of varieties of Kabbala, or zealous devotees of talmudism.[57]

The main issue, he goes on to explain, is the attainment of spirituality, religious vitality, and the correlation between the "duties of the limb" and the "duties of the heart." While Prof. Twersky is reporting and explicating medieval and early modern Jewish views on talmudism, rationalism, and spirituality, one cannot help but feel that the words are not only objective historical description, but existential positions with which he strongly identifies as well.

## AGGADA AND ITS INTERPRETATION

Another theme that Prof. Twersky saw as central and repercussive is rabbinic Aggada[58] – its use, interpretation, and authoritative status.

---

56. Isadore Twersky, "Talmudists, Philosophers, Kabbalists: The Quest for Spirituality in the Sixteenth Century," in *Jewish Thought in the Sixteenth Century*, ed. Bernard Dov Cooperman (Cambridge, MA, 1983), 431–59. The citation is on p. 440.
57. Ibid., 439. See also Isadore Twersky, "Law and Spirituality in the Seventeenth Century: A Case Study of R. Yair Hayim Bachrach," in *Jewish Thought in the Seventeenth Century*, ed. Isadore Twersky and Bernard Septimus (Cambridge, MA, 1987), 447–68.
58. Twersky, "Kaspi," 234–35. See Isadore Twersky, "R. Yedaiah ha-Penini and his Commentary on the Aggadah" in *Studies in Jewish Religious and Intellectual History Presented to Alexander Altmann*, ed. Raphael Loewe and Siegfried Stein (Alabama, 1980), Hebrew section, 63–82.

In geonic times, its authoritative status was questioned, probably due to the influence of rationalist thought. When conflict was sensed, *Geonim* often mitigated the status of the aggadic source and advised ignoring it when it contradicted reasonable logic.

In the twelfth century, when Christian clergy began to understand that Judaism is not primarily based on the Bible, but rather on the Oral Law, attacks upon the Talmud became frequent, with particular emphasis on aggadic sources.[59] Both the need to justify Aggada rationally and the need to defend it against outside attacks generated a great deal of hermeneutic activity. Rationalists attenuated its literal meaning using their allegorical tools; polemicists either took exception to Aggada's canonical status or presented apologetic interpretations in order to defend the honor of the rabbis. Kabbalists often stripped Aggada of its simple meaning, and it assumed a complex, mystical character in their hands.

Prof. Twersky's insight into the process of how Aggada was read – not as rationally indefensible innocent legend that could easily be dismissed, but rather as sophisticated rational allegory or an array of complex mystical symbols – leads to an understanding of how this theme continued to preoccupy thinkers and apologists continuously throughout the generations. A clear and unapologetic awareness of both the richness of Aggada as a wellspring for ideas and ethical insights, as well as a realization of the limitations of Aggada as a source for the fashioning of a contemporary world outlook, informs Prof. Twersky's writing. This insight into the complexity of Aggada, its status, and its meaning has not only historical importance, but contemporary significance as well.

## THE VARIETY OF BELIEFS AND OPINIONS IN THE HISTORY OF JUDAISM

What follows from Prof. Twersky's view of Jewish intellectual history is that there is a wide variety of beliefs and opinions that have characterized Jews and Jewish life throughout the generations. This would be

---

59. See Amos Funkenstein, "Changes in Christian Anti-Jewish Polemics in the Twelfth Century," in *Perception of Jewish History* (Berkeley, 1993), 172–200; Jeremy Cohen, *The Friars and the Jews: The Evolution of Medieval Anti-Judaism* (Ithaca, NY, 1982).

## Halakha and History, Intellectualism and Spirituality

a commonplace to the academic historian, but would be contrary to accepted belief within dogmatic religious circles.

Prof. Twersky did not shy away from dealing with unconventional ideas that appeared in the writings of medieval Jewish scholars. One example is his explication of Rabbi Yosef ibn Kaspi's new and radical interpretation of the concept of *dibbera Torah kilshon benei adam* (the Torah speaks in the language of men). Ibn Kaspi was a biblical exegete, philosopher, and ethicist who lived in Provence in the fourteenth century. This statement in its original talmudic context accounts for biblical repetitions by explaining that the Bible reflects ordinary human speech, and therefore nothing can be derived or insinuated from such repetition.[60] Maimonides, following Rabbeinu Bahya ibn Pakuda and Rabbi Avraham ibn Ezra, interpreted the statement, at variance with its original talmudic sense, to mean that anthropomorphic phrases and sentences were not meant to be taken literally, but rather as metaphors and allegories. Biblical language uses concrete anthropomorphic terms because of the limitations of the popular human imagination, but they are meant to convey abstract ideas. Kaspi went beyond the Maimonidean formulation and claimed, in Prof. Twersky's words:

> Many scriptural statements, covered by this plastic rubric, are seen as errors, superstitions, popular conceptions, local mores, folk beliefs, and customs, statements which reflect the assumptions or projections or behavioral patterns of the people involved rather than an abstract truth. In its Kaspian adaptation, the rabbinic dictum may then be paraphrased as follows: "The Torah expressed things as they were believed or perceived or practiced by the multitude and not as they were in actuality." …There is here in embryo a general historicistic position.[61]

This is not to say that Prof. Twersky adopted this historicistic position as his own. He certainly did not adopt another Kaspian notion: that one needn't expend too much effort studying halakhic sources but

---

60. See, for example, Nedarim 3a.
61. Twersky, "Kaspi," 239–240.

should rather devote himself mainly to philosophic spirituality, since practical halakhic guidance can be obtained from one's local *posek*.[62] Prof. Twersky's intellectual honesty, his appreciation of the broad spectrum of ideas and positions within the history of Jewish thought, and his genuine interest in the varieties of Jewish spirituality throughout the generations drew him to examine a broad range of positions and interpretive gestures.

## HISTORICISM AND ANTI-HISTORICISM: PROF. TWERSKY'S SYNTHESIS

Ibn Kaspi's historicism returns us to the question of Prof. Twersky's own historicism, historical methodology, and historical research. His commitment to historical research and historical thinking is unquestionable. I would like to sharpen the observations made above about his hasidic persona, and particularly about his connection with the Rav.

Rabbi Soloveitchik's rejection of historicist thinking warrants comment, since he did receive a broad humanistic education during his studies at the Friedrich Wilhelm University, in Berlin. In a passage from a eulogy in memory of his uncle, Rabbi Yitzhak Zev Soloveitchik, the Rav discusses the methodology of the halakhic thinking of his grandfather, Rabbi Hayim Soloveitchik, which his uncle and his father followed. He characterizes what became known as the "Brisker" school of talmudic study as one which Rabbi Hayim "purified" from all external influences, such as psychological, sociological, historical, or anthropological thinking, and which operates on the basis of its own ideal criteria, similar to the way in which mathematics creates its own independent universe uninfluenced by concrete reality.[63] Halakha is not influenced

---

62. See Ibn Kaspi's will in Israel Abrahams, ed., *Hebrew Ethical Wills* (Philadelphia, 1926), 151; Twersky, "Kaspi," 245.
63. Joseph B. Soloveitchik, "*Ma Dodekh MiDod*" in his *Divrei Hagut VeHaarakha* (Jerusalem, 1982), 76–77. In another, somewhat polemical context, the Rav said, "historicism...psychologism...[and] utilitarianism undermine the very foundations of *Torah umesora*, and it leads eventually to the most tragic consequences of assimilationism and nihilism, no matter how good the original intentions." See "*Talmud Torah* and *Kabbalas Ol Malchus Shamayim*: Partial transcript of an address of Rabbi Joseph B. Soloveitchik to the RCA Convention, 1975, on the topic of *gerut*,"

by changes in historical situations. The only effect that history has on halakha is that it provokes questions that arise from new situations. The principles of halakha are eternal and unchangeable.

Rabbi Soloveitchik was not alone in his rejection of historicist methodologies, nor was his position limited to the world of traditional Judaism. There had already been a strong anti-historicistic trend among modern Jewish thinkers, including Hermann Cohen, Franz Rosenzweig, and Isaac Breuer. As David Myers writes, a "diverse array of European and American intellectuals have given voice to their own concerns over the effects of historicism."[64]

In this light, Prof. Twersky's commitment to historical approaches is all the more interesting. While adhering to hasidic tradition and remaining personally, intellectually, and religiously close to his father-in-law,[65] he never retreated from his historical methodology. One might argue that because of the focus of his interests and the way he applied his historical methodology, there was no basis for direct conflict with his father-in-law's positions. The Rav's opposition to historicism was out of concern for the integrity of the halakhic process and his reluctance to view halakhic decisions as arising out of historically conditioned necessity. Prof. Twersky, in his writing about halakha, as mentioned above, did not deal directly with *pesak,* halakhic decisions, but with the literary and more broadly cultural aspects of halakha. Similarly, he did not deal with the biblical and talmudic periods, which would have required the historian to confront dogmatic aspects of Jewish tradition. Was this

---

http://www.parsha.net/pdf/Devarim/Vaeschanan66.pdf, p. 2. This *derasha* has been widely circulated and translated into Hebrew as an indication of Rabbi Soloveitchik's "anti-academic" position.

64. Myers, *Resisting History*, 159.

65. In *Introduction* (p. xv), he writes, "My father-in-law, Rabbi Dr. J. B. Soloveitchik, deserves special mention. I repeatedly benefited from his immense and genuinely effervescent learning and was warmed by his unfailing devotion. He has, in short, given me so much over the years that it would be folly to assume that a formal acknowledgement would be fully expressive." See above, n. 13, and his dedication of the posthumous article "LeDemuto shel HaRambam," *Asufot: Annual for Jewish Studies* 10 (1997): 9, where he dedicates the article to "My father-in-law... the Rambam of our generation." Prof. Twersky's consistent avoidance of hyperbole makes his description all the more significant.

intentional? There is no question, as he himself once said in conversation, that a scholar has the right to choose his area of research. Once it is chosen, then his commitment to truth must be uncompromising.[66] He chose the medieval period.

Prof. Twersky used critical historical tools not to give Judaism "a decent burial," in the phrase attributed to Moritz Steinschneider,[67] nor to change halakha, nor to transform or reform Judaism into a "modern" religion, nor to weaken faith in the validity of tradition, but to sharpen our understanding of the richness of Jewish tradition, of its sophistication and depth, of the spiritual treasures that it has to offer, and of the ongoing freshness and contemporaneity of Judaism. Utilizing the tools of philological, historical, and literary analysis with precision, he sought to generate an understanding of Judaism's dynamics, emphasize its uniqueness, give us an appreciation of the dazzling multifaceted halakhic personalities that have guided Jewish tradition in the past, and draw from the wellsprings of moral and ethical insight that Judaism has to offer. All this was accomplished with the "carefully lined notebook of the historian or analyst," without acting as "preacher or partisan."[68]

## PARTICULARISM AND UNIVERSALISM

I think that it would be fair to say that one could characterize Prof. Twersky's scholarship as he himself analyzed Maimonides' *taamei hamitzvot*. In his *Introduction to the Code of Maimonides*, Prof. Twersky notes Maimonides' unique interpretation of the following verses:

> Behold I have taught you statues and ordinances...that you should do so in the midst of the Land to which you go in to possess it. Observe therefore and do them; for this is your wisdom and your understanding in the sight of the peoples, who, when

---

66. This is the gist of a conversation I had with him.
67. See, however, the nuanced reassessment of Steinschneider's statement by Charles H. Manekin, "Steinschneider's 'Decent Burial': A Reappraisal" in *Study and Knowledge in Jewish Thought*, ed. Howard Kreisel (Beersheba, 2006), 239–51.
68. Isadore Twersky, "Some Aspects of the Jewish Attitude Toward the Welfare State," *Tradition* 5 (1963): 137.

## Halakha and History, Intellectualism and Spirituality

they hear all these statutes, shall say, "Surely this great nation is a wise and understanding people" (Deut. 4:5–6)

Prof. Twersky carefully traced the history of the interpretation of this verse.[69] Which wisdom is referred to here? According to one talmudic view, the antecedent of "this" in "this is your wisdom" is the calculation of cycles and planetary courses.[70] Ḥazal here tried to identify "a universal subject of study where Jews and gentiles meet on common ground and are united in scientific achievement."[71] Maimonides in the *Guide* cites the context of the verse in explaining that the antecedent of "this is your wisdom" refers to the statutes, the *ḥukkim*, which you should see not as irrational, but rather as rational and purposive and which, with proper philosophic interpretation, will have universal resonance and will impress all the nations. This will ensure that the response of the nations of the world will be "surely this great nation is a wise and understanding people."[72] Similarly, in Maimonides' introduction to *Perek Ḥelek*, the last chapter of Tractate Sanhedrin, he also uses the verse to defend the importance of interpreting Aggada allegorically for the outer-directed purpose of showing the universal significance of the Torah.[73]

While I am not attributing apologetic motivations for Prof. Twersky's historical research, there is no doubt that setting his analysis of classical Jewish sources within the universal orbit of the humanities and using critical historical categories of analysis accomplished an end similar to that which Maimonides attributed to his allegorical and philosophical methodology. Jewish cultural life can be widely understood and broadly appreciated using universal categories of literary, philological, and historical analysis.

Prof. Twersky functioned within the orbit of two secular scholarly institutions, Harvard University and the Hebrew University,[74] and

---

69. Twersky, *Introduction*, 380–87.
70. Shabbat 75a.
71. Twersky, *Introduction*, 382.
72. *Guide of the Perplexed* III:31.
73. See Twersky, *A Maimonides Reader*, 407.
74. As mentioned above, he studied in his youth at the Hebrew University. He maintained a close association with its scholars throughout his career and eventually received an honorary doctorate from the university.

not within the framework of religious academic institutions, such as Yeshiva University or Bar-Ilan University. His creative work in the field of Jewish education was also not done exclusively within an Orthodox framework. There is no doubt as to his passionate commitment to traditional Judaism, to halakha, and to Hasidism. Indeed, his academic work privileged halakhic creativity, which was perceived by many scholars as the most parochial of Jewish concerns. Yet he succeeded in analyzing halakha and its history specifically and Jewish creativity generally, using universal or outer-directed categories.[75]

This creative tension between the awareness of "outer-directed tendencies of the Jewish historical experience" and the need to explicate "inner-directed forces and experiences"[76] is probably the best key to understand Prof. Twersky's academic oeuvre.

---

75. See his reference to the outer-directed aspect of Judaic studies in a university framework in Twersky, "Harry Austryn Wolfson (1887–1974)" (n. 8 above), 107: "Jewish studies in the university are difficult and demanding, and – indeed like Judaism itself – require dialectical deftness. They should be universalist, should strive to correlate, as Edmund Wilson put it, 'the adventures and achievements of Jews with those of the rest of the world,' should bring the outer-directed tendencies of the Jewish historical experience into clear focus, and try to develop a panoramic and synoptic view which sees the interplay of forces and help integrate the study of Jewish and world history."
76. Ibid.

# Music of the Left Hand: Personal Notes on the Place of Liberal Arts Education in the Teachings of Rabbi Aharon Lichtenstein*

Rabbi Shalom Carmy with
Rabbi Shlomo Zuckier

### PART 1: INTRODUCTORY BIOGRAPHICAL SKETCH[1]

**1.**

First things first: The words of the mishna, "*Talmud Torah* is equivalent to all [of the commandments],"[2] stand at the center of Rabbi Aharon

---

* Rabbi Lichtenstein passed away on Rosh Ḥodesh Iyar 5775 (April 20, 2015), shortly before this volume went to print. The present tense is retained throughout the article.
1. This article, originally commissioned for *Torah and Western Thought*, was prepublished as two separate articles in a tribute issue of *Tradition* honoring Rabbi Aharon Lichtenstein: Shlomo Zuckier and Shalom Carmy, "An Introductory Biographical Sketch of R. Aharon Lichtenstein," 6–16, and Shalom Carmy, "Music of the Left Hand: Personal Notes on the Place of Liberal Arts Education in the Teachings of R. Aharon Lichtenstein," 223–39, both in *Tradition* 47, no. 4 (2014). See that issue of *Tradition* for additional valuable studies of Rabbi Lichtenstein's thought. See also the tributes to and eulogies of Rabbi Lichtenstein collected at http://haretzion.org/about-us/rav-aharon-lichtenstein-ztl.
2. Mishna Pe'ah 1:1.

Lichtenstein's thinking. Torah study is the noblest of pursuits, an overriding commandment, and the royal pathway to the knowledge of God. The primary arena of Torah study, for Rabbi Lichtenstein as for the mainstream of Jewish thought, is the study of legal texts: Talmud, and its commentators and codifiers. And when Rabbi Lichtenstein extols Talmud study, he has particularly in mind the Talmud study pursued in the Eastern European tradition and as developed in the past century under the flag of the Brisker school. To ignore or minimize the emphasis on Torah study, and especially on Talmud, in Rabbi Lichtenstein's thought simply because he has championed broad universal concerns and advocated the study of the liberal arts as a vehicle to religious wholeness is a distortion of his teaching to the point of making it unrecognizable.

Because Rabbi Lichtenstein's theoretical position on general studies is so bound up in his life and overall way of thinking, it is impossible to move on to the task of discussing his view of general studies without offering something of his biography, his massive contribution to the study and teaching of Talmud, and his propagation of Judaism, as well as his other public activities.

Rabbi Lichtenstein was born in 1933 in France, from which his family escaped in 1941 to the United States, finally settling in New York. As a youngster, he made his mark at Yeshiva Rabbi Chaim Berlin. There he studied with and was deeply influenced by Rabbi Ahron Soloveichik and Rabbi Yitzchok Hutner. Entering Yeshiva College at the age of sixteen, he studied with Rabbi Moshe Shatzkes and, more fatefully, with Rabbi Joseph B. Soloveitchik, known as "the Rav." Following graduation, having been urged by the Rav to pursue graduate studies, Rabbi Lichtenstein took a doctorate in English literature at Harvard (from 1953 to 1957), where his primary mentor and thesis advisor was Prof. Douglas Bush. He focused on seventeenth-century writers, including John Milton, and submitted a thesis on the theologian Henry More.[3] During this period, he continued to study privately with the Rav at his home in Boston. He married Tovah Soloveitchik, the Rav's daughter, in 1960.

---

3. It was later published in book form as *Henry More: The Rational Theology of a Cambridge Platonist* (Cambridge, MA, 1962).

Returning to Yeshiva University in 1957, Rabbi Lichtenstein taught English literature at Stern College for Women while serving as the Rav's *shiur* assistant, reviewing the lectures and aiding students when Rabbi Soloveitchik was not available. In 1961, Yeshiva University reopened its kollel, with Rabbi Lichtenstein, at 28, as Rosh Kollel. Two years later, when he began teaching a daily Gemara *shiur* in the yeshiva he continued to offer college courses on an occasional basis. Rabbi Lichtenstein was an active participant in the discussions about Torah and the secular world taking place in Yeshiva University throughout the 1960s and wrote several important articles during that decade.

By 1970, Rabbi Lichtenstein and his wife were prepared for *aliya*. He accepted the invitation of Rabbi Yehuda Amital, who had recently founded Yeshivat Har Etzion in the Gush Etzion region, and joined him as co-Rosh Yeshiva in 1971. For nearly forty years, the two jointly built and sustained the most influential *hesder* yeshiva. Rabbi Zerach Warhaftig, the noted *talmid ḥakham*, legal scholar, and Israeli minister of religion, later observed that Rabbi Lichtenstein brought "a new style of learning: clarifying *sugyot* (subjects for study) in depth in an orderly and precise way."[4]

During his first forty years at Har Etzion, Rabbi Lichtenstein had an extraordinary schedule of teaching, in addition to his leadership role in the yeshiva. He delivered *shiurim* for advanced students several times a week from the time of his arrival until April 2011 and gave general *shiurim* and *siḥot* to the entire yeshiva on a regular basis. Beginning in 1976, Rabbi Lichtenstein also served as the Rosh Kollel at Yeshiva University's Joseph and Caroline Gruss Kollel in Jerusalem, teaching there weekly.

Rabbi Lichtenstein has published widely over the course of his career, producing scores of formal articles on a remarkably broad range of talmudic subjects.[5] In addition, students have published

---

4. Rabbi Zerach Warhaftig, *Ḥamishim Shana VeShana: Pirkei Zikhronot* (Jerusalem, 1998), 153.
5. His bibliography is accessible at http://etzion.org.il/vbm/archive/Bibliography-web.htm. As of March 13, 2012, 1,067 publications were listed, most of which were student-written versions of lectures he gave on topics in halakha or *hashkafa*.

multiple volumes of his lectures, thus creating a permanent record of the decades of *shiurim* that molded generations of students at Yeshivat Har Etzion. Based on the careful notes of students, eight volumes have been published to date,[6] and the raw material for dozens more exists. Rabbi Lichtenstein has also written scores of programmatic essays on important topics concerning Jewish learning and life, as well as on his hashkafic perspective on a range of other issues. Many of these presentations are collected in a three-volume series – *Leaves of Faith* 1 and 2, and *Varieties of Jewish Experience* – as well as in two volumes of collected lectures and discussions.[7] The most important of his studies in Talmud were recently collected under the title *Minḥat Aviv*.[8]

Rabbi Lichtenstein's children, four sons and two daughters, are all involved in Jewish education.[9] Rabbi Lichtenstein considers his family to be his proudest achievement.[10] His educational progeny, graduates of Yeshivat Har Etzion, have gone on to found and teach in many other *hesder* yeshivas, and numerous graduates occupy prominent positions in academia and elsewhere in Israeli society. Rabbi Lichtenstein's strong influence on many of them extends to the substance and method of Talmud study as well as to their outlook and approach to many crucial issues of individual, communal, religious, ethical, and national import. Students who acknowledge Rabbi Lichtenstein's crucial influence currently occupy positions in many institutions of higher Jewish learning,

---

6. As of 2013, books have appeared on Tractates Pesaḥim, Gittin, Zevaḥim, Teharot, and Horayot; *Perek HaShoel*, ch. 8 in Bava Metzia, and *Perek Ḥezkat HaBattim*, ch. 3 in Bava Batra; and *Dina DeGarmi*.
7. *Leaves of Faith* (vol. 1): *The World of Jewish Learning* (New Jersey, 2003); *Leaves of Faith* (vol. 2): *The World of Jewish Living* (New Jersey, 2004); and *Varieties of Jewish Experience* (New Jersey, 2011). Also, *By His Light: Character and Values in the Service of God*, based on addresses by Rabbi Aharon Lichtenstein, adapted by Reuven Ziegler (Jersey City, NJ, 2003); and Haim Sabato, *Mevakshei Panekha: Siḥot im HaRav Aharon Lichtenstein* (Tel Aviv, 2011).
8. Aharon Lichtenstein, *Minḥat Aviv: Ḥiddushim VeIyunim BaShas*, ed. Elyakim Krumbein (Jerusalem, 2014).
9. See http://etzion.org.il/en/HaravAharon.
10. "Reflecting on 50 Years of Torah Leadership: An Interview with Rabbi Aharon Lichtenstein," accessible at http://blogs.yu.edu/news/2011/10/11/reflecting-on-50-years-of-torah-leadership/.

both in America and Israel, and his belief system is seen by many as the most authentic representation of Modern Orthodoxy in this generation.[11]

Due to his wide scholarly output and his complex and developed positions on contemporary issues, Rabbi Lichtenstein is considered by many American Modern Orthodox Jews to be their *gadol hador*, like his father-in-law Rabbi Soloveitchik before him. If the Rav bestrode American Orthodoxy like a colossus,[12] Rabbi Lichtenstein has been a remote polestar, projecting his influence from a distance, as his votaries ponder his every word, rendered all the more precious by his unwillingness to meddle uninvited in American affairs. Rabbi Lichtenstein has often been asked to present the hashkafic overview at the annual Orthodox Forum gathering and at many other Rabbinical Council of America (RCA) and Yeshiva University conclaves, with the justified presumption that his position carries authority for Modern Orthodoxy.

In Israel, Rabbi Lichtenstein's primary influence has been through Yeshivat Har Etzion and several satellite yeshivas set up by students. Yeshivat Har Etzion has also founded an affiliated teacher's college and women's beit midrash, each of which served as a model for similar programs in other *hesder* yeshivas.[13] His stature as talmudic scholar and teacher has been publicly recognized through the award of the prestigious Rav Kook Prize for Torah Literature (5773) and the Israel Prize for Torah Literature (5774).

His study and teaching of Talmud is rooted in the Brisker method, which is "fixed upon the fundamental problems...recognizing the halakhic phenomenon, analyzing, formulating, defining, classifying, and

---

11. Alan Brill ("An Ideal Rosh Yeshiva: *By His Light*: *Character and Values in the Service of God* and *Leaves of Faith* by Rav Aharon Lichtenstein," *Edah Journal* 5, no. 1 [2005]) identifies Rabbi Lichtenstein with Centrist Orthodoxy rather than Modern Orthodoxy; as the former label never became popular, we will use the latter term.
12. Rabbi Lichtenstein used this phrase to refer to Rabbi Soloveitchik on at least two occasions: *Leaves of Faith*, 2:290, relating the Rav to other *gedolim*, and "Take Rav Soloveitchik at Full Depth," *Forward*, March 12, 1999, 6, relating the Rav to American Orthodoxy as a whole.
13. See Esti Rosenberg, "The World of Women's Torah Learning – Developments, Directions and Objectives: A Report from the Field," *Tradition* 45, no. 1 (2012): 13–36, for the development of women's learning programs.

categorizing it."[14] In line with the Brisker tradition, Rabbi Lichtenstein's goal is to analyze halakha in terms of underlying abstract principles. Commentators on his distinctive contribution have discerned a shift of focus, already initiated by Rabbi Soloveitchik, according to which conceptual clarification becomes the primary goal of study rather than serving as an instrument to resolve contradictions.[15] The volumes of Rabbi Lichtenstein's collected *shiurim* should be understood less as textual analyses than as topical essays, in which fundamental questions are posed at the outset, logical possibilities are mapped out, and these are applied to the textual canvas occupied primarily by the *Rishonim*. The sources treated as primary texts include a wide gamut of *Rishonim*, including some *Ḥakhmei Ashkenaz* who were often overlooked in the prior Brisker literature (e.g., Raavya, Raavan); *Aḥaronim* are used sparingly, most often to complement or supplement the analysis.[16]

In the United States, the Brisker approach to Talmud is widely admired and sometimes emulated in Modern Orthodox circles, in part because of the Rav's precedent and in part because of the relatively homogeneous student body. Training in Rabbi Lichtenstein's approach is often regarded as the ideal. In Israel, there has been criticism of this method, partly due to the visibility of more academic or more "spiritualistic" religious and intellectual alternatives, which respectively perceive Brisk as either intellectually elitist or insufficiently historicist. Other reservations stem from greater sensitivity to the frustration of students who are exposed to Talmud just enough to know they dislike it, a situation that Rabbi Lichtenstein has responded to – despite the painfulness of the message to him – by reexamining whether advanced Talmud is really for everyone.[17]

---

14. Aharon Lichtenstein, "*Kakh Hi Darkah shel Torat HaRav*," *Alon Shevut Bogrim* 2 (5754): 108; trans. Elyakim Krumbein, "The Evolution of a Tradition of Learning," in *Lomdus: The Conceptual Approach to Jewish Learning*, ed. Yosef Blau (NY, 2006), 252.
15. Krumbein, "The Evolution." See several other articles by Krumbein for more on Rabbi Lichtenstein's *derekh halimmud*.
16. For Rabbi Lichtenstein's reflections on his method of Talmud study, see "The Conceptual Approach to Torah Learning" and "*Torat Ḥesed* and *Torat Emet*," in Lichtenstein, *Leaves of Faith*, 1:19–88.
17. For an English rendering of a dialogue between Rabbi Lichtenstein and Rabbi Shagar, a prominent exponent of a more spiritualistic approach to Talmud who

## II.

For Rabbi Lichtenstein, as noted, the central and ideal religious experience should be the study of Torah. Learning Torah, especially Talmud and halakha, allows one to be "exposed once again to his Master's commanding presence."[18] Gemara should be seen as the central text in this connection, due to its position as the basis of all halakhic literature and its authoritative nature. Rabbi Lichtenstein's vision of Gemara study explicitly engages the traditional mode of study, apprehended as a holistic system with the *Rishonim* as the primary interpreters; while recognizing some contributions of academic scholarship, he opposes those who "pass judgment upon" Hazal's work instead of being ennobled by it.[19] Learning for its own sake is linked to a view of the halakhic system as the ground of one's outlook on the world. Rabbi Lichtenstein, following the Rav, presents halakha as fundamental axiology.

In the three substantial articles referred to below on the integration of secular studies and Torah education,[20] Rabbi Lichtenstein emphasizes that Torah ideals must remain both supreme and central to an observant Jew's life, and Torah study similarly as important to his or her thinking.[21] Within this frame of reference, Rabbi Lichtenstein identifies several valuable contributions of a general education. One is

---

combined it with selective use of academic methods, see http://www.lookstein.org/articles/shnayim_ohazim.htm. See also the symposium on Rabbi Shagar in *Netuim* 17 (2011), the articles in *Tradition* 45, no. 2 (2012), and the dialogue between Rabbi Lichtenstein and Rabbi Yehuda Brandes in *Notes from ATID: Talmud Study in Yeshiva High Schools* (Jerusalem, 2007).

18. Lichtenstein, *Leaves of Faith*, 1:6.
19. Ibid., 11. For more on Rabbi Lichtenstein's focus on Torah learning, see "Why Learn Gemara," in *Leaves of Faith*, 1:1–17.
20. Aharon Lichtenstein, "A Consideration of Synthesis from a Torah Point of View," *Commentator*, April 27, 1961, reprinted as "A Consideration of General Studies from a Torah Point of View" in *Leaves of Faith*, 1:89–103; Aharon Lichtenstein, "Torah and General Culture: Confluence and Conflict," in *Judaism's Encounter with Other Cultures: Rejection or Integration*, ed. Jacob J. Schacter (New Jersey, 1997), 217–92; and Aharon Lichtenstein, "*Tova Ḥokhma im Naḥala*," in *Mamlekhet Kohanim VeGoy Kadosh*, ed. Yehuda Shaviv (Jerusalem, 1989), 25–43.
21. Following in the footsteps of his mentor Rabbi Soloveitchik, Rabbi Lichtenstein has championed serious Torah study for women, including in-depth study of Talmud, and has arguably done more than the Rav to further it on a practical level.

that exerting a positive religious influence on society requires genuine understanding of the social milieu. Another is that Torah study itself is, at times, aided by deploying analytic tools developed in the academy. Most importantly, moreover, "the humanities deepen our understanding of man: his nature, functions, and duties."[22] The observant Jew who studies what Matthew Arnold called "the best that has been thought and said in the world,"[23] is more likely to become an edified, spiritually ennobled person with an enhanced sense of human complexity.

Some may attain such insight without liberal arts study. Rabbi Lichtenstein regularly refers to Nahmanides' introduction to the Torah, which extols a penetrating understanding of the human world without championing philosophical studies as a means to it. If we agree with Nahmanides about the need for such understanding and are honest enough to recognize our limitations, we ought to avail ourselves of the tools provided by general culture. To be sure, the dangers of corruption and distraction through such endeavors cannot be dismissed. The student must, therefore, redouble his or her effort and commitment to Torah and *avodat Hashem* in order to overcome these perils.[24]

Because Rabbi Lichtenstein's argument for general studies is so strongly tied to his sense of moral and religious growth and self-examination, his own living example is not irrelevant to his position. Rabbi Lichtenstein's thinking and writing on all subjects, both in Torah study and in his perspective on the moral and social worlds, is indeed marked by a sense of complexity and a striving for thoroughness, honesty, humility, and accuracy, nourished by the breadth and scope and discipline of his study. He has acknowledged areas where his thinking about issues of Jewish significance has been affected by his general education, by his knowledge of the world, and by his appreciation of the best it has to offer.

---

22. Lichtenstein, *Leaves of Faith*, 1:93.
23. Matthew Arnold, *Culture and Anarchy: An Essay in Political and Social Criticism* (Minneapolis, 1903), 299.
24. See Lichtenstein, "To Double Business Bound: On the Divided Lives of *Ovedei Hashem*," in *Varieties of Jewish Experience*, 269–90, for some of the challenges of integrating two areas of study. For particular fields and Rabbi Lichtenstein's views on how they can be integrated into a life of *avodat Hashem*, see Lichtenstein, "Torah and General Culture."

Like other close *talmidim* of the Rav (such as Rabbi Walter Wurzburger), Rabbi Lichtenstein has been much occupied throughout his career with the place of morality in relation to halakha. His early essay "Does Judaism Recognize an Ethic Independent of Halakha?"[25] utilizes a broad range of Jewish sources, as well as some philosophical argumentation, to conclude that "Judaism demands of the Jew both adherence to halakha and commitment to an ethical movement that, though different from halakha, is nevertheless of a piece with it and in its own way fully imperative,"[26] leaving open the question of whether that moral standard is best viewed as a supererogatory category within halakha (*lifnim mishurat hadin*) or an internal one. This understanding of the position of morality within Judaism was central to his views on an additional range of issues, from the morality of war[27] to universal moral duties;[28] from understanding the command to wipe out Amalek[29] to the existence of a humanistic element within religious Judaism.[30]

This sensitivity to the human condition affects Rabbi Lichtenstein's approach to *pesak halakha*.[31] Though Rabbi Lichtenstein sees halakha as an autonomous closed system in which only internal halakhic concerns govern a *posek*'s decisions, the system itself integrates humane considerations such as *she'at hadehak* (a time of pressing need), *tzorekh gadol* (a great need), and *pikuah nefesh* (the saving of

---

25. In Marvin Fox, ed., *Modern Jewish Ethics* (Columbus, 1975), 62–88, reprinted in Lichtenstein, *Leaves of Faith*, 2:33–56.
26. Lichtenstein, *Leaves of Faith*, 2:52. See also "Being *Frum* and Being Good: On the Relationship Between Religion and Morality," in Lichtenstein, *By His Light*, 101–33, which deals with many of these issues.
27. "War and Morality – A Panel Discussion with Rabbi Dov Lior, Rabbi She'ar Yashuv Cohen, Rabbi Dr. Yaakov Hasdai, and Rabbi Dr. Aharon Lichtenstein," *Tehumin* 4 (1983): 184–96.
28. See "To Cultivate and to Guard: The Universal Duties of Mankind," in Lichtenstein, *By His Light*, 1–26.
29. See Lichtenstein, *By His Light*, 126–27.
30. See Aharon Lichtenstein, "*Mah Enosh*: Reflections on the Relation Between Judaism and Humanism," *Torah u-Madda Journal* 14 (2006-7): 1–61 (written in the 1960s); and "*Ki BeTzelem E-lohim Asa et HaAdam*: Is There Religious Humanism?" in Sabato, *Mevakshei Panekha*, 125–40.
31. See Lichtenstein, "*Mah Enosh*," 1–61, and Lichtenstein, "The Human and Social Factor in Halakha," in *Leaves of Faith*, 1:159–88.

life), such that "differential *pesak*"[32] is called for, when necessary. Thus, although "halakha, as a normative order, can never be superseded by external pressures, a specific halakha may be flexibly applied – and, in a sense, superseded – by the internal dynamics of the halakhic system proper."[33] This understanding rejects the "where there is a rabbinic will there is a halakhic way" position as an "insouciant view of the totality of halakha, verg[ing] on the blasphemous,"[34] as Rabbi Lichtenstein calls for sensitive and responsible *posekim* to apply the law judiciously.

## III.

Religious Zionism holds an important place within Rabbi Lichtenstein's *hashkafa*. Indeed, it was his deep belief in this ideology that inspired him to move to Israel, leaving a stable position for the unsure terrain of a new yeshiva. It is no coincidence that this yeshiva combines Torah study with army service, for Rabbi Lichtenstein was an early proponent of *hesder*; early in his career at Yeshivat Har Etzion, he wrote a seminal programmatic essay on its ideology.[35] Rabbi Lichtenstein's Zionism is not predicated on messianic imminence, but rather on the conviction that building a Jewish nation and future on its own soil is in itself a valued endeavor and a prized opportunity. At the same time, Rabbi Lichtenstein notes the multifold halakhic benefits of living in Israel, as discussed by several *Rishonim*, primarily Nahmanides.[36] In addition, the State of Israel connects a Jew to generations of other Jews who have lived in Israel, as well as to the living Jewish nation as it actively builds the Land. Furthermore, life in Israel affords a more integrated life than is possible in the Diaspora, a greater sense of wholeness, since there is societal and religious value even to the mundane aspects of one's daily existence.[37] Rabbi Lichtenstein's passion for the Land of Israel expresses

---

32. Lichtenstein, *Leaves of Faith*, 1:168.
33. Ibid., 170.
34. Ibid., 174.
35. Aharon Lichtenstein, "Zot Torat HaHesder," *Alon Shevut* 100 (1982): 9–33, translated as "The Ideology of *Hesder*," *Leaves of Faith*, 1:135–58.
36. Lichtenstein, *Varieties of Jewish Experience*, 294–98.
37. Ibid., 299.

itself in his assertion that every Jew should at least aspire to move to Israel, to nestle, as it were, in the bosom of the Divine Presence.[38]

In Israel, Rabbi Lichtenstein has been categorized as a political moderate, partly because he adopted the Rav's view that territorial compromise is permissible in the Land of Israel for the sake of peace. He has refrained from entering the partisan political arena. He has adamantly refused to allow politics to overshadow Torah in yeshiva life; even when Rav Amital was a candidate for the Knesset, the students at Har Etzion, unlike those at many other yeshivas, were discouraged from curtailing their Torah study in order to canvas.

Yet Rabbi Lichtenstein, from time to time, has taken positions on urgent public issues and has presented general perspectives on matters prompted by the occasion. Invariably, when he has lifted his voice, it has not been to cheerlead for those with whom he finds himself in agreement. Rather, he has repeatedly called into question one-sided, often popular opinions. For example, during the first Lebanon War, in 1982, after the Christian militiamen who enjoyed Israeli support massacred Palestinian refugees, Rabbi Lichtenstein wrote an open letter to Prime Minister Menachem Begin calling upon the government to investigate whether Israeli officials had failed to exercise restraint over the marauders; the letter first appeared in the religious nationalist newspaper *HaTzofeh*.[39]

Some years later, when Rabbi Elazar Menachem Man Shach publicly attacked secular Zionism, and labor Zionism in particular, during an Israeli cabinet crisis, it was to readers of the secular *Maariv* that Rabbi Lichtenstein explained that his world was that of Rabbi Shach and Ponevezh, and that he differed from his ḥaredi confreres primarily insofar as he insisted on recognizing and celebrating the accomplishments of secular Zionism.[40] While others are tempted to magnify the gap between Religious Zionism and the ḥaredi community, Rabbi Lichtenstein went out of his way to define that gap narrowly. He revered

---

38. See Aharon Lichtenstein, "On *Aliya*: The Uniqueness of Living in *Eretz Yisrael*," *Alei Etzion* 12 (2004): 15–22, accessible at http://etzion.org.il/en/aliya-uniqueness-living-eretzyisrael.
39. "Haḥzarat HaGaava HaLeumit UZkifat HaKoma HaYisraelit," *HaTzofeh*, Oct. 15, 1982, 5. The Rav phoned the prime minister's office in the same cause.
40. "Shefayim UShfiyyut," *Maariv*, June 21, 1991, B13.

and pursued personal relationships with major figures in the non-Zionist Orthodox community – most notably, with Rabbi Shlomo Zalman Auerbach, but with others as well – and has lamented the unwillingness of other Religious Zionist *rabbanim* to do likewise.[41] Similarly, he has repeatedly criticized the inclination of Orthodox spokesmen to derive unholy comfort from phenomena of malaise in secular society, as if its decline were necessary for our self-confidence.[42] The lesson, to at least some of his students, is that engagement in public affairs is sometimes a duty, but never an occasion to play to the galleries.[43]

In recent years, Rabbi Lichtenstein has been more forthcoming on burning issues; he opposed rabbinically backed calls to disobey orders in the army[44] and questioned a prohibition on renting land to Arabs.[45] These stances possibly constituted a reaction to the increasing tendency of militant and separatist streams of Religious Zionist culture to seek out areas of potential divisiveness between themselves and the government or society, and to use these areas in a manner that magnifies the fissures in Israeli society and politics, thus estranging those who reject these positions. The recently published book *Mevakshei Panekha*,[46] a presentation of Rabbi Lichtenstein's views in conversation with Rabbi Haim Sabato for a popular Israeli audience, has reached a large secular Israeli population interested in learning about a rabbinic authority who treats them and their culture with respect and understanding.

Beyond his intellectual prowess and dedication, Rabbi Lichtenstein's attractiveness as a religious and ethical role model is very much connected to his remarkable personal qualities. It has been lamented that

---

41. See Lichtenstein, "A Portrait of Rav Shlomo Zalman Auerbach, *zts"l*," in *Leaves of Faith*, 1:247–50; and Lichtenstein, "The Israeli Chief Rabbinate: A Current Halakhic Perspective," in *Leaves of Faith*, 2:261–77.
42. Sabato, *Mevakshei Panekha*, 141–56.
43. Another example is his criticism of Rabbi Dov Lior's eulogy for Baruch Goldstein; see "A Rabbinic Exchange on Baruch Goldstein's Funeral," *Leaves of Faith*, 2:255–60.
44. Aharon Lichtenstein, "A Rabbinic Exchange on the Gaza Disengagement," *Tradition* 40, no. 1 (Spring 2007): 17–44; and *Tradition* 40, no. 2 (Summer, 2007): 49–70.
45. "Response to the Esteemed Rabbis, Signatories of the Letter Forbidding the Sale of Homes to Gentiles in the Land of Israel," accessible at http://kolharav.blogspot.com/2010/12/rabbi-aharon-lichtensteins-response-to.html.
46. Sabato, *Mevakshei Panekha: Siḥot im HaRav Aharon Lichtenstein* (Tel Aviv, 2011).

the intellectual brilliance of R. Lichtenstein may, at times, obscure his moral and human greatness. His personal integrity, depth of character, humility, indomitable enthusiasm, attentiveness to the dignity and needs of other human beings, and truly and unfailingly humane comportment are an abiding inspiration and ideal for many whom he has taught and influenced. If this is what a life dedicated to *avodat Hashem* is about, it is hard not to want to share in that quest.

It is, of course, difficult for *talmidim* to expatiate on the character of their mentor, particularly in the context of a brief preface to an essay dealing with other matters, and especially when so much of what we would speak about pertains to private exchanges and painstaking individual guidance. For the insider, elaboration is inadequate and superfluous; for outsiders, it smacks of hagiography and bragging that does not fit the humble, down-to-earth qualities of the individual being praised. It may be best to give the floor to an outsider, one who abandoned Talmud and Orthodoxy for the analytic philosophy of language and who, decades later, seeking a way back, looked up his undergraduate teacher. He provides the following anecdote:

> Rabbi Aharon Lichtenstein, a talmudic scholar, Harvard PhD in literature, and published scholar of Cambridge Platonism, invited my family to his home at 7:00 AM on a Sunday, before he headed out to his yeshiva. When I tried to thank him for all he had done for me – Talmud with him was like boot camp for analytic philosophy – his humility inserted itself; he lowered his head and changed the subject. The contrast with much of academia could not have been more stark.[47]

## PART 2: ON LIBERAL ARTS STUDY
### I.

> For the quest for virtue must involve the whole man, the intellect included.... In our concern for practical effects, we may forget the religious principles upon which, from More's point of view as from mine, true morality must be based – "La morale," as Loisy

---

47. Howard Wettstein, *The Significance of Religious Experience* (Oxford, 2012), 22–23.

said, "étant comme impliquée dans la religion, qui en inspirait et sanctionnait les préceptes."[48]

It has been said – in fact, Rabbi Lichtenstein said it – that the occupational hazard of every scholar is the temptation to exaggerate the importance of his subject.[49] The Circe of the student writing about an authoritative and formative master is the temptation to exaggerate the overlap between the teacher and the student. This is not merely the inclination to egregious revisionism, when facts are suppressed and positions are misinterpreted with insouciance, as is not uncommon in current discourse. Especially in dealing with a thinker like Rabbi Lichtenstein, who exemplifies intellectual nuance and personal balance, the student may meet a reasonable expectation of accuracy, avoiding error or misinterpretation, without attaining precision; you may get a good account of what the student learned, but not a full or balanced assessment of what he was taught. One of the great talmudists of the modern era wrote, in a similar context, "In judging, where the falsehood is only in the estimate of the mind and not regarding what is perceived, deception is easier."[50] It is thus a matter of full disclosure to say something about my point of entry to this discussion.

From Rabbi Lichtenstein and from my other mentors at Yeshiva University, I gained the conviction that human life is about action rather than contemplation and that therefore the intellectual activity mandated by Judaism centers on thought allied to potential action – thus confirming the traditional concentration on the study of halakhic texts, so that a life apart from such learning is religiously impoverished. I gained an indelible appreciation of the traditional approach to learning, one that prevented me from succumbing to the notion that *lomdut* is somehow less "sophisticated" than the methods promulgated in the academic community and that one "transitions" from the former to the latter. Of course, such training made it impossible for me to be attracted to the

---

48. Lichtenstein, *Henry More*, 203–4. The French statement means: "Morality being thus implicated in religion, which inspires it and sanctions its precepts."
49. Ibid., ix.
50. *Or Sameaḥ*, Laws of Sanhedrin 23:6.

suggestion that one may, in good conscience, compartmentalize one's intellectual life: *frum* in the beit midrash, academically antiseptic in the library. Having said this, my nominal professional position is in a department of academic Jewish studies and the bulk of my contribution to Torah studies is in Jewish thought and Tanakh; I teach regularly in the humanities division and publish frequently on topics that are not explicitly religious in journals that are read mostly by non-Jews. A student of Rabbi Lichtenstein who had described a different career would probably focus on different points.

Moreover, at the time I was fortunate to enter Rabbi Lichtenstein's *shiur* at Yeshiva University, I was already strongly convinced that one ought to seek out the truth wherever it is. One of the urgent questions in my mind was whether traditional Judaism was capacious enough to accommodate that which could be learned from a plenitude of sources. Once I reached something approximating my present theological position, the question was how to sustain this breadth and scope, first for myself and then in teaching others. This angle of approach is significantly different from that of an individual wholly enfolded in the ethos of the yeshiva world who inquires whether and why room should be made for other studies, even if, a lifetime later, we seem to have arrived at the same destination.

A sense of complexity is the hallmark of Rabbi Lichtenstein's worldview. It is naturally very much in evidence when he addresses the question of how to think about complexity, which is at the root of our topic. Rabbi Lichtenstein's many painstaking essays on the subject, written over the course of half a century and in the context of his major productivity as a teacher and author in Talmud and halakha, defy executive summary. An "abridged and improved version" of Rabbi Lichtenstein on general studies (as the old Yiddish thespians bragged of their performances of Shakespeare) would mislead the uninitiated and scandalize those who know better. There is no substitute for picking up his texts yourself and sitting at the master's feet.

In the hope of encouraging and facilitating that encounter, I will bring those texts to your attention, in more or less chronological order. I will then turn to several areas of interest to me, where further discussion may facilitate your reading.

## II.

Let me begin with an unpublished source that played a role in my own growth. In the late 1960s, Rabbi Lichtenstein gave a number of Sunday talks to the students in his *shiur* on the place of general studies within a religious context. These were loosely organized around H. Richard Niebuhr's *Christ and Culture*. Niebuhr's method, which reflected and influenced other theological work, was to define multiple models of interaction and then analyze and evaluate each one in isolation in order to construct, in effect, a broader framework able to draw constructively on the truth of each model.

The two extreme positions are accommodation, in which religion adopts culture uncritically, and rejection. There are three intermediate categories. The first is hierarchic, where human culture has value that is of a lower level than that provided by revelation; Niebuhr identifies this position with Aquinas. Dualism (identified with Luther) is keenly sensitive to the evil of human culture, but regards engagement in culture as unavoidable, given the fallen nature of man. Conversionism (tied to Calvin) is the most idealistic model; it looks to the elevation and sanctification of culture. These categories are not always mutually exclusive; different activities may fit one better than the others, and the same activity may be justified and appreciated under more than one rubric. Judaism, with its commandment of Torah study, mandates a further perspective on these rubrics, insofar as it is important both to determine the value of an activity in itself and to justify devoting time to it. While Rabbi Lichtenstein does not explicitly employ Niebuhr's classification elsewhere, the terminology it supplies may prove helpful later on.

By the time he gave these lectures, Rabbi Lichtenstein had already written, for the *Commentator* (the student newspaper of Yeshiva University), the first of three general works on "secular studies." It was entitled by the editors "Synthesis: A Torah Perspective"[51] in deference to the prevalent Yeshiva University catchword of the time, despite the fact that "synthesis" was not one of the five thousand words in the article due to the author's dissatisfaction with the term, which implied, in his opinion, a kind of Hegelian progression through which Torah was somehow

---

51. *Commentator*, April 27, 1961, 5–6.

converted into a putatively higher entity through its combination with *madda*.[52] This article was followed twenty years later by the Hebrew "*Tova Ḥokhma im Naḥala*" ("Wisdom is good together with inheritance," Eccl. 7:11).[53] Finally came "Torah and General Culture: Confluence and Conflict," a seventy-five-page treatise that is the constructive part of a volume whose other chapters deal with the interaction of Torah and general culture in various periods.[54] I will take this culminating effort, the latest and most comprehensive of Rabbi Lichtenstein's treatments, as representing his settled views.

Two other books must be mentioned. Rabbi Haim Sabato recently published a volume of conversations with Rabbi Lichtenstein.[55] This book is declaredly intended to convey a message that is more accessible to the uninitiated public. To that extent, one might minimize its value on subjects treated at length elsewhere. Nonetheless, as Ḥazal taught, if the table talk of a *talmid ḥakham* requires study, the simplified formulations of a master educator, addressing an audience not predisposed to appreciate the full dimensions of his message, bear their own kind of significance, especially in the case of a teacher as relentlessly responsible and self-conscious as Rabbi Lichtenstein. We will draw on it accordingly.

Going back to the beginning, of course, leads us to Rabbi Lichtenstein's dissertation on the seventeenth-century savant Henry More, his only extended essay in English studies. Because this work shows him engaged in and contributing actively to Western culture, and

---

52. See J. J. Schacter, "Torah u-Madda Revisited: The Editor's Introduction," *Torah u-Madda Journal* 1 (1989): n. 49.

53. See above, n. 20. Note also Rabbi Lichtenstein's essay from the same period, in *Leaves of Faith*, 1:105–17. Torah Umadda is the slogan of Yeshiva University. Left to his own devices, Rabbi Lichtenstein would have preferred *ḥokhma* (wisdom) to *madda*, insofar as the former is the term used by Ḥazal, and also has broader connotations, including human wisdom, whereas *madda*, in modern Hebrew, connotes science. Of course the German *Wissenschaft* is appled equally to natural science and *Geistwissenschaft* (science of the spirit). Rabbi Ahron Soloveichik defended the use of the word *madda* because it appears in Daniel and need not be interpreted in the narrow sense, in his opinion.

54. See above, n. 20.

55. See above, n. 46.

because of the book's relative inaccessibility, it is worth reviewing its argument and implications for Jewish thought in general, as well as its model of religious liberal arts study in particular.

*Henry More: The Rational Theology of a Cambridge Platonist* began as a doctorate under the sponsorship of Prof. Douglas Bush at Harvard, of whom Rabbi Lichtenstein has always spoken with admiration.[56] More was a significant intellectual figure in his time; he merits attention in the history of seventeenth-century science and philosophy and religious speculation. Rabbi Lichtenstein is attracted to More's personality: "He is thoroughly dominated by that quality which he probably prized above all others – the quality of sincerity."[57] This quality also guarantees that his religious struggles are real. Yet More makes little or no contribution to what is ordinarily regarded as literature. If Rabbi Lichtenstein finds "life in these dry bones and a vital message in these dead leaves," it is not thanks to the aesthetic excellence of More's writing. If you didn't know the doctorate was in English literature, you would certainly take it for an essay in intellectual history about a "minor writer" who dealt with "major problems." Accordingly, Rabbi Lichtenstein has hardly anything here about the value of literature for religious insight and growth; rather, he is concerned with a better knowledge of and interpretation of the cultural past.[58]

The book opens with a survey of More's life and work. The next chapters concentrate on the "major problem" that interests Rabbi Lichtenstein. It is about the place of intellect in religious life, a timeless question, but one especially pertinent to a Jew preoccupied with the study of Torah. Even timeless questions, of course, exhibit unique

---

56. William Pritchard, who studied at Harvard during the same period and went on to become a scholar of American literature, wrote a memoir in which he refers to Bush as an openly Christian humanist in a secular department. He singles him out as showing personal concern for students and as virtually the only one to display a critical spirit in the classroom. See *English Papers: A Teaching Life* (St. Paul, MN, 1995), 55–57.
57. Lichtenstein, *Henry More*, 18. In my subsequent discussion of *Henry More* in this section, page references will be incorporated in the text.
58. The exception is p. 146 n117, contrasting, with respect to the question of providence and evil, Milton's *Paradise Lost* with Leibniz's *Theodicy*, to the advantage of the former; see Lichtenstein, "Torah and General Culture," 249.

configurations and reflect particular historical circumstances. More, according to Rabbi Lichtenstein, was a transitional figure. He was educated early in the seventeenth century, but his thinking gradually came to anticipate the religious outlook normally associated with the eighteenth century. Understanding how these pressures affected More and how attitudes toward the role of intellect in religion correlate with other changes in religious atmosphere and commitment may help us understand how similar pressures influence twentieth-century responses to the centrality of Torah study and how these correlate with other religious challenges of our times. This is Rabbi Lichtenstein's implicit agenda in this book; from time to time, he avows it openly.[59]

The development in More's thinking, which Rabbi Lichtenstein at one point calls a "literal disintegration" of his outlook, is described in two chapters entitled "The Simplicity of Comprehension" and "The Simplicity of Exclusion." The first chapter revolves around the idea of "deiformity," the ability of the human being to become like God, to attain "a pure goodness directed by pure reason." This overall conception, Rabbi Lichtenstein avers, "acknowledges the validity of both human reason and human will, and furthermore, it recognizes the necessity of employing both in the exercise of the religious life" (88). "Not in vain," he comments, "has More's name found its way into the histories of rational theology. The attempt to approach religious problems philosophically, often scientifically, is evident throughout his works" (55). It is an optimistic outlook: deiformity, asserted one-sidedly, lacks a sense of radical evil in human nature and is liable to dissolve the gap between God and man, and the inherent difference between revelation and the truth discovered by unaided human reason.

---

59. The notion of decline in the middle and late seventeenth century is still known to students of English literary history in connection with T. S. Eliot's idea of a "dissociation of sensibility" occurring somewhere between the Metaphysical poets, of whom Donne is perhaps the best example, and Milton, which entailed lowering Milton's prestige. Douglas Bush was not a proponent of this notion, which explained literary change entirely through aesthetic categories and which was not grounded in detailed historical investigation. Despite the fact that Rabbi Lichtenstein frequently quotes Eliot's writings approvingly, particularly regarding the proper relationship of religion and culture, his name is not mentioned in *Henry More*, nor is the dissociation of sensibility discussed.

More's later writing, in Rabbi Lichtenstein's judgment, shows a retreat from the earlier affirmation of the integration of intellect and will, to the point of being anti-intellectual. He argues that these statements go beyond the awareness that is normal among "all religious humanists" (inter alia, he devotes some attention to Milton, who was More's contemporary), that "man's absorption in his intellectual pursuits may become all-engrossing, thus in effect obscuring his higher destiny" (98). Rabbi Lichtenstein traces this tendency in More to two principles: the first is More's emphasis upon morality as the dominant element of spiritual life; the second, his "democratic" conviction that what knowledge is necessary for religion is fairly simple and easily attainable.

In the last and longest chapter, "From Religion to Moralism," More's texts continue to be central, yet the effort to understand More within the general context of the English thought that came before and after becomes the focus, and the tendency to engage the broad sweep of European religious thought down to the twentieth century becomes more prominent. As he traces the tension between the deiform elevation of man, including the intellect, on the one hand, and the de-emphasis of strenuous intellectual activity in the name of morality and religious egalitarianism, on the other, the number of passages articulating Rabbi Lichtenstein's judgment increases. Consider the following:

> Where idolatry itself is denounced as immoral rather than as sinful, it would appear evident that religion proper is conceived as an essentially moral relationship. To this extent, the unique character of religion as a distinct, purely sui generis entity is denied. (164)

> While deiformity no doubt represents the noblest of ethical and religious ideals, its quest may be beset by numerous pitfalls. Chief among these is the danger of overreaching oneself, of seeking – and asserting – not deiformity but deification; or to use the Miltonic expression, of "affecting Godhead." (165)

> It may be rejoined that the Platonists' once-born mold – their weakened sense of sin, their failure to appreciate the "numinous" – is simply the obverse side of their undoubtedly laudable emphasis

upon deiformity. And this is unquestionably true. But we must recognize that it is the result of a one-sided emphasis. (165)

It was indeed to the development of manners that the [eighteenth-century] religious community turned, and with results that were not altogether happy. With the ensuing concentration upon external conduct, the inner religious core came increasingly to be neglected or forgotten; and, with its dehydration, the vitality of English religious life was seriously sapped. (200)

In emphasizing social conduct we move, in short, from the proper ends of religion toward the logical goals of a secular morality – from the worship of God to the service of man, and from the realm of inner vision to the world of outer action.... Conduct is vital, both as an expression of character and as means to its formation. Inextricably interwoven with the essence of religious faith, it is at once cause and effect, an indispensable element in that constant interplay of the inner and the outer man, of faith and works, through which the religious personality rises to ever greater heights. But the concern with conduct may lead to abuse, and it is precisely this that confronts the student of Augustan religious life. Foremost is the possibility that conduct may be taken as an end – nay, with Tillotson, as *the* end – of religion, rather than as a means... that only the hollow shell will remain while vital inner power shall have been dissipated.... Secondly,... there is a danger that the role of conduct will be distorted by the omission or diminution of some other element of the religious life.... Cut off from the roots of knowledge and the search for it, conduct gradually loses its vitality and its content. A growth of righteousness must be accompanied – nay, must be intermeshed with – a growth in knowledge. For the quest for virtue must involve the whole man, the intellect included. Disregard this, and the result is disproportion; and disproportion, as the Greeks knew, brings first chaos and then desiccation. Thirdly,... the isolation of morality as a self-contained unit may occur not only in our experience, but in our thinking; it may affect not only our conduct, but our conception of morality proper. (201-4)

Rabbi Lichtenstein is rightly viewed as a vigorous advocate and a living exemplar of the importance of moral considerations in human relations. His encouragement of the study of the humanities is largely based on the belief that when properly utilized, this exposure increases moral sensitivity. His paper in defense of *hesder* for Israeli yeshiva students has become a classic not simply because it justifies military service under present conditions, but because he explains *hesder* in the context of a larger philosophy of social and national responsibility.[60] An enormous attentiveness to civility comes to expression in numerous public positions and pronouncements, many of which earned him unpopularity within the Religious Zionist community to which he belongs. It may seem puzzling for those who know him *only* for these acts of advocacy to discover that his years at Harvard bore fruit in a critique of "moralism," and that his narrative of the transition to the world of Augustan Enlightenment is a story of decline.

The incongruity, of course, is wholly in the eye of the beholder. As usual with Rabbi Lichtenstein, the question of one-sidedness versus balance is key. This is evident even in the excerpts reproduced above. But there is a deeper point here. The Modern Orthodoxy with which he is willing to be identified (and, unlike the Rav, he has at times accepted the label), is not about adapting Orthodoxy to modernity or about finding a formula that enables one to "live in two worlds." To the contrary, "the quest for virtue must involve the whole man" – the intellect included, social responsibility included. One particular vice of Enlightenment religion is to treat religion as a handmaiden of social conduct, "morality with frosting." One particular vice of the yeshiva world is the tendency to regard our responsibilities to outside society as insignificant. Both must be combated. As Rabbi Lichtenstein writes in his *Commentator* article, in every Garden of Eden lurks a serpent, and to contend with the serpent, it is useful to study a treatise on serpentine psychology.[61]

Earlier in *Henry More*, Rabbi Lichtenstein surveys several solutions to the "democratic problem":

---

60. Lichtenstein, "*Zot Torat HaHesder*," *Alon Shevut* 100 (1982): 9–33, translated as "The Ideology of *Hesder*," *Leaves of Faith*, 1:135–58.
61. "A Consideration of General Studies," 93.

> Stated briefly, [the problem] is simply this: Religion must be accessible to all; some definitive intellectual content must enter into religion; and yet the great majority of men cannot or will not reason profoundly about religious or metaphysical questions. (107)

The solution he finds most satisfactory is described as "Judaism," which has required not only service of the heart and hand, but also of the intellect. Torah study is a universal obligation; none may forego the attempt. "Decision, Jewish tradition has of course reserved for competent authority; if there is no royal road to knowledge, neither is there a demotic. But the *peregrinatio* is the duty and destiny of all" (109).

The ideal of *talmud Torah* was not available to the seventeenth-century Platonists, but the pressure to make religious fulfillment possible for everyone was urgent for many reasons. The result, according to Rabbi Lichtenstein, is that the Platonists, although they did not participate in the decline of religion, nevertheless contributed to it. The fact that their legacy was so different from their positions is, in his opinion, indubitable. More, for example, was far from deism, yet his downplaying of definitive dogma opened the door for it:

> Dogma, ritual, intellection – whatever one may think of them – at least set an objective floor for religion; it can sink so low and no lower. These, however, the Platonists tended to minimize. They placed almost all their eggs in one basket, and it proved to have a sizable hole. (30)

Any reader of the book would assume that the phrase "rational theology" in the subtitle conforms to common usage among historians and philosophers. In the closing pages, however, Rabbi Lichtenstein rejects this terminology. The prevalent attitude views reason not as a participant in religious life, but as an umpire: "It does not play the game, but rather sets up the rules and then referees" (209).[62] The goal is social

---

62. Rabbi Lichtenstein therefore does *not* endorse the common idea that it is desirable to subject religious doctrine to doubt as a way of testing or fortifying one's faith.

conduct, marked by "especially lavish praise for toleration," largely on pragmatic grounds, and disdain for dogma as unnecessary and socially divisive. Against this, Rabbi Lichtenstein's view of the rational theology worth pursuing is "something else entirely." It applies to a theology for which "thinking is a genuine religious experience," and incorporates the search for knowledge, "whether as an end or as a means – as a facet of the religious realm proper" (210).

## III.

We have caught a glimpse of how the study of the humanities is practiced. "Torah and General Culture"[63] surveys a broad range of disciplines and addresses the theoretical questions facing *benei Torah* or *benot Torah*[64] preparatory to engaging in such study. The earlier sections of the essay discuss the positive value to be gained from such study. The later sections focus on the impediments and dangers – the apportionment of time, the corruption of morals, the corrosion of faith, the chilling of fervor. My opening caveat about the dangers of trying to paraphrase and simplify Rabbi Lichtenstein's thought is even more in place here, where so much is covered, and even more important, where the theoretical analysis is meant not only to inform but to influence individual decisions. For those who are making these decisions or revising and fine-tuning them, Rabbi Lichtenstein's careful exposition rewards equally careful examination. I will limit myself to discussing several areas of special interest to me. I hope that my discussion will encourage vigilant reading on your part.

### The George Steiner Problem

For as long as I can remember, Rabbi Lichtenstein has been troubled by the question raised by George Steiner: If culture is humanizing, how can a man read Goethe or Rilke, play Bach and Schubert, and do his

---

Nor, of course, does Maimonides (see *Mishneh Torah, Laws of Idolatry* 2:2). See my "The Nature of Inquiry: A Common Sense Perspective," *Torah u-Madda Journal* 3 (1991–1992): 37–51.

63. Unless indicated otherwise, page references in the text of this section are to this essay.
64. Note the gender difference with respect to the obligation of Torah study.

work at Auschwitz?[65] On this Rabbi Lichtenstein comments, "This is, no doubt, a terrifying question for believers in the self-sufficiency of secular humanism – and a formidable one even for advocates of religious humanism" (249).

It is not obvious why this is a problem for advocates of liberal arts study within a religious framework in general, and where the primacy of Torah is recognized in particular. In defending his position against champions of "Torah only," Rabbi Lichtenstein has frequently resorted to the parable of the bread and the butter. A hungry man is offered a slice of bread, then another slice; at last he asks for butter, only to be told that bread is, after all, the staff of life, and that he should therefore ask for another slice of bread: "Spuriously rigorous logic dictates that more of the best is always best. But sound common sense knows that additional bread does not take the place of butter" (265).

Nonetheless, by the logic of the analogy, certain foods may make a positive contribution to one's nutrition only as part of a balanced diet; butter unbuffered by bread may be worthless or harmful. It should not be surprising that art and science unlinked to a moral center do not humanize. For religious humanism, and particularly for Judaism, with its main dishes of "bread and meat,"[66] the Steiner problem should not arise.

In fact, Rabbi Lichtenstein himself employs a version of this argument to counter one line of religious anti-intellectualism he finds in More:

> As More himself so often eloquently declares, knowledge *within* a moral context is very different from knowledge without it, and that within such a context, the quest for wisdom and its possession may be essential aspects of right human character.[67]

---

65. Steiner also discusses works of artistic excellence produced by immoral people. On the connection between intellectual greatness and moral character, see below. Steiner's question appears in the preface to his *Language and Silence* (London, 1967), as well as in later writings. Rabbi Lichtenstein discusses it, inter alia, in Lichtenstein, *By His Light*, 227ff.
66. See Maimonides, *Mishneh Torah, Laws of the Foundations of the Torah* 4:13.
67. Lichteinstein, *Henry More*, 105.

Here are three suggestions why the Steiner problem should trouble even religious humanists:

1. From a logical perspective, to be sure, it is not always true that a complex whole expresses the qualities of its constituent parts; water has no qualities in common with either hydrogen or oxygen. Yet it is counterintuitive, at a human level, that the experience of great art alone should have no wholesome quality whatsoever. If high culture really is morally indifferent in the presence of horrific evil, then one wonders whether it is ever worthwhile.
2. Religious humanism, for Rabbi Lichtenstein, is not only a matter of religious Jews gaining benefit from the products of general culture. It is also about human dignity and the value of human endeavor.[68] The bankruptcy of modern culture, its failure to deter or even its complicity with moral horror, casts a shadow on the dignity of the human being, and this should trouble not only naive believers in the power of culture alone, but all of us who value the image of God and human achievements.
3. The Steiner problem demonstrates that intellectual excellence and its appreciation can be wholly divorced from moral decency. The intellectual pursuit mandated by Judaism in the service of God is meaningless absent the effort to integrate of will and mind. Yet Ḥazal speak of a generation when those who embraced the Torah did not know God, who did not recite the "blessing on the Torah" prior to their study.[69] How far such corruption of the cultural personality proceeded in Europe during the 1940s is thus a sobering admonition to us all.

---

68. "Humanism is a worldview which values man highly.... In this formulation, 'values' must be understood in two senses, both as 'appraises' and as 'cherishes'.... Achilles respected Hector but had no concern for his welfare, while Sonya worried over Raskolnikov but could have had but scant esteem for him" (Lichtenstein, "Mah Enosh," 3).
69. Bava Metzia 85b.

## Information versus Edification

The occasional utility of natural scientific information for halakha is rarely disputed. Rabbi Lichtenstein observes that sociological and psychological tools are valuable both to enhance one's ability to evaluate human beings and their situations, and to understand mentalities and ways of life different from our own (234ff.). Such understanding is especially urgent in confronting a secular culture. While some opponents of liberal arts may balk even at reliance on the social sciences, preferring to rely on their untutored or, as they would have it, their Torah-true intuitions, rather than on humanly fallible and often deceiving academic results, others may accept the social sciences as they would the natural sciences. They would nevertheless dismiss the humanities as subjective and as a waste of time, airy nothings significant only to their local habitations, to say nothing of their dangerous seductive powers.

At the risk of oversimplification, I would point to three elements in Rabbi Lichtenstein's response.[70] First, if knowledge of God's world is valuable as a way to know God, and if the human being, created in the image of God, is a prominent part of that world, it makes little sense to embrace the natural sciences while turning away from the creative achievement and insight that is distinctively human: "The notion that Shakespeare is less meaningful than Boyle, Racine irrelevant but Lavoisier invaluable, remains very strange doctrine indeed" (243).

Second, one may argue that imaginative artists often do a better job of illuminating human nature, and especially the morally and spiritually distinctive dimensions of the human condition, than do scientists or even philosophers. This may be due to the advantages of literary language over technical jargon, the attention of art to concrete reality rather than abstraction, or to other factors. In any event, "Not only...have [they] described more powerfully but also because they have probed more deeply. For sheer insight, can Locke or James[71] compare with Dickens or Dostoyevsky?" (248).

---

70. In "Torah and General Culture," Rabbi Lichtenstein distinguishes the first theme I list, but he groups the other two together.
71. William James, I presume.

Finally, Rabbi Lichtenstein asks, "How much more telling... is the element of power at the prescriptive persuasive level?" (249). By this he does not mean argumentation or rhetoric aimed directly at persuasion. One might wish to speak of the inspirational or elevating effect of art, as long as this is not taken merely as emotional exhortation or sentimentalism. It is, of course, these claims on behalf of literature that engender the Steiner problem.

There are differences between the vision of humanistic study derivable from the second factor alone and the attitudes consonant with the first and the third. The second strand in the exposition states, in effect, that the best literature of creative imagination does the same work that the social sciences do, only more profoundly, more concretely, more probingly – at least sometimes.[72] This does not entail that the subject matter of such literature is particularly edifying or that reading it is uplifting. From this viewpoint, the differences in depicting egotism between the outlooks of Ayn Rand and Dreiser, and Nietzsche, and the way Milton depicts Satan depend only on differences in psychological perspicuity and artistic execution. Nor, likewise, should the wholesomeness of the author be pertinent as long as he or she probes deeply and knows whereof he or she probes. In H. R. Niebuhr's terminology, this element in the justification of cultural engagement is dualistic; it takes culture as fallible and requires a relentlessly critical attitude toward it. If, by contrast, we read to know God or to be inspired and elevated, not all subject matter, however instructive, serves this purpose. One may be instructed without being ennobled, and we may not be oblivious to the peculiar relationship between the person who lives and suffers, and the one who also creates.

In *Henry More*, Rabbi Lichtenstein is exploring a noble idea – the place of intellect in the life of religious devotion. He finds More a sympathetic, inspiring figure, despite his limitations and deficiencies. Yet, although he treats More and Cambridge Platonism with the vigorous and probing solemnity befitting a noble human attempt to get at religiously momentous truth, the goal of his inquiry is not to be persuaded

---

72. I stipulate that classical works of social science often share the virtues of the humanities. That is precisely why Tocqueville or Adam Smith or Keynes are not superannuated by state-of-the-art empirical studies.

by what is noble in it. To the contrary, it is to enlighten us with the story of a noble failure and to analyze, as accurately as possible, its causes and consequences, with an eye to their ongoing lessons.

If one compares *Henry More* and the early essay on general studies with "Torah and General Culture" and the interviews in *Mevakshei Panekha*, it seems to me that in the earlier writing, the study of culture is more oriented to the critique of culture and the analysis of ideas, with less emphasis on the sheer glory of the Arnoldian "best that has been thought and said," whereas more recent statements have appreciated and cherished the best in culture, even while continuing to devote attention to the possible negative consequences of engagement in culture. Take the following:

> There are human beings, including gentiles, whose historical mission is a mission of creativity – literary creativity, moral creativity. There are people in whom you see greatness, greatness of soul, moral greatness.
>
> How can one not be impressed by Samuel Johnson? A man who emerged from the London mud and reached a level of charity that I wish I could attain. Must I ignore this because he was a non-Jew?[73]

Perhaps this perception is exaggerated, a projection of my own development, or perhaps it reflects accidental factors. If there is indeed a subtle significant shift, it could be explained in a number of ways. Perhaps the more critical approach to general culture is too demanding in terms of investment or acumen, or too daunting for a large part

---

73. Sabato, *Mevakshei Panekha*, 85. He goes on to mention Frost's "Stopping by Woods" and Milton's sonnet "On His Blindness." In recent years, he has also discussed particular poems before students. See "'The Woods Are Lovely, Dark and Deep': Reading a Poem by Robert Frost," *Alei Etzion* 16 (2009): 129–34, on Frost's poem. One may argue that correspondence between the person and the work is more important in choosing to read Johnson and More, who are primarily prose writers, whose sincerity is a condition of their credibility, rather than poets, novelists, or historians. The value of Dostoyevsky's insight, for example, does not depend on his biography in the same way.

of the likely audience. It is thus better to concentrate on texts that can be appreciated without reservation.

Rabbi Lichtenstein is fond of the example of T. S. Eliot, who during his years as a philosophy graduate student was immersed in Sanskrit, but abandoned the study, despite persisting interest, because it was drawing him in directions he did not care to pursue (287). It may well be the case that "dualism," for many of us, is an important motive for study in one's youth, when it is important to determine what one ought to believe and why, to discover what others believe and why, and to trace the implications of all this. As we move ahead with our lives, even if we do not wholly outgrow these concerns, the pressing question is not what to read, but rather what to reread, and the criteria change accordingly in favor of the texts that inspire and elevate us and help us live the lives we ought to lead.

Lastly, as noted above, the advocacy of general education is only part of Rabbi Lichtenstein's message. Religious humanism is about the appreciation and cherishing of the human being. Our current educational challenge is not solely the blight of intellectual narrowness and the ensuing deficiency in our understanding of ourselves and others. We are also called upon to counter the tendency to derogate the human being, and within Orthodox society, the tendency to deprecate outsiders, non-Jews, or *ḥilonim* (secular Jews), to make light of their contributions and dignity, and to disparage those aspects of human nature and destiny that we share, *volens nolens*, with the outside world. It is for this reason that Rabbi Lichtenstein is so vocal in insisting on the *hakarat hatov*, the sense of gratitude, that all Jews owe for the constructive work of secular Zionists, and it is for this reason that he is distressed by the glee with which religious Jews sometimes greet reports of moral communal breakdown outside our walls, as if our flourishing requires their desolation.

## The Distinctiveness of Torah

If liberal arts disciplines can confer the benefits in moral and religious sensitivity and for the knowledge of God of which Rabbi Lichtenstein speaks, it is tempting to play down the radical difference between the kind of knowledge and insight gained through such studies, and the experience of Torah study.

One characteristic of rationalism, in the sense that More exemplified and that Rabbi Lichtenstein rejects, is to value universal truths and concomitantly to avoid the absolute distinction between the wisdom accessible through nature and the knowledge given through revelation:

> Certainly, with respect to morality and religion, any blurring of position must be categorically rejected on both metaphysical and psychological grounds. A sense of the unique "otherness" of God – and consequently of the sui generis character of man's relation to Him – must be seen as a fundamental element of any truly profound religious consciousness. (172)

In our own age, the failure to observe that distinction is less often posed by the universality of natural science than by comparative and other relativistic methods of the humanities or social sciences that treat the content or experience of divine revelation as commensurate with other human cultural artifacts or experiences. Where we lose sight of it, the experience of the presence of God, the sense of divine providence, is etiolated, as the uniqueness of God is dissolved in the universal categories of deism. It also has a deadening and alienating effect on the encounter with God through the study of Torah. It is not surprising that the discussion of God in *Mevakshei Panekha*,[74] over half a century after *Henry More*, stresses this recognition.

## IV.

A word about the title of this chapter: it refers to Milton's famous statement that he wrote poetry with his right hand and prose with his left. By implication, Rabbi Lichtenstein's right hand is stretched forth in the pursuit of *talmud Torah*, while his engagement in liberal arts is the work of his active but subordinate left hand. From my reading of *Henry More* forty years ago, I recalled that Rabbi Lichtenstein had used the same image in describing the writing of the book.

In fact, Rabbi Lichtenstein did not borrow the image from Milton. "With a second hand" is a phrase of Spenser's (Sonnet 75), where

---

74. Sabato, *Mevakshei Panekha*, 18–27, esp. 23–24.

he wrote his love's name on the sand, and, when it was washed away by the tide, wrote it again "with a second hand" but with the same result. Rabbi Lichtenstein's aim is to offer More the tribute of recognition and bring to life a chapter of intellectual history partially effaced.[75]

Can Milton's image be transferred to Rabbi Lichtenstein's life's work in the manner I remembered? Milton's formula presupposed two projects – the poetry being the goal to which he wished to devote his life, the prose being the product of occasion and the task imposed by necessity – both directed by the same executive intelligence, but neither interacting with the other.[76] It seems to me that Rabbi Lichtenstein's general culture, subordinate as it is to the pursuit of Torah and the life of mitzvot, nevertheless exhibits a greater degree of interaction than Milton's image implies. In *Mevakshei Panekha*, Rabbi Lichtenstein considers the ways in which the broad horizons of Western culture, subjected to rigorous critique and self-examination, may have helped him think through certain halakhic decisions or enriched his experience of Tanakh or certain aspects of religious and ethical life, to say nothing of the linguistic resources such education made available to him.[77] And yet, because these advantages are so evidently subordinate to the absolute imperatives of Torah and *talmud Torah*, because he is so strongly averse

---

75. A gentle reminder that even the unbiased memory of a well-meaning student is not infallible!
76. In *Henry More*, Rabbi Lichtenstein writes: "Faith and reason are not [for More], as in Donne, a right and left hand; they are intermeshing roots…" (74). In other words, two hands do not represent genuine integration.
77. See Sabato, *Mevakshei Panekha*, 125–30. Rabbi Lichtenstein's preface to his *Dina De-Garmi* and to his *shiurim* on Tractate Gittin contain reflections on the advantages and disadvantages of adopting a colloquial style in writing about Talmud and organizing the material topically rather than following the order of discussion in the Talmud itself. How many Rashei Yeshiva, whatever their final conclusions, would so carefully consider the consequences of diction for the experience of Torah study, and need one ask how many would bring to such a discussion their knowledge of analogous shifts in prose style from Burton and Milton at the beginning of the seventeenth century, to Dryden at its end? For that matter, how many would include in a volume on Gittin a *shiur* on the permissibility of divorce in halakha alongside *shiurim* on classic topics relating to agency (*sheliḥut*) and the authority of legal documents (*shetarot*), and with the same rigor? Or conclude a series of *shiurim* on the tort law of indirect causation an appendix recognizing that Nahmanides' elegant analysis,

to the notion that Torah needs to be "improved" by some additional ingredient, it is impossible to think of Western culture as anything like an independent force in Rabbi Lichtenstein's worldview.

Hesitantly, I chose to refer to the "music of the left hand." From one perspective, the left hand in a piano composition is unimportant: the melody, after all, is carried by the right hand, which suffices to communicate the tune. If the left hand played alone, if the bass were amplified and the treble clef relegated to the background, the result would be unrecognizable. At the same time, the left hand, in its subordinate role, adds so much to the beauty and coherence of the music.

As Rabbi Lichtenstein has repeatedly reminded us, a broad education is not a sine qua non of a profound religious life: "It would be not only impudent but foolish to impugn a course which has produced most *gedolei Yisrael* and has in turn been championed by them" (291). Yet, for those who, like Rabbi Lichtenstein, have experienced the value of such an education, I hope this image of interaction captures something of the truth. In any case, for a combination of reasons, some of which have been alluded to in this essay, Rabbi Lichtenstein's "sense of the need for *Torah Umadda* has sharpened, particularly in light of public events throughout the Jewish world." Nevertheless, he continues:

> So, however, has my awareness of the difficulties of realizing it; of the very considerable spiritual and educational cost – regrettably, far in excess of what is inexorably necessary – which the proponents of *Torah Umadda* often pay for their choice. Jointly, these conclusions – and I am not alone in subscribing to both – pose a challenge which needs to be conscientiously and creatively confronted. (291)

---

which served as the basis of the book, may not provide satisfactory solutions for practical contemporary problems, which might be better served by other halakhic sources?

# Index

## A
Aaron the High Priest, 192
Abaye, 60
Abba Oren, 120
Abba Oshaaya of Tiriah, 100
Abortion, 146, 147, 150, 162–7, 178, 240
*Adas Yisroel*, 112
Aggada
    Halakha and, 41, 161–2, 211, 226, 240, 266, 267
    Interpretation, 273–4, 279, 316
Agnon, S. Y., 30, 71, 251
*Agudath Yisrael*, 5, 43–44
Ahistoricism, 129–31, 265
Aliya, 8, 9, 25, 183–6, 283
*Alma deperuda*, 12, 24
*Alma deyihuda*, 12, 13
Alter, Robert, 136
Amit, Yairah, 137
Amital, R. Yehuda, 176, 179–217, 283, 291
Anselm of Canterbury, 89–90
Aristotle, 14, 89, 163, 239
Arlosorov, Chaim, 6
Arnold, Matthew, 288, 309

*Arpelei Tohar*, 8, 23, 24, 32
Arras, John D., 159
Artificial insemination, 146–7, 150–1;
    *see also* ethics
Auerbach, R. Shlomo Zalman, 157, 292
Auschwitz, 183, 200, 205, 208, 211, 305
Autonomy
    Bioethics and, 153–8, 236
    Education and, 178
    God and, 91
    Human rights and, 30, 39, 145, 150
Autopsies, 147, 155, 171–3; *see also* ethics
*Avoda begashmiyut* (worship through corporeality), 197, 245
*Avodat Hashem* (divine service), 207, 288, 293

## B
*Bagrut*, 141–2
Bahya ben Asher, R., xi, 98
Bahya ibn Pekuda, R., 207, 209, 275
Balfour Declaration, 5
Bar Ilan University, 112, 239, 280
Baumol, R. Yehoshua, 223–4
Beauchump, Tom L., 158

# Index

Beit Din, 61, 71–4, 77, 175
Berdichevsky, Micah Yosef, 3
Berlin, R. Naftali Zvi Yehuda (Netziv), 3, 4, 115, 125
Biblical emendation, 117
Bill of Rights, 95–6, 107
Bin-Nun, R. Yoel, 139, 141–2, 188, 190
Bioethics, 147, 149–59, 163, 173; *see also* ethics
Board of Deputies, 5
Breuer, R. Mordekhai, 116, 184
Brill, Alan, 196, 217, 285
*Brisker derekh* (method), 115, 182, 276, 282, 285–6
Broda, R. Aryeh Leib, 53
Buber, Martin, 116, 125, 135
Buddhism, 163

## C

Callahan, Daniel, 147, 150
Capital punishment, 80, 165
Cassuto, Umberto, 116, 120, 125
Casuistry, 158–9
Chabad, 2, 191
Chajes, R. Zvi Hirsch, 62
Chief Rabbinate
    Creation of, 5
    Rabbi Herzog and, 42
    *Takkanot* and, 68–9, 73, 75
Childress, James F., 158
Christianity
    Abortion and, 163
    Communism and, 50
    Discrimination against, 48–52, 96
    Idolatry and, 49
    Oral law and, 274
    Saints, 266
    Truth and, 93–4
Conscription, 66–7
Constitution, American, 84, 91–2, 95–6, 240–1
Conversion, 78–9
Conversionism, 296
Cosmetic Surgery, 169–71
Cover, Robert, 154–5, 161–2

## D

De Tocqueville, Alexis, 105, 308
*Degel Yerushalayim*, 6
Deiformity, 299–301
Democracy
    America and, 84–5, 91–2, 106–7
    Halakha and, 47, 50, 54, 68, 70, 75, 81, 97, 104
    Israel and, 43, 46, 79, 217
    Religion and, 300, 302
*Derash* / *derush*, 132–4, 225–6, 231, 233, 247
*Devekut* (cleaving to God), 197–8, 234–5, 246
Diaspora, 45, 77–8, 109, 114–6, 196, 215–6, 290
*Dina demalkhuta dina* (the law of the government is law), 72
Discrimination, 47–62, 70–1; *see also* equality
Diskin, R. Yitzhak Yeruham, 6
Divine providence, 5, 169, 201–3, 207, 215, 298, 311
Dogma, 94, 260, 265, 275, 277, 303–4
Dualism, 296, 310

## E

*Ein Aya*, 7
*Ein Sof*, 11, 32, 233
*Eiva* (harmonious relations with gentiles), 49, 53–4, 68
Eliot, T. S., 299, 310
Emancipation, 86, 106
Emden, R. Yaakov, 156, 254
Enlightenment
    Effect on religion, 79
    Period, 122, 154, 262, 302
    Unity through, 13
*Enoshiut* (Humanity), 191–7
Epistemology
    God, 11, 210
    Humility, 197, 216
    Limitations, 16, 30
    Unity, 18
Equality
    Freedom and, 39–40
    Democracy and, 47, 85, 97–98

# Index

Torah and, 85, 98, 107
Ethics; *see also* morality
    Aggada and, 270–5
    Divine, 195, 197, 199, 300
    Ethical message, 115, 122–3, 127, 130, 135
    Ethical people, 25, 59, 201, 210, 292, 312
    Ethical universalism, 184, 214–6
    Halakha and, 98, 101, 111–2, 258, 289
    Jewish, 99, 102–7, 117, 182, 204, 212, 266, 278, 284
    Medical, 145–178
    Principles, 190, 192
Euthanasia, 146–51, 160–2, 178; *see also* ethics
*Ezer kenegdo* (helper against him), 88–90, 94

# F

Faith
    In God, 195–6, 205, 214–7
    In Halakha, 40
    In Torah, 126
    Nature of, 89–96
    Principles, 45, 38, 59
    Religious, 1, 28, 35, 202, 209–10, 301, 304
    Restoring, 245–8
    Tenets, 10, 86
    Truth and, 32
Federalist Papers, The, 91
Feinstein, R. Moshe, 157, 166, 170
Fifth Amendment, 241
First Amendment, 96
First Lebanon War, 291
First World War, 5, 44
Flattery (*ḥanifa*), 208
Fletcher, Joseph, 150–1
Fox, Marvin, 159, 289
Fragmentation, 21, 232
Freedman, Benjamin, 154, 157–8
Freedom
    And equality, 1, 39–40, 107
    European Emancipation, 86
    Human, 150, 155, 178
    Jewish, 45
    Religious liberty, 85–9, 92–7
    To change, 168

French Revolution, 39
Freud-Kandel, Miri, 176, 224

# G

Gentiles; *see also* equality
    Halakha and, 39–40, 74, 78–80, 98, 100, 103–5
    Imitation of, 56, 76
    In Israel, 43, 47–54, 69–70
    Influence on Jews, 63–4, 77, 86
    Righteous, 128
    Wisdom, 279, 309
*Ger Toshav* (stranger and neighbor), 47–8, 85–7, 96, 106
Germany, 77, 95, 112, 148
Gifter, R. Mordechai, 102
*Gilyonot* (sheets), 114, 137
Glasner, R. Moshe Shmuel, 181–2
*Gush Emunim*, 6, 9, 204, 214, 216
Gush Etzion, 187, 283

# H

*Ḥadash asur min haTorah* (novelty is forbidden by the Torah), 38, 79
Ḥafetz Ḥayim, *see* Kagan, R. Yisrael Meir, 4
*Haganah*, 184
*Hakarat hatov* (gratitude), 207–9, 310
*Ḥalitza*, 74
*Ḥalutzim* (pioneers), 27
Ḥanina ben Teradyon, R., 161
Harvard University, 250–4, 258–9, 279, 282, 298, 302
*Hashavat aveda*, 98, 101, 103
Hasidism
    Halakha and, 240
    Interest in, 140–1
    Madda and, 243
    Rabbi Lamm and, 231–4, 245
    Rabbi Twersky and, 250, 257, 262, 276–7, 280
    Rav Amital and, 190–1, 197–8
Ḥayim of Volozhin, R., 64, 219–20, 233–5, 243–6
Ḥazon Ish, 61, 64, 79, 80, 210

# Index

Hebrew University, 112, 123, 126, 224, 227, 250–1, 279
*Hefker beit din hefker*, 59, 61, 71
Heinemann, Yitzḥak, 129, 132
Heresy; *see also ger toshav*
    Truth and, 23, 32
    Zionism and, 27
    Science and, 237
    Secular Jews and, 58, 65, 209
Herzog College, 141, 184
Herzog, R. Yitzhak, 37–82
Heschel, R. Abraham Joshua, 93–4
*Hesder*, 185–9, 283–5, 290, 302
*Hester panim* (hiding of [God's] face), 205
*Heter mekhira*, 4, 48
Ḥevesh Pe'er, 7
Ḥibbat Tziyon, 4
Ḥiddush (innovation), 84, 244
Hildesheimer, R. Azriel, 112, 148
Ḥillul Hashem, 52–4, 156, 200, 216
Hirsch, R. Samson Raphael, 112, 115, 176, 243
Historical study of Judaism, Historicism, 260–2, 276–8
Ḥitzoniyut (externality), 193
Hoffman, Yair, 115, 119, 136
Holocaust (*Shoah*)
    State of Israel and, 44–5, 67, 203–7, 213
    Memorial, 75
    Aliya and, 183–5
    Response to, 196–7, 207–16
*Horaa* (halakhic decision-making), 174
Human cognition, 14, 19, 22, 33, 195
Human Rights, 97, 150, 154–5
Humanism, 196–7, 216, 252, 276, 289, 300, 305–10
Ḥuppa, 74–7

## I

Ideology, 17, 39, 41–2, 57, 133, 217
IDF, 185–8, 213
Idolatry, 48–52, 56, 99, 136, 140, 300; *see also* gentiles in Israel
Industrial revolution, 39

Infinity, 11, 162
Informed consent, 154–60
Inheritance, 69–75, 81
Ish Shalom, Benjamin, 4–5, 34
Israel
    Land of, 4, 6, 26, 43, 45, 68, 130, 138, 184, 196, 201, 204, 212, 256–7, 290–2
    Prize, 113
    State of, 25, 42–59, 65–75, 79, 82, 188, 196, 199–213, 227, 256, 290
*Ittur Soferim*, 7
*Ivrit Be'Ivrit*, 112

## J

Jabotinsky, Ze'ev 76
Jacob, Benno, 116, 125
Jaffa, 4
Jakobovits, R. Immanuel, 145–78
Jakobovits, R. Yoel, 153, 156
Jefferson, Thomas, 84, 85, 88, 107
Jerusalem
    Beit Din HaGadol in, 72–3
    Dr. Zornberg and, 140
    Prof. Leibowitz and, 112–3
    Prof. Twersky and, 257
    Prophecy and, 200–1
    Rabbi Jakobovits and, 171
    Rabbi Lichtenstein and, 283
    Rabbinate, 4–6, 29; *see also* Chief Rabbinate
    Rav Amital and, 184
Johnson, Samuel, 309
Jonsen, Alfred R., 158

## K

Kabbala
    Burial and, 76
    Halakha and, 272–4
    Interest in, 140
    Prof. Twersky and, 264–6
    Rabbi Lamm and, 222, 231–5, 240
    Rav Amital and, 198
    Rav Kook and, 3, 4, 10–3, 21, 26–8
*Kabbala (ne'eman alai abba)*, 59–60

# Index

Kagan, R. Yisrael Meir (Ḥafetz Ḥayim), 4
Kant, Immanuel, 18, 84, 148
Kaplan, Lawrence J., 2, 9, 13, 24, 34, 159, 231, 232
Karo, R. Yosef, 244, 262
Kass, Leon, 167–8
Kaufmann, Yehezkel, 116
*Kavod habriyot* (dignity of all human beings), 97
*Kehal Yisrael* (Congregation of Israel), 67
*Kelippot*, 12
Kesef Mishneh, 48
*Keter Elyon*, supernal crown, 21
*Kiddush Hashem*, 176–8, 211
*Kiddushin*, 72–3
Kierkegaard, Soren, 84, 89–90
Kirschenbaum, Aaron, 242
*Kiruv*, 27
Knesset, 50–56, 59, 177, 215, 291
*Kohanim* (Priests), 63
Kook, R. Avraham Yitzhak HaKohen (Rav Kook)
   Biography, 2–7
   Halakhic position, 48, 190–1
   Kabbala and, 232, 243
   Monism and, 10–14, 216–7
   Prize, 285
   Writings and methodology, 7–10, 14–24, 35–36, 41, 181–4, 194–5, 197, 199–203, 205–7, 214, 227
   Zionism and Secular Judaism, 25–35, 63–5, 210
Kook, R. Zvi Yehuda, 141, 184, 196, 198, 204
Krumbein, R. Elyakim, 198, 206, 207, 286

## L

Lamm, R. Norman, 219–47
Landau, R. Yeḥezkel (Noda BiYehuda), 171
Leibowitz, Nehama, 109–43
Leibowitz, Yedidyah Lipman, 112
Leibowitz, Yeshayahu, 109, 111
Leiter, Brian, 16
Levi, R. Ḥayim Yehuda, 181, 183

Levin, Yuval, 105–6
Lichtenstein, R. Aharon, 159, 174, 175, 189–91, 213, 281–313
Literary interpretation of the Bible, 110, 116–7, 123–9, 131, 134–8, 141–2, 262–3, 268–9, 278–9
Loans to gentiles, 50–1; *see also* equality
Logic, 24, 89, 103–4, 133, 242, 274
London, 5, 6, 148–9, 309
Luchins, R. David, 102
Luria, R. Yitzhak (Ari), 11–2

## M

Madison, James, 84, 88, 91–2
Maghen, Ze'ev, 105
Maharshal, 51
Maḥazikei HaDat Synagogue, 5
Maimonides
   Christianity, 49
   Halakhic positions
      Abortion, 163–5
      Cosmetic surgery, 170–1
      Euthanasia, 160
      Gentiles, 52
      Israel, 44, 47, 67
      Knowledge of God, 89
      Love [your neighbor], 98
      Self-incrimination, 241
      Women, 57
   Philosophy, 195, 240, 243–5, 250, 256–9
   Principles of Faith, 38
   School, 255
   Writings, 182, 199, 206, 238, 252, 265–75, 278–9
Malbim, 115, 125
Maritain, Jacques, 228
Maya, Moshe, 195, 205–6
Medan, R. Yaakov, 141
*Meimad*, 215
Meiri, R. Menahem, 51, 53
*Melekhet shamayim*, 266
Meltzer, R. Isser Zalman, 185–6
Merkaz. *See* Yeshivat Merkaz HaRav
*Mesora*, 63

# Index

Messiah, 21, 24–8, 44, 46, 73, 184, 186, 196, 203–4, 206–7, 214, 209
*Midbar Shur*, 7
Midrash, 43, 121–2, 125–6, 129, 131–6, 199, 226, 229
*Milḥemet mitzva* (commanded war), 44–5, 65–8
*Minhag*, 79
Minyan, 62
Mir, 3
Mirsky, Yehudah, 3
Mishneh Torah, 182, 265, 268–70
*Mishpat*, justice, 98, 100
*Mitzvat Re'iya*, 7
Mizrachi, 4, 43–4, 113, 182
Modern Orthodoxy, 1–2, 35, 109, 121, 178, 217, 228, 231, 285–6, 302
Modernity, 37–82, 228–31, 256, 302
Monism, 10–4, 17, 23–6, 28, 32, 35, 232–3
Monotheism, 10, 146
Montagu, Edwin, 5
Morality
    Contemporary, 143
    Halakha and, 240, 258
    Henry More and, 300–11
    Judaism and, 176–8, 212, 278
    Lessons, 136, 236–7
    Medicine and, 145–73
    Moral Gentiles, 51
    Moral interpretation of the Bible, 117, 127, 129, 132, 133
    Natural, 216–7
    "New", 227–8
    Personal, 29, 61–2
    Rabbi Lamm and, 226
    Rabbi Lichtenstein and, 288–9, 293–4
    Rav Amital and, 190–7, 199–200, 206–7, 214
    Responsibilities, 79, 98, 101
    Systems of, 31
More, Henry, 282, 293–4, 297–305, 308–12
Moses, 40, 127, 192
Moshe of Coucy (Semag), R., 100–1
Multiplicity, 10–4, 19–20, 26

Muslims, 48, 52; *see also* gentiles
Mysticism; *see also* Zohar
    Aggada and, 274
    Modern Orthodoxy and, 231
    Prof. Leibowitz and, 117, 140
    Rav Amital and, 197–8
    Rav Kook and, 2, 12–3, 20–1, 24, 30, 33, 35–6, 243

# N

Nahmanides, 68, 125, 127–9, 137, 140, 142, 195, 288, 290, 312
*Nashim daatan kalot* (Women are light of mind), 57
Nataf, R. Francis, 142
Nationalism, 8, 29, 44, 184, 199
Naturalness, 189, 191–7
Nature, 13, 86, 168, 237–9, 247, 260
The Nazir (Rabbi David HaKohen), 9
*Nefesh*, 26, 28, 164, 210
Nehamas, Alexander, 19
Nehorai, Michael Z., 2
Netziv. *See* Berlin, R. Naftali Zvi Yehuda
New Critics, 124, 126–7, 129, 131–2
Niebuhr, H. Richard, 296, 308
Nietzsche, Friedrich, 32, 308
Noda BiYehuda. *See* Landau, R. Yeḥezkel

# O

Old Yishuv, 6
Ontology, 6, 11, 89–91
*Orot HaKodesh*, 8–9, 194
*Orot HaTeshuva*, 8
*Orot*, 6, 8–9, 27

# P

Palestine, 5, 111–2
Pardes [physics and metaphysics], 244–5
Parmenides, 10
Particularism, 5, 9, 104, 217, 229, 278–80
Perspectivism, 15–6, 34
*Pesak*, 37–8, 42, 75, 174–5, 242, 267, 277, 289–90
*Peshat*, 121–3, 132–4, 226

# Index

Phillips, Jonas, 95–6
Philosophy
   Henry More and, 298
   Jewish, 231
   Maimonidean, 195, 270
   of *Torah im derekh eretz*, 148, 176
   Plato's, 238
   Prof. Leibowitz and, 112, 127, 141
   Prof. Twersky and, 251–6, 264, 266–8
   Rabbi Lamm and, 219, 221, 223, 239–40
   Rav Ahron Soloveichik and, 83–4
   Rav Kook and, 3, 7–8, 10, 15, 19
   T. S. Eliot and, 310
Piety, 183, 185, 194, 217, 235, 246
*Pikuaḥ nefesh*, 65–6, 68, 289
Plato, Platonism, 238, 293, 298, 300, 303, 308
Pluralism, 1, 30–36, 143, 243
Pollock, Benjamin, 22
Polygamy, 74
Ponevezh, 3, 291
Postmodernism, 131–4, 138, 140–1, 146, 178
Pragmatism, 1, 25, 34, 304
Preferential love, 104–6
Principlism, 158
Promised Land, 21

## Q
Queen Shlomtziyon, 55

## R
Raavad, 48, 286
Rabbi Isaac Elchanan Theological Seminary (RIETS), 224
Rabbinate (Israeli), 5, 29, 42, 55, 60, 68–75
Rabbinical Council of America (RCA), 84, 86, 94, 285
Rabinowitz, Raiza Rivka, 4
Rabinowitz-Teomim, Batsheva, 3–4
Rabinowitz-Teomim, R. Eliyahu David (Aderet), 3, 51
Radak, 129, 253
Ramsey, Paul, 150–1, 169
Rashbam, 121–2, 125, 129

Rashi, 120, 125, 127, 129–31, 134, 137, 142, 164
Rashkover, Randi, 93–4
Rationalism, 122, 271, 273, 311
The Rav. *See* Soloveitchik, R. Joseph B.
Rav Kook. *See* Kook, R. Avraham Yitzhak HaKohen
Rava, 61
Ravitzky, Aviezer, 25
Redemption, 12, 23, 27, 34, 45–6, 184, 202–7, 214
Relativism, 31, 35, 93
Religious anxiety, 194
Religious involvement in politics, 9, 182, 211–5
Ridbaz, 42, 64
Righteousness. *See Tzedek*
*Rodef* (pursuer), 164
Rosenzweig, Franz, 22–3, 116, 125, 277
Ross, Tamar, 23, 33
Roth, R. Meshulam, 67
Routine, 199, 258, 262
Rozenson, Israel, 120–1
*Ruaḥ*, 28, 210
Rush, Benjamin, 96

## S
Sacks, R. Jonathan, 36, 146, 220
Samet, R. Elḥanan, 138
*Sanhedrin*, 69, 72, 81
Schatz, Rivka, 8
Scholem, Gershom, 8, 251
Science
   Halakha and, 307
   Medical, 149, 152, 168, 172, 270
   Modernity and, 39
   Prof. Leibowitz and, 120–1
   Prof. Twersky and, 256
   Rabbi Herzog and, 80
   Rabbi Jacobovits and, 149
   Rav Kook and, 16
   Religion and, 64, 145, 233
   Social, 307–8
   Study of Judaism, 112, 116, 259, 262
   Technology and, 227–30

# Index

Secular Judaism / Jews (ḥilonim); see also democracy, Halakha and
    As witnesses, 60
    Contemporary, 64–5
    Prof. Leibowitz and, 109
    Rav Amital and, 210–1, 215
    Rav Kook and, 2, 9, 25–30, 34
    Rabbi Herzog and, 43–4, 58–65, 69
    Rabbi Lichtenstein and, 310
    *Shogegim*, 61
Secularism, 1–36, 229–30
*Sefirot*, emanations, 21, 233
Segal, Moshe Zvi, 116
Semag. *See* Rabbi Moshe of Coucy
*Semikha*, 72–3
*Serara* (female appointments to public offices), 54–5; *see also* equality
Shabbat
    Gentiles and, 47, 53, 80n.106
    Violation, 61–2, 78, 210
    IDF and, 65–6, 185
    Jewish medical ethics and, 147
Shatz, David, 2, 34–6
*She'at hadeḥak* (a time of pressing need), 54, 289
*Shekhina*, 13
Shema, 10, 199
*Shemitta*, 48, 50
*Shemona Kevatzim*, 9
*Shevirat hakelim*, 12
Shimon bar Yoḥai, R., 226
Shimon ben Shetaḥ, R., 99–103
*Shitat yaḥid* (minority opinion), 68
Shulḥan Arukh, 7, 51–2, 59, 244
Six-Day War, 187, 200, 203–4
Soloveichik, R. Ahron, 83–5, 97–107, 282, 297
Soloveitchik, Haym, 38, 174
Soloveitchik, R. Joseph B. (The Rav)
    America, views on, 95–96, 99–102, 106–107
    Approach to learning, 285–7
    Biographical, 41, 83–84, 213, 219, 224, 226n.24, 252–3, 255, 258, 262, 282–3
    Equality, 97–98, 104–106

Ethics, 102–104
Faith, 89–91
Halakha, 159, 291
Historicism, 276–7
Madison and, 91–92
Pluralism, 16
Religious confrontation, 83–95
Religious freedom, 85-9, 95–96
Soloveitchik, R. Yitzḥak Zev, 276
Sonnenfeld, R. Yosef Chaim, 6, 27
Specialization, 14, 232
Spinoza, Barukh, 13
St. Gallen, Switzerland, 5
Stavsky, Avraham, 6
Steinberg, R. Avraham, 178
Steiner, George, 304–8
Strauss, Aryeh Ludwig, 125
Strauss, Leo, 112
*Studies in the Weekly Sidra*, 114
Suffrage, 6, 35, 56
Synagogue, 56, 76–7, 81

## T

Taḥkemoni school, 4
*Takkanot* (Enactments), 38, 59, 68–75, 78, 81
*Talmidei ḥakhamim*, Torah scholars, 68, 187, 266
Talmud Torah, 219–47, 256, 259, 270, 281, 303, 311–2
*Tefillin*, 7, 8, 45, 104
Tel Aviv University, 112, 119, 123
Tendler, R. Moshe, 157
Teshuva, repentance, 27, 63, 65, 207
Textless Torah, 243–5, 247
Theocracy, 46
*Tikkun*, 12, 27–8, 32
Tolerance, 30–5, 45, 49, 58, 107
*Torah im derekh eretz*, 114, 148–9, 176
*Torah lishmah*, 219, 221, 234, 238, 246
*Torah Shebe'al Peh* (Oral Law), 40, 55, 77, 233, 244
*Torah Shebikhtav* (Written Law), 77, 233
*Torah Umadda*, 219–47, 297, 313

# Index

*Torat Eretz Yisrael* (the Torah of the Land of Israel), 141
Toulmin, Stephen, 158
Truth, divine, 19, 23, 32
Twersky, R. Isadore (Yitzhak), 249–80
Tzaddok HaKohen of Lublin, R., 237
*Tzedek* (righteousness), 60, 97–8, 100–2, 107, 128, 199, 215–7, 221, 301
*Tzelem Elokim*, 135, 182, 214
*Tzeniut* (Jewish modesty), 56
*Tzimtzum*, 12

## U

Ultra-Orthodoxy, 2, 25, 109, 178, 186
United Nations, 46, 54
Unity, of God, 10–5, 18, 20, 22–4, 27–8, 30, 33
University study, 14, 117, 223, 234–7, 247
Urbach, E. E., 137

## V

Vilna Gaon, 63–4, 219, 243

## W

Waldenberg, R. Eliezer, 156, 166, 170
War of Independence, 67, 185
Washington, George, 95
Weiss, Meir, 116, 125, 136
Weizmann, Chaim, 76
Will, George, 85
*Wissenschaft des Judentums*, 3, 112, 260–2, 297; *see also* science, study of Judaism
Witnesses, 55, 58–61, 69, 73, 75, 241
Wurzburger, R. Walter, 173, 233, 289

## Y

*Yeridat hadorot*, the decline of the generations, 243–4; *see also* secular Judaism, *shogegim*
Yeshiva University, xii, 190, 219, 222, 224, 228, 234, 280, 283, 285, 294–6
Yeshivat Har Etzion, 141, 180, 184, 187, 190, 203–4, 215, 283–5, 290–1
Yeshivat Merkaz HaRav, 5–6, 184, 187, 204, 213
*Yibbum*, 74
R. Yishmael, 163
Yom Kippur War, 203–4, 206
Yosef Ibn Kaspi, R., 129, 263, 266, 275–6

## Z

Zeimel, 4, 7
Zionism
  Political, 2
  Prof. Leibowitz and, 111–3, 140
  Rejection of, 43–4
  Religious
    IDF and, 188
    Prof. Twersky and, 251, 256
    Rabbi Herzog and, 80, 82
    Rabbi Lichtenstein and, 290–2, 302
    Rav Amital and, 181–2, 184, 186–9, 197–8, 202–5, 211–6
    Rav Kook and, 4, 6, 8, 25–9, 200
  Secular, 44, 64, 115, 291, 310
Zohar, 10, 12–3, 63, 195, 234
Zornberg, Avivah, 139–41

# Contributors

**Rabbi Shalom Carmy** teaches Jewish Studies and Philosophy at Yeshiva University. He is editor of *Tradition*. He received his BA and MS from Yeshiva University, and his rabbinic ordination from its affiliated Rabbi Isaac Elchanan Theological Seminary (RIETS), studying under Rabbis Aharon Lichtenstein and Joseph B. Soloveitchik. He has edited some of Rabbi Soloveitchik's work for publication. He edited the Orthodox Forum volumes on *Modern Scholarship in the Study of Torah: Contributions and Limitations* and *Jewish Perspectives on the Experience of Suffering*, as well as several other works. He writes a regular personal column in *Tradition* and contributes regularly on Jewish and general subjects to *First Things* and other journals.

**Dr. Stuart W. Halpern** serves as the Assistant Director of the Zahava and Moshael Straus Center for Torah and Western Thought of Yeshiva University, and the Assistant Director of Student Activities of the Bernard Revel Graduate School of Jewish Studies. He received his BA from the University of Pennsylvania, an MA in Psychology in Education from Teachers College at Columbia University, an MA in Bible from Revel, and his EdD from the Azrieli Graduate School of Education and Administration. He is the co-editor of the *Mitokh Ha-Ohel* series, and

Contributors

editor of the *Derashot LeDorot* series, and also serves as a member of the Steering Committee of the Orthodox Forum.

**Rabbi Dr. Carmi Horowitz** was born in New York in 1943, graduated Yeshiva University High School for Boys, studied in Yeshivat Kerem B'Yavneh, graduated Yeshiva College and Bernard Revel Graduate School, and was ordained at RIETS; he earned his PhD at Harvard University under the guidance of Prof. Isadore Twersky. From 1979, he taught at Ben-Gurion University for nine years, partially overlapping with the eighteen years he taught at Bar-Ilan University. In 1986, he established the Jerusalem branch of the Touro Graduate School for Jewish Studies and served as its dean until 2004. In that year he led the Touro branch in Israel in its transition to Lander Institute, Jerusalem Academic Center, an independent college of higher education recognized by the Israel Council of Higher Education, and served as its founding rector, a position he held until his retirement in 2010. Rabbi Dr. Horowitz is former president of Givat Washington Teachers College and presently professor of Jewish Thought at Michlalah Yerushalayim. He has written and edited books and articles in the field of medieval Jewish intellectual history, with particular emphasis on the history of the sermon literature and aggadic interpretation. Recently, Touro College New York and Lander Institute published a jubilee volume in his honor on the theme of the history of aggadic interpretation, edited by Professors Michael Shmidman and Joseph Tabory.

**Dr. Alan Jotkowitz** studied at Yeshiva University, Yeshivat Har Etzion, and Yale University School of Medicine. He is currently professor of medicine and director of the Jakobovits Center for Jewish Medical Ethics and associate director of the Medical School for International Health, Ben-Gurion University of the Negev; and a senior physician at Soroka University Medical Center, both in Beersheba, Israel. He is associate editor of the *European Journal of Internal Medicine* and the author of over one hundred peer-reviewed papers in such journals as the *American Journal of Medicine*, the *American Journal of Bioethics*, the *Journal of Medical Ethics*, the *Journal of Contemporary Religion, Tradition,* and *Modern Judaism.*

# Contributors

**Dr. Yehudah Mirsky** is associate professor of Near Eastern and Judaic Studies at Brandeis University. He studied at Yeshivat Har Etzion and Yeshiva College, and received rabbinic ordination in Jerusalem. He was a law review editor at Yale University and completed his PhD in religion at Harvard University. He worked in Washington, DC, as an aide to then Senators Bob Kerry and Al Gore, and at the Washington Institute for Near East Policy, and served in the Clinton administration as special advisor in the US State Department's human rights bureau. From 2002 to 2012 he lived in Israel and was a fellow at the Van Leer Institute and the Jewish People Policy Institute. He has written widely on politics, theology, and culture. He was a Red Cross chaplain after the events of September 11, 2001, and is active in *HaTenua HaYerushalmit*, the movement for a pluralist and livable Jerusalem. He is the author of the widely acclaimed volume *Rav Kook: Mystic in a Time of Revolution* (New Haven, CT, 2014).

**Dr. Daniel Rynhold** is director of the doctoral program and associate professor of Modern Jewish Philosophy at the Bernard Revel Graduate School of Jewish Studies. Educated at the Universities of Cambridge and London, Dr. Rynhold has previously held positions in the Department of Theology and Religious Studies of King's College London, and at the renowned Jews' College of London. He has published a number of articles on various topics in Jewish philosophy, including the problem of evil, Nietzsche and Jewish philosophy, and the thought of Moses Maimonides and Joseph B. Soloveitchik. He is the author of *Two Models of Jewish Philosophy: Justifying One's Practices* (Oxford, 2005) and *An Introduction to Medieval Jewish Philosophy* (London, 2009).

**Rabbi Dr. David Shatz** is University Professor of Philosophy, Ethics, and Religious Thought at Yeshiva University, editor of the *Torah u-Madda Journal*, and editor of the series *MeOtzar HoRav: Selected Writings of Rabbi Joseph B. Soloveitchik*. He has edited, coedited, or authored fifteen books (including a volume of his collected essays), and has published over seventy articles and reviews dealing with both general and Jewish philosophy. His work in general philosophy focuses on the theory of knowledge, free will, ethics, and the philosophy of religion, while his

## Contributors

work in Jewish philosophy focuses on Jewish ethics, Maimonides, Torah and science, Judaism's view of other religions, and twentieth-century rabbinic figures. After graduating as valedictorian of his class at Yeshiva College, Prof. Shatz was ordained at RIETS and earned his PhD with distinction in general philosophy from Columbia University. He has appeared on several episodes of a Public Broadcasting Service television series featuring distinguished scientists, theologians, and philosophers, and was named a winner in the John Templeton Foundation Course Competition in Science and Religion. He is a member of the Orthodox Forum steering committee and of the editorial board of *Tradition*. In recognition of his achievements as a scholar and teacher, he was awarded the Presidential Medallion at Yeshiva University. A book concerning his life and thought will appear in The Library of Contemporary Jewish Philosophers, a series that the publisher Brill states "showcases outstanding Jewish thinkers who have made lasting contributions to constructive Jewish philosophy in the second half of the twentieth century."

**Rabbi Dr. Meir Y. Soloveichik** is director of the Zahava and Moshael Straus Center for Torah and Western Thought at Yeshiva University, and rabbi at Congregation Shearith Israel in Manhattan. He graduated summa cum laude from Yeshiva College, received his *semikha* from RIETS, and was a member of its Beren Kollel Elyon. In 2010, he received his doctorate in religion from Princeton University. Rabbi Dr. Soloveichik has lectured throughout the United States, in Europe, and in Israel to both Jewish and non-Jewish audiences on topics relating to Jewish theology, bioethics, wartime ethics, and Jewish-Christian relations. His essays on these subjects have appeared in the *Wall Street Journal, Commentary, First Things, Azure, Tradition,* and the *Torah u-Madda Journal*.

**Yael Unterman** holds a BA in psychology and Talmud from Bar-Ilan University, an MA in Jewish history from Touro College, and an MA in creative writing from Bar-Ilan University. She has published pieces in a variety of genres, including prose, fiction, poetry, and book reviews. Her first book, *Nehama Leibowitz: Teacher and Bible Scholar* (Jerusalem, 2009), was awarded the category of finalist in the 2009 National Jewish Book Awards. Her second book, *The Hidden of Things*, a collection of short stories revolving around the search for personal and religious connection, was published by Yotzeret Publishing in 2014. Yael is also an international lecturer and creative educator, facilitating workshops in bibliodrama, an experiential technique that has been likened to "spontaneous midrash." She has performed a solo show that she authored, *After Eden: The First Family Conflict*, in venues worldwide.

**Rabbi Dr. Itamar Warhaftig** studied at Yeshivat Kerem B'Yavneh, where he received *semikha*, as well as Yeshivat Har Etzion. He studied at the Hebrew University in Jerusalem, where he earned his doctorate in Jewish law. Rabbi Dr. Warhaftig lectures at Bar-Ilan University and teaches at the "*Mishpetei Eretz*" Institution in Ofra, Israel. He is one of the editors of *Teḥumin* and has written numerous books and articles on Jewish law.

**Rabbi Reuven Ziegler** is chairman of the editorial board at Koren Publishers Jerusalem and director of research and archives at the Toras HoRav Foundation. A founder of Yeshivat Har Etzion's renowned Israel Koschitzky Virtual Beit Midrash, he has served as its editor-in-chief for two decades. He is author of *Majesty and Humility: The Thought of Rabbi Joseph B. Soloveitchik* (Jerusalem and New York, 2012) and editor of many volumes, among them works by Rabbi Joseph B. Soloveitchik, Rabbi Yehuda Amital, and Rabbi Aharon Lichtenstein.

**Rabbi Shlomo Zuckier** is associate rabbi at the Joseph Slifka Center for Jewish Life at Yale University and codirector of the Jewish Learning Initiative on Campus (JLIC) at Yale, as well as a PhD student in Yale's Ancient Judaism program. He studied for several years at Yeshivat Har Etzion and received ordination from RIETS, as well as MA degrees in Bible and Talmud from the Bernard Revel Graduate School for Jewish Studies at Yeshiva University. Rabbi Zuckier is editorial assistant for *Tradition: A Journal of Orthodox Jewish Thought*, and a graduate of the Wexner, Tikvah, and Kupietzky Kodshim Fellowships.

*The fonts used in this book are from the Arno family*

*Maggid Books*
*The best of contemporary Jewish thought from*
*Koren Publishers Jerusalem Ltd.*